THE
MESTIZO
MIND

SERGE GRUZINSKI

THE MESTIZO MIND

THE INTELLECTUAL DYNAMICS OF COLONIZATION AND GLOBALIZATION

LA PENSÉE MÉTISSE

TRANSLATED FROM THE FRENCH BY DEKE DUSINBERRE

Routledge
Taylor & Francis Group

NEW YORK AND LONDON

Published in 2002 by
Routledge
29 West 35th Street
New York, NY 10001

Published in Great Britain by
Routledge
11 New Fetter Lane
London EC4P 4EE

Routledge is an imprint of the Taylor & Francis Group.

Printed in the United States of America on acid free paper.

Ouvrage publié avec le soutien du Ministère français de la Culture Centre
National du Livre./This book received a translation grant from THE FRENCH
MINISTRY OF CULTURE-CENTRE NATIONAL DU LIVRE.

Library of Congress Cataloging-in-Publication Data

Gruzinski, Serge.
      [Pensée métisse. English]
      The mestizo mind : The intellectual dynamics of colonization and
globalization / Serge Gruzinski ; translated from the French by Deke Dusinberre.
            p. cm.
Includes bibliographical references and index.
      ISBN 0-415-92878-8 (Hardcover : alk. paper) — ISBN 0-415-92879-6
(Paperback : alk. paper)
      1. Latin America—Civilization. 2. Mestizaje—Latin America. I. Title.
F1408.3 .G7813 2002
980--dc21
                                                                        2002002618

FOR THÉRÈSE

C ONTENTS

ACKNOWLEDGMENTS

The subjects covered in this book were extensively discussed in my seminar at the École des Hautes Études en Sciences Sociales, in Paris, from 1994 to 1998. Criticism and comments by Carmen Salazar, Louise Bénat-Tachot, Sonia Rose, Juan Carlos Estenssoro, Mary del Priore, and Guilia Bogliolo Bruna helped me to correct and enrich the realms that we explored together. Several chapters were presented and discussed in conferences organized by Manuel Ramos and the Centro de Estudios de Historia de México de Condumex (Mexico City); Berta Ares and the Escuela de Estudios Hispanoamericanos (Seville); Eddy Stols and l'Université Catholique de Louvain (Belgium); Clara Gallini and the Associazione Internazionale Ernesto de Martino (Rome); Adauto Novaes and the Funarte Foundation (Rio de Janeiro); and Janice Theodoro da Silva, Laura de Mello e Souza, and the University of São Paulo. Décio Guzmán, my first reader, and his colleagues at the federal University of Pará and the Museu Emilio Goeldi in Belém enabled me to discover a new world, the Amazon. Photographs by Gilles Mermet and Marc Guillaumot provided me with a new perspective. The Instituto Nacional de Antropolgía et Historia (Mexico City) and its director, Señora María Teresa Franco, made its treasures available to me. Finally, I would like to thank Agnès Fontaine at Fayard for welcoming and patiently rereading this new manuscript.

THE
MESTIZO
MIND

INTRODUCTION

A priest was celebrating mass in the little church of Acoma, among the Hopi Indians of New Mexico. The congregation included a German visitor, Aby Warburg, one the founding fathers of art history, an eminent specialist in the Renaissance who was the scion of a very rich family of bankers established on both sides of the Atlantic. Warburg noted the native murals on the walls: "During the service I noticed that the wall was covered with pagan cosmological symbols. . . . "[1]

A photograph taken by Warburg, moreover, shows "a very ancient and universal motif for representing the growth, the upward and downward motion of nature."[2] Another photo shows the interior of the church—Hopi women dressed in black like Spanish peasants, praying before a baroque altar laden with statues of saints whose painted colors can be imagined.

Warburg had not made the journey in order to explore how Native American beliefs had been transformed or "contaminated."[3] And yet he had discovered the existence of a hidden link between "primitive [Amerindian] culture" and the civilization of the Renaissance. "Without studying their primitive culture, I would never have been able to provide a broad foundation to the psychology of the Renaissance."[4]

Having traveled to United States to attend the wedding of his brother Paul (to one of the daughters of the Loeb banking family), Warburg soon tired of East Coast society and set off on an exploration of "pre-Hispanic, savage America," a comparative quest for eternal nativeness and mythical imagination.[5] And, naturally, he found them. The distance he traveled from Hamburg and New Mexico seemed as great as the one separating his own century from the Renaissance, even though he was aware that modernity was about to give birth to "fateful destroyers of our sense of distance."[6]

Thus Warburg blithely combined the paths of anthropology and art history. He had even become a field-worker who used native informants, as did Franz Boas (whom he would meet in New York) and specialists from the Smithsonian (who gave him a warm welcome in Washington). Warburg was a pioneer, and still remains one to the extent that even today his anachronistic approach surprises people: we are little accustomed to dealing with the native American past and sixteenth-century Europe in the same way, and even less inclined to look to the indigenous world for keys to a better understanding of the Renaissance.

A century later, it is hard not to want to pick up Warburg's study where he left off, starting this time from a series of clues that he unwittingly left behind: the photograph of the baroque altarpiece, allusions in his notes to "Hispano-Indian layers," and a cutting from the *Saint Louis Daily Globe*, dated December 14, 1895, recounting the miraculous appearance of the skeleton of the patron saint of a church in Isleta, New Mexico. All these details clearly point to something other than "pre-Hispanic, savage America." They raise the question of whether Warburg's intuitions perhaps had a historical basis, whether the link between Native Americans and the Renaissance traced a path that existed elsewhere than solely in his imagination—namely, the dusty path from the south once taken by missionaries from Mexico, bearers of an art and a faith whose many signs can still be seen in this region of the United States. Perhaps the "primitive cultures" that Warburg thought he was observing were cultures already permeated with European features, perhaps they were "mestizo" cultures. This is what we can learn from the history of New Mexico, the culmination of four centuries of confrontation between European invaders and indigenous societies which led to a mixture of colonization, resistance, and mestizo processes.

Warburg's travels among the Hopi converge with the themes that run throughout this book: Amerindian societies, Renaissance Italy, and the search in America for keys to an understanding of the Renaissance, plus the overall context of globalization—of which the Warburg family was an emblematic figure in the late nineteenth century—not to mention the difficulty we still experience in "seeing" mestizo phenomena, much less analyzing them.

With the triumph of the U.S. version of economics—what Geminello Alvi calls the "American age"[7]—or faced with what is less forthrightly called globalization,[8] phenomena that scramble our usual landmarks have been proliferating: the mélange of the world's cultures, multiculturalism, and a defense of identity in forms ranging from simple preservation of local traditions to bloody expressions of xenophobia and ethnic cleansing.

At first sight, the distinctions seem clear. The fragmentation of nation-states weakened by the global system has been met by the reaffirmation of ethnic, regional, and religious identities, as demonstrated by ethnic or identity-affirming movements among indigenous, minority, and immigrant populations. The link between local crisis and globalization has even been made explicit, as in Mexico where the Zapatista movement in Chiapas constantly proclaims its rejection of economic globalization.

Mestizo processes are often associated with uniformization and globalization. By speeding up transactions and transforming every type of object into merchandise, the world economy allegedly triggers a ceaseless circulation that feeds a henceforth planetwide melting pot.[9] The hybrid and exotic products disseminated by "World Culture" reportedly constitute a direct manifestation of globalization, a vein systematically worked by the mass-culture industries. For that matter, such products fit as comfortably into "New Age" trends (which claim that everything is "fusion") as they do into the multicultural cosmopolitanism displayed by the new international elites.[10] Mestizo mechanisms therefore tend to be set against identity affirmation: they are alleged to be a deliberate or imposed extension—in the cultural sphere—of globalization. The defense of local identities, in contrast, rises up against this new, universal Moloch.

In fact, the picture is much more complex. Not all affirmations of identity represent a rejection of the New World Order. Many of them are reactions to the dismantling of a prior order of a national, neocolonial, or socialist type, as seen in the Yugoslavian wars. Furthermore, many interests sympathetic to the identity issue are far from hostile to triumphant free trade and the American empire—Hollywood's recent infatuation with Native Americans has shown that a concern to respect and glorify those peoples can fill producers' coffers (see the documentary series hosted by Kevin Costner, *Five Hundred Nations*). Finally, everyone knows that many apologists of "political correctness" and "cultural studies," from the shelter of the American empire's academic ivory towers, have developed the notion of a world rigidified into watertight, self-protecting communities.[11] In short, the imposition of a universal mold, the standardization of the world, and the flattening of a reality reduced to merchandise (with abstract financial networks and electronic links) could perfectly well go hand in hand with an imaginary pluralism, with an illusory diversity maintained at all costs, indeed with "traditions" concocted or reconstructed out of whole cloth.

Conversely, whereas certain mélanges suit the new free-trade ethic by providing new sources of profits and weakening any opposition it might encounter, others forthrightly resist globalization. Such is the case with local mestizo phenomena that constantly outflank World Culture's efforts at recuperation. Most syncretic inventions stemming from the suburbs of Los Angeles and the poor quarters of Mexico City and Bombay escape commercial recuperation and mediatized distribution. Which is why the finest offerings of Mexican and Russian rock remain unknown to fans in London and Paris.

Cultural hybridization therefore covers disparate phenomena and extremely varied situations which may be found in the wake or fringes of globalization. But this process—which clearly transcends the sphere of culture—raises another issue so obvious that it is often overlooked: Through what alchemy do cultures mix? Under what conditions? In what circumstances? In what ways, at what pace?

These questions presuppose that cultures are "miscible," a presupposition that goes without saying if, like A. L. Kroeber, you feel that "cultures can blend to almost any degree."[12] But things seem less obvious in light of the conclusions drawn by Claude Lévi-Strauss at his seminar on identity: "Between two cultures, between two living species as close as imaginable, there is always a differential gap and ... this differential gap cannot be bridged."[13]

As for myself, I will approach such matters by roundabout paths, aloof from both cultural sociology and anthropology. First I will attempt to deal with the issue as an historian—although one convinced that history should not be confused with a superficial expertise in contemporary matters and the immediate past—by focusing on a period that entertains a special relationship with today's world. If we knew the sixteenth century better—the century of Iberian expansion, not just of French religious strife and Loire-style *chateaux*—we would no longer discuss globalization as though it were a new, recent situation. Nor are the phenomena of hybridization and rejection that we now see on a worldwide scale the novelty they are often claimed to be. Right from the Renaissance, Western expansion has continuously spawned hybrids all over the globe, along with reactions of rejection (the most spectacular of which was the closing of Japan in the early seventeenth century). Planetwide mestizo phenomena thus seem closely linked to the harbingers of economic globalization that began in the second half of the sixteenth century, a century which, whether viewed from Europe, America, or Asia, was the Iberian century *par excellence*, just as our own has become the American century.[14]

This glance backward is merely another way of discussing the present, because the study of yesterday's mestizo mechanisms raises a series of questions that remain topical. Here, in no particular order, are a few of them: Did the mélanges spawned by Western expansion represent a reaction against European domination? Or were they an inevitable repercussion of that domination, indeed a clever way of insinuating European customs among subject populations? To what extent can Western society tolerate the proliferating spread of hybrid processes? At what point will it seek to halt them, at what cost will it manage to control the phenomenon and employ it as the basis of its supremacy? What meanings, what limitations, and what pitfalls lie behind the convenient metaphor of the melting pot? Finally, if a mestizo way of thinking does indeed exist, how does it express itself?

Before going back in time to address these questions, we must discuss the obstacles that hinder our understanding of mestizo mechanisms. Some problems are related to ordinary experience, while others stem from intellectual habits and mental reflexes that the social sciences sometimes have difficulty overcoming.

PART I

MÉLANGE,
CHAOS,
WESTERNIZATION

1 AMAZONS

> *Sou um tupi tangendo um alaûde!...*
> (I'm a Tupi who plays the lute!...)
> —Mário de Andrade "O Trovador,"
> *Paulicéia desvairada (1922)*

This line by Mário de Andrade long trilled through my mind, as though it might help me unravel the feelings I had about certain regions of the Americas—such as a remote island south of the Amazonian delta, discovered in the course of an academic trip.

The tranquility of the place was conducive to reverie and reflection. Only the air seemed to be prey to constant motion: in the sky, between wind-twisted palm trees, my eye encountered scudding clouds that slowed only at dusk. But the endlessly blowing wind hardly threatened the torpor of the village of Algodoal, where I was staying. Algodoal, meaning "cotton plantation": when uttered by natives, the name of this village carried Afro-Indian resonances that charmed me even before the boat had set me on its shore.

The village was just as I had expected—salt-eroded carcasses of boats, a few plank shacks, and scanty electricity composed a "preserved" landscape whose exoticism reminded me of my first Mexican trip long ago, back in the 1970s. Days passed in measured steps. In the morning, donkey-drawn carts carried merchandize and supplies. Sometimes bleached boats arrived to drop penniless young people on the island, attracted by the vast ocean beach.

The shore ran as far as the eye could see, beyond the great white dunes overlooking the channel. At high tide, it could only be reached by hailing a dinghy, unless you wanted to risk swimming across the muddy waters of the narrow strait. At dusk, on the village beach, groups of dark-skinned, half-naked teenagers indulged in a ritual contest called *capoeira*. Their movements responded to the insistent tunes of the *berimbau*, a simple musical instrument made from a wooden bow stretched with a metallic string that passed through a colorfully painted coconut. In the distance, pursued by the rising tide, a herd of livestock would cross the beach at a lively pace, escorted by a rider whose silhouette could barely be discerned in the pink mist of dusk. Once night fell, the constellations of the southern hemisphere lit up the sky. On land, the flickering glow of candles illumined a few patios where hammocks were swinging. Far away, the rhythms of a *carimbó* were stifled by the yawning wind.

This idyllic picture is only a delusion, however, since it eliminates everything startling about a village that I wished had been stranded in the nineteenth century. Every evening, a news program on the Globo TV channel spewed forth images of blood, money, scandal. Early in that month of September 1997, the death of Princess Diana stirred the islanders' imaginations, bringing them into line with the rest of the globe. The deadly streets of Paris had followed me to Algodoal, bedecked for the islanders in an exoticism both glamorous and funereal. My mirage of powdery sand and sunny poverty had to make room for the remembrance of a princess.

Many parts of the Americas such as Algodoal continue to belong to the past—that, at any rate, is how we describe everything that appears archaic and rustic to our eyes—even while sharing global dreams on a daily basis. In order to account for these contrasts—which are blithely perceived as contradictions—people usually just see Tradition holding out against the ravages of Progress and the contaminations of Civilization.[1] How can this reflex be explained, this irresistible tendency that spurs us to seek archaism in all its forms, to the extent of overlooking—willfully or not—whatever concerns modernity in any way? It is almost as though we take malicious pleasure in creating difference.[2]

Despite reflecting on all that, television still struck me as out of place in Algodoal, in the same way a calculator seems out of place among the Chiapas Indians or Ray-Bans on the nose of a Siberian Yakut. Yet television was part of the island's reality just as much as the ocean-worn colors on its worm-eaten wooden boats.

Nor was it possible simply to contrast village "timelessness" with big-city "modernity." With two million inhabitants, Belém, the capital of the western Amazon region, is itself a mélange of eighteenth-century colonial town planning (designed by an Italian architect), of Belle-Époque Paris, and of chaotic modernity ringed by shantytown *favellas*. Neoclassical palaces by Bolognese architect Antonio Landi, decrepit early-twentieth-century dwellings, middle-class high-rises, and neighborhoods of shanties with open sewers all compose an ensemble as heterogeneous as it is unclassifiable. In the middle of Republic Plaza, the Teatro da Paz—an opera house every bit as fine as the one in Manaus—rises like some strange vestige of a turn-of-the-century civilization, a lavish wreck that washed up on Amazonian shores.

How should we deal with these mixed societies? First, perhaps, by accepting them as they appear to us, instead of hastily reordering and sorting them into the various elements allegedly making up the whole. This dissection—what is called an analysis—not only has the drawback of shattering reality, but most of the time it also introduces filters, criteria, and obsessions that exist only to our Western eyes. Archaism is often, if not always, an illusion. Many features typical of native societies in Latin America come from the Iberian peninsula rather than some distant pre-Hispanic past to which nostalgic ethnologists try to assign them.

"I'm a Tupi who plays the lute! . . . " On Algodoal, the notes of a "primitive" harp accompany the gestures of the boys dancing the *capoeira* on the beach. But the singer's chant picked up on a song played over the air by Brazilian radio stations; the lyrics, referring to "Brazilian culture" and "national culture," owed more to the spread of social-science vocabulary than to obscure Afro-Brazilian traditions—which I was forced to admit with a pang of regret.

Accepting, in its globality, the mongrel reality before one's eyes is a first step. But this effort often leads to a realization that can produce a kind of anguished impasse: mélanges are apparently always placed under the sign of ambiguity and ambivalence. Such is the supposed curse hanging over the heads of composite worlds.

Writers have used it to fine effect. Macunaíma, the protagonist of a novel by Mário de Andrade, is "an ambivalent, indecisive character, torn between two value systems."[3] The story of this multifaceted being, an archetype of Brazilians and Latin Americans torn between antagonistic options—Brazil versus Europe—wavering between cultures yet belonging simultaneously to both of them, is exemplary of this fracture. It is hardly surprising that Macunaíma's world is riven all the way through: "He is, in fact, a layered man who cannot manage to meld two highly diverse cultures."[4] In fact, the obsession with the gap between the two worlds pertains to Mário de Andrade as much as to his protagonist, Macunaíma. In every chapter of the book—on almost every line—the fissure recurs clearly and almost palpably, and "the themes are almost always organized in pairs."[5]

The twists and turns of the plot of *Macunaíma* illustrate the impossibility of escaping the contradictions and dilemmas of a double heritage. The protagonist hesitates between two worlds when looking for a wife: he first chooses a Portuguese woman, then a native South American, Dona Sancha. But his choice resolves nothing. If he is finally attracted to the indigenous woman, that is only because her mother, Vei do Sol, made her look like a European—Macunaíma falls into a trap that Vei do Sol set for him.

The protagonist's mistake conveys the complexity of situations generated by the confrontation of two worlds. Yet on closer inspection, Macunaíma's contradictory decisions do not cancel one another out. The two successive choices, the two sequences, "nonetheless form a perfectly organic whole within the structure of the tale."[6] To Macunaíma, the opposing elements appear to be "two sides of the same coin." So they cannot be separated. Like the residents of Algodoal, Macunaíma is fully exposed to the appeal of the Western world. He belongs to it just as much as they do. The line by De Andrade cited above powerfully sums up this interconnection:

I'm a Tupi who plays the lute....

It is possible to be a Tupi—an indigenous inhabitant of Brazil—and still play a European instrument as ancient and refined as the lute. Nothing is irreconcilable, nothing is incompatible, even if the mélange can sometimes be painful, as *Macunaíma* shows. Just because lutes and Tupis come from two different backgrounds does not mean they cannot be brought together by a writer's pen or within an indigenous village administered by Jesuits.[7]

In fact, just as a diagnosis of roots often leads to debatable attributions, so avowed incompatibilities lumber unusual combinations with interpretations that owe more to our ways of seeing than to reality itself. This further complicates any approach to mongrel worlds, which combine as much as they contrast the elements that go into them.

Nor is that all: the sophisticated literary techniques used by the author of *Macunaíma* appealed to Brazilian critics,[8] but such techniques were not merely an expression of immense talent or a personal crisis of identity. The art of Mário de Andrade expresses not only "a terrible rift...on every level of the tale,"[9] the forms he invented also make it possible to explore a polymorphous reality composed of multiple identities and constant metamorphoses. De Andrade manages this by playing on the indeterminacy generated by the superimposition and fusion of characters. In *Macunaíma*, Rainha da Floresta is by turns "Empress of the Virgin Forest," an Amazon, and an Icamiaba Indian. There is nothing incoherent or contradictory about that. De Andrade's writing convinces us that whatever may appear incoherent may perfectly well have a meaning and that the true continuity of things resides deep within metamorphosis and precariousness.

MESTIZO PHENOMENA IN THE AMAZON

On the island of Algodoal, I used that line by de Andrade ("I'm a Tupi who plays the lute") as an antidote to the images and fantasies I projected on both people and places. It was less a key for explaining what I saw than a kind of safeguard against employing the attractive but simplistic filter of exoticism.

Exoticism is not merely a purveyor of clichés. In the best circumstances—that is to say, when the land and indigenous population have miraculously escaped colonization, exploitation, and evangelization—it is the way the West generally sets its seal on everything: "Evidentemente, il mondo era nostro."[10] If the Amazon remains a good example of this, that is because it provides fertile soil for our mania for overlooking "proximate" in our effort to flush out the "remote," our quest for archaism and otherness. The immense forest is one of those reservoirs that has long fed our thirst for exoticism and purity. Many people have been fooled by this, and I cannot claim to have escaped it.

Everything contributes to the illusion: at the mouth of the Amazon River, the marriage of land and sea confounds our normal landmarks and renders the terrain almost impenetrable; the stormy waves merging into the Atlantic have the freshness of river water; inland, the sea of greenery over which you can fly for hours on end inevitably evokes the virginity of nature still protected from civilization and its pollutions. Unlike Mexico and the Andes, whose populations were hybridized very early on, the Amazon seems to extend the ramparts of its gigantic forests and interminable rivers to a humanity long isolated from the rest of the continent, thought to have been exposed to white covetousness only recently.

As though that were not enough, right from the Renaissance the mysteries of the great forest have stirred Spanish, Portuguese, French, English, and Italian imaginations—the earliest explorers sought either the female warriors known as Amazons, or Eldorado, or the garden of the Hesperides.[11] To which could be added our own childhood memories every time the misfortunes of indigenous peoples revive the myth of the Noble Savage that a humanist, literary, and academic France has cultivated since the days of Jean de Léry and Michel de Montaigne. Finally, the threats now looming over this region of the globe add dramatic tension that makes it appear even more appealing. The Amazon is now becoming, or has already become, a lost paradise.

It is hard to avoid fantasizing about this timeless world. The Amazon is often invoked when couching indigenous creativity in terms of survival, when conceiving of mankind in general as "the symptom of a troubling conservatism" in a manner so abstract that it overlooks the uniqueness of specific situations.[12] Writers, poets, and filmmakers have constantly exploited these clichés to weave dreams for a public ever hungrier for primitive worlds and permanence. Hollywood and the media, displaying a timely humanism, have jumped on the bandwagon with their usual success.

Modern science has not always dismissed these fantasies and preconceptions. By understating the historic and prehistoric changes experienced by Amazonian populations, by minimizing their capacity for innovation and spread, by ignoring the federations that unite tribes into larger units, and by overlooking the impact of widespread movements that have animated the forest, anthropologists have sustained the image of societies frozen in their traditions.[13] The stress placed on a group's adaptation to its environment has led to oversights concerning not only interactions between peoples but also the repercussions of European presence.

Structuralist anthropology thus made the Amazon a preserve of "uncivilized mentalities," churning out scholarly theories and monographs. No doubt these thinkers—led by Claude Lévi-Strauss—made a crucial contribution to the social sciences in the twentieth century. But their contribution has come at a cost. With overstressing of a distinction between "cold societies" supposedly resistant to historic changes and "hot societies" that thrive on change,[14] a myth has been created which reinforces the clichés mentioned above, just as it discourages closer study of a prehistory now known to extend back over ten millennia. That is also the reason why "other" Amazons, more mixed and more exposed to Western influence, have remained in the background; archives show that these "contaminated" Amazons date back to the seventeenth, indeed very late sixteenth, century.[15]

Everything has changed down through the ages—environment, demography, social and political organization, cosmologies. As Anna Roosevelt points out, the destabilization of indigenous political structures during the Conquest, as well as the deculturation and decimation provoked by the missions, profoundly modified Indian culture and forms of settlement.[16] Although Amazonian Indians were not "Tupi[s] who play the lute," they nevertheless had European merchandise in their hands at a very early date, from French machetes to Dutch guns, and were even more quickly in contact with germs. By the Renaissance, Europeans were heading up the Amazon River, and in the first half of the seventeenth century they were sailing both up and down it—Pedro Teixeira's expedition left Belém in 1637, made its way up the river and its tributaries as far as Quito, then returned to its original port two years later.

That was when Europeans began frequenting the heart of the great forest, the Rio Negro region of the Amazon, establishing commercial and political links with the indigenous elites. But they had been preceded by objects from the Old World. Without waiting for the arrival of whites, trade routes thousands of miles long had opened the forest to Dutch, Spanish, and French items. Slaves were used as a unit of exchange everywhere— throughout the seventeenth century, indigenous peoples along the Rio Negro might be slave traders or, in turn, become slaves of the Dutch or Portuguese.[17] During certain years, the Portuguese managed to round up a good thousand of them, whom they transported in dreadful conditions to Belém and Gran Pará, at the eastern edge of the forest. Survivors mixed with the local populations in a melting pot that increased over time.

In the eighteenth century, the Portuguese crown's well-informed policies led to the militarization of the heart of the Amazon. Rio Negro occupied a strategic position on the frontier between Portuguese Brazil and the Spanish empire, as well as being a route of access for the Dutch in Guyana.

This buildup translated into military construction and a tighter European grip, leading to the deportation of populations who were forced to supply their labor. Early urban development resulted, and an administrative capital, Barcelos, was even built from scratch on the site of the town of Mariuá. It became home to architects, draftsmen, scholars, and civil servants charged with studying the region in all its physical and human aspects, including individuals of the stature of Bolognese architect Landi and members of the Hispano-Portuguese commissions responsible for establishing the line of demarcation between the two empires. In 1753, with the arrival of Mendonça Furtado, governor of Pará and brother-in-law of the all-powerful Portuguese politician Sebastião José de Pombal, the young capital enjoyed unprecedented liveliness.

The intensification of the Portuguese presence had numerous consequences for the Amazon basin. In the floodplains of the lower Amazon River, missionaries created a new ethnic group, the Tapuyas. In the center of the region, colonization accelerated the intermingling of indigenous populations: Indians from the Içana, Xié, and Vaupés rivers were forced to go to Barcelos to work for the Portuguese—while some built the city, others grew manioc and *salsa parilha* (sarsaparilla) on behalf of the colonizers.

The Portuguese authorities then had great difficulty preventing these indigenous peoples from returning to the forest "to live in their huts like the savages they once were."[18] These constant migrations, even as they prevented the natives from settling down, exposed the inner forest to influences transmitted by all those returning from the world of whites. The ten or so towns dotting the Rio Negro were active centers of penetration. The small groups of soldiers and mestizo traders living there overlooked no opportunities to drive deeper into the forest to exploit the local natives.

Starting in the 1760s, the construction of new forts and growing numbers of Carmelite religious establishments further increased European pressure on the Amazonian milieu. From that period dates the spread of Catholic holidays, such as the Feast of Saint Joachim, in the upper Rio Negro. Caught between Spanish and Portuguese ambitions, the indigenous peoples were subjected to the exactions of soldiers and the ventures of missionaries, and were drawn to small towns full of European merchandise and Christian images. Fewer and fewer of them were able to remain untouched by time or by whites.

Then the effects of biological cross-fertilization began to be felt. In a desire to mitigate hostile reactions and to keep the natives in Christian villages, Portuguese authorities encouraged soldiers posted to the forest to marry the daughters of indigenous dignitaries, "so that the Indians will be more inclined to live in the villages."[19]

Yet it should not be imagined that the Amazon was entirely colonized. The Portuguese in the eighteenth century lacked the resources of the rubber

barons of the Belle Époque and the multinationals of today. It is nevertheless undeniable that ever-increasing zones were undergoing a series of influences, penetrations, and shocks that had repercussions on the deepest parts
of the forest. As elsewhere on the American continents, this first wave of
colonization occurred under the sign of chaos and mélange. One need only
skim the travel journal by Brazilian scientist Alexandre Rodrigues Ferreira,
Diario da Viagem Philosophica, to appreciate the instability and insecurity
then reigning in Rio Negro country—relations between the groups were
steeped in wariness and suspicion, there was general impunity, and the practical impossibility of monitoring the region made it all the easier for the
Portuguese and mestizos to violate laws forbidding the enslavement of
Indians.

Although the Amazon has a very old history, it is only very recently that
historians and archaeologists have begun to unearth and describe it.[20]
Paradoxically, written sources abound, since the gigantic expanse of the
great forest aroused the interest of Europeans at an early date—numerous
accounts have been left by explorers, administrators, and missionaries in
search of Eldorados to conquer, slaves to raid, or souls to save. The issue of
delineating the border between the Spanish and Portuguese empires itself
mobilized great energy. Since resolving the dispute required reconnaissance
of places and populations, the two bureaucracies carried out inquests deep
into the heart of the Amazonian region; bundles of papers mounted up as
the conflict dragged on.

Gaps or inadequacies in research until quite recent years cannot therefore be explained by a lack of archives.[21] Rather, they result from a tendency
to overlook history in certain parts of the globe or to accord it only a
negligible role in the fate of those regions. By ignoring history, we deprive
ourselves of a crucial perspective, overlooking the effects of Western colonization in all those lands and, consequently, the reactions it triggered.
Either we totally fail to see the mestizo phenomena that occurred or, once
they become dominant and irrefutable, they are hastily described as "contamination" or interference.

THE KASSEL INDIANS, SEPTEMBER 1997

History has no monopoly on demystification—contemporary art has often
preceded it down that path. In a matter of days, the vagaries of academic
invitations would propel me from Amazonian Brazil to the borders of the
former East Germany, namely to Kassel, a middling-sized town that is
invaded every four years by contemporary art during its Documenta exhibition. Another coincidence—but was it really a coincidence at an event
devoted to the major issues of the recent half-century?—meant the exhibi-

tion devoted significant space to Brazil and the Amazon, juxtaposing objects and photographs.

The work of German photographer Lothar Baumgarten has incisive qualities.[22] The artist showed aspects of the daily life of Yanomami Indians without his photographer's eye ever lapsing into the analytic gaze of the anthropologist or the voyeuristic stare of the tourist. The shots were presented in such a way as to compose a personal album where a private diary might be kept. With a remarkable sense of efficiency, Baumgarten eschewed the exoticism ordinarily sparked by the sight of naked Indians in the forest. He did not try to lock them into an organic totality but rather to inspire a sense of proximity and familiarity with the people he photographed.

It was not the first time that Baumgarten had shown the extent to which our eye and our sensibilities are easily fooled. Between 1973 and 1977 he made a film, *The Origin of the Night*, based on a local Tuyi myth, which plunged audiences into a two-hour experience of the Amazonian jungle—or at least, of a set that imitated it. For at the end of the film, the enthralled audiences discovered that they had been exploring a Rhineland forest.

Several years earlier, while studying under Joseph Beuys, Baumgarten had already played on the viewer's lazy eye. He took a series of photographs of the tropical forest, labeling each one with the name of an indigenous people of South America. In fact, this scholarly encyclopedia was nothing other than a series of compositions concocted from broccoli! Baumgarten's artistic output, employing highly varied media, employs humor and hoax to pursue a project both aesthetic and intellectual: to examine forms of interaction between Western civilization and remote societies, without sacrificing the respective identity of either.

Documenta X presented other works related to Brazil. Alongside Baumgarten, it featured a retrospective of the oeuvre of Hélio Oiticica, whose work in the 1960s was related to the concerns of the "anthropophagic" movement.[23] This modernist trend of the 1920s—to which Mário de Andrade belonged—felt that it was up to the colonized individual (here, the Brazilian artist) to digest the colonizing culture into order to merge with indigenous cultures all the better. Starting from these principles, Oiticica salvaged and recycled popular materials in order to strip them of their exotic or folkloric veneer, endowing them with a universal significance. This can be seen in his use of large *parangolés*, costumes worn by Brazilian dancers during samba parades. Oiticica turned these silly, colorful outfits into living sculptures that paid tribute to major figures such as the popular soccer star Pelé. Thanks to stylization and metamorphosis, a mélange of forms produced original, unclassifiable objects. *Tropicalia*, a labyrinth created by Oiticica in 1967, displayed the divergences and dualities in Brazilian society by producing an indeterminacy that prevents any stabilization of meaning—its fragmentary images forestall recuperation by consumer and market mechanisms.[24]

What struck me at Kassel was not the fact that a photographer and sculptor had attacked exoticism by using humor and irony,[25] it was the way artistic creativity, via technical procedures and aesthetic decisions, spurred reflection on the clichés of exoticism. The way in which Lothar Baumgarten neutralized exotic aspects and the way Hélio Oiticica sublimated them through a mélange of items tell us not only about the sources of exoticism but also the ways it can be defused (Baumgarten's use of mockery, Oiticica's production of a Brazilian—therefore mestizo—artwork). Their art does not stop at a critique of a situation, it dismantles the very mechanisms and then exploits that working knowledge to devise other setups designed to shatter stereotypes.

Baumgarten and Oiticica reject exoticism, challenge categories of knowledge, and invent ways of liberating the gaze via the manipulation of unusual materials or the use of unexpected viewpoints or compositions, thereby playing on perceptual pitfalls. They were preceded down this path by the literary oeuvre of Mário de Andrade, employing other techniques.

Perhaps this means that within the realms discussed here—the study and understanding of mélange—artistic creativity, whether conceived in visual or literary form, has as much to teach us as the social sciences, which so often stick to the well-worn paths of discourse and theory.

2 MÉLANGE AND MESTIZO

> An eclectic mélange of *punk rock* and *world music*—
> of global raga-rock, if you will—the third album by
> these Englishmen of Indian stock, who henceforth
> work as a duo, is a perfect antidote to the sham "spiri-
> tuality" of groups such as Kula Shaker. Tjinder Singh,
> leader and *songwriter*, explores a weave of multiple
> influences here, ranging from a wonderfully pop
> *Brimful of Asia* (which suddenly reincarnates
> Cornershop in a Tandoori-Beatles form) to *cheap* '70s
> funk, via equally *cheap* techno licks, a few kilograms
> of cannabis-scented hip hop, and some northern
> Indian folk.[1]

Music reviews like this one can be read in many French newspapers today, and are distinctive as much for their style and swift-paced ideas as for the subject they address. Readers are spared nothing: the cascade of technical terms, the dropping of English words into a French text (indicated here in italics), the nod to world culture, and the stress on hybridism ("Englishmen of Indian stock ... a Tandoori-Beatles form") all fuel a prose that apes the music it is discussing. The accumulation of terms cannot disguise the diffi-culty of defining this album by Cornershop—the commentary refers only to "mélange," "eclecticism," and "weave of multiple influences." This passage reveals the poverty of representations and discourse spurred by the acceler-ation and intensification of planetwide intermingling.

A PLANETWIDE IDIOM

The fact that "hybrid" and "mestizo" (sometimes in its Spanish form, *mes-tizaje*) are now commonly used alongside "ethnic" in cultural studies is not merely an indication of the confusion gripping our minds. The phenomenon also betrays the appearance of a "planetwide idiom."

Beyond its vagueness, this increasingly common discourse is not as neutral or spontaneous as it appears. It could be seen as a language of recognition used by new international elites whose rootlessness, cosmopolitanism, and eclecticism call for wholesale borrowings from "world cultures." It supposedly reflects a social phenomenon, a growing awareness of groups accustomed to consume everything the planet can offer them, for whom hybridism seems to be supplanting exoticism.[2] It represents a new way—unless it is viewed as a variation on old European cosmopolitanism—to get some distance on one's original milieu and to stand out from the rest of the crowd.[3] It is also a way to place new products on the market, wrapping them in a seductive glow. The French advertisers for Jungle for Men, a scent launched by a major Japanese fashion designer, adopted a messianic tone to describe a new earthly paradise "teeming with color": "It's the city, it's graffiti, it's mestizo. It's the country, it's poetic, perfectly peaceful. . . . It's the world of tomorrow, authentically mestizo." Obviously, it is nothing other than the world of Kenzo customers.

This planetwide idiom is also the expression of a more elaborate rhetoric which claims to be postmodern or postcolonial[4] and which argues that hybrids make it possible to break free from modernity, condemned for being too Western and one-dimensional.[5] Its spokespeople see the intermediate zones situated between the West and its former possessions as the site of emerging "hybrid conceptual frameworks from which new ways of knowing emerge."[6] These ideas are prospering on American campuses and in intellectual circles with roots in lands formerly colonized by Western Europe.[7] Praise for Creole culture in the French West Indies constitutes another version of this stress on "the transactional and interactional amalgamation of Caribbean, European, African, Asian, and Levantine cultural elements that history has yoked together on the same soil."[8]

It is worth taking this "planetwide idiom" into account, if only to get some distance on the fashionable language and ideologies that are playing an ever-increasing role. Postmodern criticism, in spite of its excesses, has sometimes hit the nail on the head,[9] while many creative artists and writers have shed new light on the world's mélanges (a light not always provided by the social sciences). The work of Edouard Glissant, to cite just one example, is noteworthy.[10]

Whether the effect of fashion or not, the phenomenon of mélange is objectively incontrovertible, from Brazil to Paris and from Mexico City to London. Even admitting that every culture is hybrid and that mélanges date back to the origins of human history, it cannot now be dismissed as merely a fashionable ideology stemming from globalization. The phenomenon is simultaneously straightforward and complex. Straightforward, because it can be found at various levels throughout human history and is today ubiquitous. Complex, because it becomes hard to grasp once we try to go beyond the confining effects of fashion and rhetoric.

THE UNCERTAINTIES AND AMBIGUITIES OF LANGUAGE

Still relatively little explored—and therefore little familiar—this mélange of individuals and mind-sets is called *métissage* in French. It is hard to know exactly what this "mestizo effect" covers—its dynamics are not really questioned. Mixing, mingling, blending, crossbreeding, combining, superimposing, juxtaposing, interposing, imbricating, fusing, and merging are all terms associated with the mestizo process, swamping vague descriptions and fuzzy thinking in a profusion of terms.

The word "mélange," meanwhile, suffers not only from the vagueness of the concept to which it refers. In principle, a mélange is a mixture of pure elements such as primary colors, that is to say homogeneous bodies free from all "contamination." Perceived as a shift from homogeneous to heterogeneous, from the singular to the plural, from order to disorder, the idea of mélange therefore carries connotations and assumptions that should be avoided like the plague. The same is true of the term "hybridity."

These resonances recur in the notion of mestizo crossbreeds, and the distinctions usually made between "biological crossbreed" and "cultural crossbreed" only increase the confusion. Biological crossbreeding presupposes the existence of pure, physically distinct human groups separated by barriers that are broken by the mélange of bodies driven by desire and sexuality.[11] By activating transmission and exchange, by stimulating movements and invasions, history would thereby put an end to what primal, biological nature had allegedly defined. But this is an embarrassing presupposition for people seeking to free themselves from the notion of race. As to the notion of "cultural crossbreeding," it is heavy with ambivalence linked to the very concept of culture, to which I will return later.

Nor are the connections between biological crossbreeding and cultural crossbreeding very clear: the birth and increase of mestizo individuals is one thing, the development of mestizo lifestyles stemming from various sources is another (and not necessarily linked to the first). Furthermore, by raising the issue in these terms, we overlook the connections between biological/cultural on the one hand, and social/political on the other. Add to all this the increasingly common use of the word *métissage*, and it becomes clear why the confusion has led some people to reject such a heavily connotated concept.

THE CHALLENGE OF MÉLANGE

The phenomenon of mélange has nevertheless become an everyday reality, visible in our streets and on our screens. Multifarious and ubiquitous, such mélanges combine individuals and images that nothing would normally unite. The blend of styles and cities within Belém is not an isolated example.

Nowadays, in a few hours you can go from Moscow's mélange of Calvin Klein posters and Lenin statues to Mexico City's mélange of Indian women strolling among Reforma's high-rise buildings, then back to Tourcoing (in northern France, where I was raised), where a North African population comes to terms with the vestiges of proletarian housing blocks and the arrogant, incongruous shell of a school of contemporary art. Everywhere, standard frames of reference are being shattered by these surprising and sometimes awkward juxtapositions and presences. Does that mean a homogeneous and coherent modern world has suddenly given way to a fragmented, heterogeneous, and unpredictable postmodern universe?

The social sciences are beginning to supply clues and insight into this question. Anthropologists finally freed from their fascination with uncivilized peoples and sociologists sensitive to the mélange of lifestyles and attitudes have taught us a good deal about the scope and meaning of the crossbreeding that is taking place before our eyes. Jean-Loup Amselle's pioneering book, *Logiques métisses*, showed what the African experience could contribute to a debate whose terms he fully helped to clarify.[12] More recently, Michel Giraud, a specialist of the Caribbean region, has published similar reflections on that part of the world.[13] Meanwhile, François Laplantine and Alexis Nouss have pointed out the importance of mestizo processes in the history of human societies, stressing the singular features of what is both a field of observation and a mode of thought.[14] A few years ago, Carmen Bernard and I undertook a reinterpretation of the history of the New World by focusing our approach on mestizo phenomena, for which we established an initial inventory.[15]

Yet can any single field fully address the issue of mestizo processes? What is needed is "nomadic" scholarship, ready to range from folklore to anthropology, from communications to art history.[16] Historical demography, family histories and genealogy, and social history are as concerned with this issue as are religious history and linguistics.

This intermingling of fields has yet to occur, and much remains to be done, even though significant contributions have already been made by both cultural anthropology and religious anthropology.[17] The former has pointed out that "cultures can blend to almost any degree and not only thrive but perpetuate themselves."[18] Anglo-American anthropologists have taken an interest in the issue of cultural change, spread, assimilation, and "acculturation,"[19] drawing up a typology of methods of contact ("attrition, adjustment, and penetration") and spread ("dissemination, dispersal"). They have also elaborated a series of categories that make it possible better to define the conditions and modalities of mélange, if not shed light on its mechanisms.

Yet it was Mexican anthropologist Gonzalo Aguirre Beltrán who first linked mestizo processes to acculturation. At the conclusion of a remarkable historical analysis of the "process of acculturation" in colonial and modern Mexico, Aguirre Beltrán showed that mestizo phenomena are the result of "the struggle between colonial European culture and indigenous culture.... Opposing elements of the cultures in contact tend to be mutually exclusive, confronting and opposing each other; but at the same time they tend to interpenetrate, combining and identifying with each other."[20] It is this very confrontation which permitted "the emergence of a new culture— the mestizo or Mexican culture—born of the interpenetration and combination of opposites. This culture developed through countless vicissitudes that led to its definitive consolidation with the triumph of the revolution of 1910."[21] By bringing to light the development of a mestizo medical tradition, Aguirre Beltrán concretely described the emergence of a coherent system of ideas and practices.[22]

One special type of mélange has sparked much research: the cross-fertilization of beliefs and rites, otherwise known as religious syncretism. The term itself has a long history, dating back to Plutarch.[23] In the field of religious anthropology, it is particularly appreciated by specialists in Afro-Brazilian religions, which represent fertile terrain because they combine influences from African, Amerindian, and Christian forms of worship. A recent study listed no fewer than 150 books on the subject of religious syncretism.[24] Some people think Brazilian syncretism simply masks the survival of ancient rites, others perceive it as a veritable strategy of resisting Christianization by "salvaging" aspects of local paganism. Still others, analyzing its mechanisms, present it as a patchwork, a do-it-yourself religion, an "indigestible amalgamation."[25] The better to identify the specificity of these phenomena within the Afro-Brazilian world, controversial notions such as scission have also been raised by theorists such as Roger Bastide.

A look at these studies shows that the term syncretism has multiple, indeed contradictory, meanings, and that it can be applied to highly disparate situations of beliefs and practices: intersection, parallelism, mélange, fusion, and so on. In fact, these terminological distinctions offer little insight into the complexity and variability of given situations. Is it really possible to propose overall categories if "each case is unique"?[26] Moreover, a single phenomenon may take several forms: the Afro-Brazilian rite called Tambor de Mina, held in the Casa da Mina in São Luis do Maranhão, displays syncretisms that have been analyzed in terms of parallelism yet also in terms of convergence. On closer look, many syncretist rituals appear to display a kind of unstable but lasting "equilibrium" between various traditions, rather than clear-cut, easily classifiable states.

When it comes to Mexico, the proliferation of definitions and categories generated by researchers is equally perplexing.[27] Syncretism is alternately described as a conscious or unconscious process, objective or subjective, permanent or temporary. It can apply to elements that are structurally analogous or totally incompatible. The conclusions drawn by specialists are similar to the ones for Brazil, referring to "the fluid and dynamic nature, the constant evolution, of the various indigenous and mestizo realities."[28] "Far from resolving existing ambiguities, the negotiation (and potential conflict) that occurs between groups adhering to different models constantly creates new ones." Although it is undoubtedly true that syncretism concerns shifting, contradictory situations, describing them as "fluid and dynamic" does not offer sufficient tools for grasping those contexts and relations.

The picture has been further complicated by the extension of the term "syncretism" to other spheres. In medicine, literature, philosophy, science, and the arts, many forms of syncretism have been identified. Moreover, concepts such as "approximate arrangement" (Balandier) and "double causality" (Bastide) spur people to view every situation as syncretic. All things considered, perhaps reality as a whole is syncretic, which would make the concept of syncretism so general as to render it superfluous.

It is therefore hardly surprising that the very idea of syncretism appears problematic, indeed pointless.[29] Accused by certain anthropologists of being simplistic or impressionistic,[30] often weighted with negative connotations, syncretism winds up designating a confused and artificial phenomenon synonymous with hodgepodge, impurity, and contamination.[31] The terms mélange, mestizo, and syncretism create the same sense of confusion or even doubt and rejection. How can we explain this?

BERLIN 1992: CONCEPTUALIZING THE IN-BETWEEN

Difficulty in conceptualizing mélanges is not limited to the realm of the social sciences. Even a physical phenomenon apparently as straightforward[32] as the mélange of fluids—which could hardly be compared to mestizo individuals and cultures—remains an "imperfectly understood process" according to scientists.[33]

Our confusion is not due solely to the complexity of the social and historical world. An understanding of mestizo processes runs up against intellectual habits which favor monolithic ensembles over "in-between" spaces. It is obviously simpler to identify solid blocks than nameless gaps. It is easier to think that "everything which appears ambiguous is only apparently so, that ambiguity does not exist."[34] The simplicity of dualistic and Manichaean approaches is appealing, and when they dress themselves in the rhetoric of otherness, they soothe our consciences even as they satisfy our thirst for purity, innocence, and archaism.

The history of the conquest of the Americas could thus be reduced to a destructive confrontation between good natives and evil Europeans, with all the conviction and good faith formerly invested in distinguishing the savage natives from civilizing conquerors. This way of viewing things stultifies and impoverishes reality by eliminating all kinds of elements that play crucial roles: not only the exchanges and intersections between the two worlds, but also the groups and individuals who act as go-betweens, as intermediaries, who move between the large blocks that we are happy to identify. In reality, these intermediate spaces have played a key role in history, as has been noted in terms of the colonization of the New World: "the spaces in between produced by colonization [provided the] location and energy of new modes of thinking whose strength lies in the transformation and critique of the 'authenticities' of both Western and Amerindian legacies."[35]

The interest currently shown in the issue of borders partly reflects these concerns. As many examples demonstrate, a border is often porous, permeable, and flexible—it moves and can be moved. But it can be the most difficult thing in the world to conceptualize, so much does it seem simultaneously real and imaginary, unbreachable and retractable—somewhat like that almost invisible borderline that still separated the two Berlins in 1992. Although the Berlin Wall had been demolished three years earlier, a borderline somewhere between Kreuzberg and Mitte, along Heinrich-Heine Strasse, continued to separate ways of walking, seeing, motioning, dressing. The sudden passage from one world to another—from one sidewalk to another, one drabness to another—now entailed little more than a physical impression or feeling of strangeness. The once-divided parts had been joined together, yet were still not a single unit.

This feeling of incompleteness—but in terms of which model of reference?—was perhaps only an illusion born of an inability to conceptualize in-between worlds. Was there a process of hybridization gestating beneath the apparent triumph of the West? What go-betweens and intermediaries were skirting between the two cities and their unnatural pasts? Where, for example, should we place the Asian vendors whose snow-covered stalls crowded the subway station at Schönhausen Allee? Where do we put the gypsies begging beneath Alexanderplatz Station? Berlin's jumble of historical periods constitute other borderlines: the passerby who dwells on the remains of Anhalt Station, once the city's largest and most famous train station, should be aware that it was bombed in 1943, closed by the Soviets in 1957, dynamited by West Berlin's Senate in 1961, and finally reduced to its mummified appearance of an ancient ruin. Such complexity is an affair of both space and time.

The film *Europa* magnificently evoked this in-between state. Director Lars von Trier revealed the chaos of a society bled dry, just emerging from a totalitarian regime, of a Germany devastated by war and thrust into the unknown, prey to an nameless future. In Von Trier's own words, the Germany of *Europa*—that of 1945—was a "strange zone." It was emblematic of those intermediate worlds that arise in the aftermath of catastrophe, staggering between a disintegrating system and a recomposition brutally imposed by a triumphant West.

The hard sciences offer us images of these indistinct regions—transitions between colors, for instance, offer gradations of indescribable complexity.[36] Each time two colors seem ready to connect and merge, a third erupts between them. A study of the Mandelbrot set—that collection of points forming a skein of convoluted shapes and threads, allegedly "the most intricate object in mathematics"—shows that an apparently smooth border, once enlarged, is in fact composed of a chain of spirals.[37] Molecular biology, too, shows that the thresholds separating the lively from the inert, the living from the dead, and human life from nonhuman life are eminently problematic.

Borders may wander before settling into definitive places, just as they may go through random or transitory phases. Some continue to shift in an indefinite cycle, such as the borders separating the various ethnic groups in colonial America. In the eighteenth century, there was such a diverse range of mixtures of populations of European, indigenous, and African origin that a need was felt to distinguish a whole series of groups and subgroups. Painted illustrations of *castas* claimed to provide Europeans with a description of all these varieties, constituting a new genre that represented the unfulfillable task of establishing categories already overwhelmed by reality (and therefore ignored, in everyday life, by those concerned).

A THREADBARE CONCEPT

When coming to grips with mélange, we should be wary of the term "culture," now threadbare through use by generations of use by anthropologists, sociologists, and historians. Progressively endowed with highly diverse meanings, taken up by philosophers,[38] adopted by historians often less concerned than their anthropological colleagues with the content they gave it, the term wound up invading the media and the corridors of bureaucracy. Originally applied to premodern, primitive worlds, "culture" was later extended to modern societies and contemporary realities, becoming a kind of carryall term increasingly difficult to pin down. Not that it is easy to abandon the term[39]—it sticks to the pen and may well be encountered in these very pages. And it sustains the belief—whether avowed, unconscious, or secret—that a "complex set" exists with a coherent, stable totality of tangible contours, able to condition behavior: culture. Whatever the place or period, one need merely define the content of this culture, revealing its "logic" and shedding light on its functions and virtualities, simultaneously taking care to reveal its hard, unchanging core. Yet this "culturalist" approach tends to stamp reality with an obsession for order, analysis, and formulation that is in fact specific to modernity.[40] By stressing specificities and differences at the expense of everything that links one culture to other groups—near or far—we quickly broach the rhetorics of otherness and multiculturalism that defend the "cohabitation and coexistence of separate, juxtaposed groups, resolutely turned toward the past, which must be protected from any encounter with others."[41] Now, study of the history of any given human group alone demonstrates that, while acknowledging that a set of practices and beliefs possesses some autonomy or other, it is more like an amorphous cluster in perpetual movement than a well-defined system.[42]

The category "culture" is a perfect example of slapping a Western concept onto realities that it transforms or effaces. The routine use of the term minimizes the fact that such realities inevitably and irreversibly contain foreign "contaminations," influences, and borrowings acquired from elsewhere. It suggests that mestizo processes are mechanisms that occur on the edge of stable entities labeled cultures or civilizations, or are a kind of disorder that might suddenly scramble impeccably structured—and allegedly authentic—units.[43]

"A PROPER GENTLEMAN IS A MAN OF PARTS"

Yet another pitfall awaits researchers: the notion of identity, which assigns every human being or group characteristics and aspirations—also highly determined—supposedly based on a stable or unchanging cultural substrate. Such a definition may be provided by the people concerned or by the conditioned reflex of an observer; and it can be simplified in everyday language to a curt label which soon turns into caricature.

Conceiving the history of Mexico as a confrontation between "Aztecs" and "Spaniards" is just one example: by stressing false categories, we overlook the multiple, mobile, and stratified groups to which the protagonists of that history belonged. A "Spaniard" was also—and perhaps primarily—an individual from Andalusia, Castile, Extremadura, Aragon, or the Basque country. Within each region, these Spaniards defined themselves first of all by the *patria* (land) and town from which they came: we know how staunchly conquistadors from the city of Medellín, led by Hernán Cortés, opposed clans from other towns. On a smaller scale, being a member of a specific lineage—all the descendents of a common ancestor from a well-known house (*solar conocido*)—often counted as much as social background, region of birth, town or "nation" of allegiance. When it came to "Indians," insofar as sources provide a clear picture, it seems that the same diversity of affiliations and social positions obtained. Yet out of habit or ignorance, we continue to identify all the populations of central Mexico as Aztecs, a term that refers exclusively to the mythical ancestors of the founders of Mexico City.

Every human being is endowed with a series of identities—or equipped with more or less stable bearings—that can be successively or simultaneously brought into play, depending on context. A "gentleman is a man of parts," said Montaigne.[44] Identity is a private story, itself dependent on relative ability to interiorize or reject instilled norms. Socially, a person constantly deals with a galaxy of individuals, each of whom has multiple identities. The variable geometry and intermittent nature of these configurations[45] mean that identity is always defined on the basis of multiple interactions and relations. It was the context of conquest and colonization of the Americas that incited European invaders to identify their adversaries as "Indians," thereby subsuming everyone under one unifying, simplifying label.

Identity and culture: everything covered by those two terms is constantly in danger of being fetishized, reified, naturalized, and elevated to the status of absolute.[46] This is sometimes deliberate—with well-known political and ideological consequences—yet may often be due to mental inertia or inattention with regard to clichés and stereotypes. In fact, if such categories so color our vision of things and provide an apparently satisfactory analytic grid, that is because they stem from deeply rooted modes of thought.

Those mental habits recur throughout historic analysis and proceed in the same fashion everywhere,[47] leading people to speak of a "baroque America" or an "ancien régime economy" as though these were homogeneous and coherent realities whose original characteristics merely needed to be established. Or people may study "pre-Hispanic religions" without worrying about the validity of that framework, even though it merely apes the concepts and practices of Western Christendom. Elsewhere we have shown how sixteenth-century chroniclers and their successors, based on more or less debatable analogies, used Western categories and subcategories (religion, god, pantheon, temple, sacrifice, myth) to classify traits wrenched arbitrarily from the Amerindian context.[48] Now, that view presupposes that there exists an underlying model—universal and timeless, although defined in the West—called religion, composed of identical reference points independent of period, region, or society.

This approach—Aristotelian in origin[49]—spurred specialists to discuss content without querying the existence or degree of reality—indeed, relevance—of the envelope they thought they were filling. Hugues Neveux has provided convincing examples of this in his book on peasant revolts in Europe.[50] Specialists in economic history, meanwhile, have also decried the latent fetishism of categories, proposing to "question the concepts used by historians (on the formation of prices, money, links between economy and demography)" the better to expose "their relative timelessness" and "the difficulty of using them to construct a specifically historical temporality."[51]

In short, the historian's tools must be subjected to a severe critique and a reexamination of the canonical categories that organize, condition, and often partition research: economy, society, civilization, art, culture, and so on. Such a critique is beyond the scope of this book, but it would be useful to keep it in mind when embarking on the seas of culture, identity, and mestizo processes. If the latter strongly resist analysis, that is because the usual categories—society, religion, politics, economy, art, culture—incite us to separate what cannot be separated and to overlook phenomena that straddle the standard divides.[52]

THE INERTIA OF ETHNOCENTRISM

Vague vocabulary and the accumulated impediments of mental habits do not explain everything, however. History, in fact, has generally ignored mestizo phenomena. Although it has taken an interest in nationalist movements, in the emergence of identities, and in the relationship between pop culture and scholarly culture, history has rarely dealt directly with the effects of mélange within non-Western societies and the dynamics it triggers. European historians generally favor Western history over that of the rest of the world, the history of Europe over the rest of the West, and, even more commonly, national history over that of neighboring countries. Whatever the reasons for such ethnocentrism, it has hardly encouraged exploration of mélanges.

Might historical anthropology be an exception? Having arisen on the fringes of history and ethnography, historical anthropology has taught us to go beyond the Eurocentric discourse of the colonizers and to adopt the view—or "vision"—of the vanquished peoples, an approach embodied by the work of Miguel León-Portilla and Nathan Wachtel. Such work has revealed the wealth of forms of thought and modes of expression that had been developed in the Americas prior to the European invasion.

Yet can we exhume the "vision of the vanquished" and reveal its complex workings without questioning the impact of the intellectual constructs and interpretations of reality that these foreign societies deployed against Western experience? Today it is no longer possible to describe the intellectual clash between Renaissance chroniclers and Amerindian societies as a merciless duel between the truths of reason and the mistaken ways of primitive societies. And it must be recognized that ancient American societies had developed modes of perceiving time—or, more accurately, what we Westerners call "time"—as sophisticated as our own, in other words as complex and efficient as the one we still use to record history.

By their presence alone, and by the many traces they have left, these conceptual constructs challenge the alleged universality of our vision of things, because they yield forms of temporality and historicity irreducible to our own.[53] This confrontation sheds light on the extent of ethnocentrism and artifice in the notion of culture and its frequent inappropriateness to non-European realities.[54] In the case of Mexico, indigenous accounts reveal that the idea of a Nahua culture or Meso-American culture is a pure construct by Western observers.[55] Such a challenge cannot be lightly dismissed simply because it is promoted by advocates of postmodernism and postcolonial studies.[56] The planetary melting pot so present in everyday life reminds us that were are not alone in the world of ideas, that "Western" certainly no longer means "universal." We must therefore learn to relativize our modes of thought by practicing what Italian anthropologist Ernesto De Martino called "critical ethnocentrism."[57]

In order to understand the "vision of the vanquished," scholars logically focused on the Amerindian side, how it survived and resisted colonization, by showing how Western borrowings were absorbed into indigenous tradition. This attitude, adopted and amplified by "cultural studies," has sometimes locked indigenous society into a purely native and exaggeratedly homogeneous framework by systematically excluding mestizo phenomena from the field of observation. This represents an idealized framework in the sense that some advocates of "political correctness" and "the Indian voice" have set Amerindian philosophy—which they have themselves exhumed—above Western rationality, itself reduced to a simple tool of domination at the service of European nations.[58]

Now, giving precedence to everything Amerindian over everything Western merely inverts the terms of debate instead of changing or reinvigorating it. Furthermore, this denunciation of European Eurocentrism barely masks a new imperialism promoted by an academic philosophy spawned in the best U.S. universities. Although this school of thought readily proclaims its distance from Europe, it nevertheless remains fundamentally Western in form and content. Above all, the indigenous philosophy that countered European domination was far from possessing the sharp outlines, "purity," and authenticity attributed to it. Only rarely was it not mixed with features of Western origin, did it not make room for a more or less mestizo vision of the world.

ORDER AND TIME

Still other conceptions impede our understanding of mélange and mestizo processes. The complexity of these phenomena accords poorly with a positivist tradition that maintains a vision of time based on linearity. The notion of culture emerged from an evolutionist viewpoint,[59] one that long pervaded history. Historians often tend to interpret past periods as the product of linear movement, evolution, indeed progression or progress. As though at every point, a new phase was supposed to develop forces whose seeds could be found in preceding phases. Thus the Renaissance stemmed from the Middle Ages and paved the way for the modern era. This linear history carries in itself the perpetual question of roots, which itself implies the idea of a past purity or authenticity that must be recovered. We must therefore be doubly cautious when seeking to pinpoint the early signs—in sixteenth-century Iberia—of the mestizo phenomena and globalization that now seem to us to occupy the center of the worldwide stage.

Yet mestizo mechanisms disrupt that linearity. They arose in sixteenth-century America at the junction of distinct temporalities—those of Western Christendom and Amerindian societies—which they brought into brutal contact and mutual interpenetration. Here the metaphor of contiguity, succession, and replacement that subtends an evolutionary interpretation is no longer valid, not only because the temporality of the vanquished was not automatically replaced by that of the victors, but because it could coexist with it for centuries. By suddenly merging societies long held to be distinct, the intrusion of mélange undermines portrayals of historic development as a unique evolution, and sheds light on the crossroads, side streets, and dead ends that should all be taken into account.[60]

The idea of linear time is usually accompanied by a belief that an order of things must exist. We have a hard time abandoning the idea that every system possesses a kind of primal stability toward which it inexorably tends. Thus economic history is often based on "strong, implicit hypotheses such as an evolution in terms of equilibrium—every movement correspond[s] to a momentary disequilibrium resolved in the context of a movement of greater span."[61] It is not surprising, then, that the complexity and mobility of mélange phenomena and conflated temporalities provoke images of disorder. Yet by placing mélange alongside disequilibrium and perturbation, we relegate it to the status of a transitory or secondary phenomenon, in theory infinitely less revealing than the structure within which it allegedly occurs.[62]

Reality hardly matches this view of things. Instead of dealing with occasional perturbations within an underlying order ever ready to reassert itself, most systems display behaviors that fluctuate between various states of equilibrium, without the existence of any mechanism for a return to "normal."[63] On the contrary, the return to apparently identical or similar states winds up creating new situations in the long run. The more perturbed the conditions, the more the oscillations between distinct states occur, provoking the dispersal of the system's features, which wander in search of new configurations. The system's movements fluctuate between absolute regularity and absolute irregularity, maintaining a wide margin of unpredictability.[64]

Viewed from this angle, mélange and mestizo phenomena lose their appearance of temporary disorder and assume a basic dynamic of their own. In my opinion, this interpretation is the one best adapted to the complexity of mélange and the significance of mestizo processes. Yet it also makes studying them difficult, since it runs up against not only our rigid categories but also our normal perception of time, order, and causality. Mestizo processes belong, in fact, to a class of objects that leave historians fairly disarmed.

Ilya Prigogine, in *Les Lois du chaos* (*The Laws of Chaos*) refers to Karl Popper's discussion of "clocks and clouds." Classical physics was interested primarily in clocks, today's physics, mainly in clouds.[65] Prigogine explains that the precision of clocks continues to haunt our thinking by making us believe that it can attain the precision of the particular and practically unique models studied by classical physics. Yet what predominates in nature and our environment are clouds—those desperately complex, fuzzy, changing, fluctuating, ever-moving forms. Mestizo mechanisms relate to that order of reality.

THE CLOUD MODEL

The concern to grasp reality in all its complexity requires that we distance ourselves from the rampant positivism and determinism inherited from the nineteenth century, along with its largely superseded science. The cloud model supposes that all reality includes an unknowable element and that it also contains a dose of uncertainty and randomness. For social historians, the uncertainty involves the lives of players unable to predict their fates or the accidents that befall them. Randomness is the outcome of the interaction of the countless components of a system.[66] If, with the help of a microscope, we observe a speck of dust suspended in water, we will see it shaken by incessant movement in all directions. This motion is due to the thermal agitation of the water molecules, which are so numerous and so invisible that it is impossible to predict the trajectory of the speck of dust. The trajectory therefore appears random. Randomness is not linked to the multitude of elements present, for it can also be found in simpler systems composed of a limited number of observable elements.[67]

Historians do not always take uncertainty and randomness into account, even though both processes played key roles in situations such as the discovery of America, where totally separate worlds suddenly came into contact. It is the presence of randomness and uncertainty that lends mestizo processes their ungraspable nature, paralyzing our efforts to understand them. For how can the diversity and multiplicity of mestizo phenomena feed back into the play of classic causality? Can we perceive a "logic" at work behind mélanges of all kinds, or does that term confer the implacable, automatic nature of a law on things somewhat slow and regular?

Complexity, unpredictability, and randomness therefore seem inherent to mélanges and hybrids. It might be hypothesized that they possess a chaotic dimension, as do many other social and natural phenomena. That is why our intellectual tools, inherited from the Aristotelian sciences developed in the nineteenth century, leave us unprepared to face them. The question of mestizo mechanisms is not just one of objects, of whether or not they exist. The study of mestizo phenomena also—and above all—raises a problem of intellectual tools: how should we conceptualize mélanges?

HINTS FROM THE PAST

Given this series of pitfalls and problems, what is a historian to do? I shall discuss mestizo mechanisms and their intellectual wellsprings within a specific historical and geographical setting, namely Renaissance Europe and the conquest of the Americas, in particular Spanish Mexico. The reasons for this choice were mentioned above: the first waves of global cross-fertilizations were contemporary with the establishment of the first world economy between 1570 and 1640.[68] In a matter of decades, the Spanish and Portuguese managed to dominate Western Europe, much of the Americas, and the coasts of Africa even as they asserted their ambitions in the Philippines, in Nagasaki, in Macao on the Chinese coast, and in Cochin and Goa on the Indian Ocean.

The term "mestizo" will be used to designate the mélanges that occurred in the Americas in the sixteenth century—mélanges between individuals, imaginative faculties, and lifestyles originating on four continents (America, Europe, Africa, Asia). As to the term hybridization, it will be used for mélanges that occurred within a single civilization or historic ensemble—Christian Europe, Meso-America—and between traditions that had often coexisted for centuries. Mestizo and hybrid mechanisms concern not only objective processes observable in various domains but also the awareness that individuals had of them in that past, as expressed through the manipulations they effected, the constructs they developed, and the arguments and criticisms they advanced.[69]

3 THE SHOCK OF CONQUEST

> When we saw the land through our inner vision, it
> appeared filled with great shadows, thrust into the
> mayhem of transgression and total disorder.
> —Motolinía, *Memoriales*

The mestizo processes triggered by the conquest of the New World[1] seem
intrinsically linked to two other major sixteenth-century phenomena in the
Americas: on the one hand, what is generally called the "shock of conquest," and on the other, what I designate by the term "Westernization,"
namely the multifarious undertaking by which Western Europe, in the wake
of Castile, conquered the souls, bodies, and lands of the New World.[2] The
fact that mestizo mechanisms arose during Europe's expansionism, in a context of colonization, means that they cannot be limited to cultural phenomena. If we want to understand them, we cannot overlook their links to the
concomitant conquest and Westernization. The nature of those links needs
to be specified.

WORLDS TURNED UPSIDE DOWN[3]

The mestizo processes of the modern era normally appear against troubled
a background, against a setting of shattered identities. Although not all
mestizo phenomena are necessarily the product of conquest, those stemming from Western expansion into the Americas inevitably arose from the
rubble of defeat.

In 1521, that "sad and dreadful year,"[4] Mexico City fell to Spanish conquistadors and their indigenous allies. We owe the best description of that
period to a Franciscan monk whom the local natives called Motolinía, "the
poor [man]." One chapter of Motolinía's chronicle details the repercussions
of the fall of Mexico City in the early 1920s: "God struck this earth with
ten terribly cruel plagues to punish the harshness and obstinacy of its inhabitants who held prisoner the daughters of Zion, in other words, their own
souls, under the yoke of Pharaoh.... The first of these plagues was ... the

arrival, on one of the ships, of a Black infected with smallpox, an illness unknown in these lands."⁵ The ensuing epidemic among the natives was so virulent that entire regions lost half of their inhabitants. Many people then died of hunger. "Since everyone fell ill at the same time, they could not care for each other and there was no one to prepare food." In many places, entire families were wiped out: "to halt the stench, since they could not bury [the dead], they demolished the houses over them, turning their homes into their tombs." Smallpox was known as the "great leprosy" because people "were covered from head to foot in sores that made them resemble lepers." As had occurred in ancient Egypt when the waters, springs, and streams were transformed into rivers of blood, "this land became the blood of death." The disease killed young and old. That was God's chastisement for past atrocities, namely the practice of human sacrifice: "In this land there reigned immense cruelty, and the blood that was spilled was offered to Satan, the demonic angel."

The second plague was the death of indigenous warriors. "The muddy waters of the lagoon of Mexico produced frogs instead of fish: the dead floated, swollen with water, their eyes bulging like frogs, devoid of eyelid and eyebrow, staring in opposite directions, a sign of the sinner's dissoluteness." Corpses cluttered the waters of lakes like rotting fish, poisoning air and food. Indigenous accounts corroborate this terrifying vision: "And broken bones lay on the paths. Hair was scattered around. The roofs of houses collapsed, their walls reddened. Worms thrived in streets and squares while the walls were spattered with brains. The water was reddish as though it had been dyed. We drank it as it was. We even drank brackish water. . . . We were all alike in this, whether young, priest, woman, or child. . . . "⁶

The hecatomb was followed by famine. "Hunger was cruelly painful, swelling and twisting the stomach and intestines until death followed. . . . This great famine killed many among the poor and people with little."⁷ Disease, war, famine—the Horsemen of the Apocalypse were exterminating the Indians in their homeland.⁸

The disorganization of production caused by these destructions and the collapse of farming were compounded by the ravages of the new system of exploitation and payment of tribute. Black slaves and overseers tyrannized the Indians in the same way that "Egyptian oppressors had made the people of Israel suffer. . . . They poisoned and corrupted everything, stinking like meat infested with flies, due to their evil examples." Invaders who had been merely peasants in Spain acted like lords and began issuing orders to Mexico's "native" leaders; blacks "made themselves more served and feared than had they been the lords of these folk."⁹ The disintegration of social hierarchies was accompanied by other, equally uncontrollable phenomena. Gold fever drove Spaniards "into the bonds and chains of the devil from which they could not escape without suffering severe wounds."

Mexico City, the former native capital that became "the head of New Spain," was at the center of the maelstrom. Reconstructing the city was a gigantic task "which, in the early years, required more people than the building of the Temple of Jerusalem in the days of Solomon." It mobilized swarms of men exhausted by the tasks imposed on them: "As they worked, some were hit by beams, others tumbled into the void or were carried off by collapsing buildings that were being demolished here to be rebuilt there." As in the Apocalypse, peals of thunder and lightning split the city into three parts, delivering it to "the desires of the flesh, the desires of the eyes, and the arrogance of the living." That is how Motolinía's pen denounced the vanity of victors impatient to build gigantic homes that their forebears would never have imagined.

Many Indians were reduced to slavery. Parents sold their children in order to pay tribute. Many were persecuted so that their property could be extorted; they were thrown into jails which they would never leave alive, "because the Spaniards treated them in a beastly way and cared less for them than their animals and horses."[10] Everywhere, gigantic herds of humans converged toward Mexico City, where they were branded with a hot iron. That was the eighth plague, though not the least, for the ninth was even worse—forced labor in the mines. Motolinía's description needs no comment: "As to the slaves who died in the mines, their stench was such that it provoked the plague, especially in the mines at Huaxyacac. There, for half a league all around and on a good portion of the road, you walked only on corpses and bones. The vultures and ravens that came to devour the bodies of the dead and satiate themselves on this cruel butchery were so numerous that they darkened the sun."[11] Meanwhile, villages were emptying as Indians sought refuge in the mountains. It was a time of "dreadful, opaque clouds."

The crisis also struck the ranks of the victors. Trouble arose from rivalries between the conquerors; "dissension and factions" brought the country to the brink of civil war. That is why the plagues of Mexico were worse than those of Egypt—they lasted longer, caused more deaths, and were due more to human cruelty and greed than to divine wrath.[12]

CATASTROPHIC IMAGERY AND MILLENARIAN SIGNS

Motolinía borrowed his imagery and interpretations from the biblical books of Exodus and Revelation (Apocalypse). His rhetoric of catastrophe and chastisement was first of all designed to anchor the events of the Conquest in a metaphysical and providentialist context. The recollection of the plagues of Egypt and the evocation of the second, sixth, and seventh angels of the Apocalypse lent universal scope to his account and underscored the singularity of the events. Putrid waters, rivers of blood, foul stenches issuing from the mouths of dragon and beast, thunder and lightning, historical parallels with the fall of Jerusalem and its destruction by Titus—everything was employed to convey the confusion at the time, to paint the ravages of disease and war, to describe the corruption of social relationships and the unchallenged reign of gold and silver.

Ever since the Middle Ages, apocalyptic texts and images provided a means of conceiving disorder and visualizing its fearful repercussions, as exemplified on the walls of Capella Nuova in the cathedral of Orvieto, Italy. It was in this chapel, in the closing years of the fifteenth century, that Luca Signorelli depicted the reign of the Antichrist, which art historians have discussed at length.[13] Signorelli's frescoes and Motolinía's text are a Christian way of describing and explaining global upheaval. For Motolinía, the crises gripping post-Conquest Mexico, prey to spectacular mutations and unheard-of calamities, could be expressed only in the extreme terms of an apocalyptic account.[14]

It is not the millenarian angle that interests us here, but rather the way Motolinía interpreted unforeseen situations.[15] The apocalyptic and Old Testament allusions supplied him with a model of the catastrophes triggered by the Conquest, even if he recognized the model's lack of precision: "On looking closely, there are major differences between these plagues and those of Egypt." Motolinía was trying to establish relationships between the series of events he recounted. Far from arbitrary, the successive plagues that struck Mexico constituted a detailed series of related crises: epidemic, ravages of war, famine, tyranny of middlemen, extortion of all kinds, mad rush for gold, murderous reconstruction of Mexico City, reduction to slavery, labor in the mines, divisiveness among the victors. The immediate repercussions of the Conquest, identified with the three first plagues, were later joined by the destabilizing effects of Spanish domination. Installing the new settlers caused widespread instability—the demands and construction of a colonial infrastructure exhausted the indigenous labor force. Reducing a large part of the conquered population to slavery ruined old social hierarchies even as conflicts between conquistadors brought the land to the brink of disaster: "Revolts and plagues so thoroughly destroyed the land that many houses were abandoned. There was no one who was spared the pain and tears which lasted for years."[16]

According to Motolinía's account, the disintegration was characterized by its swift pace and acceleration. "Great was the haste with which the Spaniards made slaves in the early years... [and] the impressment they imposed on the Indians." The monk took care to distinguish exogenous, military, and epidemiological shocks directly related to the invasion from endogenous perturbations caused by Spanish settlers. This chronic instability dominated the social landscape throughout the early decades of colonization.

Finally, instead of contenting himself with a providentialist explanation—God's chastisement of the Indians—Motolinía reintroduces human responsibility into the series of disasters sparked by men. And the men in question were Spaniards as much as Indians. Whereas the epidemic and even the war appeared to be divine punishment against various layers of the indigenous population, other ills befell innocent, powerless, terrified losers. The monk's target changes from the third plague onward. He compares the Spanish conquerors to "Egyptian oppressors who afflicted the people of Israel," to torturers who treated the natives like animals, to worshipers of the Golden Calf who fell into the clutches of the Devil. It was now a question of "trials and tribulations inflicted upon the Indians." The "vision of the vanquished" had replaced that of the victors.

In his conclusion, however, Motolinía challenged even this perception of things. The chapter concludes with a description of social chaos: the Spaniards were divided and ready to kill one another, surrounded by Indians ready to swoop on their conquerors.[17] By rejecting dualistic or Manichaean interpretations, Motolinía conveyed the instability and disturbances of the world he observed in the 1520s. Unlike Hispanophile or Indianophile versions of the Conquest, both equally simplistic, his account makes it possible to grasp the past in its disorder and complexity, without Motolinía ever abdicating his own profound convictions. His depiction of the past—not to be confused with the reality it depicted—reveals that a Renaissance monk was no less well equipped than we are to describe the shock of conquest.

THE DISORDER OF THINGS

Around 1530, had we viewed Mexico City from the top of the still superb ruins of the pyramid of Templo Mayor, we would have seen a kind of freak city, a composite architecture composed of crumbling remains and newly erected buildings. War, followed by the construction of a Spanish-style town, abolished the regular lines of the pre-Columbian city. Yet it did not become a Castilian town firmly rooted upon the ruined palaces. Instead, the urban horizon united, juxtaposed, and—more often—superimposed a heterogeneous pile of abandoned remains, destroyed or renovated Indian buildings, and strongholds endowed with Castilian-style towers or crenellated ramparts. This new city—Hispano-Indian and medieval-Renaissance—arose in the vague interstices between the vanquished conurbation (the pre-Hispanic *altepetl*), the models envisioned by the conquerors, the urban ambitions of the new overlords, and the effective possibilities of reconstruction. The composition of the city's population would have been equally surprising: Indian nobility, indigenous slaves and servants, conquistadors from every part of Spain, and blacks from Africa rubbed shoulders in the streets, houses, and public buildings, mingling their bodies, scents, and voices.

Spatial disorder was accompanied by a confusion of temporal frameworks, born of the confrontation of different time systems. In those years of conquest, time systems appeared to be exactly what there were, namely constructs proper to each world, representations of passing time expressed through institutions, rites, and techniques of measurement. Pre-Hispanic society placed great importance on "counting time," which played a key role in cosmology. Elaborate calendars recorded passing time in order to identify the uninterrupted series of festivities that marked the Indian year. These celebrations enabled Nahua priests to act on the cycles of time, which they were able to speed up or slow down according to circumstances. The pace was accelerated by hectic races organized between cities of the valley, whereas the calculated slowness of a sacrificial victim's climb up the steps of a pyramid before meeting the blade of an obsidian knife temporarily delayed the moment of death. Extravagant offerings and sacrifices helped to prolong the lives of the gods who fed on the blood that flowed generously from human victims.

The sudden arrival of the Spanish and the abolition of grand festivities—outlawed along with human sacrifice or henceforth impossible to celebrate due to lack of participants, resources, and freedom of action—plunged the indigenous masses into a growing void. In a matter of years they saw themselves deprived of ways of measuring and influencing the passing of time. Time—or rather the indigenous equivalent of it—was dwindling away.

Now, indigenous time systems could not be instantly replaced by Christian temporality.[18] A strange period arose, disturbed by apparitions of the old gods as well as the new devil. While it is difficult to analyze the strangeness of this intermediate situation, it is even more awkward to imagine the awkwardness it generated.

At the risk of anachronism, let us return to Lars von Trier's film, *Europa*. It would never occur to us to associate the defeat of Hitler's Germany with the fall of indigenous Mexico. Yet Von Trier's filming technique represent a fully successful attempt to evoke, through imagery, the apocalyptic conflation of two clashing worlds. One astounding scene illustrates the collision of collective memories and times: on a train racing through the rubble of conquered Germany at night, there emerge figures wrenched from the world of concentration camps (wretchedly familiar images of skeletons dressed in prison tatters, piled on their pallets). *Europa* hitches the immediate postwar period to the Nazi past like the wagons of a train, establishing inconceivable continuities.

In Mexico City, disorganized urban life and scrambled time systems accentuated the social and political disorder. Throughout the 1520s, the failure of the polices adopted by the new authorities increased the general confusion. Either impotent or indifferent to the demographic hemorrhage decimating the indigenous population, the Spanish authorities had to improvise a society for which they had no precedent, unless the colonization of the West Indies and its subsequent disaster was taken as a harbinger of the occupation of Mexico. How could Mexico City be spared the fate of Caribbean towns, deserted as swiftly as they were founded, sometimes becoming the haunts of ghosts who terrorized passing visitors?

"STRANGE ZONES": CONQUEST AND CHRONIC INSTABILITY

In Mexico, as everywhere in the New World, the sudden appearance of Europeans was initially synonymous with chaos and disorder. Zones of severe turbulence were created in the West Indies (1493–1520), the Andes (1532–1555), and Portuguese Brazil. Neither the evolution of colonization nor the mélanges triggered by the Spanish Conquest can be understood if this basic fact is overlooked.

Troubling "novelties" created "discord," according to chronicler Fernández de Oviedo.[19] Shaken by dissension, revolts, and civil wars, disturbed by a radical disruption of ancestral hierarchies and political systems, in a mere matter of years these "strange zones"—to use Von Trier's expression—became the scene of the disjunction of local communities and an accelerated metamorphosis of society. They were wracked by all kinds of fluctuations and perturbations, most of which were beyond human control, such as the ravages of disease and death on native populations devoid of immune defenses against European pathologies. The epidemics brought by Europeans cut down generations and collective memories more efficiently than swords of steel or deafening cannon of acrid smell.

In the wake of conquest, "strange zones" emerged on Caribbean islands, in Mexico, then in Peru and Brazil. They cannot be correctly described as "colonial societies," for that term supposes a certain state of accomplishment and relative stability that would be attained only after one or several decades had passed (not to mention the death of millions of individuals). Instead of such societies, there appeared indefinable "agglomerations" of uncertain future. Motolinía reported that the Indians could have swept the Spanish presence away at any moment had God not maintained them in a "state of blindness" and miraculous passivity. True enough, the balance of power long remained unpredictable, even if a retrospective illusion of inevitability—as described by philosopher Raymond Aron—makes us perceive the Conquest as an ineluctable fact. These "agglomerations" went through more or less intense periods of turbulence of varying duration—sometimes intensified through human catastrophe (three million deaths in the West Indies between 1494 and 1508)[20] or constant war (Peru), sometimes evolving toward progressive stability (as in Mexico).

The agglomerations arose from the brutal collision, then forced interpenetration, of groups and societies which the Conquest threw into chronic instability. The invaders, too, were subject to precariousness and powerlessness. As soon as they arrived in the West Indies, the craftsmen on whom the construction of new establishments depended were weakened and disorganized by disease (while the earliest colonists, staunchly attached to their status as *hidalgos*—gentry—refused to pitch in manually); most of the craftsmen "were ill, thin, and famished, and could do little because they lacked the strength."[21] In Mexico, the European invaders were just a small cohort cut off from its island bases (Cuba and Hispaniola) and far from its Iberian roots (Extremadura, Andalusia, the Basque country, and so on).

"How is it that there were survivors among all those who left to settle countries so far from their homelands," wondered Oviedo, "leaving behind them all the charms to which they had been accustomed since childhood, exiling themselves far from friends and relations?" Day after day they were thrust into the unknown, the unpredictable. The unpredictability of exploration: having landed on the tropical coast of Veracruz in April 1519, by November the invaders found themselves in snowcapped mountains facing a huge metropolis that was probably the largest city in the world, Mexico-Tenochtitlán. The unpredictability of conquest: dissension within the ranks of the Spanish camp was in fact as dangerous to Cortés and his troops as was the reaction of indigenous peoples.

Attacked, felled, and vanquished, the indigenous societies were politically mutilated, socially dismembered, and decimated by war and epidemics. One of the Nahua peoples called the Mexica (incorrectly known today as Aztecs) lost the dominance it had managed to wield over most of central Mexico. Yet even indigenous collaborators with the Spaniards, who were little better off, soon became aware of the precariousness of their situation and the uncertainty hanging over them.

The relationships between victors, vanquished, and collaborators—all coming from worlds with such dissimilar trajectories—and the consequences they engendered were of unprecedented complexity. Unprecedented because the medieval hybridizations that had occurred on the Iberian peninsula were different from the mestizo processes of the Conquest. Although the peninsula's history was long the product of conflicts, exchanges, mélanges, and coexistence between the three worlds—Christian, Jewish, and Muslim—contact had been established over a period of time; the inhabitants of Spain had been "seeing one another" for centuries and had emerged from a shared background of ancient paganism followed by monotheism.

In the Americas, the shock was as brutal as it was unforeseen. It cannot be reduced to a question of simple discrepancy nor to a clash between to stable systems, one of which was suddenly disturbed by the intrusion of the other. There was nothing monolithic about the social milieu embodied by the conquerors. The invaders perceived themselves socially as a jumble of "different kinds of people."[22] If their own chroniclers are to be believed, most of the time they were scarcely commendable individuals. "In the beginning, for every noble man of illustrious blood there came ten coarse men and others of low and obscure lineage."[23] Many rootless, delinquent characters poured into the Spanish Indies; others composed the bulk of the Portuguese population that settled in Brazil.[24] Social differences were compounded by regional disparities: Castilians, Basques, and Extremadurans cordially detested one another and had a great deal of difficulty getting along.

The diversity of indigenous and European protagonists—on religious, linguistic, physical, and social levels—and the tensions between them produced a heterogeneity further accentuated by the disruption of defeat and a deficient political framework. Traditional local authorities, militarily defeated and deprived of their ancestral aura, suffered from a crisis of legitimacy, whereas the new Hispanic authorities struggled to define and impose themselves. The Conquest ultimately eroded all authority. The control exercised by the new sovereign authority—incarnated by Emperor Charles V, who ruled from either Spain or the Netherlands—was limited, not to say nonexistent. Continental and maritime distances slowed the transmission of information and order.

Motolinía felt that this distance made Mexico frankly ungovernable: "One cannot govern such a large country from so far away; a thing so separate from Castile and so distant cannot maintain itself without being exposed to great desolation and without collapsing day after day for want of a king and a leader at its head."[25] Corruption was widespread, morality was loose, the Spanish Inquisition had no foothold. The strongest did as they pleased.[26] At any moment civil war might erupt between conquerors divided into "leagues and cabals," "factions," "parties," and "clans," all carried away by passions and tyrannical ambitions, forming so many pressure groups that they were accused of seeking to imitate the *comuneros* of Castile.[27]

Imaginative constructs were also perturbed. The Mexica had great difficulty situating their invaders: it was only later, after a patient labor of reinterpretation, of masking and filtering facts, that they associated the arrival of Cortés with the return of their god Quetzalcoatl.[28] As to the conquistadors, they swiftly realized that the vanquished people were neither Jewish nor Muslim, and that the reality they were discovering was far more unsettling than they had first imagined. Although images drawn from chivalric romances initially provided interpretations for what they could not explain themselves, such imagery was of little use when they had to begin governing this strange, diabolical land. They dreamed for a while of the sierras of the Lady of Silver with her palace of precious metal, until they were beguiled by fabulous news arriving from Peru and by descriptions, far to the north, of the Seven Golden Cities of Cibola, a North American version of the Amazonian Eldorado.[29]

MESTIZO PROCESSES

Relationships between victors and vanquished also took mestizo forms which blurred the borders that the new authorities sought to maintain between the two groups. Right from the start, a new destabilizing element was introduced by biological mestizos—that is to say, the result of physical interbreeding—often accompanied by mestizo beliefs and practices.

The overwhelming majority of the new European immigrants were male: soldiers, priests, merchants, and adventurers of every ilk. Single or separated from their wives (who remained in Castile or on Caribbean islands), these Europeans assumed the prerogatives of all victors. They behaved all the more freely in that they found themselves in pagan territory, practically beyond the reach of the Catholic Church. European clergy was long limited to a strict minimum, and the few priests who accompanied the conquistadors did not always try to put a brake on abuses. Indian women were easy prey for the invaders, who had often violent and fleeting relations with them without worrying about the young offspring they left behind. Rape, concubines, and, more rarely, marriages generated a new category of population—mestizos—of ambiguous status. It was not clear whether mestizos should be integrated into the Spanish world or the indigenous community. In principle, these half-breeds had no place in a society legally divided into a "nation of Indians" and a "nation of Spaniards." This was all the truer in the case of mulattos born of black women and Spanish men or Indian women and black men.[30]

For all these reasons, Indians, blacks, and Spaniards had to invent new ways of coexisting—or, for the first group in particular, ways of surviving—day after day. In every sphere, improvisation won out over norms and customs. The process of Westernization therefore began in this perturbed context, which explains the constant "excesses" and lethal outbursts decried by Las Casas in his *Historia de las Indias*. Another major figure of the day, Dominican friar Domingo de Betanzos, harshly criticized "the ordeals, experiments, changes, and novelties" that were on the verge of putting an end to the Indian question.[31] The invaders' rapaciousness, combined with a total lack of colonizing skills, provoked the irreparable: gold fever, incompetence, bungling, and short-term goals (combined with a good measure of contempt and indifference) resulted in an outlandish exploitation of indigenous labor that the Spaniards did not even bother to feed. There followed an "unpremeditated"[32] genocide, which hastily implemented relief measures only intensified, leading to the massive importation of slaves from Africa.

Would Mexico suffer the same fate as the Caribbean Islands? A terse comment expressed the disorder reigning there in the 1520s: "The land is lost...all is lost already, and every day will be lost further."[33] The comment applied equally to the military events that pitted the conquerors against one another, to the unseemly behavior of the wives of royal officers, to the immodesty of prostitutes, and to the fate of debt-ridden Spaniards who were thrown in prison or condemned to wander from island to island. The consequences of this "perdition" were equally disastrous on the younger indigenous generations: "Young people from eighteen to twenty are thorough scoundrels, are shameless, drunk and thieving, have very many mistresses, are killers and disobedient villains, are ill-bred, insolent and voracious...."[34]

It is hard to describe this succession of upheavals. The difficulty of grasping them is due to not only the number of variables involved, the unpredictability of intersecting trajectories, and the disparity between colliding traditions. It also stems from the vagueness of the opposing ensembles—where does the indigenous world begin, where does the conquistadors' world end? Their borders were so intertwined that they became indissociable. Indeed, it is impossible to describe in simple or straightforward terms such diverse situations as the exchanges between a Spaniard and his indigenous entourage, the rapport between the two communities within Mexico City, or the relations between the two populations on the level of the entire country. The same degree of vagueness, precariousness, and improvisation characterized all these situations, which cannot be analyzed simply in terms of acculturation or deculturation.

FROM UPRISINGS IN PERU TO *MAMELUCOS* IN BRAZIL

The disorder was even deeper, more spectacular, and more lasting in Peru. As elsewhere, the sudden appearance of conquistadors in the Andes provoked a social, political, and religious shock. But the political instability and uncertain future of the land were accentuated by two assassinations: Diego de Almagro was beheaded in 1538, and Francisco Pizarro was assassinated three years later. A series of uprisings sustained a climate of civil war enflamed by Inca factions divided into supporters and adversaries of the Spanish. These events helped to delay the establishment of a strong, respected, colonial government. Peru thus seems to have embodied the fears aroused by the Mexican experience against a background of crisis within the native nobility, high mortality among Indian populations, and rootlessness and self-destruction on the part of the invaders.

It was not until the middle of the sixteenth century that the Peruvian situation began to stabilize, and only with the arrival of Francesco de Toledo as viceroy did the Crown definitively impose its authority on all parties. The repercussions of the Conquest and disturbances were nevertheless irreversible. In the early seventeenth century, Indian chronicler Felipe Guaman Poma de Ayala painted a dreadful picture of the city of Lima, prey to a confusion of identifying signs and groups:

> He saw the city full of Indians who had left their villages and came and went as they pleased, having become Yanacona servants or craftsmen even though they had been sent to work in the mines; Indians of low extraction were dressed like Spaniards, wearing collar and sword; others cut their hair to avoid paying tribute and serving in the mines. It was the world turned upside down....In the same way, the author saw enormous numbers of Indian prostitutes burdened with little mestizos and mulattos, all wearing skirts, ankle boots, and hats; although they were married, they lived with Spaniards and Blacks and there were even some who did not want to marry Indians or leave the city because it would mean abandoning a prostitute's life....[35]

The long series of upheavals, combined with stronger efforts at resistance by indigenous peoples, lent Peru's mestizo phenomena features distinct from those found in Mexico.

The colonization of Brazil provides yet another example, one that experienced neither the civil wars of Peru nor the clash of empires. Although hesitant colonial policies and a war-decimated Indian population would seem to link the Brazilian situation to the ones in Mexico and the Andes, the feebleness of the Portuguese presence created slower rhythms even as it left greater room for maneuver to the interest groups and individuals who settled in that new territory. Some of them were *degregados*, that is to say Portuguese convicts sentenced to overseas exile, while others were European adventurers. This explains behavior that earned the Land of the Holy Cross a scandalous reputation and a proliferating mestizo population large enough to receive its own name, *mameluco*. More than in the Andes and Mexico, the borderlines between various populations—Europeans, mestizos, converted Indians, forest Indians—were vague and shifting. But the Portuguese Crown's inability to establish any solid framework also lent wild and brutal accents to this occupation, notably when it resulted in the enslavement of the native peoples followed by the massive importation of blacks from Africa.[36]

LOSING BEARINGS

The troubled era that began with the Conquest had a lasting influence on lifestyles among Iberian-American societies. The antagonists lost many of their bearings through the force of circumstance or the effect of defeat. The weakening or crumbling of indigenous dynasties, the ravages of epidemics, the break in traditional systems of education, the outlawing of public forms of idolatry, and the unbridled exploitation to which they were subjected provoked the disorientation and collapse of native populations. Equally evident was the agony suffered by black slaves ripped from their African homeland and forcefully shipped to Mexico, Peru, or Brazil, regions more disturbed than the Iberian mainland.

Nor were the conquerors spared this loss of roots. They had broken all direct links with the *casa solariega*, the land of ancestors, with the hometown, with the cycle of local holidays, with the supernatural protectors whose worship was preserved by Iberian confraternities. A feeling of remoteness haunted Spaniards: "so distant from Castile, receiving neither help nor succor, except what comes to them by way of God's great mercy."[37] Their habits were transformed by American seasons and food, by constant contact with Amerindian men and woman. It all required constant efforts at adaptation and interpretation. "People sow and harvest at any time," noted Franciscan friar Pedro de Gante (Peter of Ghent), thinking of the harsh winters of his native Flanders. The slow evolution of traditions and lifestyles that occurred almost unnoticed in Europe was suddenly replaced by an acceleration of new experiences and new lessons. Blacks and Europeans had to grapple with unfamiliar situations that irrevocably altered the meanings of things and relationships between people.

For everyone, Indians included, a phenomenon of physical and psychic distanciation occurred, in every sense of the term. By the force of circumstance, everyone had to "adopt a certain distance" from his or her original milieu, whether that meant the Andalusian countryside, the coast of Africa, or pre-Conquest Mexico. Other, similar phenomena had effects that were equally perturbing. Many features of traditional societies and Western Europe lost the meaning originally attributed to them. Objects that transited from one world to another wound up amputated from the collective memory they incarnated; by circulating between different groups, they forfeited the tradition and sometimes the power they held. The same was true of all kinds of beliefs and practices. How could indigenous peoples interpret painted or engraved images coming from a Europe about which they had absolutely no notion? What keys could they use to unlock content, analyze forms, and grasp what Europeans intended to convey through imagery and representation?

Nor were local practices and beliefs spared such "decontextualization." It sometimes took the extreme form of disillusion, leading to a loss of both meaning and legitimacy. Beings and things were deprived of their aura or their power once the ties that linked them to a global or, so to speak, metaphysical conception of life and the cosmos were dissolved. The defeat and humiliation of indigenous aristocracies undermined the concepts that almost organically allotted them a measure of divinity.[38] The destruction of idols had an even more immediate impact—material objects were reduced to ash and mutilated debris, precious metalwork was melted into permanent oblivion. By breaking idols and demolishing pyramids, the invaders demonstrated the total impotence of the old gods. Even if such acts did not suffice to prove the gods' total nonexistence, the shock was serious. It was the brutal beginning of a desanctifying of beings and things, and it disoriented Amerindians all the more for being accompanied by the permanent suppression of major ceremonial cycles.

Alongside these spectacular aggressions came the difficulty of understanding new colonial realities and the challenge of being confronted by different knowledge and techniques. The forced conversion to Christianity obviously undermined numerous types of behavior and beliefs, yet changes extended to many other realms as well. A technical innovation such as the replacement of ancient codices by alphabetic writing, manuscripts, and books introduced a new relationship to information (or what passed for information among the Indians). The adoption of the surprisingly efficient medium of writing competed with the multiple connotations of traditional glyphs and colors. The use of alphabetic writing also modified the selection and editing of data, imposing the pace of linear narrative. Even more determining were European painting techniques, which were limited to depicting realities situated in another time or place, whereas Indian "paintings" made divine forces present and almost palpable. In this respect, the Spanish Conquest "secularized" information.[39]

In other spheres, surveys conducted by Spanish missionaries, bureaucrats, and doctors placed an interpretative grid on the indigenous environment, reducing it to the level of desanctified nature, to a "flora" and "fauna" devoid of any Amerindian pagan presence. With only a few exceptions, the "metaphysical" dimensions attributed by Amerindians to their environment were censured, ignored, or scorned by Europeans. Indigenous informants, for that matter, adopted the habit of understating or overlooking such aspects in an effort to deflect the invasive curiosity of their powerful questioners.[40] The obligation to supply answers that suited the requirements of literate Europeans nevertheless constituted a confusing and often acrobatic exercise. And this exercise recurred when indigenous painters were obliged by their conquerors to produce hundreds of maps of Indian villages. Once again, local specialists were required to provide their new masters with legible information, which meant inventing a cartography and sense of space partly adapted to European eyes.[41]

The incredible extent of devastating epidemics also perturbed the minds of local populations, disarming Mexican *curanderos* (healers). Unable to continue explaining an epidemic as the doings of indigenous gods, victims questioned by Spanish authorities wound up linking it to social and political causes. The shock of disease and the imposition of new lifestyles spurred indigenous informants to offer precociously sociological reasons and invent materialist explanations. Whether such statements reflected the deepest feelings of Indians or not, they reveal the constant pressure placed by the new order on the vanquished populations' modes of representation. Disillusion could therefore follow paths apparently less painful and infinitely more subtle than the demolition of temples—medical knowledge, cartography, writing.

But colonial pressure was also expressed in a more brutal and widespread fashion by the forced enrollment of Indian labor into markets, mines, and workshops, obliging natives to adopt production rhythms and relationships—not to mention a conception of work—with no connection to local traditions and ancient cosmologies.

And yet distanciation, decontextualization, and disillusion through loss of meaning were not experienced by blacks and Indians alone. The victors were also subject to them, if in an infinitely less tragic and often less conscious way. Spaniards who learned to eat corn were a long way from imagining the cosmic import this divine grain held for Indians; had they sought its significance, they would have had to penetrate the realm of the Indians' allegedly idolatrous beliefs. They might then have compared indigenous corn with wheat from Castile, noting that—in a fantastic switch—both grains played a central role in worship and representation. Cacao and tobacco underwent similar fates, being emptied of the divine presences in which they had been steeped; prior to the Conquest, they were eaten only by the indigenous nobility, for they enabled humans to enter into contact with the divine world. During the colonial period, these same items became simple merchandise, ultimately becoming the focus of secular sociability (and, when it came to chocolate, a feminine one at that). People began to partake of them by inventing refined "rituals" which had lost all religious dimension, becoming merely a sign of wealth and social status. Any quest for a superhuman otherworld was replaced by sensory pleasure and material lavishness in the form of chocolate services and smoking accessories.[42]

THE VAGARIES OF COMMUNICATION

The shock of conquest did not go so far as to secularize the way of perceiving the world, but it sufficed to upset time-honored customs, thereby sowing doubt, ambivalence, and indecisiveness. Loss of bearings and loss of meaning modified the conditions and content of communication between individuals and groups who were suddenly brought into contact. These losses yielded a constant deficit in any exchange that might arise, because contact occurred not between "cultures" but rather fragments of Europe, America, and Africa—fragments and shards that did not remain intact for long once they encountered others.

By augmenting phenomena of disorientation and distortion,[43] the Conquest imparted highly special constraints, dynamics, and tenor to communication between people. Communication was fundamentally "chaotic" in the sense that all exchanges were fragmentary, irregular, and intermittent in nature[44]—interlocutors appeared and disappeared, one day's arrangements no longer suited the next day. All stages of communication, from emission to reception, were constantly disrupted. Interpretations arose from chance situations, often independent of standards and frameworks established by the various traditions. Thus the way the Spaniards pictured their conquest—New Spain—constantly evolved as a function of the background of their informants and the type of information they managed to obtain.

Vagueness and confusion were more common than our sources admit.[45] The chronicler Oviedo reports an incident that occurred between a Spanish judge, *licenciado* Alonso Zuazo, and a group of Indians in Mexico City over the issue of images. Installed in the city in 1524, when Cortés was on campaign in Honduras, Zuazo received a group of Indian notables—"four men among the most qualified and wise in these provinces"—who came to complain about the destruction of their idols. Not unreasonably, they argued that the Spanish, like themselves, practiced idolatry: "The Christians also had the same idols and the same images."[46] This claim embarrassed Zuazo, who explained through interpreters that Spaniards "did not worship images for what they were, but for what they represented, which could be found in the heavens and from which we received life, death, goodness, and everything that concerns us here below." So saying, he took a picture of Saint Sebastian hanging over his bed and tore it before the Indians, "giving them many other explanations on this subject in order to undeceive them and free them of their paganism; and he told them not to believe that we worshiped images as they did." The Indians' reaction was not long in coming. "Seeing this, one of them smiled at the interpreter and said they did not think that the judge considered them to be such foolish folk; they knew well that such images were made by *amantecas* (master craftsman), as were their own; and that they did not worship them as images but, just like Spaniards, on account of the sun, the moon, the stars, and all the influences in the heavens, from which came life." This reply apparently met with no answer. Zuazo "remained somewhat embarrassed and silently prayed that God would supply him with the words to defend his cause." The judge's embarrassment was unlikely to have been a unique occurrence—it induced him to perform an iconoclastic act that might have alarmed a Church constantly on the lookout for image-smashers.

At the conclusion of their discussion with the judge, the Indians asked for an image of the Virgin "because they did not understand God and his image very well." Zuazo fulfilled their request without suspecting the misconception that this gift would engender. Many Indians thought that God and the Virgin were one: "By saying Mary or Saint Mary, [the Indians] thought they were naming God and they called all the images they saw Saint Mary." Elsewhere, in Michoacán, the cross was taken for God. This confusion between the Virgin, Christian symbols, and God strongly influenced the reception of Christian imagery in Indian lands. Although the account of the conversation between Zuazo and the Indians does not reveal the full scope of misconceptions between the Spaniard and his interlocutors (insofar as their arguments were translated and interpreted in Western terms), it betrays traces of the difficulties that arose with every discussion, however "civilized."[47]

The vagaries of communication stemmed from language barriers and the impossibility of finding term-for-term correspondences for such totally opposed conceptual universes and collective memories. The extent of the obstacle can be appreciated by studying the linguistic efforts made by Nahuatl-speaking peoples to designate new concepts and objects that arrived with the invaders.[48] In Brazil, similar confusion would be seen in the perplexed and muddled explanations sparked by a messianic movement of indigenous origin, the *santidade* of Jaguaripe in the region of Salvador de Bahia, so summary were the interpretations of Christianity by the cult's followers.[49] This is not to say that obstacles to communication were purely conceptual; they were amplified by the brutality and contempt of Europeans, often more concerned to belittle their indigenous interlocutors than to valorize their intellectual heritage.

SURVIVAL, ADAPTATION, MESTIZO MECHANISMS

These gaps in communication, which remained a long-term phenomenon, are an inextricable part of mestizo mechanisms. Although they stemmed from the lasting shock wave of conquest, they also prefigure the ways people today deal with the multiple realities of our modern world. The effort we all make to assemble fragments constantly arriving from all corners of the earth has become a global exercise, intensifying practices begun, in fact, in Renaissance Mexico—with one difference, of course: we must never overlook the context of conquest, shock, and physical violence that governed this kind of "surfing" in sixteenth-century Spanish America. For blacks and a large part of the indigenous population, creating new bearings was a question of survival, indeed a question of life and death. And even for Spaniards, an ability to adapt to the new American environment was a decisive and sometimes vital asset—the inability to take root in newly conquered Mexico induced many to pick up and move on to other lands they imagined to be richer or more welcoming.

The imperative to survive and adapt explains why the groups most directly involved in the Conquest had to learn to rely henceforth only on local, partial knowledge. The men who defeated the Mexica seized power in a land about which they knew nothing. The Spanish Empire was equally enigmatic to Indians who now depended on a mysterious regime coming from a part of the universe that their elders had said contained nothing but primal waters. Neither camp could grasp the full picture. Who can say how many Spaniards in those early days, once their material and religious demands were met, sought to acquire true familiarity with indigenous societies?

Like prisoners in a maze, Amerindians and Europeans advanced step by step, progressively resolving the difficulties and choices facing them. The complexity, intricacy, and unpredictability of situations made survival for the former and adaptation for the latter a shortsighted affair.[50] The most vital as well as the most trivial issues had to be resolved—from inventing Indian rituals devoid of human sacrifice (henceforth outlawed) to finding local sauces and condiments to go with pork, that novelty from Europe. From the summits of pyramids to the backs of kitchens, compromises, modifications, and reversals were common. The unthinkable became a tolerated and even common practice early in the Conquest, when, for tactical reasons, the Spanish accepted the cannibalistic practices of their indigenous allies (only to outlaw them as soon as they had the means).

Deduce, discover, learn: if only a partial vision of a global situation is available to someone in a maze, then the need to move forward calls for feats of skill and shrewdness. It requires constant mobilization of intellectual, creative capacities. Groups and individuals have to weave more or less extravagant and superficial links between the bits, fragments, and shards they manage to pick up. Everyone is forced to construct a personal palimpsest based on received impressions, images, and notions, endowing them with new meanings and new values. Unable to decode information received from all sides in a linear way, people acquire knowledge and practices that—set against the data and impressions thus gathered in an occasional, random way—constitute ensembles that never close on themselves.

That explains why, in multiplying errors, incomprehension, and approximations, the situation created by the Conquest was not entirely sterile and destructive. It stimulated a capacity for invention and improvisation necessary to survival in an extremely troubled, composite, and totally unprecedented context (Amer-Afro-European). This constraint forged a special receptiveness among survivors—flexibility in social practices, fluidness of eye and perception, and an aptitude for combining highly diverse fragments.[51]

This makes it easier to understand the stress placed on the early period by anthropologists such as G. M. Foster. The initial decades were a time of rapid choices and instant decisions—individual and collective, conscious and unconscious—on countless issues.[52]

The shock of conquest forced the groups involved to adapt to fragmented, fractured worlds, to endure precarious, unstable, and unpredictable situations, and to cope with often rudimentary communication. These traits strongly marked the conditions in which Spanish America's mestizo processes developed, creating an environment that was chaotic in every sense of the term and sensitive to the least perturbation. Another process, however, was playing an equally important role.

4 WESTERNIZATION

Your oyster's the universe,
no stranger to exoticness.
The world'll treat you like a guest
so upsa-daisy, off you go,
upsa-daisy, heading West.
                —Guesch Patti, lyrics to *La Marquise*

Whereas the conquerors of Spanish America were initially concerned with forcibly annexing the lands running from Florida to Tierra del Fuego and from the Lesser Antilles to the Pacific Coast, the civil and ecclesiastical authorities later toiled hard to cultivate the same lifestyles and environment that Western Europe had developed over the centuries. They even wanted to transform "native" inhabitants of the New World into Christians.

Westernization includes all the tools of domination employed in the Americas by Renaissance Europe: the Catholic religion, market mechanisms, cannon, books, and images. It adopted various, often contradictory forms, some of them overt rivals because Westernization was simultaneously material, political, artistic, and religious (the "spiritual conquest"). It called not only on institutions and social groups (conquistadors, monks, jurists) but also on families, relations, and individuals. Once in America, they all struggled to build replicas of the society they had left behind. In its Castilian version, Westernization meant the cross-Atlantic transfer of the Old World's collective imagination and institutions. The undertaking was colossal and occurred in successive waves from the sixteenth to the nineteenth century. In different guises (and with different contents, objectives, and speeds), Westernization has continued down to the present day, steadily spreading across the entire planet.[1]

REPLICATING THE OLD WORLD

Throughout the sixteenth century, then, Westernization introduced new material, political, institutional, and religious frameworks designed to control the upheavals triggered by the Conquest. The systematic construction of colonial lands and society was done through duplication. The norm of duplication is the standpoint from which we should view the reconstitution or transfer of Iberian lineages every time conquistador families and their entourages embarked upon the conquest of the New World. It is also in this sense that we must analyze the emergence of a European-style infrastructure: the building of towns, ports, roads, forts, and arsenals; the founding of universities; the gigantic building campaigns that dotted both American continents with churches, cathedrals, cloisters, chapels, and hospitals. There thus arose a New Spain (that is to say, Mexico), a New Galicia, a New Castile, and many other dominions with familiar names harking back to Iberian provinces.

The reproduction of European institutions generated networks that swiftly extended to all Spanish possessions. As in distant Castile, cities were headed by powerful municipal councils, or *cabildos*. Bishoprics and archbishoprics multiplied as the new Christendom grew. The expansion of Hispanic institutions matched the vastness of America. Nothing seemed to halt it, not even the vast Pacific Ocean, since the Spanish went on to discover and conquer the Philippine archipelago, attempting to transform Manila into an Asian outpost of Castile before turning to Nagasaki in anticipation of the conquest of Japan and China (never undertaken).

This irresistible expansion was accompanied by a policy of standardizing language and laws. From Florida to Chile, Castilian was the language of administration. It was spoken by the victors, by mestizos, by blacks, by mulattos, and also by Amerindian leaders. In his introduction to *Política indiana*, jurist Solórzano y Pereyra glorified an "empire that united so many kings, so many rich and powerful provinces, the greatest monarchy ever seen in the world because it truly contains another world."[2] Decrees destined for one part of America were applicable throughout the empire. The famous "laws of the Indies," compiled from the seventeenth century onward, were the fruit of the transplantation of Castilian laws onto two continents and two hemispheres. From California to Buenos Aires, Castilian law—or rather, Castilian law on the Indies (*Derecho indiano*)— governed daily life, established the relationship of individual and group to the state, and imposed the notion of private property and the legitimacy of profit. The Jesuit José de Acosta summed up this standardization of law in the following terms: "The multitude of Indians and Spaniards form one and the same political community, and not two entities distinct from one another. They all have the same king, are subject to the same laws, are judged by a sole judiciary. There are not different laws for some and for others, but the same [law] for all."[3]

Spanish America was a replica of a real or ideal Castile, of Roman and imperial Europe, as indicated by the title of Caesar given to Charles V in correspondence with the New World. America could innovate, in fact, because unlike Europe, it did not have to take into account obstacles inherited from the medieval past and it was free to come to terms with what remained of indigenous substrates. It laid out towns on checkerboard plans, the finest accomplishment being the imperial city of Mexico-Tenochtitlán. Crisscrossed by straight roads at right angles, towns and cities constituted a mold of total order into which colonial society merely had to pour itself. In the center of all towns rose the symbols of the supremacy of the victors: the church, the headquarters of the municipal council and the king's representative, and a large square with a fountain. Cities built from scratch, such as Puebla in Mexico and Lima in Peru, prefigured more recent urban developments in Latin America—they were Renaissance Brasilias. This policy of urban development concretized the imperial determination to inscribe the victory of a government and a faith onto the American landscape.

Did that mean it would merely erect a Europeanized stage set, designed to reproduce in America a medieval and renascent, if bureaucratic and conquering, Castile? No, for not only did this replica of the Old World not exclude Amerindian populations, it could not do without them. Legally, the vanquished peoples constituted one of the two cores and two pillars of colonial society: "the republic of Indians" alongside that of Spaniards. Institutionally, they formed communities based on the Castilian model.

The Spanish Crown divided even as it united: it cemented vanquished societies into a position of otherness, although one modeled on the Hispanic world. Everywhere, Amerindian leadership served as intermediary— often self-interested—between Europeans and the native masses. The latter supplied the contingents of labor required for the countless construction sites in Central America, the Andes, and Mexico. It was the masses who produced the staples demanded by the victors, who built the new surroundings from nothing, and who wrenched gold and silver from the bowels of the earth. Sometimes attracted by profit or novelty, but usually forced or trapped, the native populations were confronted with new ways of working at the same time that they were thrust into a market system that bound their fate to Europe's economy.

ANOTHER CHRISTIANITY

"The natives were the engine and the reason behind all the projects undertaken by mendicant orders."[4] Whether laborers, de jure or de facto slaves, servants, consumers, or colleagues, Indians not only had their place in the kingdoms of the New World but also sparked the keen interest of the best intellectually equipped group among the new arrivals: church missionaries. The integration of Amerindians into colonial society was subject to one pressing condition—the vanquished had to renounce their religious beliefs.

All of them were considered to be "idolaters," either victims of the Devil or overlooked by the Revelation. Therefore all were obliged to convert, as had the Moors of Grenada.

The Christianization of Amerindians mimicked that of the Moriscos.[5] Yet it also sought to recreate primeval Christianity, even as it presented itself as a new version of the Old Testament in its struggle against idol worship, or as a new Egyptian hermitage in its quest for asceticism within new wildernesses. One Spanish civil servant who was a great reader of Lucian and the humanist Thomas More, and would later become bishop of Michoacán, asserted that he saw "this new Church of the New World, primeval, new and renascent, as the shadow and form of the primeval Church of our world in the days of the holy apostles."[6]

Yet was conversion merely a question of salvation? For Renaissance Europeans, religion and politics were inextricably linked. The political integration of Amerindian peoples required their Christianization because faith was the sole common denominator among the subjects of Charles V, who ranged from Flemings in Ghent and Moriscos in Grenada to Basques in Bilbao. Moreover, Renaissance Christianity was more a way of life than a well-defined set of beliefs and rites. It encompassed education, morality, art, sexuality, eating habits, and social connections, also orchestrating the calendar and the important moments in life. For all these reasons, Christianization constituted a key link in the Westernization of the New World.

The tools of that conversion revealed the variety of strategies adopted by monks to subject vanquished peoples to their law and make them Christians. Whereas European-style urban development already marked a physical break and visible replacement in the eyes of indigenous populations, the physical Church truly concretized that project. Church buildings embodied a supremacy both spiritual and technical, for they respected the mold of European architecture. In the Andes and even more so in Mexico, hundreds of examples of lofty vaults stupefied and fascinated the Indians, who had never known such construction methods. This bold technique helped to demonstrate the advent of a new empire, spectacularly symbolizing the terrestrial and celestial realm claimed by the Church.[7] The proliferation of monastery-forts with crenellated walls gave a frankly military appearance to the missionaries' presence, even though it is not absolutely clear today from which enemy—Indians or Spaniards—the Franciscans sought to protect themselves.[8]

The administrators and promoters of spiritual conquest assiduously dotted the American soil with new landmarks that would constantly catch the eyes of locals: "the protective shell of nave and cloister, the prodigy of the vault, the majesty of the porch, the grid of streets intersecting at a square overlooked by the house of God (or *teocalli*) of the Christians."[9]

But this environment, this stylized replica of a European model, would assume its full meaning only if local populations received a Christian education that attacked idolatry at the roots. The arrival of the first Franciscans in Mexico sounded the starting gun for an educational enterprise highly inspired by the humanism of the first half of the sixteenth century. Schools sprouted within the monasteries; sons of the indigenous nobility learned to read and write; the best students earned the privilege of studying in Mexico City at the college of Santa Cruz de Tlatelolco, where they learned Latin, typography, and the great classics of antiquity. An Erasmus-style humanism, nurtured on the ideas of Thomas More, presided over the education of an indigenous intelligentsia that was nearly admitted to the priesthood and that provided efficient help in recording part of pre-Hispanic tradition. This elite Westernization, based on a Renaissance model, nevertheless worried Spanish laymen, who were unhappy at seeing Indians who could write as well as—and perhaps better than—they did.

The conquest of souls was accompanied by a conquest of bodies designed to subject family, marriage, and intimate practices to the universal norms of the Church. By the late 1520s, the massive promotion of Christian marriage seemed the most efficient way to obtain a swift and profound Christianization of the indigenous populations. During the decades that followed the Conquest—even prior to the Council of Trent—monks defined and adapted the system of values, rites, and conduct governing marriage and the conjugal life of vanquished peoples. As a unique, uniform code, valid everywhere regardless of ethnic background or social status, based on written tradition and law, Christian monogamy participated in the reproduction—in every sense of the term—of Westernized forms of life. Finally, monitoring souls also meant monitoring the flesh and its most intimate delights, as revealed by confession manuals written in indigenous languages.[10]

THE INDIAN COPY: PRODUCTION AND REPRODUCTION

Reproducing the West also meant reproducing its technologies.[11] This strategy accompanied the spread of evangelization from the start, because the Renaissance version of Christianization meant importing a Western way of life. The requirements of the clergy and the needs of conquistadors therefore implied a transfer of technology to the indigenous populations. The conditions of this transfer and apprenticeship were marked by the increasing role of local initiatives and by the high quality of indigenous copies.[12]

The pace of this adaptation was as surprising as its resoluteness—the indigenous craftsmen the most exposed to pressure from the invaders were soon appropriating European techniques whenever they had a chance, their skill often surpassing that of their Spanish masters. Indians sought not only to reproduce the arts of the Old World by any means possible, they raced ahead. When it came to hammered gold, for instance, instead of spending eight years of apprenticeship—the time judged necessary to become a Spanish master—the Indians "observed all the details of the craft, counting the blows of the hammer, noting where the master struck and how he turned the mold again and again; and within a year they were producing hammered gold, doing so by borrowing a little book from the master without him noticing."[13] All means of discovering the Spaniards' secrets were valid, from spying on every little act[14] to carefully decomposing and memorizing all stages of production, or even consulting arcane texts.[15]

The use of Castilian looms met with equally striking success. The Indians copied garments, furniture, and even musical instruments, which they then mass-produced: "They have made *vihuelas* and harps.... They have made flutes with the right pitch, in all the registers required for the mass and polyphonic song. They have also made pipes and cast high-quality slide trombones."[16] Bartolomeo de Las Casas was amazed at the quality of the musical instruments made by indigenous hands.[17]

There were nevertheless numerous obstacles. Making the first organs—an instrument with no equivalent in indigenous society, for which a complicated Nahuatl word had to be invented[18]—presented more than one problem. In this case, the copy was preceded by inventive substitutes: "In the place of organs, they organized a concert of flutes with so many flutes that the music resembles that of wooden organs."[19] In other instances, the Indians relied on salvage and do-it-yourself techniques: "From a candlestick they made a slide trombone."[20] The manufacture of instruments and rapid spread of Western music—"music has taken root in this land"—provided an opportunity to assess the Indians' overall copying skills: "These people are like monkeys: what some do, the others immediately copy." In medieval rhetoric, the image of a monkey symbolized the ability to imitate.

The Indians displayed the same talent for copying when it came to buildings and architecture: "Since the arrival of stonecutters from Spain, the Indians make everything they have seen our workers do: arches as well as ... gates and windows that require much work; any ornamentation with grotesques and monsters that they have seen they can produce, as well as pretty churches and houses for the Spanish." An amusing anecdote illustrates the extent and even excesses of indigenous imitation. An Indian craftsman met a Spaniard wearing the pointed cap, or *sanbenito*, imposed on victims of the Inquisition. Intrigued by what he assumed was a garment worn during Lent, the Indian immediately began making *sanbenitos* and selling them in the street, with the cry *"Ticohuaznequi benito?"* (Who wants to buy a benito?). The story greatly amused the town's residents and even inspired a proverb. The copying frenzy gripped some Indian producers to the point of making any old thing.[21]

This anecdote raises another issue, namely the Amerindians' relationship to the colonial market. Their extraordinary copying skills were more than a demonstration of gratuitous virtuosity or tireless ingenuity.[22] The manufacture of European objects supplied the demands of a clientele, both native and Spanish, eager for these items and seeking to acquire them at least expense. Native copies had an immediate impact on the competition between Spanish and indigenous artisans. It allowed the natives to break the monopoly of Spanish craftsmen by offering quality merchandise to consumers in town and country. Mimicry seemed to go hand in hand with access to a market.

Mimicry could have ambivalent effects. It hastened the integration of Indians into an economic and technical world of Western origin. And at the same time that it established dependent relationships—the copyist on the model, Mexican Indians on the Iberian peninsula—it opened the way for indigenous workers. The best qualified Amerindians enjoyed some room to maneuver and invent, which they immediately exploited.

Yet did this maneuvering room suffice to preserve ancient beliefs and habits? The multiplication of copies occurred in a deritualized context, having lost the meaning that native tradition assigned to human labor. Deritualization also explains the growing role played by European machines. If Spanish-type fabrics appeared identical to Hispanic models, that was because they were produced on machines made in Spain, according to a protocapitalist mode of production. Accelerated reproduction on a preindustrial scale and quantity was the fruit of the advent of European machinery. This was even truer of the books and engravings that came off the printing presses. Market, machine, and mimicry were therefore linked.

COPYING AND COMMUNICATING

The reproduction of the West's collective imagination via theater and dramatic ritualization provided a new dimension to the mimetic process.[23] Missionaries used the theater to explain and disseminate the content of the Christian faith. Edifying works "represented," that is to say made visible, events from the Holy Story, major figures from the Christian pantheon, and the sacred geography of the West. Once again, Indians played a direct part. Scenarios for the plays were inspired by the monks but produced by the Indians themselves.[24] The local population constructed and installed the sets, performed the music and singing, and played all the roles (often portraying themselves). Spanish observers were struck by the quality and authenticity of indigenous performances. The terms "to imitate" (*contrahacer*) and "naturally" (*al natural*) were often used when praising performances that were so faithful to the proposed model that they were often mistaken for it. For Las Casas, a Dominican friar, "they are either angels or monsters among men."[25] This time, skill at mimicry no longer suggested the caricature of a monkey, with its animalness, evoking instead the example of creatures whose abilities were superhuman—angels or monsters.

Mimicry also functioned in the sphere of Catholic worship. Motolinía recounted the admiration and amusement he felt during one visit to a village. Prior to his arrival, the Indians had called the faithful to Mass, reciting the catechism and saying prayers; they had even rung the bells as though it were the moment of offertory and consecration, "and they had been doing so for over six years." That the new converts' zeal might play nasty tricks on the Church did not seem to cool the Franciscan's enthusiasm.[26] This amazing tendency can be explained by the education Amerindians received in Franciscan monasteries. Reading and writing were accompanied by lessons in music, drawing, calligraphy, and painting. Indigenous youths learned to reproduce European imagery at the same as they entered a new universe of graphic and acoustic communication.[27]

It was significant that writing, music, and drawing were all taught together: "Many children of eleven or twelve, who know how to read and write, sing plainsong and Gregorian chant and can even note the music for themselves." The three Western modes of expression were in fact based on the same principle: alphabetical signs, notes, and "images" were designed to reproduce speech, sound, and sight. In each case, indigenous pupils were confronted with concepts and techniques unknown at home.[28] The coherence of the European system probably simplified the task of the monastic teachers. Their Mexican disciples became aware that the arrangement of figures in three-dimensional space followed the same ordered principles as written compositions and the distribution of notes within a Hispano-Flemish harmony.[29]

COPYING OR INTERPRETING

The direct involvement of Amerindians in theatrical performances explains the efficiency and impact of the shows on audiences, themselves invited to participate in the action. Yet indigenous participation also marked the limits and ambivalences of theatrical mimicry. Even if the monks were not aware of it, indigenous shows tended to deviate from the original Hispanic model because they were subject to an Indian approach to performance and staging. Actor and character became one in the minds of Amerindians, who for centuries had used the same word—*ixiptla*—for the victim of sacrifice, the god he or she incarnated, and the priest who bore the god's name. The mimesis required by the West was therefore prone to misappropriations that thrived under the mistaken appearance of carbon copies. This paradoxical outcome arose in many situations involving Westernization and indigenous reactions to it.

In fact, right from the earliest days, the concept of copy was shown to be very elastic, ranging from exact replica to fair copy to inventive interpretation. On the technical level, writing was taught by making copies so perfect that the difference between the original and its replica was imperceptible. It is significant that the first writing exercise involved making a Texcoco Indian copy a papal bull. The result was strikingly realistic, "so true was the copy." Indigenous disciples also excelled in calligraphy: "They imitated [letters] so well that no one could see the difference between the sample and the copy they made." Las Casas reported that when a Franciscan monk showed him a book written by an Indian, he momentarily thought it had been printed, so close was the quality of the handwriting to the typography of Western presses.[30] Las Casas also mentioned the example of a letter that the Indians of Mexico City had sent to him and which he showed to the Council of the Indies; the councillors were thrown into confusion because they were unable to decide whether the text had been printed or handwritten. Amerindians had become master calligraphers, rivaling the work of a machine, the printing press. Rarely has mimicry been so perfect.

When it came to painting, the results were equally clear-cut. By the 1540s, *tlacuilos* (painters) had become excellent copyists by European standards: "Since the arrival of the Christians, great painters have emerged; since the arrival of Flemish and Italian models and images brought by the Spanish...there is not an altarpiece nor image, however remarkable, that they fail to copy and imitate, especially the painters in Mexico City, for that is where everything good from Castile is destined."[31] Las Casas, probably inspired by Motolinía, was equally laudatory. "Progress" was particularly notable in the sphere of depicting humans and animals.[32] Bernal Díaz del Castillo was also full of praise for Mexican painters in his "true history" of the conquest of Mexico.[33]

We should nevertheless be careful not to think of such copies in terms of our own use of photography, photocopiers, and scanners, for we have become overly accustomed to the accuracy of mechanical reproduction. In the sixteenth century, the only sphere in which copies could be technically perfect—the only register in which they were an almost pure product of machine operations—concerned engraving and graphic prints. In all other cases (with the exception of dogma), the European concept of reproduction left considerable scope for interpretation, especially on the artistic level.

Even if the European model by nature remained a demonstration of the conquerors' superiority, the Indians were allowed the right to interpret when it came to copies. Las Casas explicitly referred to this when he praised "the highly exquisite and highly new manners they invent," adding that "everything furnishes them with material to adorn and perfect the plays they intend to perform."[34]

European painting sought above all to convey a subject with the help of a limited range of strictly essential elements, always drawn from a repertoire familiar to the majority of beholders.[35] This artistic leeway coincided with a lack of preparation on the part of Mexican painters. They had no notion of the history of European painting nor of stylistic developments, and the forms they struggled to reproduce were too new to prevail in an internally constraining manner. Their ignorance and distance constituted both a technical handicap and a source of relative freedom.[36]

CHAOS, WESTERNIZATION, MESTIZO PHENOMENA

Similar processes occurred in the Andes, although subject to time lags due to civil war and to variations related to the specificities of religious orders and conquered populations.[37] In both southern and northern hemispheres, the crystallization of the colonial situation occurred in the context of a vast reproductive undertaking—Westernization—which initially took the form of a brutal grafting of European frameworks and lifestyles, only to be reinvigorated later as successive transformations experienced in Western Europe reached and were adapted by Spanish America.

The mimetic dynamics[38] of Westernization, which occurred in environments that were perturbed, unpredictable, and uncertain, steadily channeled the disruptions caused by conquest. They enhanced effects of convergence, balance, and passive resistance, which in turn produced new modes of life and expression. All kinds of features—institutional, religious, artistic, legal, and economic—became agglomerated around stabilizing poles of attraction. Such was the case with the worship of Marian imagery (in particular the Virgin of Guadalupe),[39] which occupied a key place in colonial society.[40]

The Westernization of Spanish America thus appears to have involved the duplication of Old World institutions, the reproduction of Western items, and the depiction of Europe's collective imagination; and the same was true of New France, New Holland, and New England. But unlike the French, Dutch, and English experiments, the Spanish Conquista turned indigenous peoples into the protagonists of reproduction—for better or worse: "Who built all the churches and monasteries owned by the monks in New Spain, if not the Indians with their own hands and their own sweat?"[41] This fundamental difference—everywhere except Castilian America, Amerindians were inevitably marginalized, excluded, or exterminated— explains why mimicry automatically became a source of inventiveness and mestizo phenomena. Since the indigenous version of reproduction was always accompanied by interpretation, it triggered a cascade of combinations, juxtapositions, amalgamations, and superimpositions caught in the cross fire of mimicry and mestizo mechanisms.

Obviously, Westernization encountered resistance in various forms, from open rebellion to all kinds of latent hostility. Some "idolaters" rejected Christianity.[42] Indians who fled the "congregations" (forced gatherings of the population), who escaped into the forests of Petén,[43] or who simply sabotaged work in the mines, all demonstrated their rejection of the lifestyle that Crown and Church tried to impose on them. But these attitudes never truly threatened Spanish domination, except on border areas. And above all, they always coexisted with other types of reaction to Westernization, ones that took advantage of the maneuvering room, however slight, left to vanquished populations by Christianization and the introduction of European techniques.

The mestizo processes at work in Spanish America must therefore be understood in this global context—the chaos of the Americas immediately after the Conquest, Westernization imposed on a continental level, a mimicry performed by the indigenous peoples themselves. Understood in the triple light of *Conquista*, Westernization, and mimicry, mestizo mechanisms appear first as a survival response to an unstable, unforeseen, and largely unforeseeable situation. In this respect, they conform to the general state of fragmentation. But these "makeshift" processes also represent an effect of Westernization when they stem from indigenous replication and appropriation of European features.

Latin America's mestizo phenomena must therefore be viewed simultaneously as an effort to recompose a crumbling universe and a tendency to make local adjustments to the new frameworks imposed by the conquerors. These two trends cannot be dissociated. Neither is independent of the profoundly perturbed environment described above.

Figure 1. Centaur, Church of Ixmiquilpan, Hidalgo, Mexico (© G. Mermet)

Figure 2. Peter Greenaway, *The Pillow Book* (© M. Guillaumot/Stills Press)

Figure 3. Peter Greenaway, *Prospero's Books* (© M. Guillaumot/Stills Press)

Figure 4. Grotesques, School of Antwerp, 16th century (photo: Gruzinski)

Figure 5. Cruxifixion, Monastery of Acolmán, Mexico (photo: Gruzinski)

Figure 6. Christ in Majesty, feather mosaic, Museo Nacional del Virreinato, Tepotzotlán, Mexico City (photo: INAH)

Figure 7. Juan Gerson, *The Son of Man*, fresco, Monastery of Tecamachalco, Mexico (© G. Mermet)

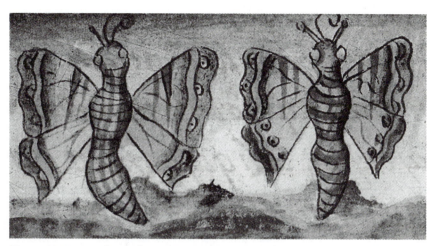

Figure 8. Mexican butterflies, in Bernardino de Sahagun's *Florentine Codex*, (photo: Gruzinski)

Figure 9. Ovid, *Tam de Tristibus quam De Ponto*, published in Mexico City by Antonio Ricardo in 1577 (photo: Gruzinski)

Figure 10. European grotesques, Veneto, Italy, ca. 1520 (photo: Gruzinski)

Figure 11. *Book of Hours of the Blessed Virgin*, printed by Pierre Ochart, 1567 (photo: Gruzinski)

Figure 12. Grotesques, Library of San Giovanni Evangelista, Parme (photo: Gruzinski)

Figure 13. Ludovico Buti, *Mexican Warriors*, Uffizi, Florence (photo: Gruzinski)

MESTIZO
IMAGERY

5 THE LADY CENTAUR AND THE MONKEY

A curious mixture of foreign and Chinese elegance
that is disturbing, arresting, and beautiful.
—Peter Greenaway, *The Pillow Book*

Mestizo phenomena invaded almost every sphere of life in Renaissance Mexico. Ordinarily, they do not lend themselves to systematic discussion, due to lack of source material and methodology. Imagery, however, is an exception. Painted manuscripts and monastic frescoes constitute a remarkable collection that is both vast and accessible (there are nearly 3,000,000 square feet of painted surface in New Spain). Art historians have often relegated them to status of curiosity, as though embarrassed by works imbued with neither the glamour of the Renaissance nor the "fascinating mystery" of pre-Columbian art.[1]

A "JUMBLE OF STYLES"

There are functional explanations for the impact of Western imagery on the newly conquered lands: whether drawn, engraved, or painted (on canvas or walls), images met the requirements of evangelization and the battle against idolatry. They helped to overcome obstacles created by linguistic and conceptual barriers; they called on skills of assimilation already developed by centuries of pictorial and pictographic practices,[2] and they slowly took the place of ancient codices. Religious orders, notably the Franciscans, lent decisive impetus to what appeared, right from the start, as a war of Christian images versus Indian idols.[3]

The spread of Western imagery brings us face to face with one of the most accomplished demonstrations of mimicry. It was employed to reproduce, in conquered lands, key features of Europe's visual ambiance and collective imagination. From a very early date, images from Europe inspired copies executed by indigenous *tlacuilos* trained in a different tradition.

These Mexican artists discovered new forms forged from surprisingly different molds, since European art in America was a combination of Spanish, Flemish, Italian, and German styles ranging from the Middle Ages to the Renaissance. Indian artists observed, copied, and reinterpreted these various models with a latitude all the greater in that, unlike their European counterparts, they were not shackled by the Old World's traditions, schools, and stylistic criteria. This explains the profusion of styles and innovations that constitutes the most striking feature of Mexico's indigenous Renaissance.[4]

Yet might the art that issued from their hands be merely an "endless jumble of styles," a shameless combination of Romanesque with Gothic, of Renaissance with Hispano-Moorish, of American with Iberian and Flemish? Or does it represent a series of skillful blendings and appropriations of forms freed from their historic context, forms as invasive and uprooted as the people who settled in the Americas? How did the mélange occur, and to what ends?

Before attempting to answer these questions, a detour via cinematographic artistry will help us to assess the scope of the phenomenon, because filmmakers create imagery that probably has as much to teach us as art history and cultural history.

THE PILLOW BOOK

Images from Peter Greenaway's movie, *The Pillow Book*, create a universe where periods and civilizations interweave. It was not the first film in which the English director juggled with historical allusions, but previously such allusions generally belonged to the European sphere, whereas the inspiration for *The Pillow Book* was Asian. Specifically, it was based on a classic of Japanese *soshi* (or "confessional") literature, widespread in tenth-century Japan. Greenaway drew a series of texts and images from this bedside book by Sei Shonagon, and used them to accompany the film's plot: in the 1970s, in Kyoto, a calligrapher celebrated the annual birthdays of his daughter Nagiko by writing his greeting on the little girl's face, signing it on the nape of her neck. Once grown up, Nagiko begins to search for the ideal calligrapher-lover who will use her entire body as a sheet of paper. Her encounter with a young interpreter allows her to swap roles; she begins to do the writing herself, fulfilling her literary ambitions by becoming a calligrapher of male bodies. These painted bodies recounts Nagiko's fatal passion in thirteen separate books.[5]

Greenaway's images constitute a "disturbing, arresting, and beautiful" mosaic: visions of the tenth-century Japanese court, borrowings from Japanese movies of the 1950s, and a contemporary fashion show in late twentieth-century Hong Kong. These scenes are inserted into the main image as screens with the screen, establishing a dialogue with the primary scene by creating a flow so homogeneous that the viewer's eyes can no longer overlook this second vision. Writing and images interpenetrate in a physical way: the writing painted on the face or drawn on the human body becomes an animated book; or, cast as light and shadow, it is projected on the walls behind the characters. Simultaneously text and image, bodies are transformed into veritable living ideograms. Different sexualities intersect;[6] various types of international music follow one another—Westernized Chinese tunes accompany Japanese rock, French vocalist Guesch Patti's strange minuets are wed to ritual Tibetan music which, in turn, echoes an Afghan wedding chant and contemporary music. People are also mélanged: "There is a mixed Chinese, Japanese, and European audience."[7]

These shifting variations on East and West differ sharply from the way Europe usually views Asia. In *Tokyo-Ga*, Wim Wenders merely raised questions about imagery in Japan from the standpoint of a European visitor. Western films on Asia have shamelessly exploited clichés of oriental exoticism for a long time now,[8] while the Japanese industry can produce a vision sufficiently Westernized to be seen and appreciated in Western theaters, as exemplified by Kurosawa's films. More recently, Chinese directors have followed Kurosawa by playing on an aestheticized image designed to appeal to Hollywood.

Yet new options have surfaced, other than producing exotic clichés or Westernizing local tradition. The accelerating circulation of art forms has engendered composite idioms and collective imaginations comprising sounds and images drawn from the most diverse spheres.[9] The usual landmarks begin to fade. *The Pillow Book* depicts a world—Japan, Hong Kong—where the East/West clash has been radically transformed, in which notions of exoticism, center, fringe, and modernity have lost their reassuring clarity. The camera no longer poses the question of "the Other" when it presents relationships between East and West; it explores a mélange of worlds inflected by Greenaway in every form. This is his way of describing—by filming—and conceptualizing—by engendering—a mestizo phenomenon that is normally so difficult to grasp. The results are unsettling, but perhaps that is the very mark of mestizo processes. Is *The Pillow Book* a Japanese-style European movie or a parodistic pastiche? Is Greenaway seeking to render Japan exotic, or has he allowed himself to be absorbed by Asia? His vision is clearly "under the influence"—but is it English or Japanese? Mestizo processes do not permit unambiguous answers. Although Greenaway draws his imagery from the distant tenth-century roots of a non-Western society, there is nothing archaeological about his relationship to Japan's past—it immediately appears in the form of appropriation and re-creation.

Greenaway employed various techniques to achieve this end. He selected and combined three distinct screens: a CinemaScope format, in color, when relating Nagiko's life in Tokyo (the camera is placed at ground level, as in Ozu's films); a smaller screen that recounts—in black and white—Nagiko's earlier life and subsequent end; and finally, even smaller incrusted images of highly refined color, which illustrate passages from Sei Shonagon's original *Pillow Book* like so many animated miniatures from that distant period. Instead of melding into the primary image, these precious scenes exist alongside it; the interconnections produce a series of visual effects that transfigure the action. This juxtaposition of periods sheds light on and validates Nagiko's plans, while the refined colors of the past underscore or counteract the grayness of modernity.

In a different manner, though to similar ends, Greenaway's film appropriated the art of calligraphy to create a visual universe that is constantly reinvigorated through new languages and alphabets.[10] Writing systems and languages—of which there are nearly twenty—intertwine. Calligraphy abandons its purely decorative dimension, lending body to the space through which the characters move. This ornamental sidetracking frees the screen for borrowings of all kinds—the actors' bodies are inscribed with ancient Roman characters, Chinese ideograms, Indian and Islamic learning. The singular relationship between text and image established by Greenaway provides a framework for global mestizo phenomena whose components never lose their own singularity.

The Pillow Book cannot provide us with a key to the mestizo imagery of Renaissance Mexico. But, like *Europa*, the film can train the eye to detect phenomena, processes, and mechanisms that usually escape it—capturing, appropriating, interweaving, attuning.

MONKEYS, FLOWERS, CENTAURS

The *Casa del Deán*, or Dean's House, is the oldest building in the Mexican town of Puebla, so rich in colonial history. As its name indicates, the house belonged to a clergyman, Tomás de la Plaza, who was the third dean of Puebla's church from 1564 to 1589. Very little is known about the man, who nevertheless had the good taste to make his residence one of the wonders of the Mexican Renaissance.[11]

A visit to this magnificent dwelling yields many surprises. One of the two official reception rooms is covered with scenes from Petrarch's *Triumphs*.[12] The other features an elegant Hispano-Flemish decor traversed by a procession of elegant ladies on horseback, namely, sibyls. Ever since the Middle Ages, Christian art had given those ancient prophetesses a new lease on life, because they allegedly foretold the coming of the Messiah. The subject had often inspired painters, weavers, and sculptors.

The parade of sibyls runs between two friezes featuring a foliate decoration in which surprising creatures gambol: they include female centaurs with ample bosoms offering flowers to monkeys who sport earrings and crew-cut hair. These monkey-and-centaur couples bring life to scenes as entertaining as they are enigmatic.

Monkeys were nothing new in European painting. Since medieval days they had romped in the margins of manuscripts among minstrels and peasants; the ones cavorting in the floral borders of the *Spinola Hours*[13] or carefully grooming themselves on a millefleurs tapestry in the Louvre are spitting images of their Puebla cousins. The figure of the monkey was charged with symbolic meaning, and its exoticism meant that it was naturally associated with other strange and fantastic animals. Some twenty years before the Puebla frescoes were executed, Peter Bruegel the Elder executed a little oil painting on wood, now in Berlin's Gemäldegalerie, showing two monkeys squatting beneath an arch, one in profile, the other seen frontally. In the background, behind the chained animals, can be seen the Scheldt River and the Port of Antwerp. It has been suggested that this allegory symbolized the enslavement of the Netherlands under Spanish domination.

The earrings worn by the Puebla monkeys nevertheless give them an irresistibly Mexican air. Monkeys played an important role in ancient Mexico. The Indians easily tamed them and were amused by their predilection for ladies.[14] The artists who painted the *Florentine Codex* depicted mischievous creatures with pensive or amused looks on their nearly human faces.[15] Monkeys were also present in myths and rituals. Ancient Mexicans believed that an early human race was transformed into monkeys after a hurricane, the memory of which survived in Indian and mestizo chronicles of the latter half of the sixteenth century.[16]

The monkey was also one of the twenty figures in Mexico's ancient ritual calendar. Called *ozomatli*, the monkey was the sign for the eleventh day.[17] Standard depictions adorned it with an earring and crew cut like its Puebla relatives.[18] The Nahua peoples associated *ozomatli* with good luck, joy, and—in a negative connotation—a licentious life. Men born under the sign of the monkey were fated to be singers, painters, or dancers, and would have many friends in life, even frequenting lords and princes. Women born under this sign, meanwhile, would be charming, have good voices, and lead loose lives ("neither very respectable nor chaste").[19] Unlucky individuals—since the sign could sometimes bring bad luck—would die premature deaths.[20]

The two other elements in the frieze—the flower and the female centaur—are equally intriguing. The centaur clearly comes from classical antiquity, though it remains to be seen what path brought her to the Americas. As to the flower depicted both blossoming and withered, it would seem to belong to Mexican flora, perhaps a *poyomatli* (or *puyomate*), which flowers on the grimly named shrub *Quararibea funebris*, or, more likely, an *ololiuhqui* (*Turbina corymbosa*). Both these plants are powerful hallucinogens, a significant detail.[21] The presence of insects in the frescos would seem to corroborate this hypothesis, since they were included in Amerindian recipes for vision-triggering ointments.

Monkey, centaur, and flower are not arranged arbitrarily, however. The mysterious poses of female centaur and monkey comprise a scene that is repeated and inverted several times across the frieze. How should we interpret the gesture of the centaur, who bends the stem so that the monkey can grab or smell the flowers? The mere presence of the monkey—a figure charged with pagan memories—and the hallucinogenic flower is surprising enough. How can we explain their presence in the official reception room of a prelate of the Catholic Church who, moreover, was linked to the Spanish Inquisition at a time when Tridentine orthodoxy was being imposed everywhere? The centaur's bare breasts add a note of indecency to this display of Indian superstition and only compound our puzzlement.[22] When Peter Greenaway appropriated elements of Japanese tradition, his writings and overall cinematic oeuvre shed light on the mestizo imagery he developed. We have nothing comparable for Puebla. For want of sources, the artists' intentions remain unknown. At the very most, we know that the painters were probably native Mexicans and that they worked in the mid-1580s. They perhaps belonged to one of the teams who executed *romanos* (Roman-style decoration, that is to say, grotesques), traveling up and down central Mexico from the mid-sixteenth century onward.

THE CENTAURS OF IXMIQUILPAN

In the Mexican countryside you are more likely to come across centaurs than indigenous painters, even though it means traveling several hundred miles. Some fine specimens can be found in the frescoes decorating the Augustine church of Ixmiquilpan.[23] Located approximately 120 miles northwest of Mexico City, the Indian village of Ixmiquilpan[24] ("the place where *qualites* [purslane] grows") is now a small, prosperous-looking city on the road to Texas and the United States. Its main square teems with crowds on market days, and the liveliness of alleys protected from a blinding sun by awnings, where the scent of flowers mixes with the odor of *fritangas*, contrasts with the torpor of the esplanade leading to the church.

Inside the sanctuary, once eyes dazzled by the high-plains sun and the metallic blue sky have adjusted to the shady interior, you can see a long fresco running down each side of the nave, over six feet high and covering some 2,000 square feet. The content is as surprising as the friezes at Puebla. Indian warriors, naked or wearing jaguar or coyote skins, do battle, while others clash with centaurs in the midst of a setting of fantastic animals and enormous garlands of foliage that entwine wounded or dying Indians. Several warriors brandish decapitated heads. The spectacle resembles the martial arts imagery seen on the posters for Kung Fu films that line the market square outside. The frescoes are all the more surprising in that they adorn the interior of a Catholic church where the sacrifice symbolized by the mass has been celebrated for over four centuries. Ordinarily, the only decapitated heads worthy of being displayed to the faithful are those of martyred saints.[25]

European and Indian elements form a strange, fascinating, inextricable weave. The Renaissance can be credited with inspiring the garlands of acanthus leaves, the capitals decorated with what look like pomegranates, the aggressive, horrified, or anguished expressions on the warriors' faces, the grimacing, grotesque, horned heads, the nude young warriors displaying their fleshy buttocks, the centaurs, the hippogriffs, and the freakish, plantlike creatures. The poses of the defeated and dying warriors are borrowed from European models, as is the dramatic tension permeating the scenes and characters. Strangely, Christian iconography is practically absent from the main fresco, except for the three arrows wielded by the centaur, which echo the emblem of the Augustinian order that founded the church and monastery.

The Amerindian world, on the other hand, should be credited with the absence of depth, the uniform color of the background (which has faded to orange in certain sections), the stereotyped depiction of figures (heads in profile, chests shown frontally), the coloring and pigments. Turquoise blue, or *xihuitl*, although it has often degraded over time, connotes the precious, sacred beauty of divinity; it highlights leafy garlands, feather decorations, and ornaments. Dawn-pink colors the banners and the bases of the large swaths of green plumes. Glyphs of pre-Columbian origin appear here and there—volutes issuing from mouths to indicate speech or song, place-names indicating the village of Ixmiquilpan.

The warriors' weapons and costumes are Amerindian. On the Ixmiquilpan frescoes the warriors fight with clubs, obsidian swords, and traditional shields. The men are naked or covered with jaguar or coyote skins or eagle feathers. Several wear loincloths.[26] Some warriors brandish traditional banners. The chief of the "jaguar knights" is wearing the *copilli*, or tiara, worn by lords. Feet are shod in *cactli*, or Indian-style sandals.

The figure's gestures also betray Amerindian heritage and "classic" behavior: the warriors who capture prisoners are highly similar to those found in the *Codex Mendoza*. All these characters clearly belong to the

Nahua aristocracy that dominated the Ixmiquilpan region before the Spanish arrived. After the Conquest, during the new Catholic festivities, local nobles continued to preserve the memory of two elite corps known for bravery and excellence, called the "jaguar knights" and "eagle knights."[27]

Other elements taken from high-plains flora and fauna anchor the fresco to indigenous cosmology: the depiction of jaguar and eagle incarnate the "night and day" couple (the jaguar's spotted robe suggests nocturnal darkness, while the large bird evokes Tonatiuh, the sun).[28] The flower seen proliferating on the frescoes is probably tobacco, whose ritual uses were many.[29] Also present are prickly pear (an allusion to the founding of the native city of Mexico-Tenochtitlán) and *maguey* (a type of agave), whose juice was fermented into *pulque*, the drink of men, gods, and sacrificial victims.

This brief inventory highlights the composite nature of the work. Yet by separating the elements composing it, we ultimately lose sight of the strange uniqueness of the combinations. It is a centaur, rather than an Indian warrior, who is wearing Indian sandals. Pre-Conquest warriors spring from the blossoms of gigantic flowers—why? There is something special about the three arrows held by the centaurs: in theory, the ones found on Augustinian emblems are always pointed downward, sunk into a heart, whereas the centaurs' arrows are pointed upward like those of the god Tezcatlipoca in the *Codex Borgia*.[30] So are these Christian or pagan symbols? Or are they perhaps Christian signs diverted from their original meaning and thereby Indianized? Or maybe perfectly ambiguous features? Puzzlement grows when it is realized that the heart seen on the Augustinian emblem might be interpreted as an allusion to the human sacrifice performed in ancient Mexico.[31] Numerous details in the fresco link the two worlds so tightly that attributing them to one or the other runs the risk of masking their composite, polysemic nature.

RITUAL COMBAT IN MEXICO AND IBERIA

The unity of the frescoes stems largely from the warrior subject matter. The presence of these battle scenes in a Catholic church is unsettling, and their explicitly native air incites us to look to the Mexican side for an initial explanation. The Spanish Conquest did not put an instant end to all manifestations of Mexican civilization. The new civil and religious authorities allowed the Indians to retain some of their dances, as long as the content was no longer conspicuously pagan. During major Catholic holidays, nobles danced dressed as "eagle knights" and "jaguar knights." They sang war songs about fallen warriors and mimicked battle scenes.

Such festivities generally took place in front of the church but might continue inside the sanctuary, despite ecclesiastical prohibitions. Their spectacular nature, prefiguring today's folk arts, was likely to please Spanish spectators in search of new distractions. They nevertheless perpetuated ideas incompatible with the invaders' Christianity. The "jaguar knights" seen dancing on the main square of Tlatelolco in the mid-sixteenth century were heirs to a military elite dedicated not long before to the worship of the god Huitzilopochtli. The Spanish clergy was aware that during the pre-Hispanic period such dances represented cosmic struggles between the forces of light and darkness.

At Ixmiquilpan, the exuberant foliage among the battle scenes inevitably evokes the Indian notion of "flower war," a ritual form of combat designed to capture prisoners who would then be sacrificed to the gods: "Those who seized a captive did not kill him, they brought him back as tribute, then made an offering of him."[32] This was pre-Hispanic combat *par excellence*, the very type that Christianization wanted to end forever. So do the frescoes represent images of human sacrifice or glorification of the god Tezcatlipoca? That might be going one step too far. The obsessive search for pre-Columbian elements can lead to overinterpretations that impoverish a work by discarding its other dimensions.[33] It is nevertheless true that the frescoes are teeming with pre-Hispanic vestiges that allude to traditional cosmology: the undulating movement of the enormous garland weaving across the frieze from one end to the other may well suffice to evoke the gyratory motion of ancient cosmic forces.[34] Many details of European origin, meanwhile, could be read as Mexican glyphs.[35] Shortly after the Conquest, this pagan past—still so present to indigenous minds—met with competition from a new ritual that originated across the Atlantic: the *Moros y Cristianos* festival. Inhabitants of the Iberian peninsula and western Mediterranean, having done battle against Muslims for centuries, had invented festive, ritual combats that pitted figures dressed as Moors against those dressed as Christians. These combats inevitably ended with the defeat of Islam and conversion to Christianity.

In Mexico, evangelical preachers constantly inculcated new converts with crusader ideals and hatred of Muslims. In order to achieve this, they promoted the *Moros y Cristianos* festival wherever they could. As early as the 1530s, spectacular shows given in Mexico City and Tlaxcala made a lasting impression.[36] With the encouragement of monks and the collaboration of the Indian leadership, Mexicanized versions of *Moros y Cristianos* were organized and promoted throughout the countryside. The Iberian antagonists of Moor and Christian, perhaps too exotic for a native audience, were replaced by a "converted Indian" and "savage Indian" (or Chichimec). Faith went to war against barbarity and always won a smashing victory. An important detail worth adding is that the church at Ixmiquilpan was dedicated to one of the leaders of the heavenly army, the archangel Michael, who, following tradition, is depicted here wielding a sword against the Devil, whom he slays. The theme of divine war links the church's patron saint to the indigenous warriors who clash on the walls of the nave.

The Mexicanization of *Moros y Cristianos* was made all the easier since it fit both a pre-Hispanic mold and current events.[37] The pre-Hispanic precedent provided a cosmic dimension—the struggle between sun and darkness—and a historic one, since Indians were playing out an age-old antagonism between sedentary and nomadic tribes. Indigenous memory was full of migrations of Indians from the north, who attacked sedentary groups and seized power from them. The nomads bore the feared but glamorous name of Chichimecs.

And the wild, aggressive, nomadic Indian was a figure that also obsessed colonial society in the sixteenth century. Spanish expansion toward the north encountered indigenous populations who put up much tougher resistance than the Indians in central Mexico. These mobile groups knew how to profit from the resources of a desert that also served as refuge, and they preferred to plunder the newcomers' merchandise rather than submit to King and Church. Their resistance was all the more troublesome once the 1546 discovery of rich silver mines spurred a massive rush of Spaniards to the north. Miners and their supply convoys were constantly exposed to raids by Indians who knew those desert regions well.

Ixmiquilpan was located on the edge of the Chichimec world and lived with the threat of indigenous attacks, producing a siege mentality immediately perceptible in the frescoes. The region was crawling with Pames, one of the most dreaded Chichimec groups. When captured, Pames prisoners were executed or sentenced to forced labor in the mines around Ixmiquilpan.

During those troubled times, Christianized Otomis felt as threatened by massacre as the Spaniards did. Chichimecs would kill Otomi men, scalp their victims, then destroy the crops and take women and children away with them. The area seemed all the more exposed once Ixmiquilpan became a major way station on the silver route. Cargoes of weapons, corn, clothing, and tools arrived in town before setting off for Zacatecas and the mines in the north. Such traffic explains the town's prosperity and the size of the Spanish colony that settled there.[38]

OVID'S "METAMORPHOSES"

Current events, the new Christian festival, and pre-Hispanic allusions explain the importance that the *tlacuilos* of Ixmiquilpan gave to the themes of war and combat. Yet a Christian and allegorical interpretation of these clashes is also required, demonstrating it to be a struggle between good and evil. Only on that condition could the presence of these paintings inside a church be defended, in a spot visible to all and normally designed to convey edifying messages taken from holy scripture. But how could Indian elements be transformed into allegories or moralized imagery? Who conceived and executed this adaptation?

One series of puzzling features has not yet been discussed, namely the participation of centaurs in this battle. Armed with shields, bows, and arrows, these grimacing creatures did not belong to the pre-Hispanic world, where horses were unknown. Were they perhaps a decorative element borrowed from classical antiquity? Or might they represent Chichimecs, who had taken up European horses so enthusiastically that they became one with their mounts? Or might they even depict European invaders, whom the Indians initially thought were part of their horses? This last, bold interpretation would suggest that the centaurs are holding the arrows of the Augustine order to show they belong to the side of Church and Europeans.

It is possible that both interpretations of the centaurs—as Chichimecs and as Europeans—are compatible, given that both Chichimecs and Spaniards were enemies of local warriors. Whatever the case, the presence of centaurs raises questions about the origin of these freakish animals and their role in these frescoes. Such an "addition," if addition it is, might be explained as a whim of the Indian artists or their European patron—a monk or *tlacuilo* might have taken a decorative figure from a European engraving and added it to the indigenous imagery. But the inclusion of centaurs in the combat scenes is much too elaborate for this purely decorative hypothesis to suffice.

Other details seem to converge and point down the same path. The battling centaurs immediately bring to mind the famous battle between the Centaurs and the Lapiths, as immortalized on the metopes of the Parthenon. And two more equally intriguing scenes lead in the same direction—namely the proud warrior brandishing a decapitated head (from which he turns away), and the head from which a cactus plant springs.

The warrior's deed is incomprehensible within strict Amerindian tradition, since participants in the "flower war" did not immediately kill their enemies but "always tried to take them alive, to sacrifice them."[39] If we overlook the native dress, the warrior's pose recalls the exploit of Perseus, who slew the Gorgon and held aloft her head, crawling with snakes, as a weapon against his opponents: "He backward turn'd, Medusa's head reveal'd."[40] The depiction on one warrior's shield of a head seen frontally, long hair undone, would seem to be an additional allusion to the Gorgon, whose "shining hair [was] chang'd to hissing snakes."[41] In classical iconography, Medusa's decapitated head decorated the shield of Athena.

As to the other head, it perhaps alludes to the story of Daphne, whose hair grew into leaves, her arms into branches. The tuft of quetzal feathers seen on other characters and freakish animals is here transformed into a sharp-leafed *maguey* (agave). The laurel tree of the Daphne myth would therefore have been transformed into an indigenous sacred plant from which the Indians made their divine beverage, *pulque*.

Perseus, the Gorgon, Daphne, Centaur and Lapiths: all these incidents are described in Ovid's *Metamorphoses* and the many anthologies inspired by that masterpiece. The poem may have been the source of ideas that *tlacuilos* could have "Indianized" by developing an extremely refined mestizo artwork. This Indianization is all the harder to refute since the process can be glimpsed in other frescoes in the church. The pose of the "jaguar knight" wielding his club and taking a captive by the hair is the Mexican version of a motif seen on friezes in the sacristy, where a putto hanging from a branch grabs the foliate hair of a plantlike beast. The only thing Indian about it is the execution. In the large nave fresco, in contrast, a jaguar skin and Mexican loincloth mask the putto's nakedness, whereas the beast has been turned into a warrior with a shield.

This interpretation may appear overly bold or reckless. It sits uncomfortably with the image we have of Amerindian natives, torn between the splendors of pre-Columbian societies and the unmitigated collapse that followed. Nor does it correspond to the clichéd image of Spaniards as bloody, uncouth conquerors who came to destroy age-old civilizations. Furthermore, how could indigenous artists have managed to find inspiration in Ovid? This question inspires another, even more troubling, one: what use could they possibly have made of the *Metamorphoses?*

6 MEXICAN OVID

> A conscious effort to create harmony between two
> worlds separated by centuries.
> —Jean Seznec, *La Survivance des dieux antiques*

How did Ovid get to Mexico in the first place? By ship: in monks' baggage
and through booksellers' orders. In 1576 alone, no fewer than nine copies
of the *Metamorphoses* arrived in Mexico City.[1] By the late sixteenth century, the Latin poet was also being read in the Andes and in Portuguese
Brazil, in Lima and in the Bahia region.[2] There is nothing mysterious about
Ovid's presence in the Americas. Our surprise—or skepticism—is due only
to our ignorance of the sixteenth century and our growing distance from the
Latin classics. For literate people of the Renaissance and for a wider
European public than we realize, Ovid's book was both a classic and a best-
seller. It was part of general knowledge, being one of the most published,
discussed, translated, and imitated books of the day.[3]

FROM EUROPE TO THE NEW WORLD

The Middle Ages had not forgotten Ovid. On the contrary, he had been
recopied, transmitted, and discussed. With the arrival of printing and the
Renaissance, Ovid's work enjoyed even greater dissemination. It could be
found in every library and every study; popes such as Pius II had no qualms
about praising the *Metamorphoses*.[4] The book was translated into Italian
by Nicoló Agostini, Ludovico Dolce (1553), and Giovanni Andrea del
Anguillara (1563). Abridged and illustrated editions made Ovid accessible
to readers and artists throughout Europe. Spain was not to be outdone: a
Castilian version allegedly dates back to 1466, and only two years after the
discovery of America, the first Catalonian translation was published in
Barcelona.[5] Jorge de Bustamante's Spanish translation dates from 1542, six
years after the publication of *Myrrha*, a tragedy by Cristóbal de Villalón
based on Book X of the *Metamorphoses*. Spanish theater drew extensively
on mythology, as witnessed by the plays of Juan de la Cueva, packed with
borrowings from Ovid and Virgil.[6]

Popularization spread in the second half of the sixteenth century, adopting new forms. Scholars offered ready-to-use recipes and formulas to poets in need of inspiration, a method described by Antonio Tritonio in 1560: "I sought to collect mythological examples drawn from the XV books of the *Metamorphoses*, and to rewrite them in the form of common-places that could be adapted to most things when writing poems."[7] The upshot: copying and plagiarizing. A Dr. Alonso Pérez, for example, could write a second part to Jorge Montemayor's *Diana*—"a story full of pedantry and obvious imitations from Sannazzaro and Ovid"—which was read as far as way as the coast of Brazil.[8] European artists all consulted "abridged [versions] which were little more than a series of pictures."[9]

In other words, Ovid was found everywhere, in increasingly accessible form. It was hardly surprising that chroniclers, scholars, monks, Jesuits, and administrators should carry him across the ocean.[10] He was transported, read, and—better—printed. It was in Mexico City in 1577 that, for the first time in the Americas, the anthologies *De Tristibus* and *De Ponto* were published.[11] From that period onward, Ovid figured in most anthologies published in Mexico.[12] Furthermore, Ovid's image as a learned poet exiled to the edge of the known world would have appealed to the hundreds of clergymen condemned to spend the rest of their days in the Americas, thousands of leagues from home among barbarians who were no better than the peoples of the Black Sea.

All this explains the presence of Ovid in the brand-new libraries of New Spain—probably including Ixmiquilpan. The frontier town was not only a stage on the silver route, it was also the site of an Augustinian monastery (1548) and, from 1572 onward, of a school that trained young monks in theology, Latin, and the humanities. Founded barely forty years earlier in a setting worthy of a Hollywood Western, Ixmiquilpan constituted a highly respectable outpost of Western civilization.

As to the Spaniards found there, they were not all ignorant bureaucrats, shady adventurers, or uncouth miners. The extremely wealthy Alonso de Villaseca, who made his fortune in the cacao trade, spent time in Ixmiquilpan; the scope of this Spanish patron's activities included financing the development of the university in Mexico City and backing the arrival of the Jesuits. Villaseca was responsible for bringing to Mexico City his relative Cervantes de Salazar, the first holder of the chair of Latin at the university and a talented chronicler. If the "cacao king" and his entourage, plus a hand-ful of cultivated monks, were joined by several civil servants keen to main-tain intellectual standards and by a few Hispanicized native leaders, then the profile of the faithful attending services in the church differs from what might be expected of a village populated by Otomi Indians, mestizos, and black slaves. The Europeans at Mass probably had a smattering of classical education, all the more so the monks who were training at Ixmiquilpan. Many of them were certainly more familiar with Ovid than we are.

Yet they did not read him the way we do: ever since the Middle Ages, the great Latin poet had been less a source of mythical stories and relatively risqué pagan legends than an anthology of edifying morals. People had learned to read Ovid between the lines; this "moralized Ovid" hid profound truths and exemplary models beneath the finery of the ancient gods. Workshops churned out convenient condensations of Ovid's stories, producing edifying moral tales. Every canto became an allegory that required deciphering. Note how Ludovico Dolce, an Italian specialist of the day, referred to one of the figures perhaps identified on the walls of Ixmiquilpan: "Perseus denotes the worthy man who, by arming himself with prudence and wisdom, vanquishes all obstacles."[13] As one commentator explained, "under the bark of these pleasant stories is contained all the sap of morality and theology."[14] Such exercises were also common on the Iberian peninsula, where Castilian editions of Léon Hebreo's *Dialoghi d'amore* contributed heavily to the allegorical interpretation of mythology.[15] When it came to the myth of Perseus, Léon Hebreo interpreted it as the allegorical expression of psychomachia, a combat between the forces of heaven and those of earth, between mind and matter.[16]

OVID AND THE AMERINDIANS

The fact remains that the painters who executed these frescoes were not Europeans but *tlacuilos* affiliated with the indigenous nobility, whose customs and distinctive features were familiar to the artists. Unquestionably, the monks must have given their assent to the project and monitored its execution; they could hardly have done otherwise, since the church belonged to them. Unquestionably again, the results would not have displeased them. Allusions to an Indianized Ovid were highly likely to amuse the clergy who, at any rate, always read and appreciated the poet through a Christian filter, moralizing Ovid as just described; furthermore, the frescoes were painted in a style fashionable at the time—the grotesque manner—which the entire Western world was cultivating.

Indian mastery at adapting and tailoring subjects drawn from mythology may seem surprising. But it can be explained by the training that indigenous painters and nobility received following the Spanish Conquest. They were exposed to works and images derived from classical paganism, directly or indirectly. By the 1530s, the sons of the Mexican aristocracy were learning Latin, and the brightest among them became remarkable Latinists, supposedly able to rival ancient authors. Youths from the capital and surrounding valley were trained at the college of Santa Cruz de Tlatelolco, an institution of higher education founded even prior to the university of Mexico. The college library offered them access not only to a substantial number of Christian authors, but also Cato, Cicero, Juvenal, Plutarch, Sallust, Seneca, Virgil, Livy, and Flavius Josephus.[17] This institution, along with provincial colleges, turned out Latinized nobles with a smattering of humanism. During the same period, indigenous painters and musicians came to the fore, and their talent startled Spaniards as demanding as the old conquistador Bernal Díaz del Castillo. By the 1540s, the teaching of Latin was so successful that some Spaniards became alarmed, convinced that "reading and writing as are harmful as the devil." It was reported that "every day there are more Indians who speak a Latin as elegant as Cicero's...it is admirable to see what letters and colloquies they write in Latin, and what they say [in that language]."[18]

Don Pablo Nazareo was a pure product of that educational system. In March 1566, ten years before Ovid's works were first printed in Mexico City, this Indian prince from Xaltocan quoted Ovid in a long letter in Latin that he sent to Philip II: "Munera, credi mihi, capiunt hominesque deosque: Placatur donis Jupiter ipse datis. Quid sapiens faciet? Stultus munere gaudet. Ipse quoque accepto munere mitis erit." (Believe me, presents conquer men and gods. Gifts even pacify Jupiter. What should a wise man do? A gift delights a fool, and a present will soften a wise man, too.)[19]

The quotation is all the more surprising because it was taken from *Ars amatoria* (*The Art of Love*), a less edifying and less well-known book than Ovid's poems and *Metamorphoses*. Don Pablo knew his Ovid so well that he even provided the reference to the book he employed: "ut ait Ovidius ille libro tercio de arte."[20] The example of Jupiter was not a pure exercise in style or ornamentation from the pen of a relative of the Emperor Moctezuma. It was designed to appeal to the generosity of the king of Spain, whom Don Pablo compared to the god Phoebus Apollo.[21] Don Pablo was not just a tireless translator of Holy Scripture—as he insistently reminded the king of Spain—but was equally at ease in the mythological world of his conquerors: the indigenous scholar was familiar with the muses and Minerva and could quite naturally endow the Christian God with an epithet taken from Horace: *Deus Olympicus Optimus Maximus*. The neoplatonist themes, allusions, and tone of these pages radically distinguish them from the ones written by monks in Mexico yet did not spark the least censure. In the 1560s, if one were of noble origin and had the backing of the Church, one could be Indian, Christian, Latinist, and humanist, and even allow oneself a few affectations in Renaissance Europe's scholarly language when imitating the refined elegance of the Nahuatl spoken at the court of Mexico.

Don Pablo, for that matter, was not an isolated case (although we are concerned here only with an intellectual elite). The talents of Antonio

Valeriano, another student and teacher at the college of Santa Cruz, amazed his contemporaries because "even in the last years of his life he spoke Latin *ex tempore* with so much elegance and pertinence that he seemed to be Cicero or Quintilian."[22] Valeriano's education and connections enabled him to govern the Indians of Mexico City until his death in 1605.

Indian nobles nevertheless had other ways of learning about the gods of the Greco-Roman world. Translation was one of the main paths to ancient classical texts—Aesop's fables in Nahuatl reveal the extent to which Amerindians were able to penetrate the ancient text, adapting it to Mexico's conceptual framework and reality; they even explicitly indicated whatever confounded their understanding or seemed incomprehensible by adding: "I do not know why."[23]

Public imagery also played a role in the dissemination of mythology. During the funeral ceremonies for Charles V, celebrated in the large monastery of San Francisco in Mexico City in 1559, architect Claudio de Arciniega erected a grandiose cenotaph in memory of the emperor.[24] The monument was elegantly sober, decorated with inscriptions and paintings whose subjects provide a brief tour of ancient mythology: the labyrinth of Daedalus, Apollo, Jupiter, Theseus, and the Eumenides were featured. Also to be seen was "Hercules doing battle with the Lernaean Hydra, with many heads. This figure meant that Caesar had wounded and defeated Lutheran heresy, that source of various errors."[25]

Yet these figures from mythology were not alone; the cenotaph's painters had inextricably woven together the likes of Moctezuma, Atahualpa, Jupiter, Cortés, Caesar, Phoebus, Phaeton, Huitzilopochtli, Pope Alexander VI, Ferdinand the Catholic, Fame, and many others. Although the indigenous masses who crowded into the monastery of San Francisco would have had great difficulty understanding the mythological allusion of these ephemeral paintings, nobles who studied at Santa Cruz de Tlatelolco could have simply racked their school memories or questioned the monks who had taught them.

Familiarity with classical antiquity soon spurred indigenous nobles to draw conclusions that were not always favorable to the Spanish. By the 1540s, books in Latin on the background of their invaders had informed Mexican Latinists that Castilians had been conquered and converted to paganism by the Romans, and had only received baptism later. Amerindians therefore discovered that the Spanish, like themselves, had been pagans; and they wondered why a thousand years of Christianity had not turned them into exemplary Christians.[26]

By the middle of the century, educated Indians knew enough about pagan antiquity, with its literature, beliefs, gods, and role in Renaissance culture, to integrate them into their own thinking. Given this situation, can the frescos by the *tlacuilos* of Ixmiquilpan be reduced to a simple exercise in painterly virtuosity under the strict guidance of their Augustinian mentors? Those painters did not passively copy models they were shown. They adapted classical motifs in a manner that gave an antique air to Indian scenes rather than making Christian images of them. To judge by the appearance and content of the frescoes, it is hard to imagine that the Augustinians dictated it all. The overwhelming predominance of indigenous motifs limited the scope of European intervention, and references to antique paganism at the expense of Christian iconography accord poorly with an evangelistic role. Finally, the subtle marriage of Ovidian motifs with Indian motifs suggests an imaginative and intellectual effort beyond the reach of a European mentality. But why all that effort?

CAPTURING OVID

Although the Indianization of a moralized Ovid might satisfy the Ixmiquilpan Augustinians and thereby reassure suspicious minds, it probably masked less orthodox intentions. Everything suggests that indigenous artists took advantage of favorable circumstances to appropriate Ovid and, thanks to him, cover up countless pagan allusions hidden in the frescoes without sacrificing any of their spectacular nature. Classical inserts—whether straight (centaurs) or Indianized (Perseus)—diverted the eye from suspiciously idolatrous features. They generated mestizo imagery whose reassuring strangeness buried pre-Conquest allusions under antique quotations and decorative exuberance. Borrowings from mythology counterbalanced a ubiquitous Indian iconography.[27] The Indianized Ovid was perhaps therefore a kind of decoy or a disguise designed to hide Amerindian messages even as it masked the fact that pre-Hispanic images were not mere appearance in the European sense of the term, but a physical presence produced by *tlacuilo* artists. If the paintings' orange background is interpreted as an evocation of the solar heaven—*tonatiuhilhicatl*—then the frescoes suddenly plunge us into the celestial and glorious world of Indians who died in battle. If the warriors who brandish their enemies' decapitated heads are mere dancers, on the other hand, then they hark back to the Indians who performed after the sacrifice of a victim to the god Xipe Totec: "Those who were there, the priests, worthies, and masters of the slaves, began to dance...around the stone where the captives had been executed; while dancing and singing, the masters of the captives carried the heads [of the victims] in their right hand, grasped by the hair; this dance was called *motzontecomaitotía*."[28]

Espousing just one of the various interpretations suggested by the pre-Hispanic elements found in the frescoes is perhaps impossible. I can merely propose hypotheses here, because any record of the original content is preserved solely in the painted imagery. It might be assumed, on the other hand, that in the sixteenth century the imagery benefited from an oral counterpart, that it was reinforced—as had been the case in pre-Hispanic days—by chanted texts and dances similar to those from the Valley of Mexico (for which a few transcriptions survive). In this case, a good number of interpretative keys would have lain in the often hermetic songs combining Christianity and paganism.[29]

MESTIZO FORMS AND CONCEPTIONS

Thanks to the artistry of the Ixmiquilpan painters, classical mythology may well have served to revive Amerindian mythology, a conjuring trick probably performed elsewhere. The Ovidian origin of some of the scenes in the church, for instance, may help to identify the female centaurs in Puebla. The gender of these creatures makes their identification much easier, since females are far rarer than male centaurs.

Two female centaurs feature in the *Metamorphoses*. One, "the fair Hylonome,"[30] was thus named because she lived in the woods. This Greek name (*hylo*, woods) exactly corresponds to the one given to the *ozomatli* monkey by Franciscan friar Bernardino de Sahagún in the *Florentine Codex*: "he who lives in the woods."[31] The other female centaur, daughter of the centaur Chiron, is Ocyrhoe, who "utters prophetick tale[s]."[32] I am inclined to opt for this latter candidate, inspired by several coincidences: her companion the monkey is drawn from the ritual calendar used for prophecy; the sibyls who cavort above them are among the greatest prophetesses of pagan antiquity; and the main fresco prefigures episodes from the life of the Christ. The theme of prophecy is thus central to the imagery on three occasions.

The presence of these creatures from classical mythology might be explained in the same ways as at Ixmiquilpan. Mythology was used to mask indigenous components, helping to render "palatable" figures and beliefs banished by Christianity. Here, a female centaur might provide a classical alibi for the eleventh sign of the ancient Mexicans' ritual calendar; that interpretation is somewhat too brief, however, because the monkey is just an isolated figure grafted onto a clearly Westernized framework. Furthermore, maybe the animal with the earring was just a borrowed device, emptied of meaning—an exotic, decorative, "disillusioned" image. And the theory of simple camouflage raises yet another problem: it does not account for the presence of the flower, a flower doubly linked to monkey and centaur.

This flower probably holds the answer, if it we agree that it represents *ololiuhqui* or *puyomate*, powerful hallucinogens consumed by the Indians before and after the Conquest. The use of such plants, far from having disappeared under Christianity, spread to the mestizo and mulatto populations. Despite repeated condemnation, the Church never managed to eradicate the consumption of hallucinogenic plants nor even to restrict them to indigenous society. Right from the late sixteenth century, people of mixed blood, blacks, and poor whites discovered indigenous transports and tried to divine their future with these new magic plants.[33] Given this widespread infatuation, hallucinogens could link beings from both worlds and unite them in the same task. The frieze therefore portrays the complicity between a semi-goddess of classical paganism and an Amerindian god. Both are performing a prophetic ritual—the centaur Occyrhoe bends the stem of the plant toward the *ozomatli* monkey who, perhaps gripped by its intoxicating scent, foretells the future.[34]

Unlike the Ixmiquilpan frescoes, the Puebla frieze occupies only a small portion of the total painted surface. Its images cannot be abstracted from others without running the risk of impoverishing its meaning. By studying it closely, we might overlook the magnificent sibyls rising above it. As with Peter Greenaway's screen, the juxtaposition of various planes is not arbitrary. The female centaurs and monkeys who escort the parade of sibyls perhaps bear more than a purely decorative relationship to them. They may well add meaning or indeed supply the meaning for the overall ensemble.[35]

It will be recalled that each of these beautiful riders prefigured an incident in the life of Christ, which is shown in the medallions set above her head. The theme of prophecy therefore runs throughout the entire work, which superimposes three strangely symmetrical levels: the sibyl sits between classical paganism and Christianity, just as the hallucinogen establishes a link between classical paganism—the female centaur—and Amerindian paganism—the *ozomatli* monkey. Linking monkey to centaur not only lifts the Amerindian world to the same level as the classical world, it establishes an indirect relationship, via pagan figures of sibyls and centaurs, between Amerindian beliefs and Christianity.

The use of classical antiquity therefore has a different meaning here from at Ixmiquilpan. It is no longer a question of camouflaging ancient beliefs but of rehabilitating them by illustrating their continuity with Christianity in a more affirmative way and in a more elaborate discourse. This path was indicated by the sibyls, those pagan soothsayers recycled into the story of Christian revelation. Why not build bridges between Amerindian paganism and the victors' Christianity, similar to the ones built by medieval Europeans between classical religion and their own? Nothing could be more crucial if the indigenous elites hoped to span the dreadful gulf opened by conversion to Christianity, to connect the pre-Hispanic past to Mexico's Christian present, using all possible means.

Thus at Puebla and at Ixmiquilpan, *tlacuilos* in the colonial era reconceived their relationship to the past by drawing on the classical material made available to them by Renaissance art. This experiment led them to devise mestizo imagery that embodied figurative conceptualizations of amazing complexity.

PAGAN PAST, CHRISTIAN PRESENT

This highly singular use of classical mythology calls for a little detour via sixteenth-century Europe. The role accorded to Ovid's work by educated and artistic circles during the Renaissance testifies to their familiarity with antiquity. The ancient world could be perceived as a pre-Christian world as much as a pagan one; despite its remoteness in time, educated people felt no break with that period because the Middle Ages had been its direct heir and had flowered in its wake.

Despite the wariness of certain groups within the Church, classical authors continued to be copied, quoted, and commented upon. Open-mindedness prevailed in spite of railings against pagan demons by Camaldolese monks, Dominican friars, and radical individuals such as Savanarola.[36] Renaissance scholars still felt the need to establish links with the classical world, and this concern spurred "a conscious effort to create harmony between two worlds separated by centuries."[37] Recollections of the ancient gods remained vigorous; preserved and transmitted down through the Middle Ages, mythology was everywhere: painted and carved on precious objects, staged during court spectacles, and sculpted in gardens (Ovid provided inspiration for the adornment of the grounds of large Italian villas in Tivoli, Pratolino, Bomarzo, and Caprarola).

Hostile reactions arising in the sixteenth century stemmed more from a surfeit of antiquity than from a radical rejection of the ancient gods. The popes, of course, flushed out the pagan gods—Pius V banned idols from the Vatican, and Sixtus V sought to limit the presence of ancient divinities. A few artists joined in the outcry: in 1582, Bartolommeo Ammannati felt that "making naked statues, satyrs, fauns, and things of that kind everywhere is a great and most grave error." After the Council of Trent, admonitions and warnings increased. Cardinal Paleotti, in his *Discorso intorno alle imagini sacre e profane* (Bologna, 1584), challenged the habit of "putting images of gods well in view"; he advised conserving them discreetly, tolerating them only if they contributed to knowledge of antiquity.[38]

Supporters of classical antiquity counterattacked by using all kinds of arguments. Artists fought for recognition of the harmlessness of representation, stressing the distinction between preserving and worshipping. Their arguments were financial and technical: How could they ignore their patrons' enthusiasm for pagan tales? How could they avoid relying on mythology when they needed a varied and learned repertoire suited to complex decorative schemes? Their best defense, however, consisted of providing a certificate of morality: in the face of criticism of improper and "unseemly" pictures, artists stressed the allegorico-moral side of pagan imagery. It was said to possess edifying virtues and even a capacity for symbolic expression that made it highly suited for depicting vices and virtues.[39]

In the second half of the sixteenth century, gods continued to adorn the palaces of princes and prelates. Neither the polemic nor the decrees of the Council of Trent managed to eradicate antique imagery. The men of letters who commissioned or designed decorative schemes were clergymen. This was true not only of Farnese residences in Rome and Caprarola, it was also true in Spain, where Juan Pérez de Moya published his *Secret Philosophy which Contains, underneath Mythological Tales, Much Useful Knowledge...along with the Origin of the Idols and Gods of Paganism* (1585).[40] And it was also true of the Augustinian monks of Ixmiquilpan and the dean of Puebla Cathedral, who tolerated the sight of mythological creatures in their churches and homes. The antique heritage was so present that it was impossible and inconceivable to obliterate it.

Antiquity's ubiquitous presence began at school, where ancient authors could not be avoided. Learning Latin required familiarity with pagan texts, whether studied in Florence or Mexico City, in a Spanish university or the Indian college of Santa Cruz de Tlatelolco. Those texts referred to a non-Christian past that continued to enjoy considerable prestige. Like Europeans, indigenous students were confronted with a paradoxical reality as displayed on library shelves and monastic frescoes. In the Augustinian monastery of Atotonilco, to the east of Ixmiquilpan, local Indians could admire an entire wall devoted to portraits of the great philosophers of antiquity. In the Augustinian church at Acolman, the upper part of the nave was decorated with sibyls and classical youths.

Like Europeans, literate Amerindians could legitimately feel that their pagan past was more than a pre-Christian era or period of demonic darkness and, as mentioned above, some did not hesitate to remind the Spanish that their own Iberian ancestors had also been pagans. The cult of classical antiquity showed that an indisputably pagan past could enjoy glamorous status and value. Official painting took care of reminding the Indian leadership of this—in the sixteenth century, the indigenous town council of Tlaxcala held its meetings in a reception room decorated with a series of paintings of historic subjects; almost everyday local notables gazed up at Columbus, Cortés, Pizarro, and Charlemagne, along with three heroes of antiquity, Hector, Caesar, and Alexander.[41] Allegories of Fame and Memory pointed out that the recent and distant pasts were one, inviting Amerindians to incorporate their own history. In the church at Tezcatapec, it was not just Hector but the entire Trojan War that was presented to the eyes of faithful.[42]

This convergence could be taken one step further. If the pagans of classical antiquity were not excluded from Christian revelation, as demonstrated by the prophecies of the sibyls, then the pagans of America—as worthy as those of antiquity, according to Las Casas—perhaps benefited from the same favor. The Indians might have had inklings of Christianity prior to the Conquest; Spanish chroniclers speculated about the possibility of an ancient Christianization that had been forgotten. Mention was even made of Saint Thomas, the apostle of India, vestiges of whom were allegedly preserved in several regions of the Americas. The figure of Quetzalcoatl, the Winged Serpent, perhaps masked a missionary whose teachings were corrupted down through the centuries. A past not only rehabilitated along the lines of classical antiquity but also touched by grace would make it possible to ward off the darkness of idolatry even while recuperating a good deal of the traditional heritage.

Allusions to pre-Hispanic monotheism also pointed in this direction. They stressed continuity with the pagan past and minimized the rupture caused by Conquest and evangelization.[43] At the same time, mythology provided an example of a pacified relationship between Christianity and paganism, an acceptable compromise that could serve as inspiration to an indigenous nobility too attached to a pagan past to abandon it.

MYTHOLOGY AND HYBRID CONCEPTUALIZATION

Greek and Latin fable—what we now call classical mythology—historically possessed quasi-organic features that explain its role within mestizo processes. It was nourished on all kinds of mélange. From antiquity, the transmission of myths had taken a path strewn with surprises and metamorphoses, evolving in time as well as space. By the Middle Ages, mythology had forked into two traditions whose developments and directions did not always overlap: a visual tradition incorporating all the forms in which medieval artists conceived the ancient gods, and a literary tradition compiled from descriptions made by scholars, poets, and encyclopedists. Both traditions were the fruit of interpretations and reinterpretations, of oversights, misconceptions, and modifications.

That series of alterations can be explained by the plasticity of the materials and connections expressed through mythology. Back in antiquity, mythology already ignored geographical and historical indicators, mixing periods and places. Even in the sixteenth century, mythology remained impervious to nascent archaeological discoveries, rarely seeking to incorporate them or use them as a source of systematic revision. In contrast, it amalgamated the strangest information and data, as revealed by the engravings that circulated throughout Renaissance Europe. Italian manuals by Cartari and Conti extensively merged sources and traditions, drawing indifferently from the Late Empire's syncretistic heritage, from the Orient's fascinating hermeticism, and from mysterious Egypt. Mythology is an ideal medium for a conceptual approach that practices hybridization.

Compilers have always amalgamated diverse traditions, as superbly exemplified by Ovid's *Metamorphoses*. Right from the start, mythology displayed a predilection for the exotic and freakish, spurring it to favor the far-off, to cultivate foreignness, to feed on singularities. Living mythology often resembles a jumble of bric-a-brac. Its inclusiveness encourages erudite one-upmanship in terms of the strange, the deformed, the hermetic—everyone tries to contribute the most bizarre of features. It has never mattered that assembled versions contradict one another; they were collected and juxtaposed with ever-swelling commentaries and interpretations. So it was hardly surprising that, in reaction, texts that took stock of mythological knowledge—texts that Ovid was already relying on—sought to put a little order into forms and attributes.[44] This led to growing numbers of manuals as indispensable to artists as they were to scholars.

This gluttony for details, each more startling than the last, kindled by the appeal of oriental and Egyptian myths, had other effects. It not only paved the way for the rapprochements and comparisons that gave birth to comparative mythology, it also had an impact on the way the Americas were conceptualized.

MYTHOLOGY AND AMERINDIANS

Bartolomé de Las Casas's *Apologética historia sumaria* (1556) owed a lot to the mythological compilations that preceded it.[45] This key work related the gods of the Old World to those of the New according to grid based on ancient authors and the Fathers of the Church.[46] A detour through classical antiquity permitted religions of the Americas to exist, and Amerindian beliefs could be "plugged into" those of antiquity thanks to mythology. The connection was solid because classical paganism and American paganism were presented as expressions of the same phenomenon: idol worship. According to Las Casas, the former even partly inspired the latter.[47] It was this link that the Indian artists in Puebla and Ixmiquilpan would later reinterpret in their own way.

It goes without saying that the author of the *Metamorphoses*, *The Art of Loving*, and *Fasti* (Calendars) was extensively solicited for the *Apologética historia sumaria*. Among the many details and anecdotes that Las Casas took from Ovid, he recounted the story of Jupiter and Leda, and mentioned Isis, Pan, Circe, and the celebration of bacchanals. He also told the stories of Actaeon transformed into a stag and Daphne into a laurel tree.[48] These references evoke the spirit of the frescoes in Puebla and Ixmiquilpan and raise new questions: Might not the strange hooves on the female centaurs be borrowed from deer? Might the tuft of *maguey* leaves growing from a head in Ixmiquilpan be an Indian version of the myth's laurel leaves? Although Amerindians could not have read Las Casas, these "stock images" could certainly have been found in more or less accessible form in all libraries and many manuscripts in New Spain.

By the 1560s, indigenous collaborators of Franciscan friar Sahagún in and around Mexico City had become familiar with the little game of making connections between Nahua gods and classical gods (whether they merely recorded Sahagún's interpretations or actively contributed their own).[49] Thus comparisons and parallels between the two pantheons were made in the first book of the *Historia general de las cosas de la Neuva España*: "Huitzilopochtli was another Hercules...Chalchiuhtlicue is another Juno...Xiuhtecutli, another Vulcan...Tlazolteotl is like the goddess Venus."[50] Spelled out in the very titles of the chapters, these connections could not have escaped the Amerindian artists who illuminated the magnificent *Florentine Codex*—some of the plates devoted to Indian divinities display double titles, with the Nahua name to the left and its Greco-Roman equivalent to the right.[51] Classical mythology therefore served both to organize an exotic pantheon and to supply immediate and familiar reference points for European readers of the codex.[52] These comparisons were not mere exercises in style. For literate Renaissance readers, the ancient gods were all the more familiar for being considered as deified heroes[53] or as mythical godfathers of European peoples. Ancient gods and biblical prophets coexisted happily in places such as the Carthusian monastery of Pavia and the Colleoni chapel in Bergamo.[54]

In other documents, Ovid's iconography can be perceived between the lines. The torture of *aperramiento*, depicted on a manuscript now in the Bibliothèque Nationale de France, might be an evocation of a myth from *Metamorphoses*: the Amerindian lord devoured by a conquistador's dogs highly resembles Actaeon devoured by Diana's hounds.[55] This method of torture had become much too frequent for local painters not to depict it, but only on condition of finding a Western model, for the horrendous practice had been unknown to pre-Hispanic society.

"THE LAST WORLD"

Classical mythology's propensity for association and absorption was accompanied by a virtuality of an intellectual type. Because mythology was conducive to being pulled in every direction, it provided a choice platform for allegory. It lent itself to parallels as acrobatic and surprising as the one the Jesuits established between Diana and the Virgin Mary.[56] Scholars even wound up making connections so subtle that deciphering the meaning of mythological images required recourse to their writings.[57] Indigenous authors were also infected by this insatiable hermeticism and scholarly snobbism.[58]

The extraordinary potential still embodied by the Ovidian imagination is perhaps best revealed by a novel by Christoph Ransmayr, *The Last World*.[59] Ransmayr used material from the *Metamorphoses* to invent from scratch a bereft society at the edge of the Roman Empire. The novel's protagonist, Cotta, an admirer of Ovid, heads to the ends of the earth in the footsteps of the great poet. He discovers neither the genius in harsh exile nor the precious manuscripts of the *Metamorphoses*, but rather the little port of Tomi, a "town of iron" whose strange inhabitants are lost in the mists of the Black Sea. The tale so skillfully weaves the threads of mythology, ancient history, and the modern world, mixing periods and realities with great virtuosity, that the reader no longer knows if Ovid wrote the *Metamorphoses* based on the residents of Tomi or if the latter were figments of the exiled poet's tormented imagination. Every character's fate is based on the *Metamorphoses*, and every one of them, saddled with a mythological name, suffers the same end as his or her famous namesake. As at Puebla and Ixmiquilpan, in Tomi Ovid's creatures are drafted into other stories that plunge them into a world both strange and familiar, mingling the agony of war, the violence of colonization, and the strangeness of the frontiers of the West.[60]

Long before Ransmayr, Mexican painters were able to exploit the power of myths to traverse epochs and civilizations. Unlike Christianity, mythology does not exclude new or foreign myths. A female centaur can flirt with a Mexican monkey before the eyes of a Spanish prelate. Mythology provides a set of uniquely malleable references, situations, and images. It can tack the most unexpected and contradictory forms and meanings onto its portrayals and depictions. Here is how the Spaniard Juan Pérez de Moya explained several types of transformation: metamorphosis into stone signified death; into a flower, grace; into a tree, chastity. And what was to stop an Augustinian reader of Pérez de Moya from using this key to interpret the inventions of the *tlacuilos* in Ixmiquilpan?

So let us imagine the way Dean Tomás de la Plaza viewed the friezes in his residence. There can be no doubt that the fresco of the sibyls was commissioned by the clergyman, but it is less certain that he systematically dictated the decorative details; in fact, it is inconceivable that he suggested combining monkeys with female centaurs. However, they probably delighted him in the same way as they would have delighted most humanist prelates of the Renaissance. And it is highly possible that the dean saw—or wanted to see—the *ozomatli* monkey as an amusing allegorical creature. The monkey in Puebla may well have passed for a symbol of the Mexican world in all its exoticism, including idolatry.[61] This interpretation might have sufficed to explain the presence of this divine animal without raising anxiety about more heterodox combinations and meanings. And it is entirely possible that this educated Renaissance view also represents the truth about these frescoes.

THE PROPER USE OF MYTHOLOGY

Mythology has still other virtues. When allegory acquitted pagan imagery of licentious meaning, it employed an expedient making it possible to dodge censorship. Mythology thereby afforded some ease and freedom of expression which artists used and abused: it hardly matters that Titian betrayed Ovid when he showed Adonis fleeing the arms of Venus—he was not obliged to respect an iconographic canon closely monitored by the Church. Mythology offered a repertoire with far fewer obstacles than sacred art.

This freedom to create and invent might take an intellectual or philosophical turn. In Renaissance Europe, the meanings hidden below mythological scenes sometimes conveyed secret philosophy. It might transpire that a truth was crouching behind "superficial appearances."[62] This was the case, for example, with the ideas and symbolic figures associated with neoplatonism and the deciphering of hieroglyphic riddles.[63] The stakes might even be political—the paintings that Titian executed for Philip II contain allusions to the king's tyranny, scarcely camouflaged behind portraits of a power-hungry Jupiter.[64] Driven by a strong dose of pessimism and skepticism, the artist reinvested myths with the violence and brutality that popularizers of a moralized Ovid had agreed to minimize. Europa, Perseus and Andromeda, Diana and Actaeon lend their forms to a denunciation of the abuses and crimes committed by the gods.

The subversive power of mythology was thus linked to primordial worlds that it constantly resurrected. In more recent times, this has been realized by the playwright Heiner Müller, who drew inspiration from classical mythology to escape censorship in East Germany. More than a "safety exit," mythology offered Müller a "prehistorical" framework, a past peopled with the same visions of terror and violence so masterfully exploited by Titian in an earlier age.[65] Just as it has the power to provide exotic masks for "politically incorrect" ideas, mythology is skilled at conveying the precariousness of troubled worlds.

Instead of taking Ovid's repertoire as a collection of exotic, ethereal, and ornamental motifs, the Ixmiquilpan artists dwelled on images of the brutal shock, clash, and transformation of beings. Centaurs and griffins

were called upon to block the way of ancient Mexico's "jaguar knights."
These Amerindian painters were unaware of Titian's existence across the
vast ocean, yet they were working during the same period and they
explored similar paths by eschewing mythology's mellower versions.
Mythology helped them to rattle the shackles of Christian forms that had
been imposed on them, even as it became a vehicle for concepts either disguised or discreet, subversive or merely heterodox. Mythology's hybrid
nature was conducive to all kinds of appropriations and associations. By
opening pathways to subterfuge or double and triple meanings, mythology
would appeal to Indians constantly suspected of idolatry. In both Puebla
and Ixmiquilpan, its standardized, ready-to-use imagery and allegories were
able to distract overly inquisitive gazes.

7 THE INVASION OF GROTESQUES, OR, MOVING IMAGES

> At first it was only stealthy, transparent roots, then came little green fingers and deceptive blossoms, and finally sinewy arms plated with mossy bark—the wilderness was reaching out to grasp the town of iron.
> —Christoph Ransmayr, *The Last World*

Even supposing that we managed to discover the intentions of indigenous artists, we would still be a long way from identifying all the mainsprings of the mestizo mind. We know nothing of the processes leading to the visual expression of this Hispano-Indian universe, any more than we know the formal resources linking monkey to female centaur.

At first sight, there is little resemblance between the Puebla frieze and the Ixmiquilpan frescoes. In the Augustinian church, one's eyes are drawn to the battles fought by Mexican warriors at the expense of the upper Western-inspired frieze, which combines fantastic creatures. In contrast, at Puebla, the couple formed by monkey and centaur occupy a subordinate position, a margin apparently left to the decorative imagination of the indigenous artist. The parade of sibyls attracts a visitor's gaze so powerfully that the accompanying frieze is overlooked; a viewer has eyes only for the lavishly appareled ladies who ride through European landscapes of Nordic or Flemish inspiration. This might suggest that the vanquished people's world was relegated to a second level as a way of stressing the victory of Christianity over paganism.[1]

But there are at least two reasons for doubting that suggestion. The first concerns the status of borders and decoration in European art. Their importance has long been overlooked due to our anachronistic view of the medieval and Renaissance past. It is time to grant these features the role and meaning they deserve by reestablishing their occasionally humorous, occasionally subtle relationship with the main motif. A second, more local reason concerns the connections between sibyls, monkey, and female centaur. The

Amerindian elements are not systematically denatured and marginalized, even if they lack the spectacular dimension they possess at Ixmiquilpan.

The apparent differences between the paintings at Puebla and Ixmiquilpan are more superficial than they appear. First all of all, the frescoes are similar in content. They contain a "message" or, to be more accurate, they express an intention that we have tried to decipher here. Neither has a purely decorative function. And if we consider the painted space, they also present a similar staging of worlds undergoing mestizo processes. At both Ixmiquilpan and Puebla, luxuriant vegetation peopled by strange beings provides the setting for Indo-Renaissance creations. At Puebla, a hallucinogenic plant snakes along the walls of the dean's reception room, leading a horde of monkeys, putti, centaurs, and insects in its dance. At Ixmiquilpan, Indian warriors, plantlike creatures, and monsters clash in a series of scenes that unfold with the undulating rhythm of a gigantic garland. Sea horses, winged dogs, and birds with leaflike plumage ridden by putti populate the upper register. In each case, the artists invested themselves in this decoration. Yet it remains to be explained how this ornamental zone—theoretically devoted to frivolous decoration, superficial effects, and an obsession for detail—lent itself to such appropriations, and how the artists colonized it.

MOVING IMAGES AND HYBRIDIZATION

The Ixmiquilpan frescoes are animated by a compelling movement that is hard to describe in words. Only a movie might render the equivalent of this flow of fantastic images, as can indeed be seen in *Prospero's Books*, another film by Peter Greenaway, made five years before *The Pillow Book*.[2] A free interpretation of Shakespeare's *The Tempest*, the film unfolds like a gigantic frieze that parades endlessly before the viewer's eyes. By way of overture, long traveling shots reveal a procession of naked bodies, twisted, tortured, or dancing, interspersed with puffs of fire and spurts of water, advancing to the hypnotic rhythm of Michael Nyman's music. Unusual objects and strange creatures flow across the screen in an alternation of chiaroscuro effects and shimmering colors, against a background of endless columns and arcades. The characters are swept by constant movement, drawn into a complicated choreography, thrust into headlong a rush, plunged into bottomless waters. Everything is movement in *Prospero's Books*, just as everything is movement in the Ixmiquilpan frescoes that thrust their tentacular garlands between the overexcited bodies of warriors and monsters.

In Greenaway's work, "decorative" structures infuse the performance with a choreographic rhythm while establishing a fantastic reality open to the strangest inventions: nude creatures transformed into mermaids in vast aquariums, theatrical savages decked out in blood-red feathers, flayed women displaying their intestines, putti swinging overhead as they piss in Prospero's pool. Just as at Ixmiquilpan and Puebla, the unexpected and the freakish are intensely present. Caliban is the abominable brother of the *ozomatli* monkey and the female centaur, just as the Puebla putti are likeable cousins of Ariel.

With Prospero, mélange is king. Examples are provided throughout the film by the list of magic books collected by the protagonist. Prospero's learning encompasses both real and imaginary knowledge. Maps of the underworld visited by Orpheus, accounts of voyages, and myths from everywhere in the world count as much as a universal cosmography inventorying every phenomenon in the universe. Prospero's bestiary is full of "cameleopards" and chimeras. In a parody of Ovid's *Metamorphoses*, Book 13, titled *The Ninety-Two Conceits of the Minotaur*, lists the most notorious offspring.[3] It includes creatures as freakish as Caliban: centaurs, mermaids, werewolves, harpies, and vampires. In the book of mythologies, "nymphs and putti...endeavor to turn the next huge page to free the occupants of the next chapter—fauns and hamadryads who are already struggling to get out."[4]

Hybridization runs throughout these animated frescoes in which magic and fantasy frequent the freakish. Hybridization is to *Prospero's Books* what mestizo mechanisms are to *The Pillow Book*. The film's dynamism comes from its ability to merge the forms, genres, and registers of Western tradition. Images are superimposed on the screen, producing a zone that mingles movies, dance, opera, and theater. Prospero's island is itself indeterminate, located halfway between the fiction of mythology and the fact of earthly realms. Hybridization, like Prospero's magic, opens the way to all kinds of appropriations. It scorns ordinary logic, overturns the laws of space, time, and plausibility, is unaware of the laws of gravity, and ignores the conventions of representation at the risk of losing the audience: Is Prospero perhaps playing not only himself but all the other roles in *The Tempest?*

Hybrids nevertheless remain relatively coherent. *Prospero's Books* is not a jumble of heterogeneous and incomprehensible images. Although phantasmagoria can create quirks and surprises, it is nevertheless based on a few principles that respect "minimal formal conditions."[5] For instance, the montage of quotations and the interplay of entanglements and collages that unsettle the viewer follow the same order as the presentation of Prospero's magic books. The film's disconcerting complexity in fact rests on a limited and repetitive range of elements.

By developing the virtualities of hybridization and bizarreness, and by cultivating the power of artifice and ornament, Greenaway devised images that viewers must decipher. The screen is packed with symbols, allusions, and associations ungraspable by a superficial gaze. Prospero's twenty-four books represent dictionaries of symbols much like Cesare Ripa's *Iconologia* and Andrea Alciati's *Emblematus Libellus*.[6] Attentive viewers are invited to decipher the imagery the way an arcane text is deciphered, with the required leisure and re-viewings made possible by today's videocassette recorders. Hybridization and hermeticism are linked here, as though the effort to establish secret connections between things should overcome obstacles and remain shrouded in mystery.[7]

Hybridization, hermeticism, complexity, moving images: the concepts weaving through *Prospero's Books* suggest new questions to be asked of Mexico's mestizo paintings not only concerning the relationship between hybrid and mestizo, between organization and complexity, but also concerning the prolific trio long constituted by mannerism, grotesques, and ornamentation.[8]

THE ART OF GROTESQUES

By cultivating the art of combining the hybrid and the ornamental, *Prospero's Books* draws on mannerist ornamentation and, more specifically, the grotesque tradition. And isn't that exactly what our Mexican artists were doing four centuries earlier in their workshops in New Spain?

When *tlacuilos* began to reproduce forms imported from Renaissance Europe, they were unaware that the vogue for grotesques dated back to the late fifteenth century, when the chance discovery in 1480 of Nero's palace, the Domus Aurea, revealed frieze decoration that European artists immediately set about copying.[9] The upshot is well known. The art in the "grottoes" of San Pietro in Vincoli—thought to be the former palace of Emperor Titus—allegedly inspired Giovanni da Udine and Raphael. Thanks to these two artists, the use of "grotesque" decoration spread throughout Renaissance Italy.[10] A remarkable example in the Perseus Hall in Castel Sant'Angelo in Rome was done by Perino del Vaga (1543–1548). Publications such as the anonymous anthology *Leviores et extemporaneae picturae quas grotteschas vocant* reveal the interest and reservations sparked by this mode of representation. Giorgio Vasari, one of the first historians of Italian art, had harsh words about the new fashion: "grotesques are a kind of licentious and highly ridiculous painting which the Ancients did to decorate empty spaces...."[11] *Pace* Vasari, grotesques were not a marginal or anecdotal phenomenon. They exploited trends present in mannerism, the prevailing style in Renaissance Europe, which was to become a universal language via the Hapsburg empire.[12] Mannerism gave pride of place to decoration, as indicated by the vogue for theater with its vast stage machinery and its *inter-*

mezzi that featured fanciful choreography and dazzling apotheoses. Mannerist creations included the extravagant paintings of Arcimboldo (whose *Allegory of Fire* dates from 1566) and the burlesque poetry of Bronzino (in its search for aural and mental associations that could combine heterogeneous elements into subtle mosaics), as well as the famous *Wunderkammern* ("cabinets" of the most incredible curiosities and treasures), the sculpture of Bomarzo, and the caryatids of Milan and Genoa.[13] Preferring movement to static forms, mannerism was enthusiastic about strange, unusual, and freakish phenomena, imposing a taste for the bizarre and whimsical, for "metamorphosis and illusion."

FROM SPAIN TO THE AMERICAS

Italian grotesques swept across Europe and the Iberian peninsula. They soon found fertile soil in Castile. The tradition of the *mudéjar* and Isabelline styles, along with the fashion for plateresque work, sustained a pronounced taste for arabesques, candelabras, fantastic bestiaries[14] and Italianate medallions. As in the rest of Europe, medieval tradition had scattered freakish creatures across the margins of manuscripts and the carved walls of churches. "Plateresque whimsy" entered into ornamental compositions that repeated the same motif to satiety, producing great overall uniformity accentuated by the limited depth of relief.[15]

If Fray José de Sigüenza is to be believed, grotesques were introduced into Spain by Julio de Aquilis and Alexander Mayner, both of whom died around 1530.[16] The artists had gone to Ubeda in Andalusia to decorate the palace of the emperor's secretary, Francisco de los Cobos (1477–1547). They went on to decorate the royal palace of Alhambra in Grenada, where they left tempera and fresco paintings. From that point onward, grotesque decoration proliferated on friezes and pilasters, covered chests and altarpieces, and spread to the clothing worn by grandees, leaving no space bare. The motifs were the same as those found in Italy; "grotesques, vines, foliage, and animated things" emerged from the brushwork of more or less talented artists. That, at least, was the claim made a century later by painter Francisco Pacheco (1564–1654) in his *Arte della pinture* (1649), one of the great treatises on Spanish painting during its Golden Age.[17]

In Europe, the vogue for mannerism and grotesques was more marked in regions that had favored Flamboyant (or Late) Gothic and had been only superficially touched by the high Renaissance aesthetic—which was the case with Spain and even more so with Germany and the Low Countries.

America's mannerism flourished under the aegis of this northern and Iberian Europe, united under the scepter of Holy Roman Emperor Charles

V, followed by Philip II. By the 1540s, the art known as *romano* (or grotesque) had spread to New Spain. The Montejo palace in Merida, in distant Yucatán, was decorated with busts, medallions, and grotesques.[18] Some twenty years later, two talented European painters, Andrés de Concha from Seville and Simon Pereyns from Flanders, moved to Mexico, where they helped to popularize the new forms.[19] The former promoted the style of Luis de Vargas, a Seville-based artist who studied in Italy alongside Perino del Vaga, while the latter introduced some of the northern atmosphere inhabiting the paintings of Martin de Vos and Franz Floris.

Hispano-Flemish mannerism was not being planted in virgin soil, however. It is possible that indigenous tradition facilitated the adoption of mannerist ornamentation, much as the Flamboyant Gothic and plateresque styles had done in the Old World. Monks had already noticed the indigenous taste—*la natural inclinación*—for ornamentation (*ornato* in Spanish Renaissance terminology): "they so liked to decorate their temples that in every town, large or small, there were very pretty, well-kept ones, as prettily decorated as their understanding allowed. And, after Christianization, they took admirable care of them."[20]

This predisposition could be seen in Motolinía's assessment of indigenous painters trained prior to the Conquest: "Before, they knew how to paint only flowers, birds, and all kinds of grotesques, and if they painted a man or a horse, it was so ugly that it resembled a monster."[21] The Franciscan's view of local art included a set of motifs—plants, animals, monsters, and *romano* details—that would have had no difficulty finding its way into the composition of a grotesque frieze. In fact, by the 1540s indigenous artists were not only in contact with monks familiar with the *romano* style and with samples of the new art, but they were effortlessly producing *romanos y bestiones*, that is to say "decoration with grotesques and monsters."[22] And they were doing so with the benediction of the Church. Almost half a century later, the Third Mexican Council strongly encouraged Indians to paint "flowers, fruit, animals, birds, and grotesques...and any other thing to avoid the irreverence of poor paintings of the saints."[23] This does not mean that grotesques met with unanimous approval: by 1560, Spanish artists were complaining about the proliferation of "indecent and ridiculous" imagery; a quarter of a century later, others were still demanding that the depiction of satyrs and other mythological creatures be banished from church altarpieces.[24] It might be added that painting's ascendance over sculpture—which can be explained by technical and pedagogical factors—also helped to disseminate grotesques, even though sculpted versions did exist.[25]

Even more than artists, books illustrated with engravings and richly decorated frontispieces brought mannerist decoration to the Americas.

Printed in Spain or the Netherlands, they provided convenient repertoires that both Spaniards and Indians readily used, being unable to copy inaccessible works in distant Europe.[26] Despite the wars of religion wracking Europe, and despite the establishment in Mexico City and Lima of an Inquisition that closely monitored the trade in books, publications from Lyon, Paris, and northern Europe (Antwerp) continued to arrive in the New World; along with them arrived examples of northern mannerism, added to margins or spread across frontispieces. By 1539, these books were joined by publications straight from Mexico City's own presses. Printers originally from Italy (Juan Pablos of Lombardy), Spain, and France (Pierre Ochart of Rouen) were careful about the design of their books.[27] In addition to such books, most of which were religious in content, there were *folletos* and *pliegos sueltos*, or pamphlets and loose-leaf sheets that dealt with edifying or literary subjects. Cheaper and more numerous but more fragile than books, these publications disseminated mannerist decoration in turn.[28]

The repertoire of fantastic and grotesque imagery grew with the arrival of new shipments, and monks and Indians had merely to turn to these extremely diversified and proliferating sources. Thus books as diverse as the chivalrous novel *Tirant lo blanch*, Ferdinand the Catholic's *Constitucions*, and Antonio de Nebrija's Latin grammar all included scenes of the battle between Centaurs and Lapiths, prefiguring the Ixmiquilpan frescoes by nearly a century.[29]

Grotesques might appear in any kind of book, in some rather surprising combinations. A *Book of Hours of the Blessed Virgin*, published in Mexico City in 1567, opens with a Late Gothic engraving of the Virgin of Monserrat. The Virgin sits in enthroned above the world, with the Holy Child on her knee, and overlooks a rocky landscape dotted with crosses and a few houses.[30] This pious image is framed by fantastic and grotesque creatures whose poses and style place them at an opposite extreme from the austerely hieratic engraving in the center. The winged female sphinxes are reminiscent of ones found in the ducal hall of the papal palace in the Vatican and the Palazzo Vecchio in Florence.[31] As to the male head with horns, it is the counterpart to ones in the Hall of Apollo of Castel Sant'Angelo and the Emo Villa in Fanzola.[32] The book's printer was none other than Pierre Ochart from Rouen, France, that is to say a member of the colony of northern Europeans who were acclimating northern styles to Spanish Mexico. Several motifs in the frontispiece evoke the decorative work of Cornelis Bos (1510–c. 1570), dating from the mid-sixteenth century.[33] The upshot is a Renaissance hybrid that uninhibitedly combines pagan nudity and grinning masks with an expression of Marian piety. Yet all of this was in the air at the time—we need merely recall that it was another Book of Hours, done for Alessandro Cardinal Farnese, which was one of the first manuscripts to be embellished with grotesques.[34] Four years later, the same collage would feature in a catechism in the Huasteco language, far more likely to reach Indian hands than was the *Hours of the Blessed Virgin*.[35]

THE FREEDOM OF GROTESQUES

Ochart's frontispiece reflects both the boldness and routine of mannerist ornamentation. In Europe and Mexico, grotesque decoration provided painters with a broad range of expression within which the imagination could play freely. All amalgamations were possible, even between the most dissimilar, incongruous elements. Forms were combined in a kind of associative automatism which juxtaposed or linked elements that were theoretically far removed. In principle, the only thing that prevailed was "the impetuous power of artistic whim and an inevitable immoderateness of misconception." In principle, artists could devise "things with no rule whatsoever, putting at the end of a tiny thread a weight it could never hold, putting foliate legs on a horse or a crane's feet on a man."[36]

As "a paradigm of creative and fantastic license ever more marked as the century progressed,"[37] freed from servitude to the real or plausible, Italian grotesques rejected the constraints of decency.[38] For all these reasons, grotesque decoration allowed for a reversal of Western representation as conceived by Renaissance humanism. André Chastel argued that: "the realm of grotesques is therefore the fairly exact antithesis of the realm of representation, whose norms were defined by a perspective view of space and the distinction and characterization of types."[39]

This freedom did not go unnoticed. Cardinal Paleotti, an advocate of the Tridentine Church and a foe of antique imagery, condemned grotesques in the name of reason, nature, resemblance, and decency.[40] In Spain, artist and theorist Francisco Pacheco was alarmed by the universal popularity of a technique that invaded all spaces, both civil and ecclesiastic. The painter strongly discouraged its use in a religious context. Church decoration and religious objects should rid themselves of these hideous faces, these wild satyrs and caryatids, which should be reserved solely for the private apartments [*camarines*] of aristocratic residences.[41]

MEXICO CITY, PARMA, FLORENCE

The liberty offered by grotesques took on a new dimension once they had been transported and adapted to American soil in a climate of Westernization, colonization, and Christianization. In Mexico, indigenous painters perceived European grotesques as an inversion or negation of the visual order the Church was trying to impose, an order based on three-dimensional human space governed by the laws of gravity and favorable to systematic anthropomorphism. Grotesques pointed down another path which, by extraordinary coincidence, converged with Amerindian tradition. The features typical of grotesque decoration are indeed found in pre-Hispanic codices: "negation of space," "weightlessness of forms," and a "strange proliferation of hybrids" set against solid backgrounds. The codices also organized compositions by playing on the symmetrical arrangement of motifs at the expense of the expressiveness of figures. All these traits were common to both Italian grotesques and Mexican "paintings."

An additional factor might have stimulated indigenous interest in grotesques. Such decoration turned its back on what constituted the very goal of Western representation, namely narration. It overturned the rules established by medieval rhetoric and based on principles of imitation and resemblance. Art, according to Aristotelian texts, could be only a mimesis of truth and verisimilitude. Now, neither grotesque decoration nor Mexican codices were concerned to convey immediate reality, even though grotesques borrowed fragments or elements of it (as did the codices, for that matter).[42]

A return to Italy will shed light on the formal similarity between grotesque decoration and ancient Mexican codices. Parma boasts not only monasteries with paintings much admired by art historians, but also remarkable sets of grotesque decoration that I happened to discover during a trip to Italy in the winter of 1997. The special charm of the vaulted ceiling of the library of San Giovanni Evangelista, a stone's throw from the Duomo, is truly unforgettable. Painted between 1573 and 1575, the monastic library is decorated with paintings almost as enigmatic as those found in a Mexican codex. Ordinary items, strange objects, exotic animals, and bizarre symbols are arranged against a uniform background, comprising a stupefying set of grotesques whose goal is clearly not decorative. The work resembles certain Mexican codices once they have been completely unfolded. It is arranged more like an Indian pictograph than an alphabetic text. Of course, these formal similarities cannot eliminate the distance separating Italian grotesques from pre-Columbian glyphs,[43] but such visual relationships are the basis—and sometimes the only basis—of fertile exchange between two worlds.

Florence confirmed what Parma proffered. The Uffizi Gallery is not only one of the finest museums in the world, but its walls are also covered with grotesques, some of which were inspired by the Mexican codices collected by the Medici family.[44] Visitors who manage to take their eyes off the Italian masterpieces on the walls will discover a ceiling adorned with armed Mexican warriors and fantastic serpents done in the conventional framework of mannerist decoration. American reptiles found their way into Renaissance bestiaries with the same ease that the Ixmiquilpan grotesques became Indianized. A further surprise is the realization that the tuft of feathers depicted in the hair of the dancers of the *Intermezzi* of 1589—a long-famous Florentine festival wonderfully studied by art historian Aby Warburg[45]—are similar to the ones worn by Ixmiquilpan warriors. Which is not to say that the frescoes painted in the Mexican town inspired Bernardo Buontalenti, but that in both cases, at a distance of several thousand miles, the same traditions intersected.

This appropriation remained an exceptional phenomenon even though it occurred in one of Renaissance Italy's major capital cities. It was a rare case in which European art showed itself capable of adopting Mexican forms. In any event, it is remarkable that grotesque decoration allowed for exchanges between the two worlds—the Amerindian artists of Puebla and Ixmiquilpan delved into the European repertoire at the very moment that Florentine painters were inspired by Mexican codices. To the extent that this book is intended to indicate the paths and mechanisms of mestizo processes, it would seem that we have here a connection as crucial as it is poorly studied.[46]

In the eyes of Amerindians, mannerist ornamentation could provide a potential alternative to figurative Christian art. Its peripheral or subordinate nature made it less invasive and more attractive to indigenous artists. By providing a space of relative freedom within the Western visual order, grotesques served as inspiration to Indians curious about new forms and concerned to preserve—or revive—aspects of their own tradition.

SIMPLE RECIPES

The appeal of a style and mode of expression is closely linked to its ease of reproduction. Despite their strange and unexpected air, grotesques were stereotyped creations. Paradoxically, contempt for the dominant rules— *antiregola*—had its own rules. Not only was the iconographic repertoire finite, but it was even rather conventional. The same ornaments and objects were repeated *ad nauseam*: the same leafy garlands, chimeras, festoons, protean candelabra, masks, flying or precariously balance figures, and so on.

This respect for established forms therefore soon limited inventiveness and spontaneity to technical know-how, or "manner." Henceforth, only the quality of execution sustained the illusion of constant improvisation and unbridled imagination, as though the brush replaced the liveliness of a mind teeming with fanciful ideas. That goal, however, was an ideal accessible only to the most gifted. Normally, the production of grotesques was less demanding, which constituted a further appeal to Indian assistants not necessarily comfortable with vast figurative compositions.

In both Europe and the Americas, the production of grotesques was usually a team effort based on the mechanical division of repetitive tasks and employing all kinds of reproductive devices and techniques.[47] It was thanks to traced patterns that grotesques covered the walls of Puebla and Ixmiquilpan. By repeating and inverting an initial drawing, painters could easily cover the entire surface available. To this basic design they could bring modifications or interpretations of their own devising. For example, they might enlarge a pattern; at Ixmiquilpan, the use of patterns was accompanied by a change of scale which placed ornamentation at the very heart of figurative space. The walls of the church of San Miguel Arcangel were covered with gigantic grotesques whose undulations orchestrated both the decorative arrangement and the staging of the battle scenes. In fact, Amerindian artists invented nothing; they merely exploited one spatial virtuality of this mode of expression, namely the possibility of spilling beyond the borders the way a river spills out of its bed, as a way of organizing overall representation. This was the case in Europe when grotesques exceeded their field of application to become the "codice di aggregazione di un intero organismo architettonico," just as it was the case of northern *Rollwerk* and the *estilo monstruoso*.[48] It was also the case in the Andes, where "grotesques ceased to be decoration strictly subordinate to architecture, becoming large reliefs whose importance equaled or exceeded that of the architectural elements. . . . Once enlarged several times over, grotesques made a major impact on the viewer."[49]

CREATING AND CONCEPTUALIZING HYBRIDS

Although the unforeseen, the strange, and the surprising obeyed stylistic procedures and conventions, they also implicitly pointed to a conception of nature and to the infinite possibilities cultivated by men of the Renaissance.[50] In the sixteenth century, the curiosity aroused by distant exploration, the tradition of antique paganism, a taste for the marvelous, and the power of the Christian supernatural all fueled a state of mind that was not hamstrung by verisimilitude and that believed in the mélange of species. In this respect, Ovid indeed served as the bible of a renascent "transformationism."[51] Through "all of these myths, [Ovid] would have us understand nothing less than the fact that, in the nature of things, forms are continuously transformed, matter never perishes."[52] The popularity of the *Metamorphoses* owed much to the fact that the book converged with ideas that largely transcended humanist circles and that could also be found among the clergy, doctors, scholars, and chroniclers.

Everything hybrid appealed to Renaissance minds attentive to all of nature's creations, notably those located in between standard categories and genres. That explains the interest in monsters and strange animals displayed by the likes of Gerolamo Cardano and Ambroise Paré. Nor, in fact, was this curiosity new.[53] It did not take monsters as demonic and threatening creatures straight from hell, but rather as signs that could be inventoried and deciphered by everyone.[54] Located on the borderlines between animal and vegetable kingdoms, such wonders displayed the unlimited wealth of creation, what Montaigne called "the immensity of [divine] creation." They revealed continuity where appearances seemed to erect strict borders: "The notion of intermediate nature so often used by Renaissance naturalists provided a kind of theoretical justification and meaning, within the order of things, to the existence of mermaids and centaurs, sphinxes and griffins, and many other monsters that filled grotesque decorations."[55] Grotesques thus revealed the "relationships" (Montaigne) between the kingdoms, that is to say, the correspondences between elements apparently highly incompatible and highly dissimilar. They also embodied intermediate states such as those painted by Arcimboldo, which seem to exist between the human and vegetable kingdoms, or those mentioned by the Protestant Guillaume du Bartas: "Two animals of different species, against the common order... form an animal" whose "bastard body contains many features from one part and from the other."[56] Garlands of flowers transformed into human beings are simply a different variation on this same theme.

Hybrids are not merely a mark of the continuity of divine creation. They are the product of a movement, of the structural instability of things. It is perhaps no coincidence that Ovid was more interested in the transitional forms, in the stages of change and transformation, than in the final results of a metamorphosis. A hybrid is also the spectacular result of "sympathy" within a universe full of convergences and clashes. The rules of sympathy and antipathy that ordered the Renaissance world also orchestrated Mexico's painted imagery: antipathy triggered the combat between Indians and centaurs at Ixmiquilpan, sympathy explained the proximity or rather the complicity of monkey and female centaur at Puebla.

This conception of nature was based on a form of thought that favored *aemulatio*, a type of emulation or resemblance without contact, of inner or outer similarities.[57] By stressing hidden connections, this analogic thinking explored reality and imagination with no concern for the thresholds separating or distinguishing the two. By thoroughly exploiting the multiple possibilities of a not-yet-fully realized creativity, it examined the various registers of reality and verisimilitude. Instead of rejecting everything exotic, foreign, remote—the site of an inaccessible and often demonic otherness—it sought to integrate it into presentations and representations that reconciled surprise and harmony. Sometimes, too, it took the more discreet paths of hermeticism and magic, as found in the books not only of Prospero but also of philosophy and neoplatonism.[58]

The convergences that occurred between natural history and the Renaissance's decorative idiom abundantly testify to this state of mind. Such thinking could also be easily expressed in literary and material form, as witnessed by books such as Montaigne's *Essays*, a montage that takes a mélange approach.[59] It could furthermore be seen in the *objets d'art* piled in collectors' cabinets: nautilus shells, ostrich eggs, and coral inserted into pretty settings constituted artificial creations whose studied lines and precious materials extended nature's own forms.[60]

Another example was provided by the feather mosaics that Europeans brought back from Mexico, sparking the admiration of Renaissance collectors, including the pope and prelates of the Roman Church: the natural shimmer of the feathers of tropical birds was arranged to look like a painting. In Rome and throughout Italy, scholars and collectors waxed enthusiastic over this perfect demonstration of *theatrum naturae*.[61] In Bologna, naturalist Ulisse Aldrovandi (1522–1605) devoted several pages of his *Ornithologiae* to Mexico's feather mosaics and mentioned that Cardinal Paleotti had presented him with a *Saint Jerome* that he placed in his museum in Bologna and continued to admire.[62]

Cabinets of curiosities thus contained many rare objects and bold combinations that blurred the borderlines between art and nature, between distant object and local tradition, between religious use and magical use. Their role was little different from those of the grotesques that established links between kingdoms. The creatures that populated them, despite their lack of verisimilitude, often remained highly similar to the ones adorning the plates of books of natural history and cosmography published at the time.[63]

These curiosities show that Renaissance thought was not frozen into a closed, rigid framework, which an artist or writer then imposed on the surrounding world or reality. Grotesques made this plain by cultivating paradox and contradiction, even in those small, oft-repeated motifs where the artist took mischievous delight in defying the laws of gravity. Hybrid creations of the Renaissance thus had their own lines of force and their constants: the search for continuity, the quest for "sympathy," the detection of underlying yet crucial relationships. Far from expressing arbitrary combinations or aberrant collages, they revealed hidden relationships through the playful staging of similarities.[64]

The new knowledge stemming from explorations was influenced more than is generally thought by this way of seeing things. It helped to establish bridges between the Old World and the New, if through indirect means. When Las Casas examined religions in the Americas, he did not merely make scholarly allusions to classical mythology and religions, he offered many comparisons and developed an analogical attitude which discovered similarities between things that seemed to differ in every way.[65] This state of mind produced surprising judgments on Las Casas's part, such as his admiration for the religiousness of societies that practiced human sacrifice and cannibalism. It was also the search for resemblances which led Franciscan friar Motolinía to study "the philosophers and astrologers of Anahuac [Nahuatl-speaking Mexico]," whom he compared to "the philosophers of our own countries"; for the same reason he referred to "la filosofia de Anahuac" as one of "the manifestations and signs of the natural skill of the natives of this land."[66]

And yet grotesques never constituted a true philosophy transcribed into imagery; apart from a few examples, such paintings were never "programmatic" in nature.[67] They nevertheless conveyed an openness to the world stimulated by an exaggerated taste for all kinds of combinations, provided that they underscored preexisting links and obeyed a few rules of symmetry and proportion. Such requirements channeled artists' hybrids by guiding permutations, transpositions, and conjunctions. In short, Renaissance Europe could not only conceptualize hybrids,[68] it was able to produce them in the form of grotesques, macaronic verse, and droll decors that were more or less ephemeral.

This mode of thought was distinct from Christian Manichaeanism without being in total opposition to it. It offered more appealing horizons to curious minds and nonconformists of all kinds, as well as to the indigenous elites of Mexico and Peru. The idea that there existed similarities and hidden relationships between spheres hardly surprised the Mexicans, even if they interpreted those similarities in a different way. Indian artists were therefore drawn to grotesques for several reasons. Grotesque decoration opened the door to their imaginations and their taste for amalgamation; it was also easy to execute and reflected an intellectual background to which some of them were probably alert. By adopting grotesque decoration, *tlacuilos* were diverting the glamour and perhaps the sacredness of the victors' art to the benefit of their own world.

8 THE LANGUAGE OF GROTESQUES AND GLYPHS

> The inference is that precisely those features of Correggio's frescoes which the modern art historian tends to put aside as anomalies or to condemn as outright mistakes may well result from a surplus rather than from a deficit of learning and sophistication.
> —Erwin Panofsky, *The Iconography of Correggio's Camera di San Paolo*

A return to Parma: the Convent of San Paolo stands halfway between Palazzo della Pilotta and the Duomo. It owes its fame to a room decorated by Correggio. Another chamber, painted earlier by Alessandro Araldi, is often overlooked even though the two rooms share the same origins.[1] In the early sixteenth century, the Benedictine abbess of San Paolo, Giovanna da Piacenza, commissioned decorative schemes as startling and magnificent as those of the dean of Puebla. Although scandals rocked the life of the Italian abbess and the youth of the Spanish dean,[2] and although both of these refined, appealing characters cultivated worldliness, it is primarily their shared passion for certain forms of art that—to our delight—unites them across the oceans.

THE PARMA GROTESQUES

Painted in highly different styles, the two chambers in the San Paolo convent reveal the way in which images and decorative effects could express philosophical ideas, linking paganism to Christianity and elegantly affirming the convictions, hopes, and victories of their patron, Giovanna da Piacenza. The abbess, who tirelessly resisted the enclosure that Rome wanted to impose on her convent, truly intended to leave a splendid reminder of her time on earth by gathering around her the finest painters and best minds of the day.

In the chamber painted by Araldi, grotesques cover almost the entire ceiling and frame biblical scenes glorifying the abbess's qualities. In addition to scenes from the Old and New Testaments, the decoration includes hiero-glyphs (taken from a famous book of the day, Horapollo's *Hieroglyphica*) and age-old *exempla* of virtue and piety. Connoisseurs would have recognized the story of the unicorn that seeks refuge in the lap of a virgin, plus the triumph over injustice (symbolized by a monkey, an animal which takes on a meaning completely different from the one in Puebla), as well as a selection of images based on pagan worship—sacrifice and offerings on an altar, veneration of a statue of Apollo, a procession of a priestess of Juno, and an evocation of the goddess Ceres searching for her daughter Persephone. Classical and Christian references are freely intermingled, creating an atmosphere in which the biblical world coexists with the pagan one, as do egocentrism and intellectual game-playing. These explicit, flattering allusions should not be surprising, even among Benedictine nuns, for they confirm the fact that Renaissance Christianity knew how to come to terms with vestiges of the cults that had preceded it by reproducing cult imagery in the very heart of its own sanctuaries. Here paganism probably represented no more than a reservoir of allegories and metaphors at the service of Christianity. And it was precisely this mode of appropriation that legitimized the presence of grotesques in an ecclesiastical building.

Such interplay even permitted a certain boldness. Ovid's *Fasti* and Virgil's *Eclogues* supplied mottoes whose allusions to blind fate seem to have enchanted the abbess at a time when this concept was Christian theology's "*bête noire.*"[3] The cult of antiquity prompted borrowings from works as licentious as the *Ode to Priapus* by the poet Tibullus, revealing the extent to which Giovanna's friends cultivated the antique spirit. It is likely that these pointed allusions remained invisible to ordinary folk but held no mystery for enlightened connoisseurs.

The grotesques decorating the splendid vaulted ceiling above the visitor's head play a full-fledged role in the decoration. Actively participating in the staging of the paintings, they resonate with the various themes of a program designed to glorify the abbess: tritons and winged putti holding a globe (symbol of power) proclaim Giovanna's triumph. Yet they also play a another, more crucial role, because they establish a link between a series of pagan subjects and a series of biblical scenes. Sphinxes, masks, putti, birds, sea nymphs, tritons, human-headed griffins—all these creatures populate an intermediate world to which each makes a lively contribution. Some explicitly relay the message of the pagan figures, such as a sea nymph, giving suck to two tiny centaurs, who overlooks Roman Charity, herself breast-feeding her father. Elsewhere, smiling, upright putti with chubby arms hold round and rectangular paintings of biblical subjects, while fantastic creatures play music and sing for Christ and the gods of the ancients.[4]

Parma is home to another work discussed earlier, namely the grotesques in the monastery of San Giovanni Evangelista. On this decorated ceiling—

whose composition and hermeticism evoke certain features of the Mexican codices—the determination to build a language based on grotesque and symbolic imagery is even clearer. On the advice of Abbot Cattaneo, artists Giovan Antonio Paganino and Ercole Pio sought to exhaust the possibilities of the genre[5] by using grotesques as a form of writing, since they used the library's vaulted ceiling to formulate a "moral and pedagogical encyclopedia"[6] that develops the theme of the *aurea mediocritas*, that is to say the Golden Mean. Linked with hieroglyphs and emblems fashionable in the sixteenth century, these grotesques rival written, alphabetical expression, as though constituting the basis of a new language.

This figurative language employed hieroglyphs drawn from the repertoires of Horapollo and Valeriano.[7] Such hieroglyphs were also part of a hybrid tradition, since they combined Christian wisdom with Egyptian wisdom. Endowed with an esoteric, sacred nature, they conveyed age-old knowledge supposed to explain—to initiates—the profound essence of things. At San Giovanni Evangelista, the hieroglyphs were combined with other lexicons that also employed symbolic or allegorical imagery, namely *imprese* and emblems, which keenly interested the decorators of the Parma library. The result is a decorative environment that combines four languages—Latin, Greek, Hebrew, and Syriac—plus an amazing quantity of objects, characters, monsters, and real and fantastic animals (elephant, stag, salamander, basilisk, and so on). The interplay of inscription and imagery presents viewers with riddles whose keys reside in relationships of adjacency or proximity, as discerned by viewers themselves.

THE LANGUAGE OF GROTESQUES AND GLYPHS

The Benedictine library's resemblance to Mexican codices is therefore not a formal illusion. Perhaps nowhere else did Europe come so close to Amerindian expressive idioms—without having sought to do so in the least.

For that matter, a Renaissance comment on hieroglyphs could easily be applied to those codices: "Images replace the meanders of reasoning, they express and fix in memory the transcendent unity of the concept, they become part of the Idea through the metaphorical efficiency of their figures."[8] Reciprocally, the observations on Mexican codices made by Spaniard Diego Durán might well describe the Parma grotesques: "They used painting like letters, by means of paintings and effigies they wrote their histories and antiquities."[9]

In an even stranger coincidence, the Mexican glyphs for water and fire found a kind of twin in Horapollo's repertoire: "43. Purity. To depict purity, [the Egyptians] drew fire and water."[10]

In fact, the Mexicans' glyph of water and fire, *teoatl/tlachinolli*, stood for a different concept, namely sacred war, the goal of which was to provide the fresh blood and vital forces needed to fuel cosmic energies.[11] The coincidence demonstrates how European interest in hieroglyphs might intersect with curiosity awakened by discoveries in the New World—it was, moreover, an earlier admirer of Mexican objects, the artist Albrecht Dürer, who conceived the image of fire and water based on Horapollo's text.[12]

Nothing prevented codex painters from perceiving these forms as equivalents to their own tradition.[13] Grotesques provided a new and different repertoire that nevertheless allowed them to convey ideas in the same way as pictographs dating either from pre-Hispanic days or from the period of Conquest and Christianization.[14]

Of course, the metaphorical and allegorical aspect of grotesques should not be confused with the evocative powers of the ancient Mexican pictographic tradition. In particular, the Western concept of symbolism seems far removed from Mexican imagery which claimed to make the world's profound reality actually present, as opposed to merely "representing" it. The gap narrows, however, if we consider Renaissance Europe's view of hieroglyphs. They were seen not merely as a superior, codified form of expression: a hieroglyphic image literally incarnated the concept, as far as Marsilio Ficino was concerned.[15] Their strange shapes expressed the essence of an idea, they embodied the ideal of a natural language that was a very part of the world of things. In this case, hieroglyphs and accompanying grotesques could be seen to have a revelatory power fairly comparable to that credited to Mexican codices. This power was nevertheless more virtual than real once we acknowledge that the paintings in San Giovanni Evangelista went no further than a rough sketch of a conceptual system. As fascinating as the library's vaulted ceiling may be, the Western experiment of inventing a visual language based on hieroglyphs, emblems, and grotesques remained without issue.[16]

Did these surprising convergences between Mexican glyphs and Renaissance speculation arouse curiosity in Spain and Italy? Italian humanist Pietro Martire d'Anghiera was probably the first person to describe Mexican glyphs as "hieroglyphs." Around 1560, Felipe de Guevara's *Comentarios de la pintura* made the same connections.[17] But this issue still remains largely unexplored. Intriguing links are further suggested by a series of pre-Hispanic and colonial codices that wound up in Italian collections, not to mention the clues found in Italian commentary to the *Codex Vaticanus A*.[18] Then there was the 1579 publication in Perugia of a *Rhetorica Christiana* by Diego Valadés, a Franciscan born in Mexico of an Amerindian mother and Spanish father. His *summa* was accompanied by engravings showing alphabets of images, all of them being European in origin[19] except for those drawings inspired by Mexican codices; the glyph *calli*, meaning "house," was supposed to represent the letter E, whose shape it somewhat resembled. In fact, what was involved here was not the invention of a figurative alphabet designed to replace standard alphabets, but the development of a tool that would help Indians to learn Latin letters. Despite its lacuna and approximations, this attempt showed that Mexican glyphs were actually printed and appeared in scholarly books. They were a new means of expression that could enrich the Renaissance arts of memory.[20]

It hardly needs repeating that the visual languages of grotesque and codex were unrelated. Yet from a material and functional standpoint, both means of expression were a collection of images able to convey complex modes of thought by exploiting memory in a way completely different from alphabetical texts. This provided one more reason for Amerindian artists to paint what were called *romanos* and "monsters." The new figurative language made it possible to code an idea visually and therefore potentially disseminate it in a masked or indirect way.[21] This repertoire of hybrids, combined with mythology, made it possible to formulate forbidden ideas as well as to preserve the remnants of outlawed paganism—the undulating garlands on the walls of the church in Ixmiquilpan provided a clear and superb staging of pre-Hispanic belief in the gyrating movement of universal forces. Grotesques were all the more suitable insofar as their playful, harmless appearance was liable to lull the censor's attention; the decorative craft, apparently as empty of meaning as it was repetitive, focused on the falsely reassuring register of ornament and embellishment.

Grotesques were conducive to the full play of correspondences between highly dissimilar registers. Any allegorical interpretation of them, meanwhile, was double-edged: it could provide an orthodox meaning for pagan imagery even as it enabled certain people to perceive subversive message. As odd as it may seem today, the monkey on the walls at Puebla may have simultaneously signified ridicule of a submissive idolatry and the elevation of Amerindian paganism to the same rank as classical mythology. Both interpretations are certainly applicable to the appealing little animal, and still others are perhaps possible.

FROM GROTESQUES TO METAMORPHOSES

Grotesques represented an animated form of an exuberant force that they seemed to draw from their vegetal origin. In *The Last World*, Christoph Ransmayr conveyed this vitality by describing the growth of the vegetation covering Ovid's final home in Trachila: "The rioting green mimicked the forms it enclosed, playfully, mockingly at first, but then, obeying its own laws of form and beauty, went on relentlessly to obliterate all signs of human handiwork."[22]

A few lines later, a blue bindweed begins to ramble like some intelligent being, reaching out with ringlets of tendrils and pinning flowers here and there, taking possession of the house it has entered. Soon all that remains is a "web of rags, twine, and blossoms." Plants and things become as inextricably mingled as the flowery volutes and fantastic creatures in the Ixmiquilpan frescoes. At the end of Ransmayr's novel, based on Ovid's *Metamorphoses* throughout, the mythological transformations become completely bound up in the ramifications of the plot and the foliate forms devouring the ruins of Trachila.

This association, evocative of the freakish ramifications of grotesque imagery, raises questions about the relationship between sinuous shapes and freakish hybrids on the one hand, and mythological tales on the other. By adopting not only a form that was more than a decorative pattern (grotesques) but also a content that could not be reduced to an anthology of pagan anecdotes, the indigenous artists at Puebla and Ixmiquilpan created mestizo images.

Nor, in Europe, could the links between grotesques and mythology be reduced to their shared roots in the distant past of classical antiquity. They unfolded in the imagination as much as they covered painted surfaces or flowed from poets' pens.[23] Indeed, the spread of Ovid's work was largely due to engravings that illustrated the text in a mannerist style. Now these engravings, whether they illustrated the tales or simply exploited decorative devices, favored metamorphoses and hybridizations. Mannerist decoration, like mythology, was nourished on exotic allusions and disparate images. The presence of hybrids was designed to reveal correspondences between opposites. As "interpreters of Nature,"[24] grotesques drew together and merged things that nature associated only from a distance. And myths—those of Ovid more than any others—perhaps pursued the same goal by infinitely conjugating the theme of metamorphosis.

FROM HYBRID TO MESTIZO

Mythology and grotesques betray the presence of hybrids in Renaissance thought. On Mexican soil, however, in contact and confrontation with indigenous societies, hybrid gave way to mestizo. How did this additional metamorphosis occur?

The same question arises in other contexts and other periods. Peter Greenaway answered it by replacing the hybrid, yet closed, imaginative sphere of *Prospero's Books* by the open, mestizo horizons of *The Pillow Book*. The hybrid mechanisms running through Prospero's universe prefigured those that triggered Greenaway's mélange of civilizations—European,

Chinese, Japanese. By returning to the interplay of image and calligraphy, by systematizing the superimposition and insertion of screens, the filmmaker breathed life into the mestizo fresco of *The Pillow Book*. Although similar procedures were repeated, they explored other imaginative spheres and frontiers—playful acrobatics were transformed into experimental montage.

In sixteenth-century America, hybrid became mestizo through the vast expansion of horizons. This transition arose from a coincidence, from the unforeseen encounter between a specifically American phenomenon—the mestizo processes of the Conquest—and an artistic trend born in Italy and nourished on one aspect of Renaissance sensibility—the grotesque and mannerist tradition. It was not the sudden appearance of the New World that stimulated the European taste for hybrids, but rather the vestiges of an "otherworld" located in the distant days of ancient Rome. Nor was it mannerism that triggered America's mestizo mechanisms, but rather the Conquest, colonization, and settlement of lands unknown to Europeans.

The meeting of hybrid and mestizo did not occur only in the Americas. It was played out on both sides of the ocean. In Europe, a mannerist sensibility influenced the eye turned on all American realities, from the descriptions left by chroniclers to the collections kept in "cabinets of curiosities" known as *Wunderkammern*. Artistic and intellectual curiosity explains the interest displayed in codices, carvings, and feather mosaics that might otherwise not have survived down to the present.[25] The many copies produced in Mexico for export confirm the existence of a European market—limited but glamorous—for wonders of a new kind.[26]

This interest might go beyond mere curiosity and the desire to accumulate rare and exotic booty, sometimes favoring new encounters and provoking mestizo processes, however limited or fleeting. When executing the grotesques in the armory at the Uffizi, artist Ludovico Buti referred to the codices collected by the Medici family.[27] Other examples of such encounters concerned Mexican objects that collectors transformed or adapted to Western tastes. These include European copies of Amerindian codices, which attempted to make comprehensible—and therefore to Westernize—ancient Mexican beliefs and imagery. They did so by changing medium (switching to paper and ink), by employing illustrations with no pre-Hispanic precedent, and even by adding commentaries in a European language (not necessarily Castilian). That was the case with the *Codex Rios*, an "Italo-Aztec" hybrid book that severed most of its Amerindian connections without ever becoming a properly European manuscript. Yet this codex did not go unnoticed—anymore than did the Mexican grotesques in the Uffizi—since it was commissioned by a prestigious patron, perhaps Cosimo de' Medici or Pope Paul V.

In Mexico, faced with multiple mestizo phenomena in every realm, mannerist decoration remained a secondary sphere. Yet the range of technical and visual tools it offered could serve bold and heterodox ideas.

Grotesques and Greco-Latin mythology defused certain Western principles of reality as propagated by the Church, short-circuiting the formal standards imposed by the new visual order. They provided a syntax free of preconceptions, they operated on the fringes of the rigid and demanding Tridentine orthodoxy, and they allowed for different lines of approach to combinations among all the traditions coexisting on American soil. At Ixmiquilpan, the mouth of a freakish dolphin is transformed into the beak of a bird, making it resemble more closely the god of wind, Quetzalcoatl, while at the god's side is another metamorphosis: a dragon wielding a pre-Hispanic club utters sacred texts in age-old indigenous volutes.

What was the extent of such phenomena? Much remains to be written on the presence of mythological figures in the indigenous art of New Spain, Brazil, and the Andes.[28] No doubt the genealogy of the ceramic mermaids produced today by Métepec potters in central Mexico would take us back to the mannerist period.[29] Cousins of those mermaids can be found in the Andes Mountains, on the shores of Lake Titicaca.[30] In Peru and Bolivia, an art explicitly labeled "mestizo" explores the same repertoire—the Western mermaid has become a motif of endless variation.[31] Creatures from classical mythology make an appearance on silver vases of indigenous manufacture (*aquilla*), on painted or engraved vessels of wood (*keru*), and even on wool and cotton rugs (of which a few, all-too-rare examples have survived).[32] Grotesques chased into silver platters, mingling monsters with llamas, struck indigenous minds so strongly that they provoked visions in which ancient Andean divinities, *huacas*, disguised themselves as mannerist monsters. Such platters came alive, appearing to whirl in the darkness as the silver creatures decorating them sprang to life.[33]

Transported to another hemisphere, Italian grotesques were resuscitating America's ancient gods, sometimes merging them with other paganisms. Far to the east, thousands of miles from the Andes, where the Brazilian shores seem to reach for Africa, in the monastery of San Antônio de João Pessoa, polychrome sea nymphs greeted slaves who worshipped both the Virgin and Iemanja, the African goddess of the ocean. This time, Greek damsels of the sea served religions arriving from Africa, ushering them into the heart of Christian churches.[34]

AN ATTRACTOR?

The mestizo qualities seen on the frescoes at Puebla cannot therefore be reduced to the encounter, shock, or superimposition of European forms and indigenous ones. The convergence of the two worlds was not just a question of juxtaposition, masking, or transposition. It ultimately combined motifs and forms that, whatever their origin—local or European—had already been the object of one or several indigenous reinterpretations: the monkey did not come straight from the pre-Hispanic past, any more than the female centaur came straight from an Italian engraving. Neither was a pure product of the milieu in which it was conceived and disseminated. Mestizo mechanisms involve derivative materials within a colonial society nourished on imported fragments, truncated beliefs, decontextualized and often poorly assimilated concepts, improvisations, and occasionally incomplete adaptations.

Mestizo imagery, in fact, implies a third term derived from a mode of expression—grotesques—and an imaginative construct—mythology. This configuration connects a series of components that, depending on context and circumstance, may come into play or remain on the sidelines. By opening the Western sphere to the indigenous world at the same time as it set indigenous elements with a Western framework, the couple formed by mythology and ornamentation acted like a magnet that spatially united elements of European and Amerindian provenance, originally foreign to one another, and made them converge on the painted surface. In other words, it acted as a kind of "attractor" that allowed disparate elements to fit together by reorganizing them and lending them meaning.

An attractor does not merely link two worlds by amalgamating space and time, because it continuously blends indigenous and Western elements by triggering movements of conjunction and disjunction: disjunction between indigenous warrior and the centaur facing him, conjunction between the centaur's hooves and the Amerindian sandals it wears; disjunction between the putto holding a foliate-form head and the jaguar knight depicted in the same pose, conjunction between the arrows on the Augustinian emblem and those wielded by Tezcatlipoca; disjunction between the Renaissance-type shield showing a decapitated head (Medusa?) and the traditional Amerindian shield; conjunction between the Indian who emerges from a plant and the Renaissance appearance of that foliage, and so on.

From tiny details to overall ensembles, these incessant movements seem to stretch the space between motifs, then fold them back onto one another, only to disconnect them once again by running through the entire field of grotesques. Easily identifiable on painted murals, they spark a range of convergences in the minds of artists and viewers that are immediately conceived, perceived, and translated into figurative terms.[35]

The alternate stretching and folding therefore creates a "mélange." This blending motion, this oscillation, explains all the complexity and diversity. A series of folds need merely approach and reinforce one another for the Amerindian dimension to become practically indissociable from the European dimension. This yields, at Ixmiquilpan, the grotesque with the dolphin's head whose profile merges with that of Quetzalcoatl-Ehecatl—is it a European dolphin or a Mexican wind god? The animal's mouth has become the protuberant beak of the Meso-American divinity, but the reverse is equally true, even as both Western and indigenous aspects remain identifiable—the folding of one upon the other has not resulted in a fusion.[36]

Faced with such images, the views of contemporary specialists may radically diverge: some will primarily see the Western dimension of a given mestizo work while others, on the contrary, perceive its Amerindian nature. This is due to an attractor's extraordinary integrating capacities, a faculty that explains what may occur between a mestizo work and its viewer, whether that viewer be a literate, European, Augustinian connoisseur of grotesques or an Indian worshiper of Quetzalcoatl with a head still full of ancient memories. On this internal stage, monkeys and female centaurs can play all kinds of roles simultaneously, reactivating memories that are unrelated. It is the attractor that selects this or that connection, points to this or that link, suggests this or that association between beings and things. It acts as though it were endowed with its own energy and organizational abilities that, in fact, escape the awareness of its European transmitters and its indigenous receivers.[37]

FROM OVID TO PLINY THE ELDER

It was not the first nor the only time that elements of classical heritage served as "bridge" and binder between the West and indigenous America. In fact, such elements constantly supplied frameworks for interpreting Amerindian material and integrating it into the Western heritage. The work of Las Casas has already supplied one example, and many others could be cited. Take the European interpretation of the myth of the four suns that succeeded one another in Meso-American history: these four major landmarks in Indian cosmogony were systematically assimilated to the four elements proposed by classical philosophers—earth, air, fire, water. Franciscans Sahagún and Mendieta, as well as the Dominican Durán, were convinced that they discerned these ancient principles in indigenous beliefs.[38] In the same spirit, if on an entirely different register of vocabulary, Incan writer Garcilaso de la Vega used Roman terminology to describe the Inca empire (decurions, vestals, matrons, triumphs).[39]

These assimilations occurred at the cost of constant deformations and misconceptions, and certainly modified indigenous beliefs and knowledge. Images of Mexican gods painted by indigenous artists at the request of Spanish monks provide an example of this: they are humanized figures in the style of antique gods. Such modifications were inevitable. A Western eye remains a Western eye, which does not mean that the analytical grid of classical antiquity was merely a deforming mirror or opaque glass. First of all because that grid adopted a certain distance from the European reality of the day, and it allowed for a relative proximity with American societies. It also generated various mélanges between the knowledge of Spanish monks and Amerindian data, generating new knowledge, intermediate or mestizo, which developed alongside established knowledge.

These "impurities" and "contaminations" contain traces—and sometimes entire sections—of ancient Amerindian civilizations. Through them and by them we approach otherness, the "truth of the other"—if indeed such a thing exists, given the impossibility of freeing Amerindians from their Western straitjacket, whether pre-Columbian, modern, or contemporary.[40] Mexican sources, whether Indian, mixed, or Western, can never escape a mestizo influence, however slight.

It was not only in the realms of art, imagery, and religion that classical antiquity served as intermediary between Indian America and Renaissance Europe. Writing the natural history of the West Indies also required references to classical frameworks. When it came to gathering botanical and zoological information, the work of Pliny the Elder displayed features that helped to link American nature to European nature. Whether a question of form, of the goals and requirements of research, or of interpretation, Pliny offered approaches that could be easily transposed to American soil. His system relied on the experience of others, aimed at exhaustiveness, and was based on a relatively flexible organization of information that could even entertain competing explanations. His work was therefore suited for transposition into the Americas, where the unknown and unexpected had to be accounted for. In this respect, it played a role of attractor fairly similar to the one played by grotesques in Florence and Puebla, which absorbed elements drawn from American codices.[41]

But the use of Pliny also produced paradoxical results, because it wound up "cannibalizing"—to use a metaphor dear to Brazilian modernists—elements of classical tradition. That is what we learn from the experiment conducted by the great Spanish doctor Francisco Hernández. Sent to the Caribbean by Philip II to study flora and fauna, the scholar found himself in an inextricable situation. The more he followed Pliny's writings, the more he incorporated segments of pre-Hispanic knowledge that threatened the coherence of his project and made it almost unworkable.[42]

How can we explain this paradox? In following Pliny's model, Hernández called upon indigenous doctors, took their knowledge very seriously, and attempted to correlate their learning with European tradition. But the confrontation with indigenous interpretations could trigger a tug-of-war that challenged the very foundations of European knowledge. That is what happened when, noting the lack of rigor of antique classifications, Hernández borrowed an alphabetical classification derived from the Greek doctor Dioscorides, all the while adapting it to the particularities of the Nahuatl language; that language dazzled Philip II's doctor, who saw it as the natural language that Renaissance philologists had always dreamed of.[43] Another European theory, namely the nominalism advocated by Dionysus the Areopagite, then led Hernández to valorize indigenous knowledge and ultimately to write a mestizo book that the Spain of Philip II swiftly deemed unpublishable.

As in earlier examples, a stock of classical knowledge established a bridge between the two worlds and unleashed a mestizo process that in turn led to Dr. Hernández's reflections in an unfamiliar realm on the borderline between Indian and European experience. Like Ovid at Puebla and Ixmiquilpan, once on American soil, Pliny took to the hills and sowed the seeds of mestizo experience.[44]

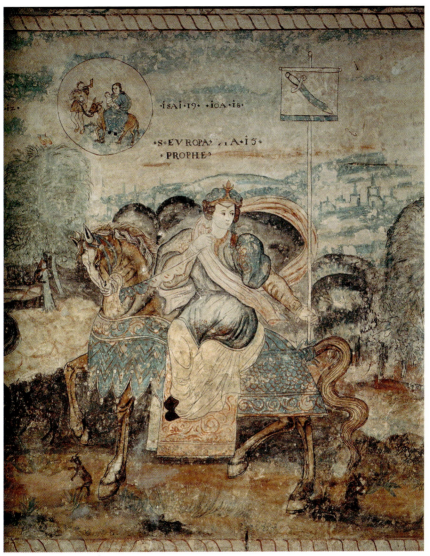

Figure 14. The European Sibyl, Dean's House, Puebla, Mexico (© G. Mermet)

Figure 15. The Lady Centaur and the Monkey, Dean's House, Puebla, Mexico
(© G. Mermet)

Figure 16. Amerindian warriors, Augustinian Monastery of Ixmiquilpan, Hidalgo, Mexico (© G. Mermet)

Figure 17. Amerindian warriors: a native Perseus (© G. Mermet)

Figure 18. Alessandro Araldi, Grotesques, Convent of Sao Paolo, Parma
(photo: Gruzinski)

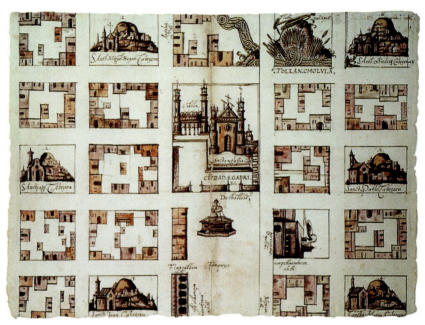

Figure 19. Map of the town of Cholula, *Relación Geográfica* (1581), Mexico (photo: Gruzinski, all rights reserved)

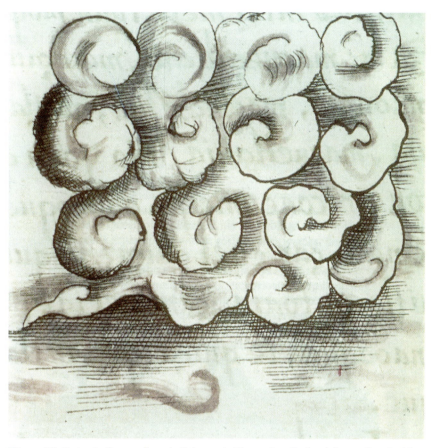

Figure 20. Rain, in Bernardino de Sahagun's *Florentine Codex* (photo: Gruzinski, all rights reserved)

Figure 21. Rainbow, in Bernardino de Sahagun's *Florentine Codex* (photo: Gruzinski,

Figure 22. Mexican "wolf," in Bernardino de Sahagun's *Florentine Codex* (photo: Gruzinski, all rights reserved)

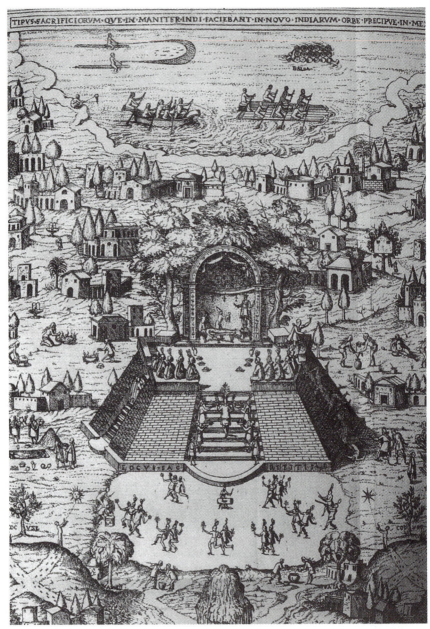

Figure 23. Diego Valadés, "Customs of the Ancient Mexicans," *Rhetorica Christiana*, Perugia, 1579 (© G. Mermet)

PART III

MESTIZO CREATIVITY

9 WOLF, RAIN, AND RAINBOW

The Augustinian monastery of Acolman, not far from the pyramids at Teotihuacan, houses a remarkable *Crucifixion* that displays the dazzling mastery of indigenous painters during the Renaissance. Mary Magdalene, clutching the cross, is so movingly noble that we scarcely notice the decorative elements assuaging Christ's last moments. On both sides of the scene, symmetrically arrayed grotesques combine floral motifs with young, curly-haired men whose lower bodies are plantlike. On their heads are baskets of flowers, topped by a geometric pattern of five white circles aligned horizontally between two white bars. This motif, repeated five times on each side of the Crucifixion, is undoubtedly of indigenous origin. If we associate the number five with the surrounding flowers, the motif might be interpreted as a representation of the Nahuatl word *macuilxochitl*, which simultaneously refers to a date and to the name of the god Macuilxochitl (Five-Flower).[1] The god Macuilxochitl, patron of musicians and singers, reigned over one of the thirteen-day weeks of the ritual calendar. Like Xochipilli, the "prince of flowers" (with whom he is sometimes confused), Macuilxochitl was closely related to Cinteotl, "the god of young corn."[2]

Hence these white circles may have transformed the flowers at the monastery of Acolman into a reminder of the divine world of the ancient Mexicans. In this case, European grotesque decoration would have once again served to integrate indigenous allusions into a Christian ensemble. It would have evoked a paradise that linked the heaven promised by the death of Christ to the flowered otherworld of ancient Mexico. This method of intimating an Indo-Christian paradise can be seen on frescoes in other Augustinian monasteries.

It is therefore possible that traces of mythology and grotesques can be found throughout Spanish Mexico. During the sixteenth century, Amerindian artists produced thousands of images for the pages of codices or in the form of feather mosaics, as well as painting countless frescoes. This impressive, extraordinary corpus of imagery contains other kinds of mestizo effects. Studying them should reveal more general mechanisms of association and imbrication perhaps common to all mestizo images.[3]

THE MANNERIST PALACES OF "AZTEC EMPERORS"

The use of grotesque decoration sometimes took a turn less complicated than those seen at Acolman, Puebla, and Ixmiquilpan. The illustrations for the history written by the Dominican friar Diego Durán testify to a less complex approach that nevertheless confirms the role played by mannerist ornamentation as go-between or, more precisely, as attractor. One indigenous artist portrayed the investitures of a series of monarchs of the Mexica tribe in highly anachronistic settings: richly worked columns, thrones with complicated moldings, cartouches decorated with foliate motifs, the occasional presence of satyrs or modest caryatids.

What is the explanation for these borrowings and appropriations?[4] Since mannerist decoration was in the air and could accommodate novelty and strangeness, it facilitated the reading of Mexican imagery without totally excluding specifically indigenous traits such as pre-Conquest glyphs, architectural features, weapons, and garments. The use of grotesque decoration made it possible to maintain a constant balance between the exotic and the familiar. It was also used to highlight a scene from the past by underscoring the majesty of the monarch and the lavishness of Amerindian palaces.[5]

This aspect assumes special meaning here. It is effectively clear that mannerist decoration borrowed from illustrated Bibles, notably from the Old Testament, projected the pomp of Babylon and Jerusalem onto the court of Mexico City. Such was the case with the thrones and royal scenes mentioned in the Book of Kings, which probably inspired one of the painters of the *Codex Durán*.[6] By making a connection between the Mexica and the Old Testament, the artist was perhaps illustrating a widely held sixteenth-century theory that the Indians had descended from the lost tribes of Israel (a theory that Durán set out in the first chapter of his history).[7] If so, the production of the images must have required close collaboration, not to say collusion, between the friar and his indigenous artists. Once again, mannerist decoration was apparently able to convey religious and political messages of startling precision. Durán's opinion was far from universally accepted; adversaries of the theory of Jewish origin rejected such connections and favored illustrations with a local—that is to say, indigenous— tone. This was done by the Jesuit Juan de Tovar, whose version borrowed heavily from Durán's writings but expunged all verbal and visual materials that might support the hypothesis of Jewish origin.

Grotesque decoration could be diverted down paths that were not always theological or political. One of Durán's indigenous painters modified the caryatids in another illustration in a more playful way[8]—no longer impassive, the caryatids turn their head toward the main scene, which shows Moctezuma receiving his new courtiers.[9] The two young women dressed in white therefore seem to be listening attentively and boldly to the speech made by the Mexicas' monarch. Similar questions are raised by the satyrs flanking a scene featuring the monarch Ahuitzotl,[10] and by the mannerist interpretation of pre-Hispanic architecture in the depiction of Mexico City's great temple.[11]

CHOLULA, A TALE OF TWO CITIES

Indian painters also produced hundreds of maps. Nothing strange initially strikes the eye on looking at the map of Cholula, an old indigenous settlement in the Puebla valley—no Amerindian divinities cavort with creatures from classical mythology. It is just a sober, austere document with bureaucratic overtones.[12] The map, which dates from 1581, was accompanied by an administrative description of the Indian town written by Gabriel de Rojas, a critically minded *corregidor*, or Spanish civil servant. Rojas was curious about the Indian past and enjoyed stories. Map and description together constituted a *relación geográfica*, that is to say a geographical report responding to official requests made by the Spanish crown in the 1570s in an effort to learn more about its American possessions.

At first glance, the map appears to be a Spanish-style one showing the Indian town in its colonial form. The community is organized around a central square flanked by ecclesiastical and administrative buildings. The impeccable regularity of the geometrical grid follows instructions issued by the Spanish crown and represents a spatial manifestation of the policy of Westernization discussed in Chapter 4.[13] In fact, archaeological research has revealed that this map was a long way from a faithful image of Cholula in 1581; instead, it reflected an ideal form to which the town was supposed to conform,[14] which also explains the outsized dimensions of the Christian buildings. The Franciscan monastery of San Gabriel, a fortified edifice,[15] and a royal chapel several aisles wide (probably inspired by Cordoba's cathedral-mosque) incarnated a double Christian presence that apparently accorded with the piety of local residents, thought to be "well disposed toward things of the faith"[16] and enthusiastic about the worship of saints: "All houses possess an altar with many images of saints."[17]

Yet if we study the map more attentively, a series of details destroy the impression of profound Hispanicness. Questions are raised by the repeated presence of a hill rising above each neighborhood on the map, along with another hill capped by a trumpet and partly hidden by reeds. The hill with trumpet is set on a stone base that indicates the site of Cholula's great pyramid, scrupulously described in the 1581 report as "a mountain so renowned and so famous." Formerly dedicated to the god Ciconauh Quiahuitl, its summit boasted "a small square that could hold a thousand men."[18] It was therefore one of the most imposing artificial mountains of the Amerindian world, an impressive site of collective memory. Thickets of reeds, watered by a stream, hid the masonry base of the edifice. The reeds had a specific meaning, for they form the glyph for Tullan, "god of reeds," one of Cholula's pre-Hispanic names. The city shared this glamorous epithet with other towns of ancient Mexico that played special political and religious roles.[19] The European trumpet, meanwhile, remains more enigmatic. It appears on the coat of arms the city received from Emperor Charles V in 1540, and is probably a Christian version of an instrument from pagan days, since prior to evangelization, the sanctuary at the top of this gigantic pyramid resounded at regular times with the sound of the sea conch, the indigenous equivalent of the Castilian trumpet.[20]

Had the heraldic prestige and Christian connotations of the trumpet—an instrument directly linked to the worship of the new god—erased memories of the former sanctuary already, or did they reinforce collective memory of the place by linking past to present? It is the latter hypothesis which seems convincing. First of all, no overtly Christian symbol—cross or church—tops the drawing of the pyramid, even though the *corregidor* Rojas mentions the presence there of a large wooden cross on a masonry base.[21] The Nahuatl term for "trumpet," *tepuz quiquiztli*, implies a notion of continuity because in order to coin it, the Amerindians—or their Franciscan teachers—employed a neologism which literally meant "metal conch," simply adding the term for copper, *tepoztli*, to the traditional word for conch shell, *quiquiztli*.[22] The similarity of the terms—reinforced when the prefix *tepuz* was dropped in the second half of the sixteenth century—minimized the difference between conch and trumpet and linked the two religious worlds with which they were associated.

Information gathered by the *corregidor* also revealed that time had not yet effaced all remembrance of the site. As moved as he may have been by the beauty of the vista seen from the top of the pyramid, Rojas was aware that the site's past continued to haunt the memories of the residents. But by 1581 the pagan past had been enriched with a Christian past, since the Indians recalled that some forty years earlier, lightning had destroyed—twice—the large cross on top. Such an event was all the less likely to go unnoticed insofar as the monks hastily explained the lightning as the effect of divine wrath against idolatry that had not yet been stamped out. This interpretation was brushed aside by Rojas, who argued that "if one considers the nature of lightning and takes into account the fact that much of it falls in this land and on this town, then one will not perceive as a miracle (as certain historians do) the fact that, on two occasions, it has struck a cross whose height exceeds by forty ells the tallest buildings in this town."[23] Had the monks adopted the *corregidor*'s critical attitude, they would not have contributed to reinforcing the collective memory of all those divine presences jostling in the din of thunder, conch shells, and copper trumpets.[24]

As to the other six hills shown on the map, at first sight they seem to correspond to other pyramids of lesser importance. But the text accompanying the map of 1581 mentions only two other mounds (*cerrillos*) instead of six. And archaeological investigations have revealed the existence of just one pyramid, located in the San Andrés quarter.[25] Yet these six hills seem to be of considerable size, because the artist has drawn a group of dwellings along a path winding up the side. Nor do these steep mounts resemble the stylized forms ordinarily used for the place-glyphs designating a quarter (*cabacera*). It is therefore tempting to interpret them as one and the same mountain, the great pyramid of Cholula, seen from six different angles.

By drawing each quarter with the great pyramid in the background, the map's artist made the pyramid the center of the community—a center that rivaled the Hispano-Christian center and that drew the gaze of residents of every neighborhood. Indeed, if we ignore the Hispanicized center, another reading immediately comes to the fore; as soon as the eye lingers on each quarter, the old wins out over the new, the pre-Hispanic over the Christian. Yet as soon as it returns to the square, fountain, and church, the Hispanic imprint on the space is indisputable.

Two distinct ways of apprehending the Indian town and space, two conceptions of the urban center, two theoretically incompatible realities may therefore coexist on the same map. We need merely look at it in a different way for its meaning to flip and suddenly stabilize around the rival pole.[26] It seems as though there perhaps exists a threshold beyond which the Spanish map becomes—or becomes again—an Indian map, as though the Westernized configuration is suddenly sucked into the field of attraction of a zone of rival meaning, of Amerindian inspiration.[27]

Yet this view of things reflects an overly simplistic dualism. Organized around a main square with fountain and Franciscan churches, the Hispanic centrality was no real innovation. The two Christian churches were built in the sixteenth century on the site of a temple to Quetzalcoatl, the largest one in the pre-Hispanic city. The discontinuity of gods and worship was balanced by continuity of holy places—the Christian center was set over the pagan center, as was often the case in colonial Mexico. Every Indian in Cholula knew this, and the Spaniards were also aware of it as they tried to make the new order of things irreversible. Despite everything, the new Christian centrality remained steeped in the past it was supposed to supplant.

Nor could an "Amerindian vision" of the map be free of colonial "contagion." First of all because it focused on the great pyramid, which, although perfectly visible, was already partly Christianized. Second, because the "artificial mountain" is linked to every neighborhood by a chapel. These churches were perhaps not as Christian as their appearance would suggest, because they were probably erected over pagan temples. Nor was the old masked by the new: in 1581, an "Amerindian" or "traditional" reading of the map necessarily incorporated the signs and symbols introduced by a Christianity that henceforth played a daily role in indigenous life and reactivated as much as it effaced the past.

The size of the churches illustrates this transposition of the pre-Hispanic past into the present of New Spain. In the upper part of the map, the Amerindian artist has placed the great pyramid between two neighborhoods, San Miguel and San Andrés, whose churches are notable for their size. Their facades are flanked by tall towers, whereas the chapels in the other quarters appear to be more modest. What is the reason for such pre-eminence? We know that the pre-Hispanic nobility lived in the San Miguel neighborhood and that the San Andrés quarter had become so populous after the Conquest that the Franciscans decided to build a second monastery there in 1557. Political and demographic weight cannot explain everything, however. It is possible that the importance of the two neighborhoods expressed the power-sharing that had characterized Cholula society since pre-Hispanic days. The location of the two large churches on either side of the pyramid may have echoed the division of chiefs to the right and left of the sacred mountain prior to the Conquest,[28] as noted on an older document. The map would therefore not only bear the imprint of Spanish governance—the *corregidor*'s house, or *audiencia*—but might also bear traces of the pre-Hispanic double government, an institution carefully described in the *relación geográfica*.[29]

The Cholula map therefore showed a city where things Amerindian were reproduced in things colonial, and where things colonial penetrated things Amerindian. These multiple dimensions also have to be linked to the indigenous town's particular history. Its pre-Hispanic past had already been full of immigrations, clashes, and mixtures of various populations. The European conquest then placed Cholula in a paradoxical situation. The founding of the Spanish town of Puebla a few miles away certainly spared Cholula's inhabitants the shock of a massive, irreversible Hispanization, as occurred in Mexico City. For it was in Puebla that Spanish institutions, wealth, and population were concentrated, leaving the Indian neighbor to live at its own pace. Yet could Cholula, so close to Puebla, truly escape the influence of a dynamic, glamorous center that would become the rival of Mexico City in the seventeenth century?[30]

The map of 1581 perhaps offers a cartographic rendering of this simultaneously strong and fragile situation. The two interpretations discussed here allude to it via the alternation of two mestizo configurations, one proceeding from the Christianization of an Indian base (the San Gabriel monastery and royal chapel occupying the foundations of the Quetzalcoatl temple) and the other from the Indianization of the Christian contribution (neighborhood churches at the foot of the great pyramid).

Hence both the Spanish and Amerindian interpretations are the product of modifications and changes. They are more complementary than contradictory. There is no frontier or threshold, properly speaking, between these two distinct mestizo meanings, just a continuum or series of modulations that entertain a broad range of interpretations from the distant and superficial Spanish view to the nostalgic, better-informed indigenous view. We can well imagine that the literate, bureaucratic view of the *corregidor* Rojas was certainly not that of the Indian painter who drew the map.

This system would have been inconceivable if the painter had not drawn up a townscape, a pictorial method that spread across Europe in the second half of the sixteenth century. Earlier, engraved examples had been produced on the Iberian peninsula, such as the city views illustrating the Spanish version of a world history written by Werner Rolewinck, *Fasciculus temporum* (Seville, 1480).[31] The somewhat later illustrations for a volume containing Ptolemy's *Geographia* and Petrus Apianus's *Chorographia*, published in Paris in 1551, may have served as models for the Cholula vignettes.[32] The Cholula *tlacuilo* thereby fulfilled the Spanish Crown's administrative request: to supply views of the town that would constitute an American pendant to the ones of Spain engraved by artist such as Anton van der Wyngaerde and Antonio de las Viñas.[33] Once again, an indigenous artist borrowed a European method to develop a mestizo image. Depicting each neighborhood as a townscape in a little rectangle favored a multiplicity of viewpoints. As with Ovid and grotesques, as with Pliny and Dr. Hernández, townscapes played the role of attractor—they visually combined different conceptions of urban space. And as with Amerindian frescoes, this attractor made it possible for a mestizo mind to express itself.

AN ANIMAL IN AN AWKWARD POSITION

The correlations between various elements of Indian and European origin were not always as elaborate as those found in the Cholula map or Puebla frescoes. The link might be less complex, more fragile.

Between 1578 and 1580, Franciscan monk Bernardino de Sahagún supervised the production of the *Florentine Codex* in Mexico.[34] Book XI, "De los animales," contained a remarkable portrait gallery of superbly illustrated Mexican animals, including a mysterious four-footed creature called a *cuitlachtli*.[35] The gray-coated animal stands in a verdant landscape with little hills in the distant mist, against a whitish sky: "This animal, by what they say, might be a bear. If it is not a bear I do not know to what animal it can be compared. It is a furry animal, with long hair. Its tail is very furry like the fox, but dark gray in color. Its fleece is snowy when it is old. Its ears are small and narrow, its snout large and round. It almost seems to have a human face...."

The animal is hard to identify; it might be an American bear[36] or a kind of wolf. Its appearance raises several other questions. The animal looks as though it should fall to the ground, because its forelegs are not standing in the same plain as its hind legs. Unlike the Cholula map, this images does not involve two skillfully interwoven registers, one being used to mask the other from European eyes. Here, the imbalance leaps to the Western eye. All the elements comprising it are clearly identifiable, but the composition is awkward due to a clear discrepancy between animal and landscape.

This image might perhaps be an emblematic expression of a deeper, pathological instability triggered by the process of conquest and colonization. The imbalance of the animal would here convey tensions between irreconcilable traditions and antagonistic groups. Such an analysis will not hold, however, for at least two reasons. First, other animals in the same chapter are shown perfectly balanced on their legs. Second, the strangeness of the combination is flagrant only to a Western eye, within a visual order based on three-dimensional perspective.

Let us try to reconstruct the Amerindian approach. The artist probably began by painting the *cuitlachtli* before adding a European-style landscape. The animal could have easily dispensed with this pretty setting, as did several other mammals in Book XI. The effect of superimposition is accentuated by the way its tail overlaps the surrounding border.[37] It is as though the "wolf" had entered the picture from the left and remained fundamentally alien to the background provided by the artist.

The mestizo image produced here is therefore not the unstable reflection of a milieu destabilized by the Spanish Conquest. Faced with antithetical traditions, the *tlacuilo*[38] simply slid a Western-style depiction of nature and landscape behind a drawing of an animal that might have been inspired by an ancient codex. And yet, as with the Cholula map, the superimposition does not merge pure elements straight from the Amerindian and European worlds but rather a European-style landscape revised by an indigenous hand and a heavily Europeanized Mexican animal. The encounter of these elements, both of which are mestizo products, yields an image whose harmony attenuates any compositional discordance.

The example of the "wolf" shows that some mestizo mechanisms may be limited to superimposition, which does not mean that such images appeared unfinished or unsuccessful to indigenous eyes.

CREATIVITY

Conversely, Amerindian and Western elements can sometimes be so tightly imbricated that artists created new forms. But how did they get from mélange to innovation? Via a path suggested by two images from the *Florentine Codex*, illustrating a chapter devoted to the Indians' "natural astrology." One shows a rainbow stretching over a sketchy landscape (*Rainbow*), the other represents showers unleashed by a threatening sky (*Rain*).

The subject matter and originality of style take us back to Italy. Both link these illustrations to a masterpiece of the Italian Renaissance, Giorgione's *Tempest*, which hangs in the Galleria dell'Accademia in Venice. Art historians continue to discuss this outstanding work; scholars are divided over the meaning and execution of the painting, but all of them stress its boldness, uniqueness, and modernity. The area devoted to the open sky, zigzagged with lightning, is as striking as the presence of enigmatic figures inhabiting the disturbing landscape. At least two other Italian works bear an uncanny resemblance to *Rain*, one of the two illustrations under discussion. Leonardo da Vinci's *Deluge*, a pen-and-ink drawing of 1515, seems to prefigure the Mexican clouds through the whirling volutes devised by an artist fascinated by the dynamics of water; the same concerns and same solutions can also be seen in Leonardo's 1514 *Hurricane*.[39]

Our two Mexican paintings, executed a good half-century later, scarcely sparked any attention even though they were preserved in Florence in the famous codex. The style of *Rainbow* and *Rain* is also highly innovative,[40] but these Mexican works, painted by Indian artists under Spanish domination, are accorded only the fuzzy status assigned to intermediate art forms. Deprived of the glamour of both "the Archaic" and "the Civilized," lacking artist's name and history, they belong to neither the heritage of the Renaissance nor the world of pre-Columbian art.

The extent of their mestizo qualities can lead to misinterpretation. Although their modern air may suggest anachronistic associations, these paintings are completely unrelated to any avant-garde trend (which—if the term were to mean anything in the closing decades of the sixteenth century—would apply more to the lugubrious, shadowy, austere work of the late Titian, who brought the Renaissance to an end by pointing to new paths for the seventeenth century). The two images from the *Florentine Codex* belong to another time frame and were executed in highly specific circumstances. Like the image of the "wolf," they were produced by indigenous workshops charged with illustrating Sahagún's *Historia general de las cosas de Nueva España*. More precisely, they figured in the chapter that the Franciscan friar devoted to indigenous "natural astrology," in which he wanted to establish a compilation of all the silly myths and tales invented by the Indians to explain celestial phenomena.[41]

How did Amerindian artists respond to the Franciscan's commission? Ignoring the pagan and ritual practices extensively discussed in the text, they depicted rain in the form of a miniature similar to a plate in a volume of natural history or a comic book: wind swirls and rain pours down from a pile of storm clouds.[42] This apparent naturalism coexists with the depiction of a series of spirals produced by the rims of the clouds, representing a trace of the Amerindian interpretation of rain expressed by the repetition of a volute that served as the glyph for water. The text explains: "These natives attributed clouds and rain to a god named Tlalocatecutli." The artist's brush merged myth with naturalism just as it combined glyphs with clouds.

The execution, meanwhile, also combined two techniques: the painted glyph, liberated from geometric rigidity, and monochrome crosshatching, borrowed from European engravings. As with previous examples, glyphs and crosshatching were not straightforward borrowings from Amerindian codices or Western art, but were already adaptations and transpositions. The painter's art involved reconciling two methods of representing the transparency of water and the formless mass of clouds. The result is as startling as it is successful.

The other image, *Rainbow*, pictures an equally complex encounter between the two worlds. The rainbow arches across the sky in the shimmering colors used in ancient codices. On the ground, the brush indicates a few tufts of vegetation, not unlike the ones seen in works by great Quattrocentro artists.[43] Yet once again the artist has transformed all these features. The Indian's brush marks are not the shapeless blobs from which Italian artists managed to draw effects so rich in meaning. Here they are all on their own instead of being an extension or abstract addition to a figurative representation, as they were in Europe. The landscape below the rainbow is just a patch, a brush stroke—no landmarks, no human forms, no trace of dwellings occupy the space. Nor is the many-colored arch truly pre-Hispanic either. Like the spiral glyphs for water that emerged from the clouds, the colors have freed themselves from tradition. They have shaken off the outlines that would have framed them in a pre-Hispanic codex. Hues overlap, run into one another, and merge in very free shading of tones.

The text, in the local language, simply offers banal meteorological and physical comments; it describes shapes and colors, and mentions that a rainbow indicates the end of a storm. Only at the end do the indigenous informants refer to the departure of the "masters of the rain."[44]

Indian artists were perfectly able to wed techniques when illustrating viewpoints ranging from recollections of myths to realistic description. For rain and rainbow, indigenous artists invented new forms based on selection and mestizo mechanisms. In *Rainbow*, the use of color and the focus on chromatic effects led to a unique visual idiom. In *Rain*, modulations of line and shading produced a similar outcome. In both instances, a style and mode of representation arose halfway between abstraction and representation. The results are worthy of a great master. "The blending of substances and the mixing of lines are such that no clear composition emerges: the horizon line has disappeared, the eye finds no vanishing point and cannot distinguish where land ends and sky begins. These nearly abstract drawings depict nothing other than movement and transformation."[45] That comment, sparked by Leonardo da Vinci's drawings, could equally well apply to these two paintings in the *Florentine Codex*.

Yet can this exercise be reduced to its purely formal dimensions? Can we dissociate technical inventiveness and stylistic discovery from a progressive transformation of concepts? As at Puebla and Ixmiquilpan, the mestizo process is the outcome of a confrontation between concepts and forms. The Indian painters hired by Sahagún discovered a European Renaissance vision of things. In this respect, *Rainbow* and *Rain* also answer the question of how to understand and depict what Europeans called "nature." It is not certain that the painters grasped the concept, which had no equivalent in either their ancient traditions or their language. And by attempting to depict this unseen and unconceptualized notion, they leaped into the unknown.

At that point mestizo mechanisms ceased to be more or less complex and more or less stable mélanges, for they gave birth to amazing creativity. The attraction became so intense that the various elements were transformed into a homogeneous ensemble in a process that nevertheless remained an exception.

Up to now, I have done little more than indicate a breach or crossing of a threshold in certain mestizo creations, without being able to explain it.[46] Creativity, in fact, supposes more than the mastery of techniques from two worlds; it implies acquiring a certain distance from the indigenous or European origins of the methods employed, as well as a strong feeling of compatibility between different traditions. Original sources are silent on all these points. And if by miracle they were to speak, the emergence of new imagery might still prove to depend on more than the personal intervention and personal psychology of an artist.

Mestizo creativity seems to have its own dynamic, partly removed from the aesthetic habits and intentions of the artist. Mélanges give birth to constraints and potentials, to antagonisms and complementarities, which result in unpredictable configurations. The source of innovation and creativity probably resides in the very freedom of these combinations.

THE JUNGLE OF INVENTIONS

The range of combinations seems inexhaustible. Even if we merely analyze a few carefully contextualized mestizo creations, we cannot help but be struck by their exceptional diversity. They range from Flemish-style Crucifixions seen on the walls of monasteries at Epazoyucan and Acolman to the drawings in books of magic used by indigenous *curanderos* for their "diabolical" rites,[47] and from works commissioned by monks to a pre-Hispanic-style calendar decorating the gatehouse of a monastery at Cuauhtinchan in the Puebla region.[48] Whereas simple mélange leads to uniformization, the full range of mestizo creations constitutes a collection, a kaleidoscope of forms, colors, subjects, and compositions whose inventory alone would require patient research. It would yield familiar landmarks and well-known motifs alongside strange objects, exotic and sometimes enigmatic forms, and innovations that arose and vanished over the years.

If all these works were classified chronologically, decisive turning points and developments could certainly be identified,[49] but in any given period an amazing diversity would also be observed in terms of format, framing, style, color, and content. Several hands were at work within the same manuscript—they might copy one another, or take divergent paths. Sometimes they were even combined on the same page. Images initially painted for one codex would sometimes be divided, fragmented, and rearranged in an entirely different way in another codex, as was the case with some of the illustrations in the *Codex Durán*. Furthermore, some manuscripts belonging to the same family display variants that cannot simply be explained as the effects of the progressive Westernization of representation. Copying a Western model might thus mark a return to an indigenous tradition, constituting a kind of "revival." That is what occurred when the painter of the *Codex Tovar* depicted the great temple of Mexico City by using the version from the *Codex Durán* that was most faithful to indigenous criteria.[50]

In another example, the painters of the *Codex Tovar* and *Codex Ramírez* both referred to the *Codex Durán* when illustrating the pre-Conquest dances performed by nobles. This manuscript offered a choice between at least two styles, one traditional and devoid of perspective and natural settings (adopted by the *tlacuilo* who painted the *Codex Tovar*), and the other more Hispanic (favored by the *Codex Ramírez* artist in composing a scene with dancers dressed like Amerindians under Spanish domination). European hands familiar with indigenous styles might therefore in turn propose versions that were no less faithful to tradition than ones by indigenous painters.[51] The degree of Westernization or faithfulness to ancient ways depended on many factors: the artist's training and skills (and political outlook), the patron's intentions, the nature of the source, and the existence or not of a pre-Hispanic model. All these variables would influence the painting of a manuscript and lead to stylistic ruptures within the same codex.

Such diversity gives the impression of irregular, often random creativity. The indigenous Renaissance that occurred in Spanish Mexico is teeming with inexplicable forms, aborted experiments, startling articulations. The absence of an overall trend in forms and combinations, amazing stylistic dispersion, and an apparently endless capacity for inventiveness all paint a complex picture full of ruptures, transformations, and bifurcations.

The multiplicity of these creations does not mean that they knew no bounds. First of all, they occurred in a colonial context as part of power struggle that we now know was irreversible, not only setting the invaders against the vanquished people of Anahuac (the Nahua world), but also setting colonial society's dominant groups—including the Amerindian nobility—against the indigenous, black, and mestizo masses. Mestizo images surfaced amid the uncertainties and difficulties of fragmented communication subject to the effect of rootlessness. Finally, they reflected the imitative pressures brought by Westernization. In other words, they were born in a space that was extremely constrained historically and that partly conditioned them. Such works, it should be pointed out again, were political and not simply "cultural."

Yet although these conditions explain the recurrent patterns that strike European eyes—the absence of overtly anti-Christian and anti-Spanish imagery is remarkable in this respect—they cannot account for either the proliferation of forms or the inventiveness demonstrated by *tlacuilos* in their search for mestizo forms and combinations. The features that characterize such works—complexity and fragmentation, nonlinear development and unpredictable patterns, an almost infinite diversity of creations—also apply to the very mestizo mechanisms that gave rise to them. Yet who is to say that what is valid for Amerindian imagery is valid in other spheres?

10 CROSSING THE SEA

I stumbled on the Floridas.
Incredible, the eyes of panthers,
Cats with human skin, stare out at you
From flowers, and rainbows stretch
Like reins attached to some green beast
Beneath the surface of the sea.
—Rimbaud, *The Drunken Boat*

Wind arises, roaring, hissing.
The ocean seethes,
and the boat goes creaking along....
—*Cantar mexicano* LXVIII

MEXICO CITY, SUNDAY JUNE 4, 1564

More than forty years had passed since the Spanish arrived. For the wedding of Don Luis de Santa María Cipac, the last successor to Moctezuma and governor of Tenochtitlán, magnificently dressed Indians performed the *atequilizcuicatl*, the "Water-Pouring" song. Groups danced, singing louder and louder as their movements became faster, accompanied by the swirling of multicolored feathers and the rhythms of indigenous drums (*teponaztli* and *ahuehuetl*).

Did the old nobility of Mexico-Tenochtitlán realize it was experiencing its final glory? Eighteen months later, in December 1565, Don Luis, grandson of the monarch Ahuitzotl, would die, leaving the throne vacant and discredited—Luis was called *Nanacacipatzin*, "he who sold out the homeland," because he allowed the Spanish authorities to gain control over the administration of the tribute paid by the indigenous population,[1] triggering riots among the people of Mexico City and Tlatelolco.[2]

It was also the 1560s that saw the deaths at an advanced age of the last nobles raised before the Conquest in a world that knew neither the presence of foreigners nor the throes of defeat. Although the Indian nobility buttressed its situation by stressing its ancient legitimacy and its new loyalties to Spanish king and Christian God, it knew it was under threat.[3] The steady loss of its privileges and its political base, the end of the dynasties in the neighboring cities of Tacuba and Texcoco, and the rise of many commoners to leading positions had weakened its hand. In a letter dated March 25, 1566, Don Pedro de Moctezuma, scion of a famous family, complained bitterly of living in *grandísima miseria* (great wretchedness).[4] Everywhere, indigenous chiefs suffered "a loss of income, power, and prestige."[5]

The living conditions of the indigenous masses, reduced to silence, were even worse. Subjected to increasing taxation, they endured the ravages of constant epidemics, while in the countryside entire groups were uprooted to form "congregations," forced assemblies of populations.[6] Within Spanish society, the leadership was also experiencing troubled times. The powerful *encomenderos* feared that they would be unable to pass on to their heirs the *encomiendas* they had been granted, and envisaged the bankruptcy of their families. Young Creoles who were involved from near or afar in the conspiracy led by Cortés's son, the marquis del Valle, trembled at the thought of the repression unleashed by the representatives of Philip II; opinion was terrorized by the executions of 1566, designed to stifle all inklings of conspiracy. This urban context must be kept in mind when studying the texts that follow, with attention to the uniqueness of a period when, after a half century of colonial domination, memory of pre-Hispanic days had not yet been lost.

Although the text of the *cantar*, or song, performed for the wedding of Don Luis de Santa María Cipac has been lost, we possess the complete version of a similar piece, probably dating from the same period, preserved along with other *cantares mexicanos* in an anthology now in Mexico's Biblioteca Nacional.[7] The long song numbered LXVIII, *atequilizcuicatl*, recounts the war against the Spanish and the memory of princes of the first half of the sixteenth century.[8] A brief excerpt will suffice to suggest the feelings stirred by many passages among listeners familiar with the refined Nahuatl spoken at the Mexican court. They would certainly have been intrigued by these reminiscences.

CROSSING THE SEA

> *Çan moquetza in ehecatl cocomocan tetecuicaya yc poçonia yn
>   ilhuicaatl huiya nanatzcatihuaya yn acallia. ohuaya ohuaya....*
> Wind arises, roaring, hissing. The ocean seethes, and the boat goes
>   creaking along.
> We see great waves flowing over us, wonderful things of God. It's raining flowers, and the boat goes creaking along.
> Friends, rejoice in these waters. You're splitting it open, O Don
>   Martín! It's broken to pieces here on the ocean.

O Life Giver, you're alive in this place of fear. The waves are rolling
    over us. Let's go perish at the navel, at the roundel.
"No one in this boat is precious, friends. Can we return?" Let's go be
    counted at the navel, at the roundel!
Alas, I grieve. The emerald dew is on us. And where are we to go?
Life Giver causes grief. If only He were my friend, if only He were a
    kinsman. No one cares anymore about anyone *here* in the boat.
Inside this boat, this place of fear, jade waters are flowing over us,
    seething. Ah, these garlands roar, these fish are flying. See them!
Ah, and yonder stands the tree of sustenance, stands our palace. And
    these garlands roar, these fish are flying. See them![9]

This passage, one of the most astonishing of *Cantar* LXVIII, sparks the
same surprise and emotion felt on seeing the frescoes at Ixmiquilpan. And
its interpretation is similarly tricky. For there is nothing quite like the
unusual atmosphere of this crossing, described in a language and with an
artistry that apparently blend memories of travel with borrowings from
Castilian poetry and allusions to ancient Amerindian beliefs.

CANTARES MEXICANOS

The passage is an excerpt from an anthology compiled under the guidance
of Franciscan friar Sahagún. Scholars long considered it as merely an outstanding, sublime vestige of pre-Hispanic poetry. The eminent historian
Angel María Garibay even published a transcription of part of the manuscript and translations that brought attention to "poetic" forms thought to
have remained free of Western influence (a few pages excepted).[10]

The anxiousness to exhume an Amerindian tradition predating the
Spanish Conquest therefore led to a discrediting of those passages that bore
the marks of the colonial period.[11] But these songs contain open allusions to
Christianity, the Spanish Conquest, and colonization, and they also reveal
the dilemmas with which Mexican nobles wrestled after their conversion to
the invaders' religion.

As John Bierhorst has now irrefutably demonstrated, we are dealing
with texts that are in no way pre-Hispanic fossils and that were reinterpreted and sometimes reformulated in the face of Christianity and colonial
society. The written form that has been handed down to us gives a frozen
image of a creative process, whereas the oral version was probably enriched
with new elements at every performance.

These songs were the work of the nobility of Mexico City and its envi-
rons. They are riddled with allusions to members of the Nahua aristocracy

who lived in the fifteenth and early sixteenth century. The military ethos, the fate of dead warriors, the remembrance of ancestors, and the enunciation of ancient lineages were certainly still of concern to the composers of the *cantares*, but all those traditional issues were henceforth raised in a totally transformed religious, political, and social environment.

KEYS TO THE TEMPEST

Study of this passage raises difficulties, as did our analysis of imagery. A text is not an image, however. It does not strike the mind in the same way as a painting, because the latter possesses an immediate obviousness that a text acquires only once it is understood.

The ocean crossing described in *Cantar* LXVIII is thoroughly puzzling. Given the form in which it has survived—a written manuscript—can it be read as a ritual text of pre-Hispanic origin? Several Amerindian features can be detected, such as the allusion to Don Martín, perhaps a historical figure who allegedly took the name of Ehecatl, the all-powerful god of wind, and thereby secretly incarnated that windy divinity. The rain of flowers ("it's raining flowers and the boat goes creaking along") adds another Amerindian touch if we accept it as an allusion to the arrival of warriors who died in combat. The "roundel" may well be the round stone on which priests executed the victims they sent to the navel of the world, that is to say the afterlife. Finally, this crossing strewn with obstacles seems like an initiatory voyage similar to the ones taken by shamans and sorcerers in ancient Mexico. At the end of his life, Quetzalcoatl, the most famous of them all, embarked on a raft—"a bed of serpents"—and headed across the sea in the direction of Tlapallan, "the place of dawn," the eastern abode of the Sun.[12]

But this "ancient" interpretation would be more convincing if the Nahuas of Mexico City lived by the sea. The grand itineraries described in their myths were usually land routes. How could Indians in the Valley of Mexico, living at an altitude of over 6,000 feet and familiar only with mountain lakes, have integrated into their realm of beliefs a maritime environment so unfamiliar?[13] They had been positively stupefied at the sight of Spanish ships, for that matter. The peoples living along the Gulf of Mexico, meanwhile, belonged to other ethnic and linguistic families; the only Indians who really set to sea in the form of coastal navigation were the distant Mayas.

Another interpretation suggests that we have a recollection of a crossing actually made by Nahua nobles who sailed for Castile. Several voyages of that type were made after the Conquest. Musicians and dancers were taken to Spain and Rome by Cortés in December 1526,[14] and the eldest son of Moctezuma went to Castile around 1528,[15] preceded by Martín Ecatzin, a nobleman from Tlatelolco.[16] This Don Martín has been identified with the other Don Martín whose name discretely evoked Ehecatl, the wind god. Yet this second interpretation is also somewhat too simple. The absence of Spaniards on the ship and the marvelous events that punctuate the crossing suggest that it is more than a simple historical allusion. The Amerindian elements mentioned above are not mere travel memories transformed by Amerindian poetry; that might have been the case with the flying fish mentioned in the *cantar*, but the rain of flowers that showered the ship give the voyage another meaning.

There remains a third interpretation of the crossing. Favoring a Western, Christian framework, it would cut away the Indian dross to reveal a recurring theme in Castilian poetry (as influenced by Italy and Petrarch): an account of the voyage of the soul, with all the heaven-sent calamities designed to put the soul to the test. Sailors and passengers on the ship would therefore symbolize humanity exposed to the assaults of lashing wind and waves. Christian moralization had in fact merely salvaged an old classical motif—the unleashing of the elements could lend cosmic significance to the adventures of ancient heroes from Odysseus to Aeneas, or it could come between a bashful poet and his beloved, as celebrated by Martial. For that matter, the theme of ocean tempest ran throughout the sixteenth century, from Rabelais's *Quart Livre* to Oviedo's *Naufragios* to Shakespeare's *Tempest*.

This theme had itself crossed the ocean, along with mythology and the finest Renaissance poetry (both secular and religious). It inspired Mexican writers and mobilized anthologists. The writings of poets in Mexico City were full of allusions to this commonplace of sixteenth-century literature. Hernán González de Eslava, who addressed it on several occasions,[17] was not the only one to describe the odyssey of the ship of faith sailing toward Bethlehem. He was probably connected to Sevillan poet Juan de la Cueva, who also evoked the dramatic effects of a tempest:

> What arrogance, what wrath
> has driven the ferocious Cerulean gods!
> Against me
> the light winds conspired,
> laden with rain and showers.
> They often roared,
> breaking rigging and ships,
> meeting no resistance.
> While my poor eyes, full of sadness,
> gazed upon the fury of their tantrums.[18]

Like the swells that lashed the Amerindian passengers in *Cantar* LXVIII, waves that flowed from the pens of European poets could become marvelous, living, and divine:

> And thus he addressed the waves,
> though they never deigned to listen:
> "Waves, since die I must, just let me reach
> the other shore, and on my return
> may your fury deprive me of life."[19]

Castilian poets, whether born in Mexico or just visiting it, lived in the same city as the performers of the *cantares*. They all went to the same churches and joined in the same festivities. So it is not impossible that literate Indians met these writers, that they attended poetry gatherings and even "colloquies," those theatrical dialogues in which González de Eslava specialized.

That, however, remains pure speculation.

Another trail seems more solid. The episode may have originated in a sixteenth-century legend well known throughout Spain, namely the pilgrimage of Saint Amaro.[20] This tale recounts the tribulations of a Spanish saint who taught Christian doctrine yet felt incapable of explaining heaven. Amaro therefore wanted to see the abode of the elect with his own eyes, and divine grace allowed him to sail to heaven—the voyage entailed crossing a sea—which he had the unique privilege of seeing. On his arrival, angels greeted him to the sound of celestial harps.[21]

This hypothesis is all the more appealing since it rests upon the existence of at least two Nahuatl versions of the tale. The story was known to the Indian world, for the Franciscans (and their indigenous helpers) adapted it to this new audience. Both Nahuatl texts offer a deliberately Indianized version of Christian paradise. In one of them, the harps are replaced by Amerindian drums,[22] and Saint Amaro sees a sacred garden filled with flowers, birds, and song—namely, a spitting image of the otherworld of pre-Conquest Indians. It might be imagined that the authors or performers of the *cantares* themselves, familiar with these Christian texts, drew on this repertoire to enrich ancient tales and to give their improvisations a tone more in keeping with a Christianized society and audience.

Shamanistic voyage? Mystical itinerary? Poetic escapade? Indianized exemplum? Or historic crossing? If we continue to dissect it, the work may cease to live. In fact, mestizo text and image converge here. Similar questions were raised by the Cholula map: Was the space it disclosed irreversibly Christianized, or did it retain its pagan organization, or was it a reformatting of desanctified, "administrative" information? Pagan or Christian? The text of the *cantares* leaves us similarly perplexed.

A MONK'S-EYE VIEW

Spanish monks sought to grasp the meaning of these *cantares*. They witnessed the dancing and singing, they heard and sometimes transcribed and translated the chants. Yet they cannot point us toward a more confident analysis, because some monks favored what they believed to be the Christian content, while other denounced the pagan nature of such practices.

Dominican friar Diego Durán, raised among the natives, was one of the most discerning observers of indigenous society. He was aware that ancient rites might be hiding underneath Catholic celebrations. According to Durán, however, this mélange of Christian and pagan festivities implied a preliminary amalgamation of the two practices. Christian appearances were not designed merely to veil pre-Hispanic beliefs and actions, but masked a product that was already composite in nature, a blend of traditional "rites" and Catholic "ceremonies."[23] Durán employed the verbs *mezclar* (mix), *entremeter* (interpose), and *revolver* (scramble) to refer to several types of equally dangerous mélange. Nothing was more alarming than people who associated Christian ceremonies with those of paganism—the "old law"—because, claimed Durán, they spawned novel practices, things "diabolical and satanic of their own invention."[24]

By devoting many pages to a description of pre-Hispanic *cantares* and dances, Durán wanted to draw his fellow Catholics' attention to the pagan drift that Indian dances might encourage:

> Should there be an Indian dance (*mitote*) and should you see one or two people stand in front of all the others, adorned differently, dancing with different counter-steps, coming and going toward those who are guiding the dance, every now and then giving amusing shouts that end with a whistle, or reciting unintelligible words, then you should know that those two Indians represent gods, gods to whom they are dedicating the dance and celebrations, both deep inside and on the outside.[25]

Durán admitted that an initial hearing of the colonial versions of the songs accompanying the dances seemed to be full of "absurdities" (*disparates*). That is the same impression we get today on reading "Crossing the Sea." According to the Dominican friar, the songs were composed of "metaphors so obscure that almost no one understands them." The same observation might easily be applied to the text of "Crossing." But such hermeticism is mere appearance, explained Durán, because behind it lay "admirable maxims that can be found in both the religious and secular songs they compose these days."[26] His interpretation was liable to lull the scruples of an attentive Christian listener; if we adopt it, "Crossing the Sea" becomes just an exotic variant on the "voyage of the soul." Its meaning then becomes clear and reassuring; any features of Amerindian paganism that we might detect are nothing more than insignificant dross or decorative fossils which present no threat to the faith.

The monk's reaction, however, was probably also a question of fashion. Our earlier discussion of grotesques revealed the mannerist penchant for hermeticism, bizarreness, exoticism. And the interest and satisfaction that Durán took in listening to the *cantares* would seem to reflect that sensibility. His view of things, moreover, led him to think that many dances of the pre-Hispanic period were mere entertainment.[27] In this spirit, he could compare the *cuecuechcuicatl*, "tickling or itching dance," to the "saraband that our own people dance."[28] Renaissance Europeans, who enjoyed their own *intermezzi* with picturesque staging and surprising stage machinery, also appreciated Indian dances. The Mexican tumblers sent to the court of Emperor Charles V, like the Tupinambas of Brazil who performed in Rouen before King Henry II of France, would have realized this, if at their own expense.[29]

These entertainments also had an intellectual appeal that Durán noted with delight—songs riddled with absurdities contained certain truths and "admirable maxims" for people who knew how to interpret them. A recurring feature of Renaissance thought surfaces here, namely a taste for symbolic languages, thanks to which an initiated reader could discover profound truths. The interest in hieroglyphs and grotesques related to the same attachment to an allegorical and symbolic tradition dating back to classical antiquity, as revived in the sixteenth century. Durán finished writing his account just a few years before the grotesques at Puebla and Parma were painted. When he translated these "absurdities" (*disparates*) into "maxims" he could admire, he was behaving just like the readers in the library of San Giovanni Evangelista when they looked up at all those droll paintings subtly filled with edifying messages.

The pre-Conquest songs and dances, described by the Dominican friar in great detail, as though he had seen them himself, were therefore very much in the air—an air that was mannerist. Mannerism can be sensed in all the miniatures accompanying Durán's manuscript and it breathed life into other contemporary works. This manner of seeing and showing things inspired an engraving executed in Italy by mestizo artist Diego Valadés in the late 1570s for the publication of his *Rhetorica Christiana*.[30] It shows pairs of feathered dancers moving to the beat of two indigenous drums. The dance is set at the foot of one of the earliest depictions of the great temple of Mexico City to be engraved in the West. The temple seems to be topped by a Roman-style cella, an elegant architectural feature that normally houses the Virgin and saints in Italian paintings, yet which here crowns a depiction of human sacrifice and a ritual dance. The representation of Mexican rites was inscribed within a vision of pre-Hispanic life manifestly inspired by classical models,[31] presenting an ordered and tranquil image of decent paganism. Valadés underscored the spectacular, majestic side of things, which did not prevent him from placing the highly delicate subject of sacrifice at the center of the image. It seems as though mannerist art made it possible to gaze upon other worlds without immediately falling into demonic caricature.

This view of things was not shared by Franciscan friar Bernardino de Sahagún, who felt that the *cantares* were impious texts. They represented "the cave, the woods, the overgrown bush" where "the Enemy" crouched, where the Devil himself hid. Sahagún wanted to forbid "the *cantares* and psalms which [the Devil] had composed and which were sung to him without anyone understanding what they say, except the Indians accustomed to that language." The upshot, argued Sahagún, was catastrophic: "people are singing everything the devil wishes."[32] For the Franciscan monk, hermeticism was the sign of a diabolic presence. The image of the bush evokes dense, impenetrable nature, dark as a cave, where people get lost in a tangle of weeds and wild growth. The reference to a cave was no coincidence—for educated Renaissance readers who knew Porphyry's *De antro Nympharum*, a cave was the symbol of chaos and confusion.[33] When condemning grotesques, Cardinal Paleotti explained that the grottoes where such decoration was found were lairs that harbored conspiracies, magic rites, and obscene acts. So this condemnation by the Franciscan Sahagún reflected a Counter-Reformation policy of systematically banishing complications and obscurities that might hinder the education of the faithful.

In Book X of his *Historia General*, Sahagún explained his attitude: "Although they perform songs which they composed after their conversion, and which deal with the things of God and His saints, these texts are mixed with many errors and heresies."[34] Here mélange takes the form of layers or wrappings (*envolver*), as though the "things of God" were buried beneath layers of transgression. Sahagún was denouncing not so much "pagan vestiges" as deformations of Christian doctrine—error and heresy. There was no question of bringing "admirable maxims" to light. The monstrosities surrounding and smothering the new converts' Christianity represented for Sahagún an amalgamation as execrable as it was irredeemable.

The Franciscan's view reflects the rigors of Counter-Reformation rather than the mannerist marveling of the Dominican. Would his unconditional rejection also apply to the text of "Crossing the Sea"? It should be remembered that this text figured in an anthology compiled at Sahagún's request. Context, however, offered no absolution. Sahagún spent much of his life documenting Amerindian idol worship the better to know it and expel it from indigenous hearts. Furthermore, his attacks were aimed more at certain practices than at a specific group; the "errors" and "heresies" he found riddling the *cantares* were not the sole prerogative of Indians in Mexico in the second half of the sixteenth century. Several poets from Castile were subjected to similar accusations and had the misfortune to fall into the clutches of the Inquisition. Their religious poetry could smack of heresy. The prosecution of Pedro de Trejo, Juan Bautista Corvera, and Hernán González de Eslava shows what *errar* meant for Castilian poets who were contemporaries of the performers of *cantares*.[35] In a society that the Council of Trent was trying to reform and that the Inquisition was monitoring, laypeople, whether Amerindian or Spanish, had no business meddling with the faith.

IRREDUCIBLE BUT NOT IRRATIONAL

What can we conclude? Should we read "Crossing the Sea" as Dominican friar Durán would probably have done, as a subtle adaptation of Christian truth? Or should we reject it, as Franciscan brother Sahagún would have us do, seeing it as diabolical, heretical waywardness? Both positions demonstrate the perplexity engendered by new forms. Each monk interpreted the texts before his eyes with the intellectual grid and ideology available to him—it would be absurd to criticize them for not seeing what they could not see.

In fact, neither friar was totally mistaken. "Crossing the Sea" is a mestizo work of the same type as the imagery discussed in earlier chapters. It is chained to neither a pre-Hispanic reading nor a Western interpretation, but glides through a special space that cannot be reduced to one or the other of these traditions. This situation does not render it incoherent, however, since the tale carried a message for its performers, its anthologizers, and part of its audience (the part sufficiently initiated to grasp its meaning), as did the "wolf" in the *Florentine Codex* and the map of Cholula.

Once again, we find ourselves confronting the same obstacle: how can we describe and understand what appears to us to be irrational, what Durán called *disparates*? Can we avoid the pitfall of reductive rationalization on the basis of a Western or supposedly Amerindian decipherment? Can we accept the fact that the *cantares* contain apparently incompatible meanings, that they play with allusions that should be mutually exclusive yet are brought together in compositions of strange beauty?

These texts are based on rules different from our own—they accept, for instance, contradictions—which does not mean that we are dealing with exotic rules belonging to other societies and other civilizations. The *cantares* belong to a new realm, a "strange zone" where new arrangements must be invented in order to allow irreducible elements to coexist without establishing veritable logic: "I'm a Tupi who plays the lute." This admission offends our mental habits because even today the presence of contradictions is considered to be "an unimpeachable sign of the irrational."[36] It is hard to acknowledge that "the laws of logic, excluded middle, and contradiction are arbitrary,"[37] that our rationality or "ordinary logic"[38] is so conventional, the product of a history, a tradition, an environment.[39] Mestizo creations by Mexican Indians sharply remind us of these obvious facts, which also mark the boundaries curbing our knowledge.

11 COLONIZING HEAVEN

Nach Rom!
—Wagner, *Tannhäuser*

"Crossing the Sea" is just one of several episodes contained in *Cantar* LXVIII. The song opens with a reference to the birth of the new world in the thunder of war and defeat. The emblematic figures of Cortés—the "captain"—his indigenous mistress Malinche, and the viceroy appear, along with Indian leaders who won fame in the war of resistance or who lived through the early decades of foreign domination. The *cantar* alludes to these events by taking up ancient themes, invoking warriors who fell on the battlefield and reminding them of their timeless task: to "water" the deity with human blood.

These beliefs constituted the cornerstone of Amerindian cosmology. Warriors who died in battle or were executed on the sacrificial altar rose to join the sun, whose path they followed during the first part of the day: "They enjoyed magnificent dwellings of the sun where they all gathered together, dressed in its sparkling light; on the shoulders of statues of the dead, Indians placed wings made of sparrow-hawk feathers, saying that it was so they could fly off every day before the sun."[1]

This glowing fate guaranteed the preeminence of warriors who sacrificed their lives on the battlefield or atop the pyramids. Spanish domination did not eliminate this belief, even though conversion to Christianity and the *pax hispanica* rendered obsolete such practices, which the conquistadors had outlawed.

THE EMPEROR'S DWELLING

Cantar LXVIII glorifies the memory of Moctezuma, killed at the start of the war against the Spanish, transforming the Mexica monarch's death into a kind of apotheosis that led to an afterlife filled with marvelous birds and magnificent flowers: "As flower shoots, as trogons [rare birds], as pine flowers, he would go off whirling his garlands...."

Had nothing changed, then? The old warrior ethic and the Amerindian vision of an otherworld seem to have survived the upheaval provoked by the Spanish invasion. Yet the *cantar* slowly fills with Christian images and references. An allusion to Castile, the intervention of a Mexica noble with a Christian name (Don Gabriel, which also happens to be the name of a warrior archangel), and the use of the Christian response "Amen," plus allusions to a single God[2] and to the Last Judgment all point the song in another direction. In this explicitly monotheistic and somewhat vaguely Christian context, the singers raise a primordial question: How can they do battle under Spanish domination since old-style war—"flowery war"—and human sacrifice have been forbidden by Christianity? A voice is then heard to explain that hymns sung in church can replace blood sacrifice, or even trigger it. The voice makes a plea for a Christian otherworld: "Let yonder be the church!"[3]

This interpretation provided warriors with a new destination, one more suited to colonial reality: the dwelling of "the Emperor." Warriors would henceforth go and pour the precious blood before the emperor. "Take heart, nephews. Cuauhtemoc! Let's go have these captured ones, our pitchers, be a raining mist of trogons.... Let us make our entry side by side with these, our carried waters. Off to the emperor!"[4]

So who was this emperor? The title suggests the figure of Charles V, whom both Spanish and Indian texts of the day often called El Emperador. Conquered by Cortés, the Mexicas recognized the sovereignty of Charles V and theoretically agreed to serve him. Grand spectacles organized by the Spanish in Mexico after the Conquest gave visual form to this allegiance. In 1539, Franciscan monks in the city of Tlaxcala had Mexican troops, led by their "native lords," parade before an Indian playing the role of emperor (*emperador romano amado de Dios*); they were then sent to do battle with other indigenous extras, dressed as soldiers of the sultan.[5]

This political, earthly interpretation is not completely convincing, though, because the song refers to warriors who are no longer of this world. The emperor of the *cantar* might therefore also be a heavenly figure, a manifestation of divinity, an expression of the God mentioned a few stanzas earlier.

HEAVENLY EMPEROR

A Christian text written in Nahuatl and Spanish sheds some light here. Franciscan friar Alonso de Molina wrote a confession manual for the Amerindians, a widely read book that provides a good example of the religious literature available to educated Indians. Molina's commentary on the sacrament of confirmation offers a series of striking analogies with the passage in question:

> Those who have received the sacrament of confirmation will an acquire excellent reputation and will obtain many honors and heavenly glory in the after-

life.... Just as we see in this world that great knights and nobles of the emperor who receive their insignia and weapons from him and who live in his royal palace are much more honored...than the plebeians and common people. Well, that is what happens in heaven, in the palace of the great emperor Jesus Christ our Lord....[6]

Comparison of the two texts helps us to imagine how the authors of the *cantares* selected Christian material when composing their work. What did Molina's manual offer them? The Franciscan stressed the value and importance of the sacrament of confirmation as well as the distinction it conferred upon the faithful who received it. Molina's argument rested on a triple comparison between the faithful and the emperor's knights, between God and the emperor, and between the honor of confirmation and military honors. These parallels between the heavenly world and the earthly one were reinforced by an assertion that directly links heaven to the emperor's dwelling: "Well, that is what happens in heaven, in the palace of the great emperor Jesus Christ our Lord." Comparison was followed by conflation: everything implied that heaven and the imperial dwelling were one and the same thing.

There was yet another connection that could be made by indigenous nobles, the people who actually read manuals and listened to sermons and commentaries. The Nahuatl terms used to translate "great knights and nobles," "royal palace," and "nobility and grandeur [of] the emperor's soldiers"[7] alluded to their own milieu and values. Molina stressed the distinction between baptized Christians and confirmed Christians by pointing out the distance separating commoners from nobles, which must have strengthened this interpretation among an aristocratic audience. A little later in his text, the friar promised that indigenous nobles who received confirmation would join the emperor, and hence God, in his heavenly dwelling. Finally, a special welcome would be given to confirmed Indians by angels, those "citizens of heaven" ("See how the one arriving here received confirmation, and is marked by it"), which parallels an oft-repeated scene in the *cantares* of dead warriors entering the Indian hereafter.

This series of images, associations, and meanings—or similar ones taken from other Christian texts—may have inspired the authors of the *cantar*. A Christian motif linking the emperor, God, heaven, and indigenous warriors filtered into the singers' lyrics without disrupting either the coherence or continuity of the song. Far from being purely and simply absorbed into a pre-Hispanic matrix, these borrowings endow ancient beliefs with a Christian tone, which itself carries a double meaning: the emperor with whom indigenous nobles will dwell is both the earthly one and the heavenly one: "We've been required right here, and this would seem to be the emperor's home."[8]

These inclusions and inflections constitute mestizo mechanisms. Other examples could be drawn from movies, such as the shifts from one world to another in *The Pillow Book*. Indeed, it is a comment inspired by the work of Hong Kong filmmaker Wong Kar-Wai that perhaps comes closest to such mechanisms: "You slide imperceptibly rather than progress, the separation between the past and future is not a rupture, and the process of going from one to the other is nothing if not fluctuating."[9]

INDIAN ROME

The route to the emperor's dwelling meant "crossing the sea": "We, mere Mexicans, are off to marvel on the sea." For warriors who arrived safely at port, for the dancers and singers transported to the otherworld—that is to say, to the emperor's world—the voyage was not yet over:

> And the emperor command[ed] us: he's told us, "Go and see the holy father."
> He's said: What do I need? Gold! Everybody bow down! Call out to God in excelsis!
> And it's just for this that he sends us to Rome. He's told us, "Go and see the holy father."
> Our hearts will be content, for he sends us on to Rome. He's told us, "Go and see the holy father."[10]

In the empire of Charles V, a visit to Caesar appropriately preceded a visit to Saint Peter. Imperial preeminence, protocol, and geographical constraints were respected (making Seville or some other Spanish harbor a mandatory port of call on the way to Italy). Here the singers seem to be recalling some historic event. The dialogue between the indigenous envoys and the emperor is anchored in a Christian, European context. Yet in the very next passage the scene shifts again, eluding a strictly factual interpretation.

The warriors arrive in papal Rome. What could be more Christian or more Western than this visit to the undisputed center of European Christendom? Rome was certainly not unknown to the authors of the *cantares*, who attended sermons by monks and archbishops. Some Indians had even visited Rome during their travels to Europe. The humanist Paolo Giovio (1483–1552) described a visit to Clement VII made by two indigenous dignitaries (*illustres gentis proceres*) who made a big impression on the Vatican court and who were showered with honors and gifts by the pope.[11]

Here Rome is presented as the home of the Holy Father.[12] That is where trumpets sound, for it is also the city of Saint Cecilia, patron saint of musicians: "There in Rome she dwells, the mother called Santa Cecelia [*sic*]."[13] It is hardly surprising that the Holy City was associated with celestial music.

European music had spread like wildfire throughout the Amerindian world. By the late 1530s, a Tlaxcala cantor was sufficiently talented to compose a complete Mass in the Western style.[14] Very early on, Gregorian chant and plainsong held no secrets for performers endowed with prodigious memories. It was often the same performers, for that matter, who chanted the *cantares*. The popularity of European music exceeded the expectations of Church and lay authorities. In 1555, the First Mexican Council had to forbid the use of trumpets during the mass, and given the proliferation of Indian cantors, it had to restrict their numbers (such activities, it should be said, brought tax advantages because *cantores* were exempt from paying tribute).[15]

Western musical practices probably influenced local genres. It is significant that the monks' translation for the concept of plainsong, the Nahuatl term *melahuac cuicatl*, appears in several titles of the *cantares mexicanos*.[16] Was there a pre-Hispanic musical form similar to European plainsong, or are we dealing with an Amerindian tradition "contaminated" by Western practices? There might be some basis to the latter hypothesis if the performers of *cantares* were also members of church choirs.

As to Saint Cecilia, Indians learned of her through sermons by missionaries and priests.[17] On her feast day, November 22, preachers would usually remind their flocks of the virgin martyr. She is mentioned in the Nahuatl catechism drawn up by Pedro de Gante and published in 1553 by Juan Pablos. Saint Cecilia was also praised by poet González de Eslava as "A lady of the court of this triumphant Zion," a saint whose grace admits her to "the divine hall" and who sings "praises to God / within her heart."[18] Finally, Cecilia was depicted in famous paintings such as the one executed by Andrés de Concha from Seville for the church of San Augustine in Mexico City, a masterpiece of New World mannerist art.[19]

We should not be misled, however, by this reference to Christian Rome in the *cantar*. As with imagery, it is not always easy to distinguish between Christian and non-Christian. For example, "trumpets" may be metallic— and therefore Western—instruments, but they might also be conch shells similar to the ones used during idol worship.[20] Prior to the Conquest, conch shells were blown from the top of the pyramid at Cholula.

The *cantar* does not present Rome solely as the capital of music. It pictures the papal city in the form of a grotto or cavern: "At the pope's, it would seem, where there stands the palace of the multicolored cavern, there are golden paintings that imbue us with life."[21] Now "cavern" (*oztotl*) was the term for the indigenous hereafter.[22] In the *Florentine Codex*, Sahagún's local informants used the term to describe the place where ancestors lived after their death, when "the deity destroyed them, hid them."[23] A grotto also served as the entranceway to Tlalocan, the watery paradise teeming with flowers and tender shoots of corn, the abode of the elect—or victims—of the god Tlaloc.[24] One of the signs of Amerindian paradise, then, was a painted cavern[25] that might have the color and consistency of either jade or quetzal feathers.[26] And yet when the authors of the *cantares* associated pope and Rome with cavern, they were probably not thinking solely of the Mexican hereafter. The connection was also based on the sculptures, engravings, and paintings shipped to (or produced in) New Spain, showing saints and indeed popes set in polychrome niches that resembled marvelous lairs.[27] Baldachins evoked the same idea, as did canopies like the one in Cholula crowning a picture of the meeting between the pope and Saint Francis. The link between Rome and the ancient Mexican hereafter was indeed the product of an indigenous imaginative faculty that had taken Amerindian models and added aural and visual features of Christian origin.

The composers and performers of *cantares* seemed unconcerned by the fact that Spanish missionaries identified their cavernous paradise with hell[28] or that European Renaissance scholars saw caves as obscure, magic, infernal dwellings.[29] Their cavern was more like the artificial grottoes that enlivened Italian formal gardens with strange, lavish, refined decoration. For that matter, this cavern-palace transformed into a heavenly music room was directly associated with other Christian figures. The pope was not the only Catholic dignitary pictured on such premises: *Cantar* XIX describes "the Bishop" (perhaps Juan de Zumárraga, first archbishop of Mexico City) singing in the cavern accompanied on the *teponaztli* drum. A cavern was also home to the Christian God (spelled *Tiox* for *Dios*), the place where His words resounded.[30]

A multicolored cavern housing Christian divinities, traditional coloring with European music: this was papal Rome elevated to the rank of indigenous paradise. Its metamorphosis recalls the way in which the earthly Jerusalem was transformed into a heavenly, marvelous city in John's vision, a story that the Indians might have learned from the monks' sermons or from studying the frescoes of churches.[31]

Rome as described in *Cantar* LXVIII is both Christian and Amerindian at once. Its author reinterpreted Christian terms and concepts even as he adapted Amerindian beliefs. Mestizo thinking was at work in a ceaseless motion that recalls the oscillations noted on the Ixmiquilpan frescoes. Papal Rome was Indianized just as the Indian hereafter was Christianized. The two processes were indissolubly linked.

HUNTING BUTTERFLIES

> Friends, willow men, behold the pope, who's representing God, who speaks for him.
> The pope is on God's mat and seat and speaks for him.

Who is this reclining on a golden chair? Look! It's the pope. He has his turquoise blowgun and he's shooting in the world.[32]

Here the Indians' song describes a scene as strange as it is implausible, inspired by images of papal splendor that the Indians could see on frescoes they often painted themselves. At Cholula and Acolman, popes sit on magnificent thrones similar to this "golden chair." But a pope wielding a blowpipe? Who would dare paint the pope of the day—Paul IV or Pius IV, promoters of the early *Index*—armed with a blowpipe in the corridors of the Vatican? Not the most boisterous surrealist, nor the boldest painter of grotesques, nor perhaps even Greenaway himself when devising Prospero's Italy.

The imagination of the composers of the *cantares mexicanos* therefore rivals the most incongruous and whimsical inventions of mannerist art. Yet there can be no doubt about the identity of this figure—he is indisputably the Holy Father, the Vicar of Christ, the head of the Universal Church, even if the phrase that affirms his primacy a few lines later ("He is Saint Peter, he is Saint Paul") conflates the two apostles, probably because the feast day of both saints was celebrated on June 29. Like the emperor discussed above, the pope was a manifestation of divinity. By inverting our usual viewpoint, the Indians' song disrupts the relationship of exoticism we normally maintain with the Amerindian world. This time it is our own universe that the indigenous imagination has colonized and transformed.

So what is this pope playing at? A few clues are provided by a passage in Diego Durán's chronicle. The pages he devotes to the rites of ancient Mexicans include a description of a dance in honor of Xochiquetzal, goddess of flowers. During the dance, the gods shoot at birds with their blowpipes. Or, to be more precise, the Indians who incarnate the presence of the gods on earth target "false birds flying in the trees," that is to say "young boys disguised as birds" who flutter around with other lads "dressed as butterflies." All wear magnificent wings made from "green, blue, red, and yellow" feathers. At the conclusion of the dance, the performers are greeted by the goddess, who has them "sit near her, showing them many signs of honor and respect."

But did the rite survive solely in the memories of elders? Durán, an ever-attentive observer, noted that "it was the most solemn dance known to this nation, and today it is a wonder to see it performed again."[33] Far from having vanished at the time the Dominican was writing, this dance was being staged during the same period when the *cantares* were performed. It was easy for indigenous singers and spectators in Mexico City in the 1560s to make the connections that startle us today. Street pageants combined Christian celebrations and pre-Conquest religious theater which was tolerated because supposedly emptied of its pagan nature. Composers and performers of the *cantares* would have had no trouble drawing inspiration from this reservoir of images, music, and tales.

As to the turquoise blowpipe, was it a pure Amerindian addition taken from the dance of Xochiquetzal or some other pre-Hispanic rite, or was it also of European origin? In the frescoes at Acolman and Cholula, as well as in an engraving by Diego Valadés, the pope can been seen holding a large cross, symbol of his mission and rank. The blowpipe could have been grafted onto this object sacred to Western Christendom, as though conflated with the cross and staff of gold described by the *cantar*: "[The pope] has his cross and golden staff, and these are shining in the world."[34]

What game might a pope hunt with a blowpipe? Butterflies, for butterflies are "souls." They must be butterflies because, a few lines later, the *cantar* describes the papal palace as a dwelling painted with gold butterflies. More precisely, these butterflies are probably the "souls" of warriors fallen in combat. A text by Franciscan friar Sahagún provides a further clue: he noted that, four years after they died, Indians who fell in battle were changed into birds or butterflies "as white as chalk or like very fine feathers." They then came down from the heavens to the surface of the earth and fed on the nectar of flowers, enjoying eternal life.[35] In the dance to the goddess Xochiquetzal, the birds and butterflies who served as targets probably incarnated these valiant warriors descended from heavenly paradise. The pope was therefore hunting deceased warriors or, "in Christian terms," sought to capture souls in order to bring them to *teocuitlantlatzaqualli*, the golden sanctuary.

Comparing the souls of the dead to butterflies was not exclusively Amerindian, for that matter. Medieval monks placed a good deal of emphasis on this beautiful insect. They lent it mystical significance by associating it with the Crucifixion—the Christian soul redeemed by Christ's sacrifice emerged from its chrysalis of sin transformed into a new being, winged like the angels.[36] Mannerist art produced angels adorned with huge butterfly wings, such as an admirable painting by Jan Sanders van Hemessen now in the Musée des Beaux-Arts in Lille, France.

At this point in the song, it is impossible to choose between an orthodox Christian or an Amerindian interpretation—the blowpipe is Mexican, the staff is Christian, the pope is Roman, the butterflies are Indian *and* Christian, souls can also be warriors, heaven is a pre-Hispanic grotto, Rome has become a new hereafter for the Amerindians, and so on.

The continuous chain of associations and the rapid shifts from one world to another sweep away the anomalies and questions raised by the papal figure's sudden appearance in the Indians' pagan world. This highly delicate operation might have produced meaningless confusion had it not thrust indigenous and Christian elements into the sphere of shining vision, had it not endowed them with the aura of an apparition and the irrefutable power of a dazzling image.[37]

A LUMINOUS HEREAFTER

Papal Rome seemed wreathed in light. A sparkle attends the scene revealed by *cantar*, music, and dance. First there is the cross and staff of gold, then there is a reference to the golden sanctuary where the pope assembles his "captives," and a vision of the magnificent palace whose walls are painted with gold butterflies. Two verbs define and orchestrate this luminosity: *peptlaca*, "to glitter, gleam"[38] (a verb sometimes associated with emeralds), and *totona*, "to beam like the sun and jewels": "It seems the pope's home lies painted with golden butterflies. It's beaming."[39]

These shimmering terms belong to the Amerindian world in which brilliance signified the supernatural and final reality of things. The Nahua afterworld was full of luminous, colorful things—tropical flowers, iridescent feathers, shimmering butterfly wings, sun-drenched gems.[40] This scintillating, radiant reality could be revealed through performances of *cantares*.

Such light was not exclusive to Amerindian tradition. Brilliance was also present in Christianity, manifested through the splendor of the Transfiguration. As a symbol of life, light radiated from the bodies of the elect after the Resurrection. The head of the Son of Man painted by Amerindian artist Juan Gerson on the frescoes of the Tecamachalco Apocalypse is a golden-rayed sun, and there were many other examples of such divine beams issuing from the brushwork of indigenous *tlacuilos*.

Divine light bridged the afterworlds all the more easily since Spanish monks had paved the way. Hoping to appeal to neophytes, Castilian missionaries borrowed the luminous effects of the indigenous palette when painting a picture of Christian heaven. In the preachers' minds, the edifying ends to which this luminosity was put effaced its pagan origin, even if they themselves perceived the irreducibly pagan aspect of all brilliance. In this case, as in others, the monks were making risky connections: describing Christian heaven with old-style light and coloring might make the Nahuas think that old and new were one and the same thing. That, at any rate, is apparently what the poets of the *cantares mexicanos* thought when they used this same coloring and light to describe the sun-heaven of warriors and the Rome of popes.

Light-drenched vision was thus shared by both worlds. They were not juxtaposed; neither had to mask the other. Divine light united them by unifying appearances, yet it was more than appearance, it was also presence. Like music, light and color could generate mestizo meanings.

CONQUERING THE HEAVENS

More surprises may be in store. In a symmetrical if inverse movement, the Indian "colonization" of Rome—its conquest of a Christian afterworld—was matched by the entrance of biblical angels into the Amerindian heavens.

> In nine [levels] dwell Your princely ones, the angels: archangels, virtues, powers, principalities, delight you, O Only Spirit.
> You're seated among them, O queen, O Santa María: dominations, thrones, ah! cherubim, ah! seraphim. Never ending, yonder, is this heaven.[41]

This heavenly hierarchy was perhaps inspired by Dionysus the Areopagite, whose teachings the missionaries might have transmitted to the Nahuas. Whatever the case, texts discussing the order of celestial hierarchies circulated in Spanish Mexico, as exemplified by those by Sahagún.[42]

But it is highly likely that the nine levels mentioned in the *cantar* had a strangely familiar ring to Nahua minds. More than a Christian geography of heaven, they express Amerindian beliefs that were at the heart of the ancient cosmology. The Nahuas were convinced that nine heavens existed, along with as many underworlds, known by the term *chicnauhmictlan*, "the nine places of death." The nine heavens were called *chicnauhtopan*, "the nine above us,"[43] and they sat above four lower heavens, the realm of stars and meteors. According to Juan Pomar, a mestizo writer from Texcoco, the supreme divinity sat above *neuve andanas*, "nine planes."[44] Diego Muñoz Camargo, another mestizo commentator, from Tlaxcala, alluded to the same system when he described Tamoanchan Xochitlicacan, the paradise of goddess Xochiquetzal, as being "above all the airs and the nine heavens."

Pre-Hispanic concepts may therefore have remained intact after half a century of colonization and of Christian and Latin education. It is hardly surprising that ancient beliefs were beginning to shows the effects of European presence and the influence of Greco-Latin mythology. The vision of the divine dwelling, the Nahuas' Tamoanchan, as described by Muñoz Camargo, was contaminated by mythology: the Indian Venus, "goddess of lovers," spent a happy life there, living in "places that were thoroughly delightful and full of entertainment.... She was waited upon by other women who were like goddesses, in delectable places" where "fountain, rivers, and woods offered every diversion, lacking nothing."[45] The Greeks' Elysian fields were not far away.

Nor was the Holy Church. Another mestizo chronicler, Don Fernando de Alva Ixtlilxóchitl, provides even more interesting information. In his chapter on the life of Texcoco monarch Nezahualcoyotl (1402–1472), he explains that the ruler acquired knowledge superior to that of the philosopher Plato, and that Nezahualcoyotl understood that beyond the nine heavens "was the creator of heaven and earth, who gave life to all creatures, a single god who created all things visible and invisible."[46] The king allegedly even built a tower of nine stories, whose ruins could still been seen in the late sixteenth century. This tale launched a tradition that slowly spread throughout the Texcoco region and among the monarch's descendents, situating pre-Hispanic heavens in a clearly monotheistic perspective. Nezahualcoyotl's heaven was a "place of boundless glory," a premonition of Christian paradise.

In *Cantar* LXVIII, mestizo mechanisms operated on coincidences between the two worlds not only in terms of luminescence but also spatially—nine Amerindian heavens for nine Christian heavens—without, of course, overlooking the influence of Christian reinterpretations of the indigenous past.

One material detail may constitute an additional connection: wings. It would have been easy for the composers and performers of *cantares* to view angels as a new kind of heavenly warrior, because in pre-Conquest days their parents or grandparents followed a tradition of placing wings made of sparrow-hawk feathers on the shoulders of the dead. Since Christian angels were often presented as warriors, the connection was all the easier. And the link would have been strengthened in Indian minds by the fact that the same indigenous craftsmen made the costumes for the dancers of *cantares*, the wings of Christian angels, and the wings of Indian *voladores*. The *volador* tradition dated back to pre-Hispanic days, but the Spaniards appreciated the spectacular, entertaining nature of this ancient ritual, converting it into a colonial celebration in which Indians wearing feather wings flew through the air, their feet attached to a rope at the top of a tall pole. The recollection of *voladores* would account for the appeal of Christian angels in the indigenous world.[47]

"THE FLOWER TREE STANDS IN GOD'S HOME"

The Christian angels of the "nine levels" did not know they were in Tamoanchan, a mysterious place that was not only one of the afterworlds, like Tlalocan, but was also the place of creation. It referred to a region where the nine levels of the sky and the nine levels of the underworld overlap. In the *cantares*, Tamoanchan appears as the paradise of creation from which came ancient heroes such as Nezahualcoyotl, king of Texcoco;[48] it can also be assimilated to Xochitlapan ("flower land"),[49] the place where drums "roar,"[50] the site of "narcotic" plants and "living pictures."[51]

But Tamoanchan did not escape Christian influence during the colonial period, since it could simultaneously be the house of God and the home of the "flower tree," Xochiquahuitl: "The flower tree stands in Tamoanchan,

God's home."[52] This twin definition tied Amerindian beliefs to Christianity once again. These were not just any beliefs, because the ancient Mexicans considered the tree of Tamoanchan to be "the hollow tree, the solid tree, the cosmic tree within which the two currents of primordial forces circulated, whirling on themselves. That is where time was generated, that is where flowers—that is to say, fates—grew."[53] Another song, *Cantar* LXXX, provides an interesting description of the tree—"the flower tree is whirling, twisting, drizzling down in this rainy house"—which is immediately given a monotheistic inflection: "in this rainy house of yours, O Only Spirit."[54]

The Indians' heaven could therefore host angels who descended along with songs from the house of the flower-butterfly.[55] In another song, it is the Virgin herself who glides among the turquoise columns of a heavenly Mexico City, giving off a light as brilliant as the sun: "Turquoise columns stand created. O Santa María! The heavenly columns stand created."[56]

Thus as we get deeper and deeper into the texts, ever more mestizo images surface, weaving Christian borrowings in and out of Amerindian frameworks. What are we to think, given a Rome invaded by hunters of precious birds and Indian skies occupied by the heavenly hosts: Are we in the presence of a forced Christianization of the Amerindian afterworld or, on the contrary, of an idolatry burrowing into the heart of the Christian world?

Although we might ultimately dismiss the angels of the nine levels as a circumstantial addition—a Christian veneer designed to mislead—we cannot overlook the Rome of the popes and Saint Cecilia without disrupting the development of the song. An Amerindian interpretation that ignores the Christian elements is thus impossible, even though it long remained common among advocates of pre-Hispanic purity.[57] Meanwhile, the opposing, "all-Christian" interpretation would reduce the Amerindian dimension to a few metaphors and empty phrases thrown onto impeccably Catholic beliefs. Yet it is very hard to attribute the division of the heavens and the heavenly armies to a reading of Dionysus the Areopagite by amnesiac Indians who had apparently forgotten the entire basis of their own cosmology. The writings of mestizo author Pomar remind us that they had a long memory, even if it henceforth stored a fair quantity of other knowledge.

SAINT JOHN AND TONATIUH

A final example may offer a better appreciation of the complexity of mélanges, the subtlety of dosages, and the vagueness that marked the phrasing adopted by the authors of the lyrics. A passage in *Cantar* LXVIII provokes simultaneous impressions of profound ambivalence and remarkable formal coherence. The weave is so tight that it is difficult to unravel the threads composing it. In a way, this passage is a literary equivalent of the map of Cholula:

> Hear him, you Huexotzincans, him, San Juan Bautista, the Great Star's [emanation]: he cries aloud, he says, "Prepare yourselves, for the True Spirit, the lord, is come." And all the precious birds are echoing him.
>
> Dawn appears: God's emanation, the sun [Tonatiuh], has issued forth. Let Life Giver be prayed to, O Huexotzincans.[58]

Diving into the mestizo maze, we shall attempt one last analysis. A superficial examination reveals that these stanzas contain Christian, Amerindian, and Indo-Christian elements all at once. The European elements include two divine figures borrowed from Christianity: God and Saint John the Baptist (Tiox and Xan Jihuan Paha). Also recognizable is a paraphrase of a famous New Testament verse; "Repent ye, for the kingdom of heaven is at hand" (Matthew 3:2) seems to have inspired the message addressed to the Huexotzincans: "Prepare yourselves, for the True Spirit, the lord, is come."

Among the Amerindian elements, it is worth noting the allusion to the morning star, one of the manifestations of the god Quetzalcoatl under his name of Tlahuizcalpantecuhtli.[59] The elders recounted how Quetzalcoatl had put an end to his life by throwing himself on a bonfire. After his death, he mounted to heaven and became the morning star. This star announces the dawn, and its breath stirs the sun into movement.[60] The star and sun form a couple in creation myths—in *Popol Vuh*, the star is even the father of the sun. Now, the morning star is also the lord of Mictlan, the first light in the world.[61] Such are the recollections that an allusion to the star would still trigger among many Indians.

Another key figure is Tonatiuh, a term that designates the sun in the forms of both god and star. It is hard to imagine that the Indians henceforth viewed Tonatiuh merely as a planet that orbited around the earth, because other *cantares* point out that the sun is the master of shields, the god who gathers up all the warriors destined to escort him along his route.[62] Several elements belong to both worlds, beginning with the divine title Ipalnemohuani, "Life Giver." The term originally designed the god Tezcatlipoca but was employed by the Franciscans for the Christian God. Here again, there is nothing to indicate that Mexican neophytes totally expunged the presence of the all-powerful pre-Columbian god from their memories.

The content of these stanzas ineluctably evokes the mestizo imagery explored in earlier chapters, for it combines words and concepts in an extremely refined way. A pair of divine figures taken from Christianity

(God, John the Baptist) encounter a pair of divinities from the Amerindian world (Tonatiuh, the morning star). However, instead of corresponding or conflicting term for term, the two pairs have broken apart, leaving room for mixed couples: John the Baptist is associated with Huey Citlali, the Great Star, whereas Tonatiuh the Sun is assimilated to Tiox ("Deos," or God). The crisscross is perfect—the saint presents the Amerindian star, then the Nahua star in turn presents the Christian god.

Two concepts make this arrangement possible. The first is Amerindian; namely *ixiptla*, which indicates a relationship of contiguity between beings and things. I will translate it as "emanation" or "manifestation" in the sense of the emergence of divine presence into the human world. The relationship conveyed by *ixiptla* suggests a shared essence in various forms. A woman may be the *ixiptla* of a mountain just as Saint John the Baptist is the *ixiptla* of the morning star. Among the ancient Mexicans, *ixiptla* might refer to priests wearing divine apparel, or else to sacrificial victims covered with the god's ornaments, or objects elaborated during a ritual.[63] The second concept is Christian, and comes from the Holy Scripture, namely the idea of precursor. It postulates the existence, within a linear temporality, of figures who prefigure the fulfillment of Old Testament prophecies—John the Baptist was the precursor of Christ.

These two concepts imply two distinct notions of time. *Ixiptla*, or emanation, belongs to an Amerindian temporality which was primarily cyclic. *Ixiptla* of gods was produced according to a fixed periodicity, described in myths and regularly embodied in rites established by calendars. The second term—precursor—relates to a linear, eschatological Christian temporality. It was at a precise moment in history—which could not be repeated—that the precursor John the Baptist announced the equally unique arrival of the Savior.

Despite everything, these two notions could converge. First of all, both related to a shared, physical reality that was observable and recognized everywhere, namely the movement of the stars. Second, establishing the relationship of cyclical time and linear time was a common exercise in colonial society—missionaries who undertook to study the indigenous calendar attempted, with varying success, to transcribe it into the Julian (and, later, Gregorian) calendar. Amerindians performed the same task, sometimes to link their temporality to the time of monks and churches, sometimes to mask ancient celebrations behind the dates of Christian feasts. Many codices illustrate these attempts by juxtaposing signs from the Amerindian calendar with Christian dates. Finally, in the everyday life of this realm of Christendom, new liturgical cycles orchestrated a repetitive temporality that could often be superimposed on the Indians' ritual time.

Other convergences are conceivable. Just as the idea of precursor was comprehensible in an Amerindian context, so *ixiptla* assumed Christian connotations. For the monks, *ixiptla* was a translation of the world *imagen*—the *ixiptla* of a saint was his image.[64] This equivalence, assuming that the Indians grasped the specificity of European images, introduced the notion of Western representation into a world that had not known it. Tonatiuh the Sun could also be understood as the image of God, rather than His emanation in the pre-Hispanic meaning of the term. This allegorical interpretation was the one suggested by European poetry and emblematics during that same period.[65]

Yet how should we interpret these interrelated figures? We know that in colonial days Amerindian tradition was always riddled with Christianity and vice versa. We also know that a mestizo process never stops at straightforward appearances. Should Tonatiuh be seen as an ancient divinity, a simple solar star, or the son of God? In other *cantares*, Tonatiuh appears in a double Christian meaning—that of the sun created by God on the fourth day[66] and that of the "true Tonatiuh," the true sun, that is to say Jesus.[67] We should probably not eliminate any one of these three interpretations—ancient divinity, sun, Jesus. Even if they were not all present in the mind of composer or performer, nothing prevented indigenous audiences from making one association or the other, from favoring one interpretation or the other.

A Christian interpretation is more awkward for John the Baptist—to claim that the saint is an image of the Great Star or its representative is nonsensical. It is exactly the opposite that seems evident—the star is the image or symbol of the saintly prophet. It thus becomes impossible to entertain two readings of this passage—one Amerindian and the other Christian—for they tend to exclude one another; no more feasible are two parallel but superimposable readings, the Christian one serving to camouflage the pagan one. It is as difficult to stick solely to a purely Christian interpretation as it is to remain with a thoroughly Amerindian one. And any double reading is equally excluded, because it would require that each interpretation be conceivable separately.

Perhaps we are dealing with incoherence, then. For Western readers, the passage seems to convey contradictory content, incompatible forms, and skewed formulations: "San Juan Bautista, the Great Star's emanation." Things seem different, however, once we recognize that we are dealing with a mestizo way if thinking that can integrate disparate and initially irreducible images and ideas. This way of thinking reactivates the ancient one, imparting fresh force to the Christian message and creating something new.[68]

The hinge, the bond, the connection here is *ixiptla*, a specifically Indian way of articulating things that appearances keep apart. *Ixiptla* creates a new meaning and an unprecedented reality: it transforms a metaphorical link—the one associating John the Baptist with the morning star in Old World religious poetry—into a relationship that, in pre-Hispanic terms, is as supernatural as it is physical. This is the art of making metonymy from metaphor.

INDIGENOUS ATTRACTORS

Ixiptla therefore constitutes one of the tools by which the worlds are linked and bonded in unexpected ways. When discussing the paintings earlier, I referred to elements that I called "attractors." A reading of the *cantares mexicanos* may allow us to go even further, for it reveals that mestizo processes find a fertile laboratory in all kinds of "otherworlds." Whereas indigenous painters exploited features of mythology in order to give free rein to their visual creativity, "composers of songs" focused on the paradises of both worlds, which they combined, mingled, and multiplied in surprising ways. The point of encounter is startling insofar as these two worlds each had, in principle, a strict concept of the afterlife. The most elaborate mestizo phenomena thus appeared where least expected.[69]

Mestizo processes also exploited the technical resources of the *cantares mexicanos*, with their evocative power, incantatory force, effective revival of the past, and ability to summon up divine creatures and beings. Indian *cantares* were not entertainment, they were a creative act that gave life to the words the singer pronounced. Music and dance infused them with an energy that propelled them into a reality that most native Mexicans were still assumed to share.

Just as the role of mythology was inextricably linked to grotesques, so the integrating power of the Amerindian afterlife seems closely related to the vocal and gestural techniques that made it real to the living. But these techniques and realms of impression have now been largely lost, and we have only the rigid and silent manuscript of a text that distances us from the actual experience of the song. The little we know of Amerindian music and dance hardly allows us to study the means of evocation or to assess transfers and exchanges with European musical forms (which the Indians knew and liked).[70] We run the risk of missing the main point by "overreading" without hearing or seeing anything.

Modern performance may help us to appreciate the scope of the phenomenon. In 1995, cellist Yo-Yo Ma commissioned Kabuki actor Tamasaburo Bando to devise a choreographic transposition of Johann Sebastian Bach's Fifth Cello Suite. Some of Western music's most striking passages were thus translated into Japanese corporality and space in the form of a performance titled *Struggle for Hope*. The play of light and shadow, a drum, a fan, and a thicket of candles (first lit, then extinguished) all created a magical atmosphere. This metamorphosis was not just a straightforward Easternization, however. It merged New Age overtones into a meditation—as physical as it was intellectual—on the rhythms proposed by Bach. Thanks to a long process of reinterpretation and absorption, it created before the audience's eyes a world whose familiar strangeness was perhaps similar to that of *cantares* performed by Amerindians who had been subjected for several generations to the influence and constraints of the Hispanic world.[71]

Whether dealing with frescoes or *cantares*, Amerindian creativity seemed to call on a double attractor that linked imaginaries to a means of expression. As with the paintings, here the attractor's two features—the afterlife and song—were inextricably linked: the proliferation of the songs was simultaneously a creative activity, a means of communication, and a way of accessing the otherworld. Singing was an act of war that transported the performer to the world of dead warriors.[72] These various mestizo creations therefore implied attractors arising from origins both European (mythology, grotesques) and Amerindian (the beyond, ecstatic dancing, the magic of words and music). It might be supposed that the overall dynamics of mestizo processes emerged from the interaction of these various attractors in an extremely complex ballet of which we are only just beginning to decipher the first act.

INDIAN METAMORPHOSES

To what extent was indigenous soil receptive to mestizo and hybrid mechanisms? When discussing grotesques, mention was made of Amerindian systems of expression. This issue, so crucial to the exploration of mestizo imagery, is raised once again by the importance of the pre-Hispanic foundations of the *cantares*.

Whereas the dogmatic version of literate Western thought insists on clear distinctions and rejects as irrational, absurd, or diabolical anything that does not bend to the rules of its rhetoric and dualism, Nahua thought—or what we can make of it through constant European mediation—appears infinitely more flexible.

According to ancient Mexican cosmology, an interdependence existed between things, beings, and deities. Countless correspondences drew together animal, human, and plant elements into a reality largely undetectable by the human senses.[73] Humans and animals all belonged to the world of *tlactipac tlaca*, that is to say of beings who live on earth.[74] This gave rise to strange combinations: on the pre-Hispanic frescoes of Cacaxtla in the State of Tlaxcala, jaguar-men confront bird-men standing on feathered snakes or snakelike cats. The efficacy of a ritual involved establishing links between realities that appearances kept apart: a human victim, a god, a statue, a set of objects. Gods usually combined features of animal, vegetable, and human origin, without the human appearance dominating the two others. The description of Tlalteotl, goddess of Earth, included an amazing image in which the goddess's dismembered body, her mouth, and her ears spurted rivers, mountains, and human food: "[The gods] made it so that all the fruits of the earth essential to men issued from her; her hair became the trees, flowers, and grasses; her skin the tiny grass and little flowers."[75] We have to turn to Italian humanist Marsilio Ficino to find a description similar to the ones recorded by the Spanish in Mexico. Ficino identified the earth with a procreative human being: "We see the earth engender, thanks to these special seeds, a multitude of trees and animals, feeding and making them grow; we see her make rocks grow like teeth, and plants like hair for as long as they cling to their roots."

For ancient Mexicans, metamorphosis was common among gods and humans graced by divinity. Less than twenty years after the Conquest, the Mexican countryside was being traversed by divinely inspired Indians who criticized Spanish domination and glorified the old days. The Inquisition decided to send Martín Ocelotl, one of these god-men, to Spain for chastisement. A rumor nevertheless claimed that he had escaped, and other men followed in his footsteps, such as Andrés Mixcoatl, who claimed to be the "brother" of the god Tlaloc or even the god Tezcatlipoca himself, when he was not claiming to be the brother, emissary, and probably the very emanation (*ixiptla*) of the prophet Martín Ocelotl.[76] Mixcoatl, juggling with masks and identities, thus incarnated a mentality open to the most unexpected transformations, combinations, and interpenetrations.

The frequent occurrence of polysemic words in Nahua tradition also facilitated hybrid—and later, mestizo—processes. Each term has multiple meanings.[77] Flowers, for example, can take on highly different meanings. A "shield flower" is not only a plant (known as *Helianthus annuus* to botanists) and an ornament for a shield, but also a captive who will die beneath the obsidian knife of human sacrifice.[78]

Archaeology reveals that these processes could take on highly concrete forms. The recycling of objects that belonged to earlier societies, distant in space or time, testifies to further propensity for mélange and hybridization. The inhabitants of Mexico-Tenochtitlán experienced no difficulty in straddling the styles and civilizations that preceded them by adopting exotic forms or by placing their own stamp—a carved glyph—on much older items.[79] They commissioned foreign artists to produce the statues that adorned their sanctuaries. Finally, glyphs themselves were constructed from combinations of all kinds of objects, materials, and features: flower and feather produced the divine name Xochiquetzal; fire and water were the glyph for war (*atl-tlachinolli*), yielding an evocative impact and freedom unequalled by the inventions of Renaissance literati.

Thanks to this permeability, the Amerindian mentality was able to absorb everything in European thought and sensibility that tended toward hybridization. This was the very reason why grotesques, mythology, and also Amerindian song, with its polysemic expressions and its ability to bring to life all the otherworlds of both universes, triggered multiple mestizo phenomena.

THE MEXICAN LABORATORY

The images and texts discussed above were the product of the encounter and clash not of two cultures—that term being too vague—but of what might be called, in a still unsatisfactory way, two modes of expression and communication. The Conquest brought face-to-face not only text and images but also complete ensembles of highly diverse components: pictograms, grotesques, ancient mythology, color schemes, effects of light, and so on. If the variety of things created by this clash seems befuddling, that is first of all due to the great number of elements that suddenly collided.

The Western ensemble—at least the one brought by monks and civil servants—was not limited to writing and imagery. It included an extensive range of alphabetical and visual expressivity. It employed varied media and styles and was based on subtle relationships that linked image to text or commentary to illustration, that contrasted spoken language with written, or that combined spoken, written, and aural expression through the performance of written music.

The same went for the ancient Nahua mode of expression, which hinged, to oversimplify enormously, on pictographic painting, frescoes, sculpture, chant, and oral transmission, plus such unexpected elements as the play of sunlight on the sculpted walls of temples.[80]

The dynamics of each ensemble emerged from the multiple interactions arising from all its components. Every ensemble—the West's alphabetical writing, ancient Mexico's pictographic notation—had its constraints and its potentialities which dictated a more or less limited realm of possibilities.[81]

The interplay becomes more complicated once we view the clash of the two ensembles within the context of Spanish Mexico. Their unexpected, brutal encounter led to a proliferation of apparently disordered and random beliefs and artistic forms, because the European ensemble had not eradicated the Amerindian ensemble. Although Western writing, music, and imagery very swiftly profited from the glamour and power of the victors, they were far from being immediately adopted by the entire population. Throughout the sixteenth century and, in differing forms, into the following centuries, the Western ensemble and the Amerindian ensemble evolved, coexisted, interacted. Fragments of one were combined with fragments of the other, forming varied, shifting configurations.

How can the secret or order or hidden alchemy of these mélanges be identified when none was the perfect copy of the ones that preceded or followed it? Both ensembles appeared to indigenous artists like the large pools fed by the waters streaming down from the mountains. These "pools" functioned like the "basins" that attracted all kinds of forms and contents, which might be more or less fragmentary, more or less steady. That is why some codices from the colonial period tended to imitate pre-Hispanic prototypes whereas others increasingly resembled European manuscripts. All indigenous productions from the colonial period were subjected to this double attraction, which always depended on power relationships; for, as will be seen below, mestizo mechanisms are always fundamentally political.

We know how the battle ended, of course. The dynamics of Western influences, constantly reinvigorated over the centuries, would finally win out. Yet they would never completely smother the capacities of local creativity, as witnessed by the history of modern and contemporary Mexico.

In the mid-sixteenth century, however, despite the difficulties weighing on indigenous populations, the outcome was not yet certain. The fertility of indigenous artistry made it impossible to think that all was lost, and hard to envisage the developments that would occur in the seventeenth century.[82]

These two "basins of attraction" were not separated by an unbreachable gulf nor by an implacable divide, as Claude Lévi-Strauss had assumed. A multiplicity of intermediate states traced a strange border that was never a clean, immediately perceptible line. The attractors often overlapped. Not content with the Mexican codices, Spaniards were soon asking indigenous painters to produce maps deemed official, designed to swell bureaucratic archives. On the Amerindian side, the glamour of Latin writing and the appeal of imagery made an impact on Mexican artists. Such indistinctness affected people as well as things, as is clear to anyone who has wondered where to situate the Mexican artists whom conquistador Bernal Díaz del Castillo ranked with Apelles, Michelangelo, and Berruguete:[83] Should they reside in the garden of Renaissance geniuses or that of pre-Columbian *tlacuilos?*

This borderline represents a zone of continual interaction, comprised of multiple infiltrations that give it a nebulous appearance. It is a fractal borderline in the sense that, regardless of the scale at which you study it, the degree of interpenetration of forms and contents remains the same.[84] Whether you consider the entire *Florentine Codex* or only a single page, image, or indeed detail or color, the mestizo process is apparent regardless of the scale chosen, without it being possible to distinguish the purely European element from the purely indigenous one.

In fact, this topology is still little more than a simplistic snapshot that betrays the continual, irreversible movement of connections and associations. Every bond represented a point of no return not so much because it led toward an inevitable Westernization (as hindsight informs us) as because it prevented a return to roots. The reinterpretations and shifts imposed by the colonial situation—the banning of Indian paganism on the one hand, the distance from Europe on the other—made a return to any given primal tradition impossible. This applied not only to Amerindian tradition but also to European art, which was only disseminated throughout the indigenous environment at the cost of many comprises.

Finally, imbrications of distinct elements, usually fragmentary and constantly reinterpreted, do not seem to be the product of chance. Beneath their chaotic and aleatory appearance we can discern zones of convergence that are relatively stable and relatively ordered, where attractors can function as though disorder were channeled into patterns constructed according to some underlying model.[85] Does there exist somewhere an "underlying model" or more or less permanent regularities? I cannot say. The identification of attractors is a long task, all the more difficult since they emerge and vanish with time and changes in society. They in no way resemble timeless or universal structures, nor do they establish long-term frameworks; the encounter of grotesques, ancient mythology, and Amerindian artists in Renaissance Mexico remained a unique phenomenon limited to the second half of the sixteenth century.

12 SIBYLLINE GROTTO

> We should thoroughly strip them of every relic and
> every vestige of their paganism.
> —Cervantes de Salazar, *Crónica de la Nueva España*

> Otherwise this country will become a sibylline grotto,
> and all the natives will become oracles who reveal
> learning.
> —Jerónimo López, Letter to the Emperor, 1541

At the beginning of this book, questions were raised about the potential
relationship between mestizo phenomena and today's globalization of free
trade. The study of sixteenth-century Mexico obviously provides no direct
answers to such questions, yet it points with insistence down a certain number of trails.

The first is political. It urges exploration of the links that exist between
mestizo mechanisms and the Westernization of the Americas. In theory, none
should exist, since Westernization sought to force the newly conquered
Americas into a European mold, obliterating the past. That was the goal of
Christianization when it brutally swept away the past and imposed a unique
set of practices and beliefs on exhausted, defeated peoples. From this standpoint, conversion to the Christian faith was synonymous with an absolute
rejection of paganism in favor of a sole, exclusive, jealous God. Any return
to the past, or any mélange of old and new, was unacceptable, indeed
satanic. Missionaries were appalled at the idea that *errores antiguos* might
creep into Christianity. Iberian society, moreover, had an institution—the
Inquisition—long charged with exterminating such errors, mélanges, and
heresies.

HUNTING DOWN MÉLANGES

Missionaries, clergymen, and laymen such as chronicler Francisco
Cervantes de Salazar worried about the mélanges that might arise from a
poor understanding of Christianity, from unseemly idolatrous practices, or

from the confusion of sacred and profane.[1] They were not thinking solely of new converts. When Erasmus-inspired Archbishop Juan de Zumárraga out-lawed the "profane dances and scarcely respectable performances" given for the Corpus Christi celebrations, his decree targeted Spanish conquerors as much as vanquished Indians.[2]

Ten years later, in 1535, the first Mexican council raised the issue of "mélanges." Implicitly distinguishing the insertion of pagan elements into tolerated practices from by spawning of aberrant interpretations, it issued instructions on the purging of dances, songs, sermons, and catechisms in native languages. It sought to exclude from the Indians' dances "anything which might leave an aftertaste of the old [ways]," such as "insignia, ancient masks, and *cantares* about their former rites and stories."[3] To this end, the clergy was charged with subjecting *cantares* to a kind of prior cen-sorship designed to eliminate all profane content. Furthermore, given the danger of the spread of a properly indigenous Christianity—that is to say, reconceived by the neophytes—the council ordered the confiscation of ser-mons in native languages that allegedly circulated among new converts, "as much because they do not understand them as because of the errors and mistakes they make in translating them." Translations of the catechism by natives or by Spanish laymen were also monitored more closely.

What did the Church mean by "mélange"? It viewed a mélange as a juxtaposition or "interposition" in which pagan elements remained discern-able from Christian elements. According to the Church, ancient texts occu-pied an intermediate place in indigenous *cantares*, because they were chanted softly in contrast to the Christian passages which were sung out loud and which began or ended the song. The Church could not imagine that Christian features might be reworked and rewoven into the pagan fab-ric. Its shortsightedness explains why clergymen thought they could elimi-nate mélanges simply by purging and stripping away: "We should thor-oughly strip them of every relic and every vestige of their paganism."[4] In fact, the relationships soon became so inextricable that any attempt at purification was difficult or pointless.

In the last third of the sixteenth century, observers as well informed as friars Sahagún and Durán raised a cry of alarm: "Superstition and idolatry are found in everything"; "saint and idol are combined." Durán the Dominican henceforth analyzed Indian festivities by distinguishing between Christian elements, pagan elements, and "mixed" elements: "a mélange of ceremonies so diverse that some come from our religion whereas others hark back to the old law and to the diabolical and satanic ceremonies of their own invention." Between the Christianity of today and the paganism of yesterday, a third set of beliefs had now clearly appeared: "the muddle and mélange that they make of their ancient superstitions and God's law and ceremonies." Durán had the intelligence to avoid seeing the indigenous elements solely in terms of vestiges—the "ancient law"—and the perceptiveness to recognize the emergence of new beliefs.[5]

Only a few voices, nonetheless, were raised in denunciation of such mélanges. Civil and ecclesiastic authorities in colonial Mexico, at least, seem to have had other fish to fry. The fact that the Inquisition, so expert in superstition and heresy, was never allowed to persecute Amerindians says a great deal.[6] Language barriers, lack of staff and time, unfamiliarity with the terrain, and resistance by Indians explain why so few churchmen were keen to seek diabolical perversions and waywardness behind the Christian façade. Accusations of idolatry normally covered old and new indiscriminately, confusing modern misconceptions with the beliefs and practices of yore.

Given the lack of a clear guide, it was not easy to distinguish between pagan vestiges and post-Conquest mélanges. The large books compiled by monks systemically inventoried pre-Hispanic beliefs in order to extinguish them, yet they showed much less interest in "errors" that arose from Christianity's intercourse with ancient cosmologies. The appendices to Sahagún's *Historia General* and the conclusions to the chapters of Durán's chronicle do mention colonial mélange, although the latter usually viewed them as only a possibility: "A mélange is perhaps likely to arise from our celebrations and theirs."[7]

In fact, Church circles did not seem to share the two monks' anxieties. Durán stressed the heedlessness of his contemporaries several times: they were "blind and ignorant," and he denounced the policy of silence and its quibbling objections.[8] "People...claim that [denouncing idolatry] will only serve to remind [the Indians] of their old rubbish and ancient rites."[9]

This *de facto* leniency, ignorance, and confusion have a political explanation. The Church regularly prided itself for having converted the Indians successfully. Concerning idolatry, Franciscan friar Motolinía loudly proclaimed in the 1540s that: "the natives have burned all their idols, public and private.... There where the teachings of the catechism have penetrated, almost nothing is left that could have any importance.... Almost no recollection of the past remains."[10] The monastic Church could admit to only a few mistakes, because belief in its almost miraculous success was the basis for defending its privileges and positions vis-à-vis the bishops and the rest of colonial society.

The Church therefore never really hunted down mélanges any more than it systematically rooted out idolatry. Following two decades in which the destruction of temples and elimination of pagan priests were conducted with full force, repression subsided to limited intensity and efficiency.[11] This policy—or rather, lack of systematic policy—toward rooting out pre-Hispanic beliefs and practices partly explains the proliferation of mélanges. Once the shock of Conquest was over, ancient beliefs were grafted onto aspects of the Christianity imposed on the vanquished populations. This forced coexistence spurred the emergence of mestizo processes everywhere.

REPLACING AND RECYCLING

To tell the truth, as paradoxical as it may seem, the Church itself was behind many of the mélanges that "distorted" the orthodoxy of its message. For centuries, the Church converted pagans by imposing a new faith that was supposed to replace and permanently eradicate the old one. Yet this policy of replacement could be only partial and gradual—it had to be accompanied by compromises that permitted transitional phases in order to help Christianity to take root. The Jesuit José de Acosta expressed this idea in the following way: "It should be admitted that it is good to allow the Indians what we can allow of their customs and habits (on condition that there is no mélange with their past errors). In conformity with the advice of the Saint Gregory the Pope, let us make it so that their feasts and festivities tend to honor God and the saints they are celebrating."[12]

The tactic was clever but carried the risk that apparently harmless "customs and habits" would ultimately turn out to be pagan worship. What would happen if everything the evangelizers thought was pure entertainment—"a kind of recreation and rejoicing"[13]—was in fact a sign of ancient beliefs?

Let us dwell on one approach, paved as it was with good Christian intentions. As mentioned above, right from the start the monks decided to Christianize Amerindian dances and songs. This tactic was not new to Western Catholicism, for the spiritual transposition of secular and popular texts had been extensively practiced in medieval Europe and extended into the Renaissance and Counter-Reformation. Most of the time, the music that accompanied poetry and especially songs was secular in origin.[14] An appealing, popular melody could become a perfect medium for disseminating a religious text.

Poets often transposed their works themselves. In Mexico City in the second half of the sixteenth century, fans of González de Eslava appreciated not only his fashionable romances and his Italianate plays but also his "deification" of popular songs, that is, their transformation into religious poems.[15] The adaptation might retain syntactic or lexical features of the original model. But the original text often gave birth to several transpositions that might vary considerably. This literary technique of composing *contrafacta* made it possible to slip easily from the secular world to the sacred one. Missionaries employed it without always realizing that its use in the indigenous context would strikingly alter its impact, for an adaptation would henceforth not merely cross the border between sacred and profane, between learned and popular, but would also effect transfers between two worlds totally alien to one another. It is hardly surprising that this European technique of hybridization yielded mestizo products.

Pedro de Gante was one of the first to employ this technique, even turning it into a method of evangelization.[16] To help Christianize the Indians, the Franciscan monk decided to replace traditional, pagan Nahua songs with Christian hymns. The replacement was only partial, however—although the text changed, the melody remained indigenous: "The brothers translated [the Holy Story] into their language, and their master cantors composed it in their fashion, in verses suited to be sung to the music of their old *cantares*."[17] What were the consequences? The musical part was unlikely to have been spiritually neutral, a mere "folk" touch. Even stripped of the words that had initially accompanied it, Nahua music remained the bearer of a pagan message. Indigenous tonalities, instruments, and rhythms certainly helped to preserve the memory of pre-Conquest rituals. If the monks thought a clear distinction could be made between words and music, that was because they were convinced that indigenous societies, like Christian ones, were able to distinguish between the sacred and the profane (which, for that matter, was far from the case in Europe of the day).[18] Yet nothing proves that this distinction was meaningful to native Mexicans before or after the Conquest.

For these several reasons, the *contrafacta* disseminated by Pedro de Gante and the young Indians he sent out to preach constituted mestizo creations with a double resonance, pagan and Christian (or "ancient and modern," to use Sahagún's term). The mélange was all the more indissociable insofar as these creations were performed in early churches up until 1539 at the same time as pre-Hispanic dances accompanied by traditional chants.

Although Pedro de Gante pioneered the mestizo process, many others followed his lead in Mexico, the Andes, and Portuguese Brazil.[19] In Peru, in the final third of the sixteenth century, Jesuits "who went among the Indians tried to adapt the things of our holy faith to their way of singing." The operation was apparently very successful, if reports are to be believed: "The natives spend entire days listening and repeating without ever tiring."[20]

MESTIZO TREND OR CHRISTIAN RETREAD?

Adapting indigenous practices and beliefs to the new "reality" also called for more subtle interventions. In the *Psalmodia*, which he wrote with the help of literate Indians between 1558 and 1560 (published in 1583), Sahagún drew largely on the Amerindian imaginative universe when he described Christian figures such as Christ, the Virgin, Saint Bernardino, Saint Francis, and Saint Clare.

Indigenous readers would feel at home with this Mexicanized literature. Saint Clare and John the Baptist lived in a warm and fragrant setting of green mountains and flowering trees, drenched in morning dew or a shower of quetzal feathers.[21] John the Baptist had become the energy source of the flower world, "he who gives us flowers." This atmosphere is strikingly similar to the one found in the *cantares mexicanos*. The descriptions in the *Psalmodia* and those in native songs celebrating the encounter of Tonatiuh and Saint John the Baptist must have quickly merged in indigenous minds. The *Psalmodia* was a great converter of ancient Amerindian deities; "Onward my friends, for Venus has risen," it read, suddenly evoking the Great Star (Huey Citlali) mentioned in *Cantar* LXVIII. The fragrant wind that cools this scene is named Ehecatl (one of the manifestations of Quetzalcoatl and the Morning Star), even though we are still in the orthodox, Church-approved context of the *Psalmodia* edited by Sahagún, that great denouncer of idolatry and decrier of mélanges.

In principle, Amerindian features were found only in the settings in which the Christian tales were told. Reference to a flowery heaven filled with Mexican foliage simply recreated familiar imagery from which all pagan connotations were supposedly eliminated insofar as they were absorbed into an unequivocally Christian orthodoxy. But the text recycled pre-Hispanic birds and flora that had formerly expressed the supreme reality of the world, a reality made accessible to human senses only through rituals and human sacrifice. There was constant use of the term *teoyotica*, "in a divine sense," which indicated the orthodox spiritual interpretation—these days we would say "politically correct" interpretation—to be applied to the metaphors and imagery. Who is John the Baptist? The *Psalmodia* replied that he is "the one who, *in a divine sense*, is the star Venus."

Alongside translations, colonial painting made a powerful contribution to the colonization of the flowery pre-Hispanic world. The frescoes in the Augustinian monastery of Malinalco are full of precious birds and flowers set among magnificently beautiful foliage.[22] Just as they strove to rediscover monastic roots in America, the monks seem to have dreamed of creating an earthly paradise in the New World, an American Jerusalem in which the imaginative universes of both worlds would merge.

COLONIAL FESTIVITIES AND MASQUERADES

In addition to the evangelists, other Europeans countenanced the proliferation of colonial mélanges. There were multiple reasons for this; some had to do with a sacrosanct respect for the past, others related to festive customs dating back to the pomp of the Burgundian and Flemish courts, and still others represented an American expression of European Renaissance trends favorable to hybridization, namely mannerist ornamentation and grotesques.

In all *ancien régime* cultures, the nobility's traditions were an inviolable heritage; in a colonial society that made the Indian nobility its official intermediary with the Mexican masses, respect for the local elite's past was a guarantee of social stability. Why outlaw practices that perpetuated the memory of the greatness of yore? Why abolish aristocratic customs? They were part of the noble lifestyle, and in this respect they seemed as necessary as they were worthy of respect. Nobles retained their palaces, their codices, their dress, their dances, and their songs. As paradoxical as it may seem, this respect for Indian traditions encouraged mélanges; the traditions, of course, had been highly modified since they had been in theory purged, shorn of any idolatrous aspects, and made to fit to the colonial context.

Europeans enjoyed festivities and anything that contributed to their glamour. The Dominican Durán and the Jesuit Acosta viewed indigenous dances and songs as forms of entertainment that were not only permitted but essential to society's well-being. This view, shared by civilian authorities, encouraged the perpetuation of traditional events and, even more, their colonial adaptation. It was the Spanish town council of Mexico City that officially invited local Amerindians to "execute an entertainment and *mitote* dance on the public square" in 1557. In the second half of the sixteenth century, Franciscans, Jesuits, bishops, and archbishops as well as representatives of the crown adopted the habit of calling on the indigenous people to enliven important events in colonial life. In 1566, when a silver statue was being presented as an offering to the sanctuary of the Virgin of Guadalupe, Indians from Mexico City sang the "Song of Fish," while those from Tlatelolco sang the "Song of War" before a distinguished audience that included judges and the archbishop. That same year, Viceroy Gastón de Peralta attended a performance of "Axochitlaca-style" songs as well as a demonstration of *voladores* in which, as described above, Amerindians threw themselves from the top of a tall pole and twirled down to the ground, their feet held by a rope.

These indigenous events were, in theory, Christianized and therefore obeyed the monks' spiritual requirements. But it was not their edifying nature that made them so popular. People liked the dances because they featured colorful costumes, feather ornaments, strange instruments, exotic rhythms, and ancient choreography. This exotic, entertaining show was enjoyed by crowds of Spaniards, blacks, and mestizos, as keen on new diversions as were people back in the Old World.

The climate of the mannerist Renaissance encouraged such events. Amerindian dances, in fact, were contemporary with the early theatrical performances that Spanish authors were trying to acclimate to Mexican soil. Such plays shipped hieroglyphs, fantastic creatures, and allegories across the ocean, along with grotesques. Hernán González de Eslava, who arrived in Mexico City in 1558, pioneered the production of numerous plays with religious themes for festivities in the new capital. The people who attended González de Eslava's theatrical "colloquies" were Spanish, mestizo, and Amerindian. The "hieroglyphic figures" they saw staged there would certainly have disconcerted an uninitiated audience: a colloquy on "The Divine Wood" presented the Son of God in the form of "a unicorn blessing the waters." Christ, the "Precious Unicorn," was explicitly identified with a mythical animal. The fifth day of the colloquy featured the "escarbuncle," an animal with a precious stone set in its forehead ("Escarbuncle is the Redeemer"). The eighth day was devoted to the figure of an elephant topped by a tower—the symbol of the militant Church—accompanied by a text proclaiming that "Christ is a powerful Elephant."[23] Even as González de Eslava's Christ was being transformed into elephant, phoenix, or unicorn, not far away in some other square or courtyard, the pope mentioned in the *cantares* may well have been aiming his blowpipe at strange butterflies. Mannerist allegory certainly had neither the same meaning nor same substance as the Amerindian idiom, but both stimulated imaginative universes sufficiently similar to allow indigenous spectators to wander and wonder within.

González de Eslava's poetry also made regular use of allegory, constantly associating Christ with the sun and the saints and the Virgin with stars. Many features of his poetry resemble the *cantares mexicanos*. As in Amerindian chants, the light wreathing Christianity's divine figures summons up a wide range of verbs, adjectives, and nouns. Allusions to a voyage or flight toward the heavens are common. The sky is a royal court ruled by God, the "the Lord Supreme."[24] It is also a "precious spring with precious gems," an image for which equivalents can easily be found in the Nahua *cantares*.

González de Eslava was not unique. Allegory and analogy abounded in Spanish religious poetry in the sixteenth century. Outdoing one another in cleverness (if not talent), monks and poets sought to explain divine mysteries via concrete images and "hieroglyphic figures," imparting a religious meaning to everyday reality and to imaginative inventions.

MISCONSTRUING AND REVIVING

This pedagogical approach carried risks, because if the intention were misconstrued then imaginations might run wild. If an Indian or mestizo simply embroidered a little on the meaning of unicorn, or phoenix, or elephant—overlooking its nature of sacred hieroglyph and theatrical prop—then out might leap a Christ as fantastic and polymorphous as a Hindu god or the ancient Mexicans' own winged serpent. Twenty years after the Conquest, one Spanish observer was already concerned about the potential consequences of teaching Latin and science to the Indians: "Otherwise this country will become a sibylline grotto, and all the natives will become oracles who reveal learning." Steeped in Latin and the classical authors, literate Nahuas might become uncontrollable.[25]

The Church wanted to weed out mélanges even as it nurtured entire spheres of ancient practice that it hoped to adapt to a Western, Christian context. But given the least backsliding or ambiguity, this policy could lead to unpredictable, irreparable effects.

By preserving pre-Hispanic melodies, rhythms, and instrumental accompaniment, the Church encouraged a kind of coexistence between forms and contents. Worse, by confiding the dissemination of Christianized *cantares* to young Indians whose Christianity was still shaky and who were usually subject to pressure from friends and families, the missionaries risked losing control at every moment over the rudiments they hoped to inculcate in the neophyte peoples. When the Church encouraged Amerindians to Christianize ancient customs, it deliberately subjected those practices to the influence of Christianity; but at the same time, it was setting Christian elements among dangerous company. In other words, the Church itself created the conditions for mestizo processes to get out of hand.

Some of its members were aware of this, however. The perspicacious Durán fully realized that Indian events, whether actively encouraged or merely tolerated, could include idolatrous allusions—which is what happened when an Indian joined the dance dressed as his idol, secretly uttering the songs formerly dedicated to that god.[26] Durán therefore called for vigilance: "It might happen and perhaps has happened." In fact, even closely monitored events sometimes strayed from the path of orthodoxy. What were the Indians thinking when, prior to performing a dance at the express request of the Franciscans, they went to get their ornaments and insignia from Cihuateocaltitlán, "The Place of the Temple of Women"?[27]

Veneration of the Virgin and saints could also get alarmingly out of hand. In 1556, when Alonso de Montufar, archbishop of Mexico City, tried to spread the cult of Our Lady of Guadalupe among the Indians, he triggered howls of outrage from the Franciscan order, which accused him of encouraging the Indians to worship a material image, of "having them understand that this image was God"—which boiled down to promoting new idolatries. In the monks' view, the archbishop's initiative was a disaster. It merely increased confusion among the less sophisticated, who were still too often inclined to believe that Santa Maria was a generic term that applied to all Christian images. "Sowing great confusion and undoing the good things we have planted" were the terms in which the order's provincial head castigated New Spain's highest ecclesiastical authority. Behind the scandal sparked by this polemic lay the rivalry between the Church secular and the still all-powerful monks regular. Several conceptions of Christianity and worship clashed. With its Marian piety and miraculous images, the Counter-Reformation had not yet managed to crush the reformist and Erasmian leanings of the monastic church. These conflicts are well known, but we tend to forget that this top-level tension fueled "confusion" and uncertainty that would long mark Amerindian Christianity.[28]

Defenders of the cult of the Virgin of Guadalupe continued to suffer reproaches and complaints from monks. The Franciscan Sahagún delivered scathing criticism in his *Historia General*. He began by pointing out that the Marian cult sprang up on the site of a pre-Hispanic temple dedicated to the goddess Tonantzin, formerly the focus of a major native pilgrimage.[29] But it was not this indigenous past that Sahagún denounced. He criticized the Spanish preachers for calling Our Lady by the name of Tonantzin, because that name "harks back to the old Tonantzin. This is something which must be remedied, for the correct name of the Mother of God, Our Lady, is not *Tonantzin*, but *Dios y nantzin*." In other words, it was the Catholic Church's priests who were responsible for confusing the Virgin with the former goddess, just as they were responsible for confusing Saint John with Tezcatlipoca and Saint Anne with the goddess Toci.[30]

The assimilation of the Virgin with Tonantzin was even described as a "satanic invention." It could hardly be otherwise, since it was the preaching itself and its vague approximations that triggered the mestizo mechanism. Sahagún felt it was the ambiguity and error of using the indigenous name for the Virgin that sparked and masked the idolatry. The demonic trick stimulated a return to the past by reviving former practices: "They now come to visit this Tonantzin from far away, as far away as before, and this worship is also suspect." Far from perceiving the radical difference between beliefs and worship, the Indians were, on the contrary, convinced that "this thing here is like the old one," which is why they were living in illusion. It was crucial to awaken them to "the error to which they have fallen victim." In their minds, not only was there no clear difference between "ancient" and "modern," but the Christian present revived and validated a pagan past that might ultimately win out: "I think they come more for the ancient [worship] than for the modern."[31] This process seems similar to the way the Christian sacralization of the Cholula pyramid revived old pre-Hispanic beliefs.

And yet the spreading of Christian imagery was done at the cost of the brutal and spectacular destruction of Mexican idols. Imposing new imagery meant rejecting any compromise with indigenous objects of worship, since Indian images were theoretically "evil, deceitful, filthy, abominable images." Whether the object of contempt or demonic presence, all idols were to be destroyed. Yet it is obvious that Amerindians did not always grasp the difference between Christian imagery and indigenous "images."

Replacing idols by images of saints inevitably led to misconceptions; it triggered comparisons and conflations that were not always completely unfounded.[32] Indians treated the new images in the same way as they had treated pre-Hispanic paintings and statues. The eye they brought to the Christs, Madonnas, and saints was closely related to an outlook cultivated over centuries, indeed millennia. To the outrage of missionaries, new converts were responding with idolatrous worship; in other words, they were developing a mestizo practice.

By asking *tlacuilos* to paint grotesques, Spanish monks encouraged the artists to exploit exoticism and develop mélanges, which enabled the Indians to take up pre-Hispanic motifs once again, giving them new life and perhaps even a new aura. The painted and carved animals that accompanied the depiction of saints in the best Christian tradition could be manipulated in countless ways and ultimately came to constitute an obstacle to Christianization. In 1585, the theologian Ortiz de Hinojosa criticized such assimilations and requested the banning of all carvings or paintings of demons, horses, serpents, sun, and moon: "as is done on images of Saint Bartholomew, Saint Martha, Saint James, and Saint Margaret." Although such iconography had been acceptable throughout Christendom because "these animals point to the feats, wonders, and miracles the saints performed thanks to supernatural virtue...the new converts do not see them in the same way, on the contrary they are returning to the old days." It was hard to reeducate such converts, "especially the old folk who learned idolatry at their mothers' breasts."[33]

Linguistic conquest had similar repercussions. Vague approximations and ambiguous translations could be as pernicious as imagery that backfired. Fray Domingo de la Anunciación alerted the Inquisition to this danger in 1572.[34] Poor translations of the concept of the Holy Trinity were sometimes inducing Indians to commit veritable heresy. How could one God be called by three different names, as suggested by Molina's *Vocabulary*, an authorized book widely used by the Spanish clergy? In addition to dubious translations by monks, others were done by literate Amerindians and disseminated in manuscript form with no ecclesiastical control.

Just as the Christianization of Amerindian elements might easily lead to mélanges, the same effect could result from the explicit denunciation of old ways, by reviving ancient beliefs and practices and "reminding the Indians of their worthless old things and rites."[35] The outcome was always the opposite of the one sought by the Church—instead of eliminating paganism, such efforts were reactivating it or, scarcely better, creating a situation of confusion and vagueness. The Indians admitted as much to the monks. They confessed to being disoriented, *neplantla*, lost between two worlds without knowing which way to turn, to their former divinities or to the saints of the invaders.[36]

WESTERNIZATION AND COMPROMISE

All this evidence suggests that we need to take a new look at the colonization of the Americas. Westernization was not merely a destructive invasion or a standardizing operation, since it contributed to the creation of mestizo forms of expression—a contribution partly deliberate and partly involuntary, but an undeniable one nonetheless.

The policy of replacement did not always entail a tabula rasa. On the contrary, not everything old was eliminated, and what survived usually merged with whatever the Church managed to impose, with whatever the Indians agreed to accept, with whatever they were able to assimilate or were unable to reject. There was an understandable exasperation and bitterness on the part of people like Sahagún, who wrote at the end of his life: "It is clear that everything is false in the very foundation of this new Church."[37] This blackly pessimistic diagnosis indicates the limitations of hard-line Christianization. Yet it also reflects a reality even harder to admit, because it negatively acknowledges the triumph of adaptations and concessions.

Spanish colonization was an endless series of negotiations and compromises with Indian reality. The vastness of the Americas, the exploitation of the land's resources, the lack of tools of enforcement, and the need to stabilize an evolving society meant that constant trade-offs had to be made in every sphere. One example was the question of indigenous songs and dances: What fate was to be ordained for these practices? They were closely linked to pagan worship, yet they also had social, political, and "artistic" dimensions of great scope. The evangelizers, as mentioned above, were convinced that dance and song were indispensable to the community's social life and well-being. A compromise therefore had to be found so that secular or sacred dance and song became acceptable. Yet two major problems had to be resolved, the first conceptual in nature, the second practical. How could practices adapted to local realities be devised, and how could they be implemented and made acceptable to the Indians? Such questions required negotiation.

Colonial cartography provides another example of compromise, resulting in Mexican maps with a "hybrid charm" so well described by Duccio Sacchi.[38] Not only did the Spanish have their maps drawn by Amerindian artists, but they allowed the painters to incorporate signs and a way of conceiving and depicting the land highly influenced by indigenous habits.[39] Indian maps from the second half of the sixteenth century sum up the efforts of various groups—indigenous leaders, Spanish *encomenderos*, European "colonists," and the Crown's civil servants—to share control of the land; the Spanish left their indigenous counterparts a good deal of maneuvering room in exchange for the community's incorporation into the Castilian legal system and the new administrative regions.[40] The Cholula map discussed in Chapter 9 provides one of the most accomplished examples of this compromise between conflicting requirements and theoretically irreconcilable traditions. This collaboration, as mentioned above, could mask ulterior motives and a good deal of nostalgia.

Every compromise entails an often unstable and fleeting equilibrium, depending not only on permanently precarious relationships of power but also on each party's interpretations of the arrangement. In Mexico, the survival of an energetic Indian nobility acting as mandatory intermediary between conquerors and indigenous masses explains the powerful mestizo creations conceived within it, just as the evangelizing dynamism of the monks reveals how they Christianized indigenous components by first destroying and then recuperating them. This political context favored the vital Amerindian Renaissance discussed in these chapters. The Mexican nobility, bolstered by the role it managed to keep, maintained a certain number of links with the pagan past from which it drew its prestige and legitimacy. The Church accepted this arrangement as long as indigenous nobles adhered to Christianity and promoted it.

The growing difficulties experienced by both groups starting in the last third of the sixteenth century had decisive, tragic consequences on the status quo: the death of most of the Indian artists and intelligentsia, a loss of impetus in their collaboration with the monastic Church, and the deterioration of the Indian nobility's position all destroyed the compromises that had been steadily reached. Other arrangements with other players then led to the creation of a baroque America whose history still remains to written from this particular perspective.

MONITORING MESTIZO PHENOMENA

The strategies implemented by Church and Crown sometimes involved selection as much as rejection, recuperation or compromise as much as extermination. Westernization then, far from being incompatible with mestizo phenomena, seems essential to them. But to what extent? It is now important to study the thin line separating a committed (or resigned) manipulation of indigenous elements from the emergence of an autonomous complex with unpredictable outcomes. In other words, what is the threshold beyond which the processes triggered, provoked, or merely tolerated by colonial authorities began to escape them?

This question complicates and complements the one raised in Chapter 9 about the threshold separating mélange from innovation.

Although social and political factors weigh significantly on the appearance and development of mélange, it cannot be reduced to the play of compromises or the history of power relationships within colonial society. The inconsistencies and illusions of successive—and sometimes contradictory—policies, the misdirected moves, the unfortunate initiatives, and the "mix-ups" all created confused and unforeseen situations that in turn influenced the selection, interpretation, and arrangement of elements. The outcry sparked by Archbishop Montufar's encouragement of the cult of the Virgin of Guadalupe is an example of a strategy that backfired, proving that the evolution of mestizo phenomena cannot be reduced to the relatively ordered interplay of Westernization policies and indigenous reactions to them. Sudden changes in direction by evangelizers could muddy the picture: in the last third of the sixteenth century, the Peruvian Church began to persecute beliefs and practices it had itself preached during the early Christianization of the Andes; mélanges originally thought to be Christian were thus forced into the shadows of idolatry and clandestinity, suddenly giving them an entirely different status. The unforeseen and accidental effects of such turnabouts or failures were just as important as active interventions and calculated manipulations.

Another factor nevertheless explains why mestizo phenomena escaped the grasp of the people who triggered them. Mestizo creativity unleashed internal processes that wrenched it from its originators. The internal dynamics of mélange may not be able totally to override the pressures of the surrounding environment, but they are able to modify or neutralize them in lasting fashion.

We saw earlier how grotesques spontaneously generated hybrids and how the merging of mannerist and Amerindian traditions vastly increased the possibilities of mélange; the repertoire available to artists acquired unprecedented scope, and potential combinations increased almost infinitely. The impact on the imagination was therefore even less controllable. It will be recalled that in Mexico City in the second half of the sixteenth century, Castilian poet González de Eslava blithely presented Christ in the form of a unicorn, in the finest Western tradition. In the same city at the same period, but drawing on pre-Hispanic traditions, Sahagún's *Psalmodia* turned the God-Child into a precious jade shining like the sun and the Blessed Virgin into a flower that shimmered in the first light of dawn. The angels welcoming Christ to heaven became "rosy spoonbills" or "divine spoonbill-angels."[41] The proliferating mestizo motifs took advantage of the simplicity and spontaneity of free-association mechanisms. Sahagún's associations clung to the sphere of Christian metaphors only through the use of the term *teoyotica* which, it will be remembered, means "in a divine sense" or "in a sacred way." Explicitly or implicitly, the term linked all evocations of Amerindian traditions to a Christian transcendence leading straight to the one, almighty God. This link obviously supposed that neophytes had already assimilated Christian notions of divinity, the sacred, and the supernatural—which explains the limitations of that artifice.

Other equally basic procedures drew Amerindian material into the Christian sphere. There was, for instance, a straightforward coupling of terms, one Spanish and the other Nahuatl. The former was designed to draw, anchor, or maintain in the Christian register the pagan entity designated by the latter. Such was the case with *teyolia/anima* couple, which established an equivalence between the Amerindian heart and the Christian soul. Originally, however, those notions corresponded to entities and beliefs that were totally unrelated. For the ancient Nahuas, *teyolia* was one of the three vital forces that inhabit human bodies, mountains, and lakes. When an individual died, his *teyolia* went either to Mictlan, Tlalocan, or the heaven of the Sun, but earthly merits had no impact on its fate.[42] It therefore has little to do with the Christian soul, unless heretical ideas are entertained. In the same spirit, Sahagún's *Psalmodia* linked the Castile rose with the pre-Hispanic marigold (*cempohualxochitl*), which meant associating a blossom favored by Christian hagiography with a flower found in all major pre-Hispanic festivities.[43] The rose thus became the "Castile marigold" (*Castillan cempohualxochitl*). Once again, an orthodox interpretation depended on the education and sensibility of the indigenous public as well as on how much Christianity it had assimilated.

THE INSTABILITY OF MÉLANGES

Teoyotica and the coupling of terms were clearly modest but efficient attractors that made it possible to appropriate indigenous expressions and concepts. The outcome was not always the one anticipated by the missionaries. In general, ease of association produced unstable mélanges. At any moment, the threshold between a Christianized mélange and an "aberrant error" might be crossed. Ignorance of the meaning given by the Church to the clausal *teoyotica*, or a simple shift of stress from the Christian element to the Amerindian element within a given couple (soul/heart or rose/marigold) would suffice to nudge the mélange into the camp of what the monks called idolatry. The unstable morphology of mélanges indisputably stemmed from a fragility intensified by the countless number of connections.

The association of elements generated by highly different experiences, brought together in the extremely tense context of colonial society, is always prone to sudden mutations. Indeed, it is rare for a recently forged mélange to crystallize in a form that guarantees its permanence and controlled transmission. The approach taken by Sahagún's *Psalmodia Christiana* remains an exception. The associations that sprang from the minds of the monk and his indigenous helpers benefited from the twin media of writing and printing. Most ecclesiastical texts, however—the Catechism and Lives of the Saints— remained in manuscript form. Even less durable and controllable were asso-

ciations made during sermons by Spanish priests. It was because the indigenous names given by preachers to the saints in the Christian pantheon were
spread *orally* that the associations on which they were based led to the
"errors of interpretation" decried by Sahagún.

Other associations were drawn with a paintbrush or carved in stone,
but that may not have sufficed to anchor their Christian interpretation permanently. Sculpted motifs from the pre-Hispanic past coexisted in plain
view—on the façades of churches, flanking the portals—with Christian
iconography and European-style decoration. They can still be admired in
many Mexican towns. But what meaning should be ascribed to them? Most
of the time these associations are part of decorative schemes carved by
indigenous sculptors. In certain cases, the intervention of monks was
designed to prevent any backsliding interpretation. The depiction of the
wounds of Christ on the Franciscan blazon, for instance, drew on pre-
Hispanic symbolism of the precious blood shed during human sacrifice, but
the monks were there, in theory, to explain the significance of this new
divine blood. The countless flowers decorating the columns and arches,
however, were perhaps less likely to draw the monks' attention. Covered by
the more innocent label of ornamentation, ancient motifs could certainly
evoke meanings or suggest interpretations of Christianity that diverged
from orthodoxy and revived ancestral beliefs. Far from anchoring representation in the Christian camp, the durability of stone might serve a purpose
opposite to that for which Christian preaching had destined it.[44]

THE IMPOSSIBILITY OF RETURN

If mestizo phenomena represent a mélange whose meanings can vary, did
this instability favor the old paganism? Did this property, by triggering reminiscences that escaped orthodox Christianity, indicate a veritable return to
the Amerindian world? I do not believe so, for at least two reasons. The
constant association of Christian heaven and Amerindian paradise, and the
many links between the Old and New Testaments and the pre-Hispanic
imaginative world, led to the coexistence and interpenetration of the two
realms of beliefs. By thrusting Christian saints into the flowery and shimmering world of pagan ancestors, Sahagún's *Psalmodia* gave birth to new
creatures who, although not sufficient to Christianize the pre-Hispanic otherworld, were sufficiently glamorous and overwhelming to modify
Amerindian beliefs. The systematic incorporation of Christian divinities
could even put some soul into the abhorred beliefs. But this pagan otherworld, like that of the *cantares*, was no longer the one that had existed prior
to the Conquest.

SIBYLLINE GROTTO   **197**

The old paganism no longer enjoyed the means to reestablish either its own "orthodoxy" or any type of "purity" (which, for that matter, had never been one of its concerns). For lack of idol-serving priests, *calmecac* schools, and resources for spreading and imposing orthodoxy, the old rites and beliefs were exposed to increasingly "contaminated" interpretations inspired by the religion of the conquistadors. As noted earlier, in the 1580s the indigenous informants of mestizo chronicler Diego Muñoz Camargo turned the paradise of the goddess Xochiquetzal into a court of celestial delights that would enchant any Renaissance Spaniard.

The proliferation and instability of mélanges wound up distancing them from the traditions and milieus that had supplied their initial components. The Mexican Church apparently had to choose between aloof laissez-faire or an impractical extermination that it never really resolved to carry out (Sahagún's attempts to cast doubt on the new cult of the Virgin of Guadalupe by linking her indigenous name, Tonantzin, to a terrifying Amerindian goddess, Cihuatcoatl, seems to have had little effect). A third possibility was the dissemination of new mélanges. The Church always retained the possibility of regaining control of the situation by constantly favoring new associations likely to appeal to the expectations of the indigenous population. One notorious example is the second launch, by the canons of Mexico City's cathedral, of the cult of the Virgin of Guadalupe in 1648, which met with undeniable success in the long run. That is the angle from which we should view this elaboration of an "Indian" version of the apparitions of the Virgin, ultimately endowing it with the solidity of dogma.

As to the Amerindians, their ability to act varied greatly but was far from negligible. There was no question of returning to the old days. History is irreversible. The way in which they could turn the mélanges they were offered to their own ends or to develop their own mestizo phenomena depended on the freedom of action they were accorded by Spanish priests, the degree of Hispanization of the community's indigenous leadership, and also the imagination of the *curanderos* (healers) and other "holy workers" in the area, who were not necessarily specialists in the ancient world. *Curanderos* introduced Christian material with an efficiency that far outstripped indigenous priests. The new dispositions required by a baroque Christianity, and the disappearance of an Indian leadership with ties to the pre-Hispanic world soon brought an end to the combinations produced in the sixteenth century. Other mestizo creations would follow the ones epitomized by the *cantares* and the frescoes. But in order for Mexicans to recover control of mélanges a demographic resurgence was required, along with a collective effort spearheaded by a bold and imaginative leader from their own ranks. Antonio Pérez's movement around the cult of the Virgin of Popocatepetl in the mid-seventeenth century, for instance, triggered new mélanges that temporarily escaped the vigilance of the Church. But this fleeting experiment was soon stifled by repression, which points again to the fragility of mélanges.[45]

Mestizo phenomena therefore appear to be mobile, unstable, swiftly uncontrollable. They can be countered only by the generally futile tactic of annihilation or by replacement by a new mélange, a new formulation that will moreover wind up, in turn, escaping the control of its instigators. The complexity of mestizo mechanisms and the wariness they spark are probably due to a capricious "nature" that often turns their inventors into sorcerer's apprentices who wander down unforeseen paths. Simultaneously social and political, mestizo phenomena in fact entail so many variables that they complicate the usual interplay of authority and tradition. They slip from the grasp of historians who hunt them, or are overlooked by anthropologists in search of archaisms, "cold societies," and authentic traditions. This complexity is also linked to the threshold crossed by mélanges at a certain point in their history, whether transformed into a new reality or endowed with unexpected autonomy. There probably exist connections between these various thresholds and the attractors that generate mestizo phenomena. Readers will not rebuke me, I hope, for postponing that question for a future book, in order to conclude with a return to the world at hand.

C ONCLUSION: HAPPY TOGETHER

> A wonderful archangel appeared to us in a dream. He informed us that the *muiraquitã* talisman I had lost was in the beloved hands of Doctor Venceslau Pietro Petra, a subject of the vice-kingdom of Peru but of thoroughly Florentine stock like the Cavalcantis of Pernambouc.
>
> —Letter from the Emperor Macunaíma to the Amazonians, São Paulo, May 30, 1926

Bridging Asia and the Americas, *Happy Together* (1997) is a film about two Chinese men in Buenos Aires. They try to survive and sustain their love affair against the backdrop of Astor Piazzola's tango music. Hong Kong director Wong Kar-Wai, by taking a Chinese look at the New World, sought to shatter the framework in which the West has tried to contain Latin America for several centuries now.

This Asian eye reveals new interconnections unrelated to the tradition of Western modernity and indifferent to the historic routes of colonization. Buenos Aires and Hong Kong, the two cities linked by *Happy Together*, have little in common except perhaps the fact that both are former colonies of Western Europe. Buenos Aires is a gateway to Latin America, born of Spanish domination and European emigration to the southern hemisphere, whereas Hong Kong is a gateway to Asia, until recently under British domination, today torn between China and the West; it furthermore represents a society living on borrowed time.

The Hong Kong filmmaker's transfer to Buenos Aires shattered the exoticism that continues to blind European and U.S. perception of Latin America, an exoticism ever ready to wax enthusiastic over marginality, difference, and otherness. So how did Wong Kar-Wai manage this? The tango bars in Buenos Aires, the falls at Iguazù, and the photographs of Patagonia provide no local color, create no distancing effect. They sketch a space reinvented by Wong Kar-Wai, simultaneously Argentinean and non-Argentinean, as real and as fictional as the composite otherworlds found in the *cantares mexicanos*, as though they were no longer geographical landmarks but instead had become parts of a recreated universe. To these effects should be added images that appear new due to their texture, speed, or slow motion, altering our usual ways of seeing. Creative, hybrid, mestizo phenomena: perhaps the observations made during our Italo-Mexican odyssey could be applied to this contemporary film.

HONG KONG MOVIES

The images in *Happy Together* provide lively testimony to the hybrid and mestizo processes produced in Hong Kong in the late twentieth century. But first of all they belong to a film industry that, since its inception, has endlessly inflected Asia's relationship with the West. In this part of the world, the face-off between East and modern West is as spectacular as the confrontation between Iberian Europe and Native America four centuries earlier. Not that the clash is any more recent; from the sixteenth century, the Portuguese, Spanish, Japanese and Chinese were encountering and opposing one another in the Far East. As Carmen Bernand and I have written elsewhere: "Asian mestizo phenomena differ from American ones. Whereas the latter built a mestizo society on a continental scale, the former are already pointing to planetary mélanges, symbolized by the globe-trotting done by individuals and families caught in the currents of a world-economy."[1]

In the twentieth century these phenomena have assumed greater scope, as brilliantly glimpsed by creative filmmaking. Imagery once again offers a special angle from which to observe the outcome of encounters and clashes. It is therefore not surprising to find that the writings of critics and filmmakers address some of the questions raised at the start of this book. In a 1997 interview, John Woo stated: "I don't think my films are based on a single culture. Nor have they ever really been. I've always straddled Asia and the West."[2] In one of Woo's magisterial works, *The Killer* (1989), a statue of the Virgin meets a fate that inspired the following comment by the filmmaker:

> [The statue] refers not only to Christianity but to the vows of purity taken by knights of Wu Xia Pian [the Chinese knighthood]. Its destruction represents not only the ultimate blasphemy but also the symbolic unification of the two worlds.... [This scene] alone sums up the multifarious universe of a filmmaker who is both Chinese and Christian, and his syncretic vision of human emotions.[3]

The metamorphoses displayed by Chinese martial arts films in the past thirty years testify to intersecting influences that have led to multiple series of "remakes." Their history can be traced in the same way as Mexico's mestizo phenomena. The genre had already undergone a dramatic evolution marked by a series of flamboyant rises and rapid declines when, in 1965, producer Run Run Shaw reinvigorated the knighthood theme by drawing inspiration from Japanese *chambara* films and North American Westerns. Injecting "exotic" elements into a traditional framework that had already been profoundly modified by historical novels and mass-magazine fiction guaranteed the popularity of a series of films based on the character of a one-armed knight. Swordplay films became "a genre where people constantly tried to outdo one another, where the most unlikely influences were blithely combined."[4]

In the early 1980s, the People's Republic of China performed one of its customary about-faces and seized upon the genre, rehabilitating the very martial arts that it had denounced as feudal up till then. *The Temple of Shaolin* put the seal on this return, developing a story about thirteen monks from Shaolin who saved the Tang emperor. Paradoxically, then, it was Communist China who revived the Hong Kong public's interest in these stories of an ancient society. This constant back-and-forth between island, continent, Hollywood, Japan, television, and film studios has fueled a nonstop series of hybridizations (within the Chinese world) and mestizo phenomena (between Japan and America). *Pace* those people nostalgic for purity and tradition, these pure Chinese products are living, composite creations just like the Indian frescoes in Central America.

The constant cracking open, shattering, and enriching of the genre—along with compromises, reconfigurations, and reinterpretations—encourage a flexibility of form and content that highly inspired directors are able to exploit. These transformations culminated in Tsui Hark's 1995 *Dao* (*The Blade*), a reinterpretation of the classic tale of a one-armed swordsman. Hark's schematic film claims to return to Japanese roots even as it challenges the genre by eliminating the geographical and historical references inscribed in the original story.

Wong Kar-Wai devised even more unusual variations in *Ashes of Time* (1994), taking mestizo imagery to a frenzy. Like his other films, this movie combines allusions and images with the same energy and creativity displayed by Mexico's Renaissance painters. Whereas the Ixmiquilpan artists revived the theme of ritual combat by casting it in the lively, Italianizing mold of grotesques, *Ashes of Time* explores a parallel path by thoroughly reinterpreting the Kung Fu genre from the standpoint of a Western: "*Ashes of Time* dismembers and extends the classic swordplay film by taking Leone's work on the western to a mannerist extreme."[5] Startling superimpositions of images create mirages that suddenly transpose Chinese bandits to the world of the Mexican Revolution. In addition to playing on imagery, these mestizo phenomena play on sound—a Western sound track in the Ennio Morricone style accompanies the imagery from this Asian universe, with results as disturbing as the aural mélanges in *The Pillow Book*.[6]

HYBRID AND MESTIZO PHENOMENA

Wong Kar-Wai sets almost all his films in Hong Kong, a colonial society living on borrowed time.[7] This city is one of the places in the world where civilizations, hegemonies, and economic systems collide—and coexist—in spectacular fashion. The coexistence of ancient China and modern China, of capitalism, neoliberalism, socialism, and postmodernity, sustains a singular situation whose precariousness is further accentuated by the uncertainty over the city's future. This problematic, unstable, and contradictory situation is probably unique in the closing days of the twentieth century. The very existence of Hong Kong defies the most basic frameworks of Western thought by mingling tradition with modernity, oriental with occidental, communism with globalization, and center with fringe, while offering the puzzle of a reality steeped in unpredictable metamorphoses.

Despite that, our eyes remain blind to the mestizo mechanisms riddling the island. Critics struggle to assimilate Wong Kar-Wai's work to Western cinema: "*Days of Being Wild* seems to be a reformulation of a modern film turned into a genre film, a kind of re-interpretation of Nicholas Ray by Antonioni." Or else his films are associated with the flow of imagery generated by new technologies. When we finally open our eyes, unsettled by the spectacle before us, we are troubled by the ambiguity in which the Hong Kong director's films are rooted, stressing as they do the problematic nature of imagery, of form, of narrative. His oeuvre is peopled by protagonists constantly torn between contradictory spaces and loyalties.[8] Ambivalence seems to be everywhere—in the use of color which is "never quite right" and in the visual polyvalence that is allegedly a sign of incoherence and disjointedness ("the image missed its rendezvous with meaning"). Wong Kar-Wai further reinforces ambiguity through a series of "uncertainties both visual and cognitive," evident from his very first film, *As Tears Go By*. Ambiguity comes to light everywhere, becoming one of the filmmaker's "epistemological" characteristics.

Yet our discussion of the Renaissance and the Mexican worlds now suggests a different approach to the specificity of Wong Kar-Wai's films. It is not ambiguity that riddles his oeuvre. What critics have sensed—without recognizing it—when they write of "the interweaving of nocturnal, urban itineraries" or "a tale made from mismatching pieces," or when they refer to the constant complexity of plot and images, are the combined effects of hybrid and mestizo mechanisms.[9] Our deep plunge into the Mexican past has taught us to recognize, if not understand, such mechanisms. We are faced here with a mestizo artwork whose reference points are no longer solely Western and Asian. Some are even devoid of an immediately graspable meaning, as in the case of the anonymous jungle that opens and closes *Days of Being Wild* or the sight of the Iguazù Falls which interrupts the flow of *Happy Together* on two occasions. Their impact and coherence are in no way diminished by that fact these images refer to no specific universe, whether familiar or exotic, that they do not function in a seemly manner, that they "slip free of all context."[10] The images "have the power to become autonomous...they persist and organize their resistance...they grow like wild, uncontrollable vegetation."[11] They remind us of artworks from Renaissance Mexico—*Rain* and *Rainbow* from the *Florentine Codex*—which thrust us into imaginative worlds that sprang from the fringes of Western Europe and Native America.

By singling out the main characters of a scene with the use of slow motion, Wong Kar-Wai constructs a hybrid image in which distinct temporal spheres coexist. A similar effect was produced in the sixteenth century in the double calendar of the *Codex Tellerianus-Remensis*, which juxtaposed Christian and Amerindian time frames; Wong Kar-Wai's images juxtapose time "by making the various elements on the screen pass by at different speeds."[12] Fast and slow motion are combined on the screen without ever depriving the image of its coherence or beauty.

Yet mestizo mechanisms apply to behavior as well as to imagery and temporality. Contrary to appearances, the filmmaker's protagonists are not torn between external loyalties; they move spontaneously within a multiple world whose hybrid and mestizo qualities cut it loose from standard moorings. These are characters "without character," like their close Brazilian cousin, Mário de Andrade's Macunaíma. If Hong Kong and Buenos Aires are interchangeable, if one exists within the other and vice versa, that is because they both belong to the filmmaker's mestizo universe. It is less a space "that seems to have lost all sense of measure...[becoming] incommensurable, unprecedented," than a composite territory of multiple dimensions.

The apparent indeterminacy or indecisiveness in the unfolding of the tale exists only in relation to our conventions and expectations. This is perhaps the same distorting, simplistic filter that earlier prompted Spaniards to see in indigenous Mexico's paintings and *cantares* what Diego Durán called *disparates* ("absurdities"). The impression of fragmentation and rupture given by Wong Kar-Wai's screenplays resides not in the screenplays themselves; it stems from a reading ill prepared to deal with a form of narration conceived on entirely different bases. And it shares this singularity with Mexican texts of the sixteenth century. We should not therefore be surprised that Wong Kar-Wai's films inspire comments that seem applicable, word for word, to the *cantares mexicanos*: "We glide around rather than progress. There is no clear-cut separation between past and future, and the process of transformation from one to the other is nothing less than fluctuating." The *cantares* contain elements that follow one another without obeying classic narrative progression; as in the films of Wong Kar-Wai, it is hard not to get lost. Neither Amerindian nor European, the *cantares* are mestizo works.

COLONIAL SOCIETIES AND MESTIZO CREATIVITY

Although separated by seas and centuries, these works share yet another dimension: their unique relationship to the colonized and Westernized lands in which they were spawned. The *cantares* show neither Mexico's colonial society as it was (or as it now appears to us today) nor the Indian aristocracy of the mid-sixteenth century. They offer no commentary—any more than do church frescoes or codices—on the post-Conquest period or the closing years of the sixteenth century in Mexico City. Nor do movies by Wong Kar-Wai claim to describe Hong Kong's final moments before it reverted to China. This aloofness stems from the multiplicity of allusions traversing these works. It is their mestizo specificity that in both Mexico City and Hong Kong, annuls any mirroring effect without, however, cutting these works off from their historical environment. They are prismlike works that capture reflections of the urban landscape, "diffracting them into so many facets."

Should this relationship be analyzed in terms of negativity, as has already been suggested? "In his films, Wong conveys a particularly intense experience of this period as an experience of negativity: the experience of an ungraspable and ambivalent cultural space, which is always just beyond our reach or just below speech."[13] His movies allegedly bear the mark of the problematic nature of colonial space, carved from an accumulation of juxtapositions, cross-breedings, and transitions between imperialism, neoliberalism, evolving Communism, and imperial Chinese past.[14] That mark, however, is theoretically more evident in modes of expression and behavior than in explicit observations or expressly political messages. Confusion allegedly arises from fluctuating and uncertain hierarchies,[15] changing rules, "transformations as irregular as they are swift," and the threat of a henceforth unpredictable future. This confusion then find its cinematic expression in the films' contradictions, spatial paradoxes, and unbalanced emotions.

In fact, the relationship appears to be yet more subtle and complex than the above analysis would suggest. It goes beyond a simple connection of cause and effect, even if perceived and expressed in terms of "negativity." The singularity and uncertainty of Hong Kong's situation is matched by a mestizo creativity whose roots are much older than the crises of the 1990s. This response cannot be reduced to a pathological accumulation of failures and setbacks. The mixed universe within which Wong's characters move possesses its own coherences and lines of force. It is a framework for new experiences that the filmmaker expresses in forms and contents that constitute more than merely disparate and heterogeneous fragments. The uncategorizable and therefore disturbing images, the mélange of acceleration and inertia, and "the subtle instability of the image" (which means that "we are never certain of what we see")[16] are not merely symptoms of disequilibrium. To a much greater extent, they are manifestations of a carefully constructed reaction to mestizo and hybrid mechanisms. By combining flexibility of structure with extreme rigor of expression, these constructions make it possible to conceptualize the complex situation in which the island has always lived and will continue to develop. In this respect, mestizo creativity is both the product of Hong Kong's formative admixtures and the only way to conceptualize and depict them. Which means that Wong's works cannot be reduced to a simple cinematic transposition of a state of things nor to the expression of a crisis of experience and narrativity. Hong Kong is not a Western world in stagnation—it is a mixed universe which is undergoing increasingly subtle and unpredictable mestizo phenomena.

THE "CULTURE OF DISAPPEARANCE"

Sociologist Ackbar Abbas coined the expression "culture of disappearance" in reference to the situation of Hong Kong in the final decade of the twentieth century. Abbas attributed several meanings to the word "disappearance." First, it denotes a mobile, fleeting, elusive reality triggered by the anguish of reversion to China.[17] Disappearance refers to "a space that is at once very much there...and not there,"[18] an already vanished time and a "skewed space."[19] This definition would make Hong Kong the island of unpredictability and ephemeral creations—by building high-rises that are demolished as quickly as they are constructed, the territory has wound up resembling magnetic tape that is constantly erased and reused.

"Disappearance" also implies a form of systematically overlooked presence, as though an external gaze ignored the existence of creative originality by clinging to traditional dualisms—those between East and West or between tradition and modernity. Hong Kong's creativity—in movies, books, architecture—is constantly disappearing not so much because it is effaced but because it is being spontaneously overlooked in favor of clichés and conventional or familiar images. People have a hard time believing that this isle of bankers could produce anything other than surplus value. It was this same shortsightedness that, by reducing Mexico's past to a history of massacres and destruction, long overlooked the highly singular and fertile products of the Mexican Renaissance, making them "disappear" by putting them in parentheses.

Disappearance: in such a shifting context, it is pointless to seek to pin down an identity. We may as well try to freeze a reality whose main feature is change, transformation, and nonstop "disappearance." Instead of musing over the fate of Hong Kong's identity, it would be preferable to explore the emergence of a new subjectivity that is not simply a psychological concept but rather "an affective, political, and social category all at once. It is...a subjectivity that is coaxed into being by the disappearance of old cultural bearings and orientations, which is to say that it is a subjectivity that develops precisely out of a space of disappearance."[20]

This tricky situation constitutes an opportunity as much as a threat. It can trigger reversals and the emergence of new forms of existence whose vitality and survival are linked to their very mobility and instability. To avoid being assimilated or reabsorbed, people have to learn to survive in a culture of disappearance by adopting strategies ready to take advantage of change, which they can then push in unexpected directions. (Amerindian nobles who wanted to avoid pure and simple Hispanicization did just that.) This reaction would not take the form of a withdrawal into the local or indigenous, nor in a flight to marginality, but rather of a hand-to-hand struggle with the pressures and constraints of colonial—or neocolonial[21]—domination. Such an attitude would avoid the pitfalls of a reified marginality whose existence only consolidates the center, just as it would shun the illusion of insularity idealized as a haven of former purity. Although the gamble carries risks, confronting the "culture of disappearance" is not necessarily paralyzing for those who brave it.

"Postcolonial" Hong Kong is not Renaissance Mexico City. Yet like Hong Kong filmmakers of today, Amerindian artists perhaps managed to take advantage of the disappearance of their universe in order to create their own world, "working with disappearance and taking it elsewhere,...using disappearance to deal with disappearance."[22] In both instances, manipulations of imagery and the visual sphere thoroughly overwhelm the artistic field to which our myopia tries to consign them. Faced with the crisis and the constraints that restrict them, Chinese filmmakers "can intervene in political debates more effectively by problematizing the visual than by advancing direct arguments about identity."[23]

Wong Kar-Wai is not the only one to challenge the visual order, for that matter. A director like Stanley Kwan evokes an already "vanished world" by reinterpreting it through ghost stories, that is to say by recreating a genre that dates back almost to the origins of Chinese cinema.[24] In *Rouge* (1988), he reinvents the traditional parameters of the genre: rather than playing on the distinction between the human and supernatural worlds, the appearance of a ghost compresses, so to speak, space-time. The film eschews any distinction between the 1930s and the 1980s, establishing a heterogeneous space in which past and present mingle. The paradox is that one of the most popular and fantastic of genres is used as a rigorous method of representing the complexities of Hong Kong's cultural space.[25] Hybridity is so strong that elements from the past and present lose their integrity to the point of merging or becoming completely interchangeable. By introducing a double time frame, reversible time as symbolized by the ghost allows for many elements of the past to be incorporated into the present. Evoking the dead in a colonial present is an exercise now familiar to us—four centuries ago, with equally remarkable ease, the composers and performers of the *cantares mexicanos* indulged in parallel games by adapting their traditional genre and projecting themselves into an already vanished time frame.

Any parallels we might draw between Hong Kong and Mexico City do not negate the countless differences separating them. But they serve to mark the "poles" of a vast mestizo space where similar issues can resonate. Mexican painters help us to appreciate Hong Kong filmmakers even as the Chinese example spurs us, in turn, to take another look at the Amerindian example. It should remind us that the indigenous Renaissance world was under attack on all fronts—economic, social, religious. It was a universe threatened with physical extinction from the devastating assaults of disease. Finally, it was a society whose leadership was deprived of its ethos, its spheres of activity (war, idolatrous priesthood, control of tributes), and its institutional frameworks (*calmecac* schools, major rituals, and so on). "Disappearance" was weakening a world subjected to ever increasing pressure from the gigantic Spanish empire.

But it never completely overwhelmed it. The context of crisis and the apparently hopeless "culture of disappearance," exposed as it was to all the vagaries of the unforeseen and unpredictable, provoked reactions of a special type. The not-very-spectacular nature of those reactions does not mean that the colonized people remained passive—they took the indirect paths whose loops and meanders we have explored. In Mexico City and Hong Kong, there seems to have been a convergence of attitudes. What has been written on the large Asian city—a critique of colonialism that "is made obliquely in the film's treatment of visuality and its relationship to genre"[26]—applies to the reactions discussed in earlier chapters of this book. Given the impossibility of subverting visual models and imposed genres, or of seizing "already vanished worlds," artists in Mexico City and Hong Kong devised new approaches to imagery even as they destabilized and deflected genres, whether addressing Renaissance grotesques or Kung Fu movies, whether recycling ancient Amerindian *cantares* or oriental ghost stories. Each of these works, instead of merely depicting or ignoring a "dead-end situation," triggered shifts and mutations that cultivated all the resources of mestizo and hybrid phenomena. The case of Hong Kong not only inspires another look at Mexico City, it also suggests a return to Italy. For in Ferrara there is a noble residence, the Casa Romei, which boasts not only a Hall of Sibyls but also ceilings with grotesques that include Mexican turkeys, monkeys, butterflies, and pumas.[27] Also in Ferrara is the Feltrinelli bookstore where, on that same day in December 1998, I came across an Italian edition of Aby Warburg's account of his voyage among the Hopi, *A Lecture on Serpent Ritual*.

Mestizo regions are vast and are begging for further exploration. They require long voyages through source materials and academic fields, across continents and pasts. For the moment, having concluded my imperfect descriptions and interpretations of an overwhelmingly complex subject, I can only encourage readers to set off for Puebla and Ixmiquilpan, to cross the Sierra de Hidalgo with the *cantares* and *Macunaíma* in hand, or to dive into the Buenos Aires of Wong Kar-Wai.

Or perhaps to follow in Aby Warburg's footsteps, the better to understand the drawing on the church wall and the old baroque altar, both being an irrevocable part of the collective memory and experience of the Hopi Indians. A mestizo approach is no panacea—its battle is never won; it must always start afresh. Yet mestizo phenomena offer the privilege of belonging to several worlds within a single lifetime: "I'm a Tupi who plays the lute! ... "

N OTES

INTRODUCTION

1. Aby Warburg, "A Lecture on Serpent Ritual," *Journal of the Warburg Institute* II: 4 (1939): 281.
2. Philippe-Alain Michaud, *Aby Warburg et l'image en mouvement* (Paris: Macula, 1998), 196.
3. Warburg (1939), 278.
4. Michaud (1998), 183.
5. Michaud (1998), 222.
6. Michaud (1998), 223.
7. Geminello Alvi, *Il secolo americano* (Milan: Adelphi, 1996).
8. Nestor G. Canclini, in *Consumidores y ciudadanos: Conflictos multiculturales de la globalización* (Mexico City: Grijalbo, 1995), stresses the fact that cultural globalization is nothing other than Americanization of culture.
9. Another example of the process of uniformization is the widespread aestheticizing trend analyzed by Remo Guidieri in *Chronique du neutre et de l'auréole: Sur le musée et les fétiches* (Paris: La Différence, 1992).
10. This new cosmopolitanism is allegedly composed of a combination of local features that make up a cosmopolitan identity. It is expressed through notions of hybridity and creolization perceived as generalized, global identities. On this issue, see the comments by Jonathan Friedman, "Global Crises, the Struggle for Cultural Identity and Intellectual Pork-Barrelling: Cosmopolitans, Nationals, and Locals in an Era of Dehegemonization," ed. P. Werbner, *Debating Cultural Hybridity* (London: Zed Press, 1997).
11. Many American universities, whether famous or not, strongly play the old Third World card, backed by their powerful presses and networks. The rhetoric of culturalism, difference, and cultural authenticity, meanwhile, has become the most widely shared thing in the world and, in an insidious and paradoxical way, helps to standardize the very discourses that claim, on the contrary, to be defending fundamental specificities.
12. Alfred L. Kroeber, *Culture Patterns and Processes* (New York/London: First Harbinger Books, 1963), 67.
13. Claude Lévi-Strauss's seminar was published as *L'Identité* (Paris: P.U.F., 1977), 322.
14. The establishment of regular maritime routes between Europe and Asia via Africa or America, the worldwide circulation of precious metals, and the effects of Chinese demand for silver on the economy of the Hispano-Portuguese Empire all suggest that this first global economy was established between 1570 and 1640. On the question of gold and silver, see, among others, D. O. Flynn and A. Giráldez, "China and the Spanish Empire," *Revista de Historia Económica*, XIV: 2 (Spring/Summer 1996): 318–324.

CHAPTER 1

1. As did Claude Lévi-Strauss in the documentary film, *A propos de Tristes Tropiques*, produced by La Sept/Les Films du Village, 1991.
2. Hal Forster, *Post-Modern Culture* (1985), 166, cited in Michael Camille, *The Margin of Medieval Art* (London: Reaktion Books, 1992), 158.

3. Mário de Andrade, *Macunaíma: O herói sem nenhum caráter* (São Paulo: Telê Porto Ancona Lopez, 1996) [Translated into English as *Macunaima* (Pittsburgh: Pitt Latin America Series, 1988].

4. Ibid., 45.

5. Gilda de Mello e Souza, *O tupi e o alaúde: Uma interpretação de Macunaíma* (São Paulo: Livaria Duas Cidades, 1979), 59.

6. Ibid., 63.

7. Recordings now provide better knowledge of musical compositions produced for Jesuit missions in the Amazon in the eighteenth century. See the collection K 617, *Musiques sacrées missionnaires*, vol 1: *Missions jésuites de l'altiplano à l'Amazonie*, and *San Ignacio, l'opéra perdu des missions jésuites de l'Amazonie*, recorded by the Ensemble Elyma conducted by Gabriel Garrido (Les Chemins du Baroque, K 617).

8. Gilda de Mello e Souza and Haroldo de Campos, to name only the most notable.

9. Mello e Souza (1979), 56.

10. "Obviously, the world is ours." Clara Gallini, *Giochi pericolosi: Frammenti di un immaginario alquanto razzista* (Rome: Manifestolibri, 1996), 122.

11. Sérgio Buarque de Holanda, *Visão do Paraíso* (São Paulo: Editora Brasiliense, 1996); Décio de Alencar Guzmán, *Les Chefferies indigènes du Rio Negro à l'époque de la conquête de l'Amazonie, 1650–1750: Le Cas des Indiens manao* (DEA thesis, École des Hautes Études en Sciences Sociales, Paris, 1998), 63.

12. Alain Badiou, *L'Ethique* (Paris: Hatier, 1993), 4.

13. Anna Roosevelt, *Amazonian Indians from Prehistory to the Present* (Tucson and London: University of Arizona Press, 1997), 3. An example of this ethnographic fossilization can be found in G. Reichel-Dolmatoff, *Amazonian Cosmos: The Sexual and Religious Symbolism of the Tukano Indians* (Chicago: University of Chicago Press, 1971).

14. See the critique by Jonathan Hill, "Introduction: Myth and History," *Rethinking History and Myth: Indigenous South American Perspectives on the Past,* ed. Jonathan Hill (Urbana: University of Illinois Press, 198), 1–17.

15. Joyce Lorimer, ed., *English and Irish Settlement on the River Amazon, 1550–1646* (Cambridge: Hakluyt Society, 1989).

16. Roosevelt (1997), 10. Neil Lancelot Whitehead, quoted in Roosevelt (34) argues that "obviously it should be our historical understanding of the last half-millennium of interaction between Europe and America that conditions our analysis of the modern ethnic groups, not the other way around."

17. Marcio Meira, "Indios e Brancos nas águas pretas, Histórias do Rio Negro." Seminar on *Povos Indígenas do Rio Nego: Terra e cultura*, Universidade do Amazonas, Manaus, August 1996.

18. Ibid., 21. Letter written by Joaquim Tinoco Valente in Barcelos, Brazil, July 24, 1764.

19. Ibid., 22, quoting Alexandre Rodrigues Ferreira (1783).

20. An excellent introduction to these issues can be found in Roosevelt (1997). See also N. L. Whitehead, *Lords of the Tiger Spirit: A History of the Caribs in Colonial Venezuela and Guayana, 1408–1820* (Dordrecht and Providence: Foris Publications, Caribbean Studies Series No. 10, Royal Institute for Linguistics and Anthropology, 1988); and Antonio Porro, "Social Organization and Political Power in the Amazon Floodplain: The Ethnohistorical Sources," in Roosevelt (1997), 79–94.

21. See the examples cited by Porro in Roosevelt (1997), 80.

22. Born in Rheinsberg in 1944, Baumgarten lives and works in Düsseldorf and New York. *Documenta X: Short Guide/Kurzfürher* (Kassel, Germany: Cantz Verlag, 1997), 30.

23. *Documenta X,* 174–175. Hélio Oiticica was born in Rio de Janeiro in 1937 and died in 1980. On his oeuvre, see Celso Favaretto, *A invenção de Hélio Oiticica* (São Paulo: Edusp/Fapesp, 1992).

24. *Documenta X,* 140–143.
25. Clara Gallini (1996) has pointed out the power of humor and irony against racism and exotic stereotypes.

CHAPTER 2

1. "Sélection disques, rock" *Libération,* October 25/26, 1997.
2. See Jonathan Friedman's essay in Featherstone and Lash, eds., *Spaces of Culture: City, Nation, World* (London: Sage, 1999).
3. Jean-Paul Gaultier's fashion shows and Peter Sellar's theatrical shows are revealing of this phenomenon as much for the audience they draw as for the models they propose.
4. On the relationship between the postmodern and the postcolonial, see Walter D. Mignolo, *The Darker Side of the Renaissance: Literacy, Territoriality, and Colonization* (Ann Arbor, MI: University of Michigan, 1995).
5. This leads to the concept of "colonial semiosis," referring to a field of study that stresses semiotic interactions, appropriations, and resistance coming from the periphery. See Mignolo (1995), 7–8.
6. Ibid., 331.
7. Homi Bhabha, *The Location of Culture* (London: Routledge, 1994); P. Gilroy, *There Ain't No Black in the Union Jack* (London: Hutchinson, 1987); D. Hebdige, *Subculture: The Meaning of Style* (London: Methuen, 1983). See also Bhabha's discussion of the concept of hybridism in colonial and postcolonial contexts.
8. J. Bernabé et al., *Eloge de la créolité* (Paris: Gallimard, 1989), 26.
9. See Néstor García Canclini, *Culturas híbridas: Estrategias para entrar y salir de la modernidad* (Mexico City: Consejo Nacional para las Artes/Grijalbo, 1990), for a revalorization of the notion of hybridity.
10. Edouard Glissant, *Poétique de la relation* (Paris: Gallimard, 1990).
11. In fact, as Carmen Bernand has rightly pointed out, the origin of the concept of mestizo goes back to a political decision rather than a biological mélange: in medieval Spain, *mistos* were Christians who preferred to ally themselves with Muslims against King Roderigo. Bernand, "Mestizo, mulatos y ladinos en Hispano-América: un enfoque antropológico y un proceso histórico," typescript, 1997).
12. Jean-Loup Amselle, *Logiques métisses: Anthropologie de l'identité en Afrique et ailleurs* (Paris: Payot, 1990). By "mestizo logic" Amselle meant "a continuist approach which... would stress the indistinctness and original syncretism" (10), "a mélange whose parts cannot be dissociated" (248). My approach is different insofar as it concerns the process of construction of mestizo phenomena.
13. Michel Giraud, "La créolité: une rupture en trompe l'oeil," *Cahiers d'études africaines,* 148: XXXVII–4 (1997), 795–811. Giraud's article contains useful bibliographic references.
14. François Laplantine and Alexis Nouss, *Le Métissage* (Paris: Flammarion, 1997). The authors defend a definition of mestizo that is also presented as an ideal: "mestizo means a composition whose components retain their integrity" (8–9). "Mestizo does not mean fusion, cohesion, and osmosis, but rather confrontation and dialogue" (10). I feel that this confines the phenomenon to overly narrow limits that are extremely difficult to establish in practice.
15. Carmen Bernand and Serge Gruzinski, *Histoire du Nouveau Monde,* vol. II, *Les Métissages* (Paris: Fayard, 1993). Also worth mentioning is the pioneering work of Richard Konetzke on biological mestizos in Spanish America, *Lateinamerika: Entdeckung, Eroberung, Kolonisation* (Cologne/Vienna: Böhlau, 1983).

16. Canclini (1990), 15.
17. Offering an assessment, however brief, of research on mestizo phenomena is not the goal of this chapter or book. I will merely raise a few of the issues that guided my reflections.
18. Alfred L. Kroeber, *Culture Patterns and Processes* (New York/London: First Harbinger Books, 1963), 67.
19. First defined by Redfield in 1935, then adopted by many North American researchers, the concept of acculturation was acclimated to France by Alphonse Dupront and Nathan Wachtel. A useful bibliography can be found in Nathan Wachtel, *La Vision des vaincus* (Paris: Gallimard, 1971) [Translated into English by Ben and Sian Reynolds as *The Vision of the Vanquished: The Spanish Conquest of Peru through Native Eyes, 1530–1570* (New York: Barnes & Noble, 1977)].
20. Gonzalo Aguirre Beltrán, *El Proceso de aculturación* (Mexico City: Universidad Iberoamericana, 1970 [1958]).
21. Ibid., 37. In another region of the Americas, namely the Caribbean, the linguistic and cultural synthesis accomplished by the inhabitants of the islands, called creolization, sparked interest in this part of the world by researchers and writers. See Giraud (1997).
22. Gonzalo Aguirre Beltrán, *Medicina y magia El proceso de aculturación en la estructura colonial* (Mexico City: Instituto Nacional Indigenista, 1973), 275–277.
23. Sérgio Figueiredo Ferretti, *Repensando o sincretismo* (São Paulo: Edusp, 1995), 90. Plutarch employed the term syncretism to designate the circumstantial union of individuals ordinarily opposed to one another; Erasmus applied it to the united front formed by humanists and Lutherans; in the seventeenth century it indicated the harmonization of various doctrines and philosophical trends.
24. Figueiredo Ferretti (1995).
25. Ibid., 88.
26. Ibid., 92.
27. See the overview by Alessandro Lupo, "Síntesis controvertidas: Consideraciones en torno a los límites del concepto de sincretismo," *Revista de Antropología Social* 5 (1996), 11–37.
28. Lupo (1996), 23.
29. Marcello Carmagnani, "Adecuación y recreación: cofradías y hermandades de la región de Oaxaca," *L'Uomo*, New Series 2 (1989), 245.
30. Lupo (1996), 12.
31. Figueiredo Ferretti (1995), 89.
32. Compared to the field of history and culture.
33. Julio Ottino, "Le mélange des fluides," *Le Chaos, dossier pour la science*, January 1995, 94.
34. Hugues Neveux, "Les seigneuries françaises et les concepts de *Grund-und-Gutsherrschaft*," *Historie um Eigen-Sinn, Festschrift für Jan Peters zum 65 Geburstag* (Weimar: Verlag Hermann Böhlaus Nachfolger, 1997), 104.
35. Mignolo (1995), xv.
36. James Gleick, *La Théorie du chaos: Vers une nouvelles science* (Paris: Champs/Flammarion, 1991), 277–278 [James Gleick, *Chaos: Making a New Science* (New York: Viking Penguin, 1987)].
37. Ibid., 281.
38. Thus, for example, in Wittgenstein's philosophy, expressed as "forms of reality."
39. This is not the place to offer a history of the concept, much less a review of all its advocates and adversaries. It is nevertheless worth mentioning Ernest Gellner's *Relativism and the Social Sciences* (Cambridge, UK: Cambridge University Press, 1985) and Christopher Herbert's *Culture and Anomie: Ethnographic Imagination in the Nineteenth Century* (Chicago/London: University of Chicago Press, 1991).
40. Amselle (1990) describes the sequence of operations within a culturalist approach that lead to "the selection of decontextualized cultural features and the transcription of discrete social units represented by the various cultures" (10).

41. Laplantine and Nouss (1997), 75. The UN's use of the term "multicultural" to describe France following its victory in the 1998 World Soccer Cup is more indicative of linguistic confusion than of multiculturalism as such.

42. Culture is "an unstable solution whose perpetuation is random by nature" (Amselle [1990], 57).

43. The preoccupation with authenticity and purity is so strong, for that matter, that it stirs even the apostles of "creolity" when they defend "the purity of basilectal creole (a syncretic language par excellence)" or glorify the preservation of an idealized heritage. See Giraud (1997), 803.

44. Michel de Montaigne, *The Complete Essays*, trans. M. A. Screech (London: Penguin, 1991), III: ix, 1115.

45. See Giraud (1997), 795–811.

46. Amselle (1990), 63.

47. On the choice of generic concepts, see Hugues Neveux, *Les Révoltes paysannes en Europe, XIVe–XVIIe siècle* (Paris: Albin Michel, 1997), 56–62.

48. Carmen Bernand and Serge Gruzinski, *De l'idolâtrie: Une archéologie des sciences religieuses* (Paris: Le Seuil, 1988).

49. Neveux (1997), 59: "Via the notion of 'substance,' [Aristotelianism] already tried to understand the world by developing generic concepts which it felt embodied metaphysical realities."

50. The subject of peasant revolts has long remained at the center of historical debate despite the lack of any clear discussion of the choice and limits of the object. Analysis of such movements is primarily geared to defining each revolt through a quality likely to express its specific nature. This ultimately means "postulating for every insurrection a 'crucial quality,' the other [qualities] represent merely masks in the midst of misadventures," according to Hugues Neveux in "Le rôle du 'religieux' dans les soulèvements paysans: L'exemple du pèlerinage de Niklashausen (1476)," *Mouvement populaires et conscience sociale* (Paris: Maloine, 1985), 79.

51. Jean-Yves Grenier, "Projet de candidature à un poste de directeur d'études à l'EHSS: Histoire économique des sociétés préindustrielles," typescript, May 1997, 1.

52. Whereas limiting mélanges to a specific, artificial register—the cultural—means masking their complexity, turning them into phenomena with multiple entries and qualities—the sociopolitical-economic-religious register—runs the risk of replacing the purported explanation of composite reality by a linguistic artifice or conceptual chimera.

53. See Hill (1988), 1–17; Richard Price, *First Time: The Historical Vision of an Afro-American People* (Baltimore, MD: John Hopkins University Press, 1991); Robin Wright, "Aos que vão naszcer: uma etnografía religiosa dos indios Baniwa," typescript dissertation (Campinas: Departamento de Antropologia, IFCH/UNICAM, 1996).

54. Roy Wagner, *L'Invenzione de la cultura* (Milan: Mursia, 1992).

55. Developed by ethnohistory and archaeology.

56. See Mignolo (1995), 23: "Descriptions and explanations of human communication across cultural boundaries confront the scholar with the limits of a linear notion of history and invite him or her to replace it with a nonlinear history." It should be mentioned that "postcolonial studies" are presented as the extension of postmodernist thought in countries that were once colonies of Europe, formerly called the Third World.

57. Ernesto De Martino, *Furore, simbolo, valore* (Milan: Feltrinelli, 1980).

58. The work of Georges E. Sioui, a Wyandot Huron, points in this direction. *Pour une auto-histoire amérindienne: Essais sur les fondements d'une mémoire sociale* (Quebec: Presses de l'Université de Laval, 1989).

59. See the assertions of Edward B. Tylor in *Primitive Culture* (New York: Harper, 1951).

60. The evolutionist vision inspired the idea that globalization of mélange was a preliminary stage of a radical loss of roots and absolute standardization leading to the "global village."

61. Grenier (1997).

62. This state of mind suggests other ideas that continue to influence our worldview. It was long believed that the universe was moving toward a state of perfect equilibrium resulting from the transformation of its energy. Challenges to the Second Law of Thermodynamics and reminders of the irreversibility of time prompted a review of these presuppositions and granted a new meaning to disorder. The model of order that spontaneously governs our thinking now runs up against the evolution of the hard sciences themselves. The awareness of chaos has notably led to new stress on concepts of probability and irreversibility, on the nonlinear effects of linear processes. See Ilya Prigogine and Isabelle Stengers, *Entre le temps et l'éternité* (Paris: Fayard, 1988), 15; and Ilya Prigogine, *Les Lois du chaos* (Paris: Flammarion, 1994).

63. This is notably the case with "dissipating structures" in which the dissipation of energy does not result in entropy but rather in a new order of things, whether they be new structures or other dynamic states.

64. These characteristics defy any narrowly determinist analysis. They relate to Heisenberg's Uncertainty Principle (the impossibility of simultaneously establishing with absolute accuracy both the speed and position of a particle) and the work of Henri Poincaré (1854–1912) showing that minute uncertainties about the initial state of systems are amplified over time, making it impossible to predict the long-term evolution of systems; see Pierre-Gilles de Gennes et al., *L'Ordre du chaos* (Paris: Belin, 1989), 37.

65. Prigogine (1994), 26.

66. An issue also raised by economists: "Many old and recent accounts (both demographic and economic) seem to display a more or less marked random dimension," according to Grenier (1997). See also his *L'Economie d'Ancien Régime: un monde de l'échange et de l'incertitude* (Paris: Albin Michel, 1996), 425.

67. See Jean-Paul Delahaye, "Le complexe surgit-il du simple," *Le Chaos* (1995), 30.

68. It was also during that period that the earliest efforts were made at "global" consideration of major issues—religion, slavery, markets—by relying on data from the entire world. When the Jesuit priest Luis de Molina questioned the legitimacy of slavery, he did not limit his inquiry to the coasts of Angola and America, but drew examples from India, China, Japan, Malacca, and Java. See Luis de Molina, *De justitia et jure* (Venice, 1594), quoted in Carlos Zeron, "La Compagnie de Jésus et l'Institution de l'esclavage au Brésil: les justifications d'ordre historique, théologique et juridique, et leur intégration dans une mémoire historique (XVIe–XVIIe siécle)." Ph.D. dissertation, typescript, EHESS, Paris, 324. On the notion of world trade and "fair price," see Patricia Nettel, *El precio justo o las desaventuras de un confesor en el siglo XVI* (Mexico City: UAM-Xochimilco, 1997), 94.

69. An effort is made here to distinguish between internal dynamics and processes stemming from the confrontation between the West and indigenous societies. There is no question of defining the "nature" of mestizo processes but rather of revealing the mechanisms of construction that operate within an historical situation marked by colonial-type relationships of power.

CHAPTER 3

1. The history of those processes is sketched in Carmen Bernand and Serge Gruzinski, *Histoire du Nouveau Monde*, vol. II, *Les Métissages* (Paris: Fayard, 1993).

2. Serge Gruzinski, *La Colonisation de l'imaginaire: Sociétés indigènes et occidentalisation dans le Mexique espagnol, XVIe–XVIIIe siècle* (Paris: Gallimard, 1988); "Las repercusiones de la conquista: la experiencia novohispana," in C. Bernand, ed., *Descubrimiento, conquista y colonización de América a quinientos años* (Mexico City: FCE, 1994), 148–171.

3. The original French expression ("des mondes renversés") was borrowed from Denys Delâge, *Le Pays renversé: Amérindiens et Européens en Amérique du Nord-Est, 1600–1664* (Quebec: Boréal, 1991). This translation obviously alludes to the tune played by British troops on surrendering at Yorktown in 1781.

4. Toribio de Benavente, called Motolinía, *Memoriales o libro de las cosas de la Nueva España y de los naturales de ella* (Mexico City: UNAM, 1971), 294.

5. "Hirió Dios esta tierra con diez plagas muy crueles por la dureza e obstinación de sus moradores, y por tener cautivas la hijas de Sión, esto es, sus propias ánimas so el yugo de Faraón.... La primera de las cuales fue que ... en uno de sus navios vino un negro herido de viruelas, la cual enfermedad nunca en est tierra se había visto," Ibid., 21.

6. Account from Tlatelolco, published in *Anales de Tlatelolco: Unos annales históricas de la nación mexicana y Códice de Tlatelolco*, trans. by Heinrich Berlin (Mexico City: Porrúa, 1980), 70–71.

7. Motolinía (1971), 25.

8. Ibid., 294.

9. Ibid., 26.

10. Ibid., 29.

11. Ibid., 29.

12. Ibid., 30–31.

13. Luca Signorelli expressed apocalyptic anxieties imported from distant Castile, later taken by Franciscan missionaries to the New World. See Jonathan Riess, *The Renaissance Antichrist: Luca Signorelli's Orvieto Frescoes* (Princeton, NJ: Princeton University Press, 1995).

14. Such terms are not the sole prerogative of monks of old—the approach of the third millennium unleased similar expressions, even if they were no longer based on knowledge of sacred texts. See Omar Calabrese, *Mille di questi anni* (Bari, Italy: Sagittari Laterza, 1992), 59–79.

15. On millenarianism in New Spain, see John L. Phelan, *The Millennial Kingdom of the Franciscans in the New World* (Berkeley, CA: University of California Press, 1970).

16. Motolinía (1971), 31.

17. "Estaban apercebidos de guerra y tenían hechas casas de armas.... En México estaban esperando que los unos desbaratasen a los otros para acabar los que quedasen." Ibid., 29–30.

18. Even supposing, for that matter, they were interchangeable. The dissemination of the Christian time system demanded long preparation—Spanish missionaries had to explain the calendar and rites of the new religion to the Indians, and install the physical setting for Catholic celebrations.

19. "A algunos de los que a estas partes vienen, luego el ayre de la tierra los despierta para novedades y discordias," quoted in Bernand and Gruzinski (1991), I: 263.

20. According to Bartolomé de Las Casas, *Historia de las Indias* [1559] (Mexico City: FCE, 1986), I: 254.

21. "Los más estaban enfermos, y flacos y hambrientos y podían poco por faltarles las fuerzas." Las Casas (1986), 376.

22. Oviedo, quoted in Bernand and Gruzinksi (1991): I. 262.

23. Gonzola Fernández de Oviedo "En aquellos principios si pasava un hombre noble y de clara sangre, venían diz descomedidos y otros de linajes oscuros y baxos." Gonzola Fernández de Oviedo, quoted in Bernand and Gruzinski (1991), I: 262.

24. Antonello Gerbi, *La Naturaleza de las Indias nuevas: De Cristobal Colón a Gonzalo Fernández de Oviedo* (Mexico City: FEC, 1978), 390; Laura de Mello e Souza, *Inferno atlântico: Demonologia e colonização, Seculos XVI–XVIII* (São Paulo: Companhia das Letras, 1993), 89–90.

25. Motolinía (1971), 222.

26. Letter from Diego de Ocaña dated July 31, 1526, *Colección de documentos para la historia de México* (Mexico City: Porrúa, 1971), I: 534.

27. Ibid., and Bernand and Bruzinski (1991), I: 353–356.

28. Susan D. Gillespie (1989), *The Aztec Kings: The Construction of Rulership in Mexica History* (Tucson, AZ: the University of Arizona Press, 1989), 228–230.

29. Letter from Alonso Zuazo dated November 14, 1521, *Colección de documentos*, I: 363; Bernand and Gruzinski (1993), II: 338–342.

30. Two forces tended to temper the destabilizing impact. In the name of the sacrament of marriage, the Church was obliged to regularize mixed unions. Furthermore, Iberian lineage, based on extended and tentacular families, was able to incorporate concubines, orphans, and indigenous bastards in the victors' camp, although in a subordinate station. Yet these forces were precious little against a phenomenon that overwhelmed both the Spaniards and the Indians as it spread.

31. Opinion of Padre Betanzos, *Colección de documentos*, II: 196.

32. Jacques Ruffié, quoted in Bernand and Gruzinski (1991), I: 256.

33. Letter from *contador* Rodrigo de Albornoz to the emperor, *Colección de documentos*, I: 509.

34. Diego Durán, *Historia de las Indias de Nueva España e Islas de la Tierra Firme* (Mexico City: Porrúa, 1967), I: 188.

35. Felipe Guaman Poma de Ayala, *El primer nueva corónica y buen gobierno* [1628] (Mexico City: Siglo XXI, 1980), III: 1025.

36. No one has better described and analyzed Brazil's mestizo mechanisms than historian Sergio Buarque de Holanda. His *Caminhos e fronteiras* (Rio de Janeiro: José Olympio, 1957) scrupulously depicts everyday characters transformed by the experience of the gigantic spaces of the Portuguese territory.

37. Bernal Díaz de Castillo, *Historia verdadera de la conquista de la Nueva España* (Mexico City: Porrúa, 1968), vol. I, 40.

38. Alfredo López Austin, *Cuerpo humano e ideología: Las concepciones de los antiguas nahuas* (Mexico: UNAM, 1980), I: 447–461.

39. On the spread of alphabetic writing and books, see Gruzinksi (1988) and Mignolo (1995).

40. See, for example, the circumstances surrounding the study done by Philip II's doctor, in F. Hernández, *Obras completas* (Mexico City: UNAM, 1960), vols. I and II.

41. Duccio Sacchi, *Mappe del Nuovo Mondo: Cartografie locali e definizione del territorio in Nuova Spagna, Secolo XVI–XVII* (Milan: Franco Angeli, 1997).

42. On the acculturation of the Spanish, see Solange Alberro, *Les Espagnols dans le Mexique colonial: Histoire d'une acculturation* (Paris: Armand Colin, 1992).

43. George Kubler described the fragmentation and decontextualization that affected indigenous art in *Studies in Ancient American and European Art: The Collect Essays of George Kubler*, ed. Thomas E. Reese (New Haven, CT, and London: Yale University Press: 1985), 71.

44. I have borrowed this idea from Omar Calabrese, *La Età neobarocca* (Bari, Italy: Sagittari Laterza, 1997), 132.

45. The first and probably last formal exchanges between Spanish monks and Mexico City's "idol priests"—at the conference of 1524—were reworked and put down in writing several decades after the conference they supposedly document. See Bernardino de Sahagún, *Coloquios y doctrina cristiana*, ed. Miguel León-Portilla (Mexico City: UNAM/ Fundación de Investigaciones Sociales A.C., 1986).

46. Gonzalo Fernández de Oviedo, *Crónica de las Indias: La historia general de las Indias* (Salamanca, Spain: Juan de la Junta, 1547), fol. CLXXXI verso.

47. Motolinía (1971), 37.

48. James Lockhart, *The Nahuas after the Conquest: A Social and Cultural History of the Indians of Central Mexico, Sixteenth through Eighteenth Century* (Stanford, CA: Stanford University Press, 1992).

49. Ronaldo Vainfas, *A heresia dos Indios: catolicismo e rebeldia no Brasil colonial* (São Paulo: Companhia das Letras, 1995).

50. Calabrese (1987), 140.

51. Stuart Schwartz has pointed out that "the process of cultural contact was often 'messy' and undirected, that it changed over time, and that it was interactive in the sense that perceptions and actions influenced each other on both sides of the equation of a cultural encounter." *Implicit Understandings: Observing, Reporting and Reflecting on the Encounters Between Europeans and Other Peoples in the Early Modern Era* (Cambridge, UK: Cambridge University Press, 1994), 6.

52. George M. Foster, *Culture and Conquest: America's Spanish Heritage* (New York: Wenner-Gren Foundation, Viking Fund Publications in Anthology 27, 1960).

CHAPTER 4

1. A first draft of these ideas appeared in my article, "Le strade dell'acculturazione: occidentalizzazione e meticciaggi (secoli XIV–XVII)," in *Storia d'Europa, L'Età moderna: Secoli XVI–XVIII,* ed. Maurice Aymard, (Turin: Einaudi, 1995), IV: 83–122.

2. "Todo un imperio que abrazó en sí tantos reyes y tan varias, ricas y poderosas Provincias, o por mejor decir, una Monarquía la mas estentida y dilatada que se ha visto en el mundo." Juan de Solórzano y Pereyra, *Política indiana* (Madrid, Imprenta Real de la Gazeta, 1776), no. 20.

3. "Universa porro Indorum atque Hispanorum multitudo una eademque respublica habenda iam est...," quoted in José de Acosta, *De procuranda indorum salute* [1588] (Madrid: CSIC, 1984–1987), 516.

4. Javier Gómez Martínez, *Foralezas mendicantes: Claves y procesos en los conventos novohispanos de siglo XVI* (Mexico City: Universidad Iberoamericana, 1997), 100. On this issue, see also Gruzinksi (1988) and (1990), as well as the bibliographies found in Bernand and Gruzinski, I (1991) and II (1993).

5. Antonio Garrido Aranda, *Organización de la Iglesia en el reino de Granada y su proyección en Indias* (Seville: Escuela de Estudios Hispanoamericanos, Universidad de Córdoba, 1980).

6. Vasco de Quiroga, *De debellandis indis,* ed. René Acuña (Mexico City: UNAM, 1988), 57.

7. This was also the case with gateway arches under which neophytes passed. Classical tradition associated such arches with the Roman arch of triumph and to the subjection of defeated peoples. See Valerie Fraser, *The Architecture of Conquest: Building in the Viceroyalty of Peru 1535–1635* (Cambridge: Cambridge University Press, 1990).

8. Gómez Martínez (1997). Meanwhile, the *atrio* designed to host large processions was a replica of the Spanish cloister, having the same function. Often even the layout of a village with its chapels would imitate the arrangement of the *atrio procesional:* "De este modo todo el pueblo de indios enfatizaba el amplio caracter conventual." Gómez Martínez (1997), 122.

9. Serge Gruzinski, *L'Aigle et la sibylle: Fresques indiennes des couvents du Mexique* (Paris: Imprimerie nationale, 1994), 20.

10. Serge Gruzinski, "Confesión, alianze y sexualidad entre los indios de Nueva España: Introducción al estudio de los confesionarios en lenguas indigenas," in *Seminario de Historia de las Mentalidades, El placer de pecar y el afán de normar* (Mexico City: Joanquín Mortiz, 1987), 169–215.

11. See the recommendations by López Medel quoted in Amos Megged, *Exporting the Catholic Reformation: Local Religion in Early-Colonial Mexico* (Leyden/New York/Cologne: E. J. Brill, 1996), 85.

12. The role of Pedro de Gante (Peter of Ghent) among the first contingent of Franciscan evangelizers is well known. This Flemish monk was trained in Northern Europe, where

spirituality was marked by the productions of the Friars Conventual. He developed training techniques aimed at indigenous youths.

13. Motolinía (1971), 240.

14. Ibid., 243. "El oficio que primero hurtaron..." in terms of making garments. To learn and imitate gilding and silvering of leatherwork—*guadameciles*—indigenous craftsmen stole samples of materials and questioned a monk on their origin: "¿Adónde veden esto? Que si nosotros lo habemos, por más que el español se esconda, nosotros haremos guadameciles y les daremos color de doreado y plateado como los maestros de Castilla."

15. Copying occurred in the most varied spheres—for example, the casting of bells according to Spanish models in terms of measures, proportions, and alloys of metals, and also the currying of leather, and the manufacture of bellows (*fuelles*). Motolinía listed with satisfaction the leather goods that local craftsmen produced handily: "zapatos, servillas, borceguíes, alcorques, chapines."

16. Motolinía (1971), 242–243. Copying was done both through minute observation and by the reproduction of tools: "Desde que la lana se lava hasta que sale labrada y tejida en el telar, y cuando los otros indios maestros iban a comer y en las fiestas, los dos tomaban las medidas de todos los instrumentos y herramientas, ansi de peines, tornos, urdinero, como del telar, peines y todo lo demás, que hasta sacar el paño son muchos oficios."

17. Bartolomé de Las Casas, *Apologética historia sumaria* (Mexico City: UNAM, 1967), I: 327.

18. Lockhart (1992), 281: *ehuatlapitzalhuehuetl*, "hide wind-instrument drum."

19. Motolinía (1971), 237.

20. Las Casas (1967), I: 327.

21. Motolinía (1971), 243–244.

22. "Cosen con una pluma o con una paja, o con una púa de metl," Motolinía (1971), 241, 242, 244.

23. Othón Arróniz, *Teatro de evangelización en Nueva España* (Mexico City: UNAM, 1979).

24. Monks in New Spain attempted to reach indigenous audiences by stage shows, the most spectacular of which were given at Tlaxcala and Mexico City in the 1530s. See Fernando Horcasitas, *El teatro náhuatl: Epocas novohispana y moderna* (Mexico City: UNAM, 1974) and Arróniz (1979).

25. Las Casas (1967), I: 328.

26. Motolinía (1971), 92. In many communities, Indians regularly subsituted themselves for the Spanish clergy.

27. "El arte fue dirigido, planificado iconograficamente y finalizado para conseguir las metas precisas," quoted in Sartor (1992), 207.

28. With the possible exception of musical notation.

29. Motolinía was alluding to this when he waxed ecstatic over an Indian's skill at playing the rebec: "Toma con el rabel entre las flautas tiple, y discantaba entre las flautas o sobre las flautas." Motolinía (1979), 237–238.

30. Las Casas (1967), I: 327.

31. Motolinía (1971), 240.

32. Ibid. Las Casas, meanwhile, does not hesitate to compare Flemish art with indigenous Mexican art: "De los oficiales que entre ellos había y hoy hay, pintores de pincel y el primor conque las cosas pintadas que quieren hacen, es ya tan manifiesto y claro que será superfluo decillo por novedad, mayormente después que se dieron a pintar nuestras imágenes, las cuales hacen tan perfectas y con tanta gracia cuanto los más primos oficiales de Flandes y otras cualesquiera naciones las pueden sacar perfeccionadas, y pintores ha habido entre ellos tan señalados que sobre muchos de los señalados donde quiera que se hallasen se pueden señalar." Las Casas (1967), I: 322–323.

33. Bernal Díaz del Castillo, *Historia verdadera de la conquista de la Nueva España* (Mexico City: Porrúa, 1968), I: 275. "Tres indios hay ahora en la ciudad de México tan primísmos en su oficio de entalladores y pintores, que se dicen Marcos de Aquino y Juan de la Cruz

y el Crespillo, que si fueran en el tiempo de aquel antiguo o afamado Apeles, o de Micael Angel, o Berruguete que son de nuestros tiempos, también les pusieran en el número de ellos." See also II: 362: "Se me significaba a mi juicio que aquel tan nombrado pintor como fué el muy antiguo Apeles y de nuestros tiempos que se decían Berruguete y Miguel Angel, ni de otoro moderno ahora nuevamente muy nombrado, natural de Burgos,... en cual tiene gran fama como Apeles, no harán con sus muy sutiles pinceles las obras de los esmeriles ni relicarios que hacen los tres indios maestros de aquel oficio, mexicanos, que se dicen Andrés de Aquino y Juan de la Cruz y el Crespillo."

34. Las Casas (1967) I: 328.
35. Michael Baxandall, *Painting and Experience in Fifteenth-Century Italy* (Oxford: Oxford University Press, 1986), 45–46.
36. And yet the gap with Europe quickly narrowed. As Old World painters began adopting the habit of relying on engravings in books more than on the slow stylistic evolution of local tradition, artists from both worlds wound up being exposed to fairly similar working conditions: the availability of engraved models tended to take precedence over other traditions.
37. Bernand and Gruzinski, *Histoire du Nouveau Monde* (1991 and 1993); Wachtel (1971).
38. I write mimetic "dynamics" rather than mimetic "logic" of Westernization, since the latter would imply an automatic, rational, indeed ineluctable dimension that the sources refute.
39. Gruzinski (1990), 180–221.
40. The colonization of the New World can be viewed as a varied process of copying, imitation, duplication, reproduction, and representation. From this angle at least, the relationship between Europe and the Americas is similar to the one between an original and a copy. But nothing is more complex than a relationship of this type, which implies a dependence that may change with time, evolving from the most total submission to a reversal of roles, indeed an irreversible break. As to duplications of an original, they are likely to occur in the most diverse forms: the production of doubles, the development of true copies or imperfect, hasty, incomplete replicas, the subversion or neutralization of the frame of reference, or even—in extreme cases—capture and reversal. These comments probably apply to other instances of Westernization, the case of Japan and Czarist Russia coming immediately to mind, even if the pace, forms, and stages differ from one context to another.
41. Gerónimo de Mendieta, *Historia eclesiástica indiana* [1596] (Mexico City: Porrúa, 1971), 422, and Gómez Martínez (1997), 100.
42. There were incidents of human incarnations of divinities throughout the colonial period. See Gruzinski (1985).
43. Nancy M. Farris, *Maya Society under Colonial Rule: The Collective Enterprise of Survival* (Princeton, NJ: Princeton University Press, 1984); Grant D. Jones, *Maya Resistance to Spanish Rule: Time and History on a Colonial Frontier* (Albuquerque, NM: University of New Mexico Press, 1989).

CHAPTER 5

1. One exception is the book by Constantino Reyes-Valerio, *El pintor de conventos: Los murales del siglo XVI en la Nueva España* (Mexico City: INAH, 1989), which includes a bibliography of publications prior to the 1990s.
2. On pre-Hispanic techniques and pre-Conquest painters, see *Fragmentos del pasado: Murales prehispánicos* (Mexico City: INAH, Antiguo Colegio de San Ildefonso/UNAM, Instituto de Investigaciones Estéticas, 1998).

3. See Gruzinski (1990) and, for iconographical evidence, Gruzinski (1992a) and (1994a).

4. Little is known of those artists: a few names, the probable existence of teams traveling across the vast distances between monasteries of a given order, and, in each indigenous population center, the presence of a *tlacuilo* able to paint maps at Spanish request. See Reyes-Valerio (1989) and Gruzinski (1994).

5. Based on a description in the French press kit, reprinted in *Virgin Mégapress* (February 13, 1997) 39. See also Sei Shônagon, *The Pillow Book,* trans. and ed. Ivan Morris (New York: Columbia University Press, 1991).

6. One couple is mixed and heterosexual (Nagiko is Japanese, her lover is Western), another is mixed and homosexual (a Japanese publisher and the same Westerner). The European's bisexuality weaves a physical link between Nagiko and the publisher.

7. Peter Greenaway, *The Pillow Book* (Paris: Dis Voir, 1996), 32.

8. On this score, the decadent magnificence of *The Last Emperor* perpetuated a tradition embodied by *The Lady from Shanghai* and *55 Days at Peking.*

9. Although Takeshi Kitano's films have explicitly "stemmed from a reaction" to the Westernization of Japan, that is not what makes the couple's voyage toward nothingness so moving in *Hana-Bi.* The regular associations of death induced by this film relate to the same shattered universe as *Breaking the Waves* (1996) by Danish filmmaker Lars von Trier and *Crash* (1996) by Canadian director David Cronenberg.

10. The calligraphic devices adorning the illustrations of Peruvian chronicler Guaman Poma, elaborated in the early seventeenth century and also astride two worlds, are no more gratuitous than those of Peter Greenaway.

11. Alfonso Arrellano, *La Casa del Deán: Un ejemplo de pintura mural civil del siglo XVI en Puebla* (Mexico City: UNAM, 1996). The best study remains an article by Erwin Walter Palm, "El sincretismo emblemático de los Triunfos de la Casa del Deán en Puebla," *Comunicaciones: Proyecto Puebla-Tlaxcala* (Puebla: Fundación Alemana para la Investigación Científica, 1973), VIII: 57–62. An initial version of the analysis developed here appeared in "Entre monos y centauros: Los indios pintores y la cultura del renacimiento," in *Entre dos mundos: Fronteras culturales y agentes mediadores,* ed. Berta Ares Queija and Serge Gruzinski (Seville: Escuela de Estudios Hisponamericanos, 1997), 349–371.

12. The subject of Petrarch's *Triumphs* could already be found in the Flemish tapestries in the church of Colegio de Niñas in Mexico City, which the inventory dates back to 1572. See Sartor (1992), 278.

13. This manuscript, now in the J. Paul Getty Museum in Brentwood, is reproduced in Michael Camille, *The Margins of Medieval Art* (London: Reaktion Books, 1992), 156.

14. Bernardino de Sahagún, *Códice florentino* (Mexico City: AGN, 1979), III: xi, fol. 9 verso.

15. Ibid., fol. 14 verso.

16. Michel Graulich, *Mythes et rituels du Mexique ancien préhispanique* (Brussels: Académie royale de Belgique, 1982), 75. Monkeys were therefore survivors of a previous humanity: "Olvidados del uso de razón, perdieron la habla y... quedaron de la manera que ahora los vemos que no les falta otra cosa sino la habla (y quedaron mudos) para ser hombres perfectos," quoted in Diego Muñoz Carmagro, "Descripción de la cuidad y provincia de Tlaxcala," *Relaciones geográficas del siglo XVI: Tlaxcala,* ed. René Acuña (Mexico City: UNAM, 1984), 202. Information on pre-Columbian monkeys can be found in Motolinía's *Memoriales,* in *Histoire du Mechique,* in *Leyenda de los Soles,* and in *Anales de Cuauhtitlán.*

17. Several species fit the description of this monkey: *Alouatta palliatia mexicana, A. villosa mexicana, Ateles neglectus,* and so on. See Bernardino de Sahagún, *Historia general de las cosas de Nueva España,* ed. Alfredo López Austin and Josefina García Guintana (Mexico City: Banamex, 1982), II: 704.

18. See the *Codex Fejérvary-Mayer*, published by Miguel León-Portilla under the title of *Livre astrologique des marchands* (Paris: La Différence, 1992), xxxi, xli. In the *Codex Magliabechiano*, fol. 56, an Indian dressed in the skin of an *ozomatli* monkey ("en su lengua cuçumate") accompanies the *pulque* god. The *Codex Vaticanus A*, fol. 6 r., shows three monkeys set in the midst of whirlwinds.

19. Durán (1967), I: 230. In the *Popol Vuh*, monkeys—"those people of yore"—were honored by artists; see Graulich (1982), 144.

20. Sahagún (1977), I: 349–350. On the baroque use of Peruvian monkeys in colonial Andean art, see Gisbert and Mesa (1997), 329–331.

21. Another possible candidate is *Heimia salicifolia* or *sinicuichi*. Ancient Mexicans associated *ozomatli* monkeys with the *ocumaxochitl* flower, offered to monarchs and gods "esperando que por este solo obsequio obtendrán de ellos abondantes gracias," according to Francisco Hernández, *Historia natural de Nueva España: Obras completas* (Mexico City: UNAM, 1959), I: lxviii, 391. It resembles the flower of the *Huacalxochitl*: "Se ofrecían en ramilletes a los heroes y a los que llamaban tlatoani porque solo a ellos les era permitido hablar en las asembleas." Ibid., I: lxv, 390. See also Robert Gordon Wasson, *The Wondrous Mushroom: Mycolatry in Meso-America* (New York: McGraw-Hill, 1980), 66–67 and 88–91; *Codex Magliabechiano*, fol. 83 r., for a picture of *ololiuhqui*; Doris Heyden, *Mitología y simbolismo de la flora en el México prehispánico* (Mexico City: UNAM, 1983), 31–34.

22. True enough, the church of Santa Maria Maggiore in Bergamo, Italy, features a marquetry inlay with an equally strange subject: a monkey and a female centaur-lioness flank Fortune's billowing sail. This *impresa*, or emblem, designed by artist Lorenzo Lotto, apparently alludes to the various states of mercury. See Mauro Zanchi, *Lorenzo Lotto et l'imaginaire alchimique: Les "imprese" dans les marqueteries du choeur de la basilique de Sainte-Marie-Majeure à Bergame* (Bergamo, Italy: Ferrari Editrice, 1998).

23. The frescoes cover the side walls of the nave and borders (*cenfas*).

24. On the etymological possibilities behind the name Ixmiquilpan (or Itzmiquilpan), see Alicia Albornoz Bueno, *La Memoria del olvida: El lenguaje del tlacuilo, Glifos y murales de la Iglesia de San Miguel Arcángel, Ixmiquilpan, Hidalgo. Teopan dedicado a Tezcatlipoca* (Pachuca: Universidad Autónoma de Hidalgo, 1994), 14–15.

25. Such as Saint Denis and Saint John the Baptist.

26. One character seen from the back is wearing Spanish-style shorts, which might have been a later addition designed to mask the naked buttocks, whereas another seems to wearing a kind of ancient Greek chlamys, or short cloak.

27. An example can be found in the *Tlatelolco Codex*; see Robert H. Barlow, "El Códice de Tlatelolco," in Heinrich Berlin, *Anales de Tlatelolco: Unos annales históricos de la Nación Mexicana y Códice de Tlatelolco* (Mexico City, 1948), 105–128.

28. No fewer than five eagles are found inside the church, including one with wings spread wide.

29. Albornoz Bueno (1994), 58.

30. Tezcatlipoca was lord of the thirteen-day calender cycle. The sign for the first day of the month of Quecholli, which shows Camaztli, God of the Hunt, also included three arrows pointed downward. See Durán (1967), I: xvii, 281.

31. The same ambiguity surfaces in one of the chapels, where the quails of Saint Nicholas of Tolentino are the same that were sacrificed to Tezcatlipoca.

32. Bernardino de Sahagún, *Florentine Codex*, trans. Charles E. Dibble and Arthur J. Anderson (Santa Fe, NM: School of American Research, University of Utah, 1951), II: 46, quoted and discussed in Yolotl González Torres, *El sacrificio humano entre los Mexicas* (Mexico City: FCE, 1985), 281. See also Ross Hassig, *Aztec Warfare: Imperial Expansion and Political Control* (Norman, OK, and London: University of Oklahoma

Press, 1988), 119. The *Codex de Huamantla* shows a victor holding his captive by the hair, without having cut off the head (other examples can be seen in Gónzalez Torres [1985], 216–217). Decapitation occurred only after the sacrifical killing and removal of the victim's heart.

33. Such is the case of the interpretation offered by Albornoz Bueno (1994).

34. The interweaving paths taken by cosmic forces were known as *malinalli*. See Lopez Austin (1980), I: 67–68, as well as his "Algunas ideas acerca del tiempo mítico entre los antiguos nahuas," *Historia, religión, escuelas* XIII (Mexico City: Sociedad Mexicana de Antropología, 1975), 296.

35. An arrow sticking in the leg of a warrior lying on the ground made be read as *temiminaloyan*, "the place where arrows are shot," meaning the ninth heaven or heaven of Tezcatlipoca. See Albornoz Bueno (1994), 90.

36. Motolinía (1971), 107.

37. Arturo Warman, *La Danza de Moros y Cristianos* (Mexico City: SepSetentas, 1972).

38. Gruzinski (1994), 54–61.

39. Juan Pomar, "Relación de Texcoco," *Relaciones geográficas del siglo XVI: Mexico*, ed. René Acuña (Mexico City: UNAM, 1986), 93.

40. Ovid, *Metamorphoses*, Book IV, trans. Garth, Dryden, et al. (London, 1826).

41. Ibid.

CHAPTER 6

1. Irving Leonard, *Los libros del Conquistador* (Mexico City: FCE, 1996), 144, 178, 212 [*Books of the Brave* (Cambridge, MA: Harvard University Press, 1949)].

2. "Confessou que tem Ovídio de *metamorfogis* [sic] em linguagem," quoted in the "Confession of Nuno Fernandes," February 1592, *Confissões da Bahia*, ed. Ronaldo Vainfas (São Paulo: Companhia das Letras, 1997), 300.

3. Michel Jeanneret, *Perpetuum mobile: Métamorphoses des corps et des oeuvres de Vinci à Montaigne* (Paris: Macula, n.d.) 124; Leonard Barkhan, *The Gods Made Flesh: Metamorphosis and the Pursuit of Paganism* (New Haven, CT, 1986), quoted in Jonathan Bate, *Shakespeare and Ovid* (Oxford: Clarendon Paperbacks, 1998), 25.

4. Jean Seznec, *La Survivance des dieux antiques* (Paris: Flammarion, 1993), 311. On the presence of Ovid in schools, see Bate (1998), 22. Ovid's *Metamorphoses* was the first book read by Montaigne, at the age of seven.

5. Julián Gallego, *Visión y símbolo en la pintura española del Siglo de Oro* (Madrid: Catedra, 1987), 39.

6. Humberto Maldonado, *Hombres y letras del virreinato, Homenaje a H.M.* (Mexico City: UNAM, 1995), 208. See M. Menéndez Pelayo, *Bibliografía hispano-latina clásica* (Santander, 1951),VII: 81 ff., for Spanish editions of Ovid, cited in Gallego (1987), 39. Worth mentioning are an early Castilian edition published in Antwerp by Juan Steelsio in 1551, followed by others in Bruges (1557) and Toledo (1558). Additional Spanish translations were issued by Antonio Pérez (1580), Felipe Mey (1586), and Sánchez de Viana (1589). On sixteenth-century mythological paintings, whether inspired by Ovid or not, see Gallego (1987), 50–51.

7. Antonio Tritonio, *Mythologia, fabulosa exempla....* (Bologna, 1560).

8. Leonard (1996), 193. Vainfas (1997), 99; *Diana* was written by Jorge Montemayor in 1559, (Confession by Bartolomeu Fragoso, in August 1591).

9. Seznec (1993), 305. Abridged and illustrated versions of the *Metamorphoses* include Gabriello Symeoni, *La vita ef* [sic] *metamorfoseo d'Ovidio* (Lyon: 1584) and an album by

Tempesta, *Metamorphoseon sive Transformationum Ovidii Libri XV* (Amsterdam, 1606).

10. On the influence of Ovid on the chronicler Oviedo, see Antonello Gerbi, *La Naturaleza de las Indias nuevas* (Mexico City: VCE, 1978), 450. In 1567, laypeople such as the second marquess of Valle were reading Ovid, according to Georges Baudot, *Utopie et Histoire au Mexique: Les premiers chroniqueurs de la civilisation mexicaine, 1520–1569* (Toulouse: Privat, 1977), 501 n. 76. Diego de Cisneros quoted him in 1618; see the *Boletín de la Biblioteca Nacional* (Mexico City, 1968), XVIII–1/4, 118.

11. Under the title *P. Ovidii Nasonis tam de tristibus quam de Ponto*. See Osorio Romero, *Colegios y profesores jesuitas que enseñaron latín en Nueva España, 1572–1767* (Mexico City: UNAM, 1979), 30.

12. For example, see the 1605 *Poeticarum Institutionum Liber* by Bernardino de Llanos, cited in Osorio Romero (1979), 75.

13. Ludovico Dolce, *Le trasformationi tratte da Ovidio* (Venice, 1554). In his edition of 1568, Dolce offers allegorical explanations for each book of the *Metamorphoses*; see Gallego (1987), 71.

14. Bate (1998), 10.

15. Gallego (1987), 72.

16. See page 76 of *Diálogos de Amor*, Garcilaso de la Vega's 1590 translation of León Hebreo's *Dialoghi d'amore*, ed. Miguel de Burgos Nuñez (Seville: Padilla Libros, 1989).

17. Miguel Mathes, *Santa Cruz de Tlatelolco: la primera biblioteca académica de las Américas* (Mexico City: Secretaría de Relaciones Exteriores, 1982), 32, 33, 58, 64, 65. Indians could also find allusions to mythology in Boethius's *De consolatione philosophiae*; see Gallego (1987), 76.

18. Letter from Jerónimo López to the emperor (Mexico City, October 20, 1541), in *Collección de documentos*, II; 149–150.

19. Osorio Romero (1990), 13.

20. "As the famous Ovid says in the third book of his *Art*."

21. During the same period, Jeronimo Ruscelli compared Philip II to Phoebus Apollo in his royal dedication to *Imprese illustri*, published in Venice by Francisco Rampazetto in 1566; see Gallego (1987), 47.

22. Gruzinski (1988), 86.

23. Probably the Latin compilation of Accursius, *Aesop Fabulae graece [sic] et latine* (1479). See Gordon Brotherston (ed.), *Aesop in Mexico: Die Fabeln des Aesop in aztekischer Sprache. A Sixteenth-Century Aztec Version of Aesop's Fables* (Berlin: Gebr. Mann Verlag, 1987), as well as Brotherston's *Book of the Fourth World: Reading the Native Americas through Their Literature* (Cambridge, UK: Cambridge University Press, 1992), 315.

24. A description of the cenotaph was published in Fernando Cervantes de Salazar, *Túmulo imperial de la gran ciudad de México* (Mexico City: Antonio de Espinosa, 1560).

25. Joaquín García Icazbalceta, *Bibliografia mexicana del siglo XVI* (Mexico City: FCE, 1981), 173; Guillermo Tovar de Teresa, *Bibliografia novohispana de arte: Primera parte, Impresos mexicanos relativos al arte de los siglos XVI y XVIII* (Mexico City: FCE, 1988), 34. On the forms and dissemination of mythological paintings, see Gallego (1987).

26. "En poner los indios en la pulicia de la lengua latina, [the monks made them] leer ciencias donde han venido a saber todo el principio de nuestra vida por los libros que leen, e de dónde procedemos e cómo fuemos sojuzgados de los romanos e convertidos a la fe de gentiles e todo lo demás que se escribío en este caso que les causa decir que también nosotros venimos de gentiles e fuemos sujetos e ganados e sojuzgados e fuemos sujetos a los romanos e nos alsamos e rebelamos e fuemos convertidos al bautismo tanto número

mayor de años y aun no somos buenos cristianos." Letter from Jerónimo López to the emperor (Mexico City, February 25, 1545), in Francisco del Paso y Troncoso, *Epistolario de Nueva España* (Mexico City: Antigua Librería Robredo, 1939), IV (1540–1546): 169.

27. The eagle and jaguar, whether painted inside the church or carved in medallions on the outer façade, form a pair impossible to overlook.

28. Sahagún (1977), I: 146. The church consecrated to Saint Michael may have perhaps been built on the site of a temple to Tezcatlipoca; see Albornoz Bueno (1994), 19.

29. These are cruelly lacking for Ixmiquilpan. We will return later (Chapters 10 and 11) to the Indian "songs" of the colonial period, whose mestizo qualities offer several analogies with those found in the paintings.

30. Ovid (1826), Book XII.

31. "Quauhtla chane." See Sahagún (1979), XI: fol. 14 verso.

32. Ovid (1826), Book II.

33. Serge Gruzinski, "Vision et christianisation: L'expérience mexicaine," in *Visions indiennes, visions baroques: Les métissages de l'inconscient,* ed. Jean-Michel Sallman (Paris: PUF, 1992), 117–149. See also Aguirre Beltrán (1973), *passim.*

34. In the *Florentine Codex,* a man on his knees smells a hallucinogenic plant—datura—and begins to speak. See Heyden (1983), 133.

35. On the relationship of ornamentation to main motif, and on its role as support for "the celebration of a meaning or function," I am much indebted to the work of Jean-Claude Bonne.

36. Seznec (1993), 308–309.

37. Ibid., 376.

38. Seznec (1993), 312; A. W. A. Boschloo, *Annibale Carraci in Bologna: Visible Reality in Art after the Council of Trent* (The Hague, 1974).

39. Seznec (1993), 313–319.

40. *Philosophia secreta donde debajo de historias fabulosas se contiene mucha doctrina provechosa a todos los estudios, con el origen de los ídolos o dioses de la gentilidad.* In the next century, according to Gallego (1987), 38, "la fábula clásica sigue ... rodeada de una multitud de comentadores y de deformadores que casi ahogan a veces a Hómero, Virgilio, Horacio, Ovidio y al dominante Cicerón." The library of Diego Velázquez included two editions of Ovid's *Metamorphoses,* one in Spanish and the other in Italian, as well as Pérez de Moya's *Philosophia secreta* (Ibid., 34–35).

41. Muñoz Camargo (1984), 47–48; Serge Gruzinski, "Le premier centenaire de la découverte du Nouveau Monde: Témoignages de la Nouvelle-Espagne," in *Mémoires en devenir, Amérique latine XIVe–XXe siècle,* (Bordeaux: Maison des pays ibériques, 1994), 86–89.

42. Sartor (1992), 215.

43. Durán (1967), I: 10; Carrasco (1982), 56–58. The glorification of the Texcoco monarch Nezahualcoyotl as a man wiser than "the divine Plato" was an example; see Fernando de Alva Ixtlilxóchitl, *Obras históricas,* ed. Edmundo O'Gorman (Mexico City: UNAM, 1975), I: 404–405.

44. Seznec (1993), 283, 306–307; Cartari (1556); Conti (1551).

45. His sources figure in Las Casas (1967), I: cxxiii–clxi (*De Deorum Imaginibus de Albricus, Mitholagiarum Libri de Fulgence,* Ovid's *Fasti,* etc).

46. C. Bernand and S. Gruzinksi, *De l'idolatrie: Une archéologie des sciences religieuses* (Paris: Seuil, 1988), 41–74. The project was announced and stressed on several occasions: "Como parecerá cuando cotejaremos ... los dioses de las otras gentes antiguas a los de estas modernas" (Las Casas [1967], I: 369), and "Resta cotejar los dioses de los unos a los de los otros" (I: 663).

47. Ibid., I: 632.

48. Ibid., I: 416, 565; see also Las Casas's *Historia de las Indias* (1986), I: 59 (Tiphys the helmsman) and II: 54 (Arethusa the spring).

49. See the comments by Angel María Garibay K. on the Palacio manuscript, in Sahagún (1977), I: 36–37. It is known that Saint Isidore of Seville's *Etymologies*, with the illustrations of the various manuscripts, played a significant role in spreading knowledge of mythology.

50. Ibid., I: 43, 50, 56, 91.

51. Sahagún (1979), fol. 10 recto–12 verso.

52. Another comparison, with the god Mars, can be found in Durán (1967), I: 15.

53. "Da noi sono stati chiamati col nome de dei," Polidoro Virgilio, *Degli inventori delle cose, libri otto* (Florence, 1592).

54. Michel Jeanneret, *Perpetuum mobile: Métamorphoses des corps et des oeuvres de Vinci à Montaigne* (Paris: Macula, n.d.), 33.

55. Alessandra Russo, *Les Formes de l'art indigène au Mexique sous la domination espagnole au XVIe siècle: Le Codex Borbonicus et le Codex Durán* (Paris: DEA thesis, École des Hautes Études en Sciences Sociales, 1997), 51.

56. Seznec (1993), 311.

57. Meaning might be supplied after the fact, by an explanatory text or inscriptions incorporated into the work. An example of this descriptive, decoding literature can be found in the passages that Luis de Cisneros devoted to the church of Los Remedios in the Valley of Mexico City: *Historia del principio origen... de la santa imagen de Nuestra Señora de los Remedios* (Mexico City: Juan Blanco de Alcaçar, 1621).

58. See Pablo Nazareo's letter to Philip II in Osorio Romero (1990), 11–12.

59. Christoph Ransmayr, *The Last World*, trans. John E. Woods (New York: Grove/Weidenfeld, 1990).

60. Ransmayr further explored this theme in *The Dog King* (New York: Knopf, 1997), where the oppressive atmosphere is not unlike the one in Lars von Trier's *Europa*.

61. In the cloister at Actopan, monkeys with the heads of demons sit in leaves forming the *nahui-ollin* sign found in the *Codex Cospi* and *Codex Borgia* (Reyes-Valerio [1978], 258) as well as on colonial-period buildings at Yautepec (Ibid., 242). See Luis MacGregor, *Actopan* (Mexico City: INAH, 1982), 109.

62. Seznec (1993), 315.

63. Ibid., 319.

64. Augusto Gentili, *Da Tiziano a Tiziano: Mito e allegoria nella cultura veneziana del cinquecento* (Milan: Feltrinelli, 1980).

65. Philip Brady on Heiner Müller's *Theatremachine* (Faber, 1995) in the *Times Literary Supplement* (December 8, 1995), 18.

CHAPTER 7

1. Palm (1973), 57, quoted in Arrellano (1996), 78.

2. On Peter Greenaway, see David Pascoe, *Peter Greenaway, Museums and Moving Image* (London: Reaktion Books, 1997).

3. This parody of Ovid's *Metamorphoses* includes only ninety-two hybrids instead of one hundred, because a weary Theseus puts an early end to the Minotaur's tale.

4. Peter Greenaway, *Prospero's Books* (New York: Four Walls Eight Windows, 1991), 57. Hamadryads are wood nymphs (Virgil).

5. Philippe Morel, *Les Grotesques: Les figures de l'imaginaire dans la peinture italienne de la fin de la Renaissance* (Paris: Flammarion, 1997), 84.

6. Cesare Ripa, *Iconologia*, ed. Piero Buscaroli (Milan: Editori Associati, [1593] 1992), André Alciat [Andrea Alciati], *Les Emblèmes* [facsimile of the 1551 Lyon edition] (Paris, Klincksieck, 1997).

7. As Allesandro Bencivenni and Anna Samueli point out in *Peter Greenaway: Il cinema delle idee* (Genoa: Le Mani, 1996), 128, "in *L'ultimat tempesta* una delle principali aree di interesse è quella per le scienze ermetiche des rosacrociani. Vi sono rappresentatti Paracelso, Bruno e i principali filosofi dell'inizio del diciasettesimo secolo que erano interessati a creare una visione globale del mondo...."

8. Mannerism but not baroque, as asserted somewhat too hastily by critics; see Ibid., 95.

9. André Chastel, *La Grottesque: Essai sur l'ornement sans nom* (Paris: Le Promeneur, 1988); Nicole Dacos, *La Découverte de la Domus Aurea et la formation des grotesques à la Renaissance* (London and Leyden: The Warburg Institute, 1969).

10. By dispersing Roman artists, the sack of Rome in 1527 gave further impetus to the phenomenon. See André Chastel, *Le Sac de Rome* (Paris: 1972).

11. "Le grottesche sono una specie di pittura licenziosa e ridicola molto, fatta dagli antichi per ornamento di vani, dove in alcuni luoghi non stava bene altro che cose in aria; per il che facevano in quelle tutte sconciature di mostri per stranezza della natura e per gricciolo e ghiribizzo delgi artefici." Giorgio Vasari, *Le Vite dè piú eccelenti architetti, pittori et scultori italiani, da Cimabue insino à giorni nostri* [1550], (Turin, 1991), 73.

12. Antonio Pinelli, *La Bella maniera: Artisti del cinquecento tra regola e licenza* (Turin: Einaudi, 1993), 83.

13. Ibid., 155.

14. See, for example, the courtyard of the Infantado in Guadalajara designed by Juan Guas, with its decor of griffons, eagles, and lions.

15. Kubler (1984), 473–474. See also Jonathan Brown, *The Golden Age of Painting in Spain* (New Haven, CT: Yale University Press, 1991).

16. *Historia de la orden de San Jerónimo* (Madrid, 1600–1605), cited in Gallego (1987), 68.

17. Zahira Veliz, *Artists' Techniques in Golden-Age Spain: Six Treatises in Translation* (Cambridge, UK Cambridge University Press, 1986), 57.

18. Sartor (1992), 70.

19. Guillermo Tovar de Teresa, *Pintura y escultura en Nueva España, 1557–1640* (Mexico City: Azabache, 1992), 61; Jorge Alberto Manrique, *Manierismo en Nueva España* (Mexico City: Textos Dispersos Ediciones, 1993).

20. "Eran tan dados a la curiosidad de ellos [los templos] que los había en todos los pueblos, así grandes como pequeños, muy hermosos y curiosos y adornados de toda la mas hermosura que su entendimento podía alcanzar y después de ser cristianos es tanto lo que en ellos se han esmerado que pone admiración." Juan de Torquemada, quoted in Joaquín García Icazbalceta, *Nueva colección de documentos para la historia de México* (Mexico City: Díaz de León, 1986–1992), II: xcix, 174–175, cited in Gómez Martínez (1997), 107.

21. "Antes no sabían pintar sino una flor o un pájaro o un labor como romano, e si pintaban un hombre o un caballo, hacíanlo tan feo que parecía un monstro," Motolinía (1971), 240.

22. Motolinía (1971), 242. "Cuantos romanos y bestiones han visto, todo lo hacen." The regulations of 1557, issued at the request of painters in Mexico City, stipulated that fresco painters had to be "examinados en las cosas siguientes de lo Romano y de follajes y figuras," Toussaint (1982), 221.

23. G. Estarda, *Ordenazas de gremios de la Nueva España* (Mexico, 1921), cited in Turrent (1993), 151.

24. Toussaint (1982), 37.

25. Kubler (1984), 436.

26. Several richly decorated examples of sixteenth-century Spanish book illustration can be found in James P.R. Lyell, *Early Book Illustration in Spain* (New York: Hacker Art Books, 1976), 171, 183, 211, 241.

27. Many books printed in New Spain contained illustrations, decoration, and ornate initial letters in the grotesque style. By way of example, see the frontispieces to Alonso de la Veracruz's *Dialectica* (1554) and *Physica*, published in Mexico City by Juan Pablos, an engraving of Saints Peter and Paul in the *Graduel* published by Antonio de Espinosa in 1576, and the initial letters used by printers Pierre Ochart and Pedro Balli. See García Icazbalceta (1981) and Jesús Yhmoff Cabrera, *Los Impresos mexicanos del siglo XVI en la Biblioteca nacional de México* (Mexico City: UNAM, 1989). It is also worth studying several fine frontispieces reproduced in *Impresos mexicanos del siglo XVI* (Mexico City: Condumex, 1995), especially pages 27 (*Vocabulario en lengua de Mechuacán* by Maturino Gilberti, 1559), 33 (*Dialectica resolutio* by Alonso de la Veracruz, 1554), 61 (*Provisiones e Cédulas,* 1563), and 67 (*Confesionario mayor* by Alonso de Molina, 1578).

28. Irving Leonard, "On the Mexican Book Trade, 1576," *Hispanic Review* XVII (1949): 10–20.

29. See Lyell (1976), 19–20: *Tirant lo Blanch* (Valencia: Nicolas Spindeler, 1490); *Constitucions fets per D. Fernando* (Barcelona: Juan Rosembach, 1494); Antonio de Nebrija, *Grammaticae introductiones* (Barcelona: Juan Rosembach, 1500).

30. A fairly similar engraving accompanied Saint Bonaventure's *Instructio Novitiorum* (Montserrat: J. Lischner, 1499), found in Lyell (1976), 98.

31. Morel (1997), 136, no. 29.

32. Ibid., 82, no. 138.

33. Fabienne Emilie Hellendoorn, *Influencia del manierismo-nórdico en la arquitectura vir-reinal religiosa de México* (Delft: UNAM, 1980), 6.

34. Other examples of such combinations could be found in the privacy of books or monastery walls. Ambrosio Montesino's *Cancionero* (Seville, 1537) juxtaposes an image of a bishop reading the Holy Scripture with two borders of freakish figures. The grotesques at Actopan even invaded the monks' cells (MacGregor [1982], 151–152) as well as appearing on the main staircase in the form of fantastic animals and a cherub armed with a club (the infant Hercules, 140); still others, of more conventional form, adorned the loggia of the refectory (125).

35. *Doctrina christiana en lengua huasteca* (Mexico City: Pedro Ocharte, 1571).

36. Giorgio Vasari, quoted in Pinelli (1993), 133.

37. Alessandro Cecchi, "Pratica, fierezza e terribilità nelle grotesche di Marco da Faenza in Palazzo Vecchio a Firenze," *Paragone* 327 (1977): 25.

38. Grotesques became the *sogno dei pittori*, which was a "metaphor for outrunning nature" according to Pinelli (1993), 133.

39. Quoted in Morel (1997), 87.

40. Gabriele Paleotti, "Discorso intorna alle immagini sacre e profane," ed. P. Barocchi, *Trattati d'arte del cinquecento fra manierismo e controriforma* (Bari, Italy [1581–1582], 1960), II: ii, 37–42.

41. Veliz (1986), 59. Pacheco, in *Arte de la pintura* (published posthumously in 1649) remained inflexible: even when cherubs, seraphim, and fruit displayed basic decency, artists had to beware of overdoing them—they were to be used only in borders, frames, and draperies, where they could be generally appreciated.

42. Both traditions stem from deliberate choices and not from any inability to copy reality. The work of indigenous sculptors prior to the Conquest proves that Mexican artists were perfectly capable of rivaling the figurative realism of the Italian Renaissance.

43. Whereas grotesques deliberately violated Alberti's compositional rules by raising "discontinuity and disjointedness to the rank of a principle" (Morel [1997], 88), the same was not true of codices, which obeyed rules of spatial organization completely independent of the Alberti-based model.

44. On Mexican objects in Renaissance Italy, see Detlef Heikamp, *Mexico and the Medici* (Florence: Edam, 1972) and Laura Laurencich Minelli, "Museografia americanista in Italia dal secolo XVI fina a oggi," *Bulletin des musées royaux d'Art et d'Histoire* 63 (Brussels, 1992) 233–239. Historians have also shown interest in the museum begun by Ulisse Aldovrandi, a doctor, naturalist, and collector, in Bologna in 1549.

45. See the chapter on "I costumi teatrali per gli Intermezzi del 1589—I disegni di Bernardo Buontalenti e il 'libro di conti' di Emilio de' Cavalieri" in Aby Warburg, *La Rinascita del paganesimo antico* (Florence: La Nuova Italia Editrice, 1996), 59–107.

46. In *La Guerre des images* (1990), I reduced European imagery to a figurative, "realist," and anthropomorphic model based on imitation and illusion, thereby overlooking the approach described here. I emphasized the ruptures and differences beween the two worlds at the risk of caricaturizing them, and I also stressed the influence of northern artists at the expense of Italian influence; I now feel that the past was more complex.

47. Such as stucco molds, traced patterns, and other tricks of the trade to suggest chiaroscuro. See Pinelli (1993), 134–135.

48. Ibid., 156.

49. Gisbert and Mesa (1997), 339.

50. Wolfgang Keyser, *The Grotesque in Art and Literature* (New York: Columbia University Press, 1981). It goes without saying that grotesques never represent a precise translation of these concepts—the whimsy, imagination, and, in an opposite direction, routine of the studios would have opposed it. But these forms proliferated in circles whose concerns could not go unnoticed.

51. Jeanneret (n.d.), 124. This should be distinguished from the fundamentally syncretic nature of medieval thought conceived as an adaption of Arabic thought (according to Alain de Libera, *Penser au moyen age* [Paris: Seuil, 1991]). Mestizo thought is illustrated by the way the work of Avicenna was translated: "There we see a Jew and a Christian collaborating on the intellectual appropriation of the text of a Persian, transmitted in Arabic. That is a form of mélange which is certainly worth others" (112). But although stemming from mélange, this philosophy attempts to produce a homogeneous, unified knowledge distinct from the hybrid mentality discussed here.

52. Barthélemy Aneau, preface to Ovid, *Trois premiers livres de métamorphose* (Lyon: Guillaume Roville, 1556), quoted in Jeanneret (n.d.), 124.

53. "In Romanesque, as in later Gothic, the realm of marginal monstruosity is irrevocably linked with the capacity of the human imagination to create and compare," writes Camille (1992), 65. See also Jean Céard, *La Nature et les prodiges: L'insolite au XVIe siècle en France* (Geneva: Droz, 1977).

54. For Montaigne, "what we called monsters are not so for God who sees the infinite number of forms which he has included in the immensity of his creation.... God is all-wise; nothing comes from him which is not good, general and regular: but we cannot see the disposition and relationship." Montaigne (1991) II: xxx, 808.

55. Morel (1997), 80.

56. Guillaume du Bartas, *La Semaine* (Paris: Abel l'Angelier, 1583) VI: 1029–1034, quoted in Jeanneret (n.d.), 20; Morel (1997), 126.

57. Michel Foucault, *Les Mots et les choses: une archéologie des sciences humaines* (Paris: Gallimard, 1966), 40–45.

58. Neoplatonism offered a theory of concord and love which appealed to the mestizo minds of Leon Hebreo and his Inca translator, Garcilaso.

59. Jeanneret (n.d.), 235.

60. Martin Kemp, "Wrought by No Artist's Hand: The Natural, the Artificial, the Exotic, and the Scientific in Some Artifacts from the Renaissance," *Reframing the Renaissance: Visual Culture in Europe and Latin America, 1450–1650*, ed. Claire Farago (New Haven, CT, and London: Yale University Press, 1995), 178–196. This can be seen in the ceramics of Bernard Palissy, although such practices and concepts were already present in late Gothic (Kemp, 181).

61. See, for example, Lorenzo de Anania's *Fabrica del mondo ovvero Cosmografia divisa in quattro trattati* (Venice, 1576 and 1582).

62. "Imaginem ... quam ne Apelles, si reviviscat, vel alius quispiam praestantissimus pictor penicillo melius exprimat," quoted in Allessandra Russo, "Arte plumaria del Messico coloniale del XVI secolo: L'incontro di due mondi artistici," dissertation (University of Bologna, 1996), 131–132.

63. See, for example, *Cosmografia* (1544) by Sebastián Munster and *Historiae animalium* (1550–1558) by Conrad Gesner. On the interest in Mexico shown by Renaissance Italy, see Maria Matilde Benzoni, "La cultura italiana et il Messico: Storia de un'immagine da Temistitan all'Indipendenza (1519–1860)," dissertation (University of Milan, 1994).

64. Morel (1997), 83.

65. On the notion of transformation and metamorphosis in his comparative analysis of magic, see Las Casas (1967), I: 476.

66. Motolinía (1971), 59.

67. On the other hand, Morel (1997), 84, argues that they conformed to "minimal formal conditions."

68. And even hybridization. Francisco de Hollanda, in his *Dialogos da pintura antiga* (1548), set out the principles that a grotesque painter should respect in even the most whimsical productions; see Morel (1997), 85. Similarly, in 1567 Vincenzo Danti explained how to produce "new mélanges."

CHAPTER 8

1. Erwin Panofsky's monograph on the Camera di San Paolo is a model of iconological exploration: *The Iconography of Correggio's Camera di San Paolo* (London: The Warburg Institute, 1961). On Araldi, see Maria Chiusa, *Alessandro Araldi: La "maniera antico-moderna" a Parma* (Parma, Italy: Quarderni di Parma per l'arte, 1996), II: fasc. 3.

2. The dean was nearly the victim of a crime of passion. See Gruzinski (1994a), 139.

3. Panofsky (1961), 29.

4. The other room, painted by Correggio, is conceived in the same spirit but in a completely different style. Although the frescoes do not use the same repertoire of grotesques, they also convey a message combining the visual language of classical antiquity with the use of metaphors. " There is, finally, some kind of underlying philosophy which lends unity and meaning to the diverse figures and episodes; but this philosophy is a set of personal convictions rather than a result of system-building thought." Panofsky (1961), 99.

5. See M. L. Madonna, "La biblioteca: Theatrum mundi e theatrum sapientiae," in *L'Abbazia benedittina di San Giovanni Evangelista a Parma*, ed. Bruno Adorni (Milan, 1979), 177–194.

6. Morel (1979), 50.

7. Horapollo, *The Hieroglyphics of Horapollo*, trans. and intro by George Boas with a new foreword by Anthony T. Grafton (Princeton, NJ: Princeton University Press, [1505] 1993). See also Patrizia Castelli, *I Geroglifici e il mito dell'Egitto ne Rinascimento* (Florence: Edam, 1979).

8. Morel (1997), 59.

9. Durán (1977), 226.
10. Horapollo (1993), 64.
11. Perhaps depicted on the wall of the church in Ixmiquilpan.
12. Rudolf Wittkower, *Allegory and the Migration of Symbols* (New York: Thames & Hudson, 1987), 117, fig. 164. The Iberian peninsula did not remain aloof from such considerations. "Hemos de subrayar la continua y facil entrada de los libros emblemáticos en la Península ya que su contenido no despertaba suspicacias con respecto al dogma por no ofrecer con él lazos demasiados directos" (Gallego [1987], 34). Plates based on Horapollo were reprinted in Jerónimo Chaves's *Chronographia o Repertorio de Tiempos* (1574 and Seville, 1588), cited in Gallego (1987), 87. Juan de Horozco's *Emblemas morales* (Segovia, 1589) also testify to Horapollo's influence in Spain (ibid., 91).
13. Other figurative practices imported into America might have been perceived in the same way. Pedro Sarmiento de Gamboa made rings covered with signs of the zodiac and inscriptions in Chaldean, for which he was prosecuted by the Inquisition in Lima; see Bernand and Gruzinski (1993), II: 60. It is also worth mentioning the role of European heraldry, which introduced Mexican nobility to a strictly codified visual language within which each form, each object, each color, and each segment of space had a predetermined meaning. The grand families of the indigenenous nobility received coats of arms accompanied by a "royal warrant" [*cedula*] which provided a detailed description; see Guillermo Fernández de Recas, *Cacicazgos y nobiliario indígena de la Nueva España* (Mexico City: UNAM, 1961), passim.
14. In the 1530s, Amerindians made confession by drawing "diversas figuras y carácteres" on used sheets of paper, to the great satisfaction of the Franciscans. See Motolinía (1971), 138.
15. Wittkower (1987), 116.
16. The no-longer-extant grotesques in the cloister of Santa Giustina in Padua represented an intellectual quest similar to the one expressed in San Giovanni Evangelista. See Wittkower (1987), 126–127.
17. Gallego (1987), 76.
18. Eloise Quiñones Keber, "Collecting Cultures: A Mexican Manuscript in the Vatican Library," in *Reframing the Renaissance: Visual Culture in Europe and Latin America 1450–1650*, ed. Claire Farago (New Haven, CT: Yale University Press, 1995), 229–242.
19. Valadés's sources included Ludovico Dolce, *Dialogo ne qual si ragiona del modo di accrescere et conservar la memoria* (Venice, 1562) and Johannes Romberch, *Congestiorum artificiosae memoriae* (Venice, 1533).
20. On Valadés, see Rui Manoel Loureiro and Serge Gruzinski, *Passar as fronteiras. II. Colóquio Internacional sobre mediadores culturais, séculos XV a XVIII,* (Lagos: Centro de Estudos Gil Eanes, 1999); and René Taylor, *El Arte de la memoria en el Nuevo Mundo* (Madrid: Swan, 1987).
21. Certain mannerist artists tried to do exactly this. Many of them showed an interest in alchemy, magic, and theosophical speculation, as found in paintings by Johannes Stradanus and Giralamo Macchietti.
22. Ransmayr (1990), 208.
23. Pirro Ligorio, in his *Libro dell'antichità,* stressed the relationship between the rise of grotesques and "poeti delle trasmutazioni." See Russo (1997), 55.
24. Morel (1997), 84.
25. Quinoñes Keber (1995), 229–242; Heikamp (1972); H. B. Nicholson and Eloise Quiñones Keber, *Art of Aztec Mexico: Treasures of Tenochtitlán* (Washington, DC: National Gallery of Art, 1983), 171–173; Christian Feest, "Koloniale Federkunst aus Mexiko," in *Gold und Macht: Spanien in der neuen Welt*, ed. Christian Feest and Peter Kann (Vienna: Verlag Kremayr & Scheriau, 1986), 173–178; Laura Laurencich Minelli

(ed.), *Terra America: Il mondo nuovo nelle collezioni emiliano-romagnole*, catalog of the exhibition (Bologna: Grafis, 1992).

26. Quinoñes Keber (1995), 233.

27. The Florentine portrait of Emperor Moctezuma can be compared to the one of the monarch Nezahualpilli done by the Indian painter of the *Codex Ixtlilxóchitl*. The highly similar subjects make it possible to measure the distance separating Western vision from the Westernized eye of a Mexican painter.

28. Gisbert and Mesa (1997), 338–339.

29. Nadine Béligand, "Déités lacustres de temps pluriels: éclosion, renaissance et disparition des sirènes du lac de Chicnahuapan, vallée de Toluca (Mexique)," *Journal de la Société des américanistes* (forthcoming).

30. Teresa Gisbert, *Iconografia y mitos indigenas en el arte* (La Paz, Bolivia: Editorial Gisbert et Ciá., 1980), 46–51.

31. Gisbert and Mesa (1997); Pablo Macera, *La Pintura mural andina: Siglos XVI–XIX* (Lima: Editorial Milla Batres, 1993).

32. Isabel Iriarte, "Tapices con escenas bíblicas del Perú colonial," *Revista Andina* I (July 1992), 88–89.

33. Juan Carlos Estensorro Fuchs has suggested a link between a silver platter made in Peru (Lima, ca. 1586, now in the church of Saint Nicholas in Siegen, Westphalia) and the vision of an indigenous chieftain, Don Cristóbal. "The *huaca*, which is generally believed to be a basically pre-Hispanic expression, appears in the form of a freakish Western image which probably, given figurative conventions, took on the dimensions of a veritable nightmare for Don Cristóbal." "Du paganisme à la sainteté: L'incorporation des Indiens du Pérou au catholicisme," Ph.D. dissertation (Paris: Ecole des Hautes Etudes en Sciences Sociales, 1998), 385.

34. On this church, see Glauce Maria Navarro Burity, *A presença dos Franciscanos na Paraíba através do convento de Santo António* (Rio de Janeiro: Bloch Editores, 1988).

35. In the analysis he offers of transformations in pre-Columbian art under Spanish domination, George Kubler (1985), 68, distinguishes several processes at work depending on the example given: juxtaposition, convergence, "explants, transplants, [and] fragments." In contrast, I feel that these processes can perfectly well coexist within a single work.

36. On dolphins in the Andes, Gisbert and Mesa (1997) note: "se trata de un elemento europeo, elaborado en América según la sensibilidad indígena" (340–341).

37. On the definition of attractors and "strange attractors" within dynamic systems, see Pierre-Gilles de Gennes et al., *L'Ordre du chaos* (1992), 40–42; Kalus Mainzer, *Thinking in Complexity: The Complex Dynamics of Matter, Mind, and Mankind* (Berlin: Springer, 1996), 4–7, 244, 276. It goes without saying that the realm of human creativity is infinitely more complex than that of systems envisaged by mathematicians.

38. Graulich (1982), 85; Sahagún (1977), I: 50; Durán (1967), I: 169; Gerónimo de Mendieta, *Historia eclesiástica indiana* (Mexico City: Salvador Chávez Hayhoe, [1596] 1945), I: 95.

39. Bernand and Gruzinski (1993), II: 101–102.

40. In this respect, the alchemists of an "Indian voice" can be as disreputable as Eurocentrist historians and those who claim that the Other belongs to an opaque, unattainable otherworld. A discussion of this issue, with bibliographic references, can be found in Cecilia F. Kline, "Wild Woman in Colonial Mexico: An Encounter of European and Aztec Concepts of the Other," in Farago (1995), 245–247. On the limitations of the European view, see Peter Mason, *Deconstructing America: Representations of the Other* (London: Routledge, Chapman and Hall, 1990).

41. In this field of study, see Carmen Salazar-Soler, "Alvaro Alonso Barba: Teorías de la antigüedad, alquimia y creencias prehispánicas en las ciencias de la tierra en el Nuevo

Mundo," in Ares Queija and Gruzinski (1997), 269–296; and Louise Bénat-Tachot, "Ananas versus cacao: Un exemple de discours ethnographique dans l'*Historia general de las Indias* de Gonzalo Fernández de Oviedo," in ibid., 214–230.

42. Jesús Bustamante García, "Francisco Hernández, Plinio del Nuevo Mundo: Tradición clásica, teoría nominal y sistema terminológico indígena en una obra renacentista," in Ares Queija and Gruzinski (1997), 261.

43. "Parece admirable que entre gentes tan incultas y bárbaras, apenas se encuentre una palabra impuesta inconsideradamente al significado y sin éthimo, sino que casi todas fueron adaptadas a las cosas con tanto tino y prudencia que oído sólo el nombre, suelen llegar a las naturalezas que eran de saberse o investigarse de las cosas significadas." See Book II, Chapter 20 of *Antigüedades de la Nueva España* in Francisco Hernández, *Obras completas* (Mexico City: UNAM, 1984), VI: 134.

44. Other attractors from classical antiquity could be added to the list. One might study, from this angle, the relationship between the work of Garcilaso de la Vega and Flavius Josephus, from whom the Inca learned the neoplatonic philosophy of Philo of Alexandria. See Carmen Bernand, "Mestizos, mulatos y ladinos en Hispanoamérica: un enfoque antropológico de un proceso histórico" (typescript, 1997), 41. On the use of a classical analytical grid in France, see Frank Lestringant, *L'Atelier du cosmographe ou l'image du monde à la Renaissance* (Paris: Albin Michel, 1991).

CHAPTER 9

1. Christian Duverger, *L'Esprit du jeu chez les Aztèques* (Paris: Mouton, 1978), 77 ff. It might also be a reference to the number five, which corresponds to the Fifth Sun and signifies the center of the universe; see López Austin (1980), I: 75.

2. The circle motif appears in the *Codex Durán*, figuring in an illustration in Chapter 63 which recounts the embellishment work done on Mexico City's great temple during the reign of Ahuitzotl. It shows the two sanctuaries at the top of the temple pyramid. One of these temples, dedicated to the god of rain, Tlaloc, is crowned by a series of five white circles on black background, similar to those seen in the Acolman grotesques. These circles, whose centers are clearly marked, are usually associated with *chalchihuitl*, the symbol of precious water; see Reyes-Valerio (1978), 275–276. The same motif can be seen on the triumphal arch of the open chapel at Tlamanalco (ibid., 284–286) and on the depiction of a lordly dwelling in Sahagún (1979), fol. 393 v.

3. It is worth comparing the stylized depiction of the Augustinian's rope along the bottom of the Crucifixion with the rope in the Mexican glyph for water, raising the question of a possible link between this mestizo symbol, grotesques, and the death of Christ. Sprinkled throughout the grotesque decoration are four-petaled flowers that might be a transcription of the sign *Nahui-Ollin*, "Four Movement," associated with the Fifth Sun; see Reyes-Valerio (1978), 246–250.

4. N. C. Christopher Cough, "Style and Ideology in the Durán Illustrations: An Interpretative Study of Three Early Colonial Mexican Manuscripts," Ph.D. dissertation (Columbia University, 1987: Ann Arbor, MI: University Microfilms); Donald Robertson, "Paste-Over Illustrations in the Durán Codex of Madrid," *Tlalocan* 4 (1968), 340–348.

5. Mannerist ornamentation can also be seen in the pages of the *Codex Magliabechiano* (Graz, Austria: Akademische Druck -u. Verlagsanstalt, 1970), fol. 5 v. (*manta de beçote del diablo*) and fol. 7. r. (*manta del fuego del diablo*).

6. Specifically, Bibles published in Lyon by Guillaume Rouillé. See Cough (1987), 337.

7. Durán (1967), II: 14. See also the connections between Incas and Jews made by Garcilaso de la Vega, in Bernand and Gruzinski (1993), II: 101.
8. The illustration to Chapter LIII.
9. Durán (1967), II: 403–404. The caryatids are similar to those seen in *Provisiones Cédulas,* published in Mexico City by Pierre Ochart in 1563.
10. Durán (1967), II: 327. The interpretation is trickier here. It is obvious that the scene does not illustrate the chapter in which it appears, since the text reports discussions over the investiture of a monarch thought to be too young to assume the diadem. Probably the satyrs, known for their lasciviousness, embody Huasteca enemies against whom Ahuitzotl went on campaign, as Durán mentions several pages later. The reputation of the Huastecas, who lived along the Gulf of Mexico, was as bad as that of classical satyrs.
11. Illustrated in Chapter XLIII, see Durán (1967), II: 333. The columns of the two sanctuaries are set on bases decorated with grimacing masks inspired by European frontispieces.
12. "Relación de Cholula," in *Relaciones geográficas del siglo XVI: Tlaxcala,* ed. René Acuña (Mexico City: UNAM, 1985), II: 121–145.
13. Cholula therefore had the appearance of "un pueblo muy formado y concertado...con las calles tan bien trazadas y derechas como un juego de ajedrez." Ibid., 126, 142.
14. "It seems reasonable to think of the huge blocks of 1581 as describing a still unrealized project," asserts George Kubler in *Studies in Ancient American and European Art: The Collected Essays of George Kubler,* ed. Thomas E. Reese (New Haven, CT, and London: Yale University Press, 1985), 93.
15. Gómez Martínez (1997), 136.
16. "Relación de Cholula" (1985), 126.
17. Ibid., 142.
18. Ibid., 143.
19. Alfredo López Austin, *Hombre-Dios: Religión y política en el mundo náhuatl* (Mexico City: UNAM, 1973), 169–171.
20. Kubler (1985), 96.
21. "Relación de Cholula" (1985), 143.
22. Lockhart (1992), 272–274, 281.
23. "Relación de Cholula" (1985), 143.
24. One legend claimed that the Cholula tower was destroyed by a piece of jade in the form of a toad. See Graulich (1982), 75.
25. Furthermore, the dimensions of the ruins are too modest to be confused with the imposing hill drawn on the map.
26. This flipping effect is reminiscent of the Necker cube, which can alternately appear to be a hollow cube (looking at the rear edge) or a solid cube (the forward edge). On these shifting images, see Omar Calabrese, "Catastrofi e teoria dell'arte," *Lectures: Analisi di materiali e temi di espressione francese* 15, (December 1984), 45–62.
27. A map made several years later (1586) shows a community organized around the great pyramid.
28. Paul Kirchhoff, Lina Odena Güemes, and Luis Reyes García, *Historia tolteca-chichimeca* (Mexico City: INAH, 1976), fol. 9 v., ms. 54–58, p. 21.
29. It might be added that the six neighborhoods seen on the 1581 map are colonial equivalents of the twelve pre-Hispanic districts, or *calpolli.* They are evidence of a double process of continuity and adaptation to the colonial context. As Barbara E. Mundy notes, "All twelve *calpolli* survived, condensed and rearranged over time into the *cabeceras* shown in the *Relación geográfica* map." *The Mapping of New Spain: Indigenous Cartography and the Maps of the Relaciones Geográficas* (Chicago and London: University of Chicago Press, 1996), 126–127.

30. The city of Cholula long managed to preserve its social and religious organization, without however escaping the effects of colonial domination and modernization. In a major book, Guillermo Bonfil Batalla defined indigenousness as the product of colonial domination and the bearer of an Indianness which mandatorily involved hybrid and mestizo processes. This sacred city should therefore not be considered a focus of pre-Hispanic remnants nor a conservatory of cultural and social fossils. See Guillermo Bonfil Batalla, *Cholula, la ciudada sagrada en la era industrial* (Mexico City: UNAM, 1973), 256–257.

31. On Iberian examples, see Lyell (1976), 3, 5, 114, including a 1564 engraving of Alicante. On the genre of topographic views, see Georgius Braun and Frans Hogenberg, *Civitates orbis terrarum* (Antwerp and Cologne: Philips Galle, 1572), described in *Christoffel Plantijn en de ibersiche Wereld* (Antwerp: Plantin Museum, 1992, p. 250). See also Svetlana Alpers, *L'Art de dépeindre: La peinture hollandaise au XVIIe siècle* (Paris: Gallimard, 1990), 265 and Bibliography.

32. Reproduced in Alpers (1990), plate 78.

33. Duccio Sacchi, *Mappe del Nuovo Mondo, Cartografie locali e definizione del territorio in Nuova Spagna, Secolo XVI–XVIII* (Milan: Franco Angeli, 1997), 121–123.

34. On the illustrations in the *Florentine Codex*, see J. Jorge Klor de Alva, H. B. Nicholson, and Eloise Quiñones Keber, eds., *The Work of Bernardino de Sahagún, Pioneer Ethnographer of Sixteenth-Century Aztec Mexico*. Studies on Culture and Society II, 1988 (Austin, TX: University of Texas, Institute for Meso-American Studies), 199–293.

35. Bernardino de Sahagún, *Códice Floventino* (1979, facsimile), II: fol. 159 v.

36. *Ursus horriacens, Ursus americanus machetes.*

37. A variant of this approach can be seen in the depictions of an *itzincuani* and a *coiametl* (Sahagún [1979], III: fol 161 r. and fol. 164 r.): the animals do not seem to be part of the landscape, which appears behind them like a stage set.

38. Two artists may also have been involved, for nothing excludes two successive hands at work.

39. On the scholarly importance of these drawings and their depictions of nature, see Jeanneret (n.d.), 68–79.

40. Sahagún (1979), II: fol 238 r. These images should be compared with *Snow* (fol. 239 r.) which combines three geometric patterns: seven spirals of clouds, circles of snowflakes, and irregular sheets of ice.

41. "Algunas fábulas, no menos frías que frívolas que sus antepasados les dejaron del sol y de la luna y de las estrellas y de los elementos y cosas elementados." Sahagún (1979), II: vii, 255.

42. The depiction of clouds in the *Primeros memoriales* was allegedly inspired by an engraving of the Last Judgment. See Ellen Taylor Baird, "Sahagún's *Primeros Memoriales*: A Structural and Stylistic Analysis of Drawings," Ph.D. dissertation, University of New Mexico, Albuquerque, 1979 (Ann Arbor, MI: University Microfilms), 168.

43. Georges Didi-Huberman, *Fra Angelico: Dissemblance et figuration* (Paris: Flammarion, 1990), figs. 12, 87, and passim.

44. Sahagún (1963), 18.

45. Jeanneret (n.d.), 76.

46. Sociological and technical interpretations cannot account for the complexity of such mélanges, even if those explanations include the training of artists, the changing generations, the conditions of creativity, and the ingeniousness of solutions.

47. See an example in a manual for eradicating idolatry by Juan de la Serna, "Manuel de ministros de indios...," in *Tratado de las idolatrías* (Mexico City: Fuente Cultural, 1953), X: 80, discussed in Gruzinski (1988), 234.

48. Reyes-Valerio (1989), 61.

49. See the pioneering work by Donald Robertson, *Mexican Manuscript Paintings of the Early Colonial Period* (New Haven, CT: Yale University Press, 1959).
50. Cough (1987), 374.
51. According to chronicler Augustín Davila Padilla, Dominican friar Juan Ferrer could read glyphs. See *Historia de la fundación y discurso de la provincia de Santiago de México de la orden de los predicadores* (Mexico City: Academia Literaria, 1955), 286.

CHAPTER 10

1. The basis of taxation was changed. All people previously exempt were obliged to pay tribute, an obligation that even extended to certain *caciques*, or chieftains. See Charles Gibson, *The Aztecs under Spanish Rule: A History of the Indians of the Valley of Mexico, 1519–1810* (Stanford, CA: Stanford University Press, 1964), 200–201.
2. Domingo Francisco de San Antón Muñón Chimalpahin Cuauhtlehuanitzin, *Relaciones originales de Chaclo-Amaquemecan* (Mexico City: FCE, 1965), 268.
3. Gibson (1964), 168–172; Chimalpahin (1965), 270.
4. Francisco del Paso y Troncoso, *Epistolario de Nueva España* (Mexico City: Antigua Librería Robredo, 1940), X: 129.
5. Gibson (1964), 157.
6. The first great wave of congregations came to an end in 1564. The forced displacement of indigenous peoples provoked a series of disturbances—rootlessness, uprooting from traditional lands, abandonment of the diversified use of natural resources. Indian populations were restricted to a lifestyle that attempted to imitate that of Spanish villages. See Enrique Florescano et al., *La Clase obrera en la historia de México: De la colonia al imperio* (Mexico City: Siglo XXI, 1980), 83.
7. Biblioteca Nacional de México, Fondo de Origen, 1628 bis.
8. Angel María Garibay K., *Historia de la literatura náhuatl* (Mexico City: Porrúa, 1971), II: 102, 109; John Bierhorst, trans. and intro., *Cantares Mexicanos: Songs of the Aztecs* (Stanford, CA: Stanford University Press, 1985), 327–341. A facsimile of the Biblioteca Nacional manuscript has been published as *Cantares mexicanos* (Mexico: UNAM, 1994). See also Louise M. Burkhart, *The Slippery Earth: Nahua-Christian Moral Dialogue in Sixteenth-Century Mexico* (Tucson, AZ: University of Arizona Press, 1988), 5; and a review of Bierhorst's book by Xavier Nogués in *Historia mexicana* 142 (Oct.–Dec. 1986), 383–390.
9. This and all subsequent translations of the songs are by Bierhorst (1985), 336–337.
10. Garibay, *Poesía náhuatl, Cantares mexicanos: Manuscrito de la Biblioteca Nacional de México* (Mexico: UNAM, 1993), vols. II and III.
11. Garibay K. (1971), II: 89–119, nevertheless includes several excerpts. It is true that the often obscure content of the *cantares* favored a classification of issues that focused on Amerindian roots, and that the change in perspective multiplies the problems of interpretation. The efforts of John Bierhorst—who has produced the only complete translation and critical study of the manuscript to date—have not resolved everything. I would not go as far down certain paths as Bierhorst does, but nor would I necessarily agree with the criticism published by Miguel León-Portilla, "¿Una nueva interpretación de los *Cantares mexicanos?* La obra de John Bierhorst," *Estudios de Cultura Náhuatl* XVIII, 385–400.
12. "Y así se fué por la mar navegando, y no se sabe cómo y de qué manera llegó al dicho Tlapallan," in Sahagún (1977), I: 291. On sources for the fate of Quetzalcoatl, see Graulich (1982), 201.

13. The presence of sea shells in the offerings at the Great Temple in Mexico City neverthe-less demonstrates that the people of the *altiplano* were not unaware of maritime spaces.

14. Bierhorst (1985), 479–480; Robert Stevenson, *Music in Aztec and Inca Territory* (Berkeley, CA: University of California, 1968), 89, 224–225; Díaz del Castillo (1968) II: 282, 286–287.

15. Rafael García Granados, *Diccionario biográfico de historia antigua de Méjico* (Mexico City: UNAM, 1995), III: 135–136. Don Martín allegedly made two trips to Spain.

16. "A Ecatzin empero lo llevaron a Castilla. Prestó homenaje al gran soberano, al emper-ador. Porque no le fue dada muerte don Martín Ecatzin Tlacatécatl Tlapanécatl Popcatzin regresó. A los cinco años vino aquí, a Mexico Tlatelolco," in *Anales de Tlatelolco: Unos anales históricos de la nación mexicana y Códice de Tlatelolco*, ed. Heinrich Berlin and Robert H. Barlow (Mexico City: Rafael Porrúa, 1980), 12. Don Martín Ehecatl—or Ecatzin—was reportedly governor of Tlatelolco from 1523 to 1526 (according to Barlow) or from 1528 to 1531 (according to Sahagún). He was one of the ringleaders of the resistance against the Spaniards during the siege of Mexico City, and Cortés took him as a hostage to Honduras. See Robert H. Barlow, "Los caciques coloniales de Tlatelolco 1521–1526," *Obras* (Mexico City: INAH, Universidad de las Américas, 1989), II: 359–362.

17. Hernán González de Eslava, *Villancicos, romances, ensaladas y otras canciones devotas*, ed. Margit Frenk (Mexico City: El Colegio de México, 1989), 240–241, 391. See notably colloquies II and VII and *villancico* 91 ("Ensalada de la flota"):
    La flota está de partida
    quien se quisiere embarcar
    venga, que podrá ganar
    tesoro y bien sin medida....

18. "Oda de Jhoan de la Cueva," in *Flores de varia poesia*, ed. Margarita Peña (Mexico City: SEP, 1987), 429.

19. Ibid., 186–188, from a sonnet by Jhoan de la Cueva titled *Passando el mar Leandro el animoso*. On Juan de la Cueva, see ibid., note 102.

20. Louise M. Burkhart, "The Voyage of Saint Amaro: A Spanish Legend in Nahuatl Literature," *Colonial Latin American Review* IV: 1 (1995), 29–57.

21. The tale was published in Burgos, Spain in 1552, then in Santo Domingo in 1593.

22. Instead of *ynmecahuehueh* (harps or stringed instruments), the text reads *huehuetl* (drums); see Burkhart (1995), 54, note 20.

23. Durán (1967), I: 236–237.

24. Ibid., I: 17.

25. Ibid., I: 18.

26. Ibid., I: 195.

27. "Todo fingido para dar placer y solaz a las ciudades, regocijándolas con mil géneros de juegos que ... inventaban de danzas y farsas y entremeses y cantares de mucho contento." Ibid., 194.

28. Ibid., 192.

29. As inferred from the *Somptueux ordre plaisantz spectacles et magnifiques theatres dresses et exhibes par les citoyens de Rouen....* (Rouen: Robert le Hoy and Jehan dict du Gord, 1551).

30. Valadés (1989), between fol. 176 and 177.

31. Perhaps the mosaics of Palestrina.

32. Sahagún (1977), I: 255 (Appendix 6 of Book II).

33. Jeanneret (n.d.), 151.

34. Sahagún (1977), III: x, 164.

35. Pedro de Trejo, *Cancionero*, ed. Sergio López Mena (Mexico City: UNAM, Instituto de Investigaciones Filológicas, 1966), 10–74.
36. Gilles-Gaston Granger, *L'Irrationnel* (Paris: Odile Jacob, 1998), 175.
37. A somewhat painful conclusion that "is nevertheless true" according to Wittgenstein, quoted in Granger (1998), 178.
38. Granger (1998), 175.
39. This probably explains our determination to discover "logics" everywhere, both inside and outside the West.

CHAPTER 11

1. Durán (1967), II: 288–289.
2. By the name of Ycelteotl.
3. Bierhorst (1985), 330–331.
4. Ibid., 332–333.
5. Motolinía (1971), 112–113.
6. Alonso de Molina, *Confesionario mayor en lengua mexicana y castellana* (Mexico: Antonio de Espinosa, 1569), fol. 92. r.
7. Ibid. ("Inipillohuan, initlatocayouan, tecpan, nitiacuauan, nipilohuan.") Another example of this militarized, warriorlike vision of Christian heaven can be found in Bernardino de Sahagún, *Coloquios y doctrina cristiana*, ed. Miguel León-Portilla (Mexico City: UNAM, [1564] 1986), 95, 182–187.
8. Bierhorst (1985), 338–339.
9. Jean-Marc Lalanne et al., *Wong Kar-Wai* (Paris: Dis Voir, 1997), 22.
10. Bierhorst (1985), 340–341.
11. Paolo Giovio, *Elogia virorum bellica virtute* (Florence, 1551). Bibliothèque Mazarine, Paris, ms. 6765. This information was generously supplied by Maria Matilde Benzoni. Rome was written in Nahuatl as *Loma* or *Lomah* in *Cantar* LXVIII.
12. *Patele Xanto* in Nahuatl, see Bierhorst (1985), 340 (fol. 59 verso, l. 28)
13. Ibid., 341.
14. Motolinía (1971), 327.
15. *Concilios provinciales primero y segundo*, published by Francisco Antonio Lorenzana (Mexico City: Antonio de Hogal, 1769), LXVI: 140–141.
16. Bierhorst (1985), 44; Robert Stevenson, *Music in Aztec and Inca Territory* (Berkeley, CA: University of California Press, 1968); Gabriel Saldivar, *Historia de la música en México: Epocas precortesiana y colonial* (Mexico City: Cultura, 1934).
17. See the *Santoral* in the Biblioteca Nacional in Mexico City, cited in Roberto Moreno, "Guía de las obras en lenguas indígenas existentes en la Biblioteca Nacional," *Boletín de la Biblioteca Nacional* XVII: 1–2 (1966), 91; Pedro de Gante, *Doctrina cristiana en lengua mexicana* (Mexico City: Centro de Estudios Históricos Fray Bernardino de Sahagún, [1553] 1981), n.p.
18. González de Eslava (1989), 284.
19. Now in the Pinacoteca Virreinal de San Diego in Mexico City. See Tovar de Teresa (1992), 86.
20. Alonso de Molina, *Vocabulario en lengua castellana y mexicana y mexicana y castellana* (Mexico City: Antonio de Espinosa, 1571), fol. 104 r. gives *tepuz quiquiztli* as trumpet, while fol. 90 r. gives *quiquiztli* as shell used as a horn.
21. Ibid.

22. Heyden (1983), 69.

23. Sahagún (1969), VI: 131.

24. Graulich (1982), 252.

25. *Cantar* LXXI, 28, in Bierhorst (1985), 355. The term is used in the sense of "crypt" in Bernardino de Sahagún, *Psalmodia christiana y sermonario de los sanctos del año en lengua mexicana* (Mexico City: Pedro Ocharte, 1583), 193 v.

26. *Cantar* LXIV, 2 in Bierhorst (1985), 313; *Cantar* LXXXIV, 12 (Ibid., 387). Translated as *dosel de plumas* in Garibay (1993), III: 56.

27. Andrés de Concha painted saints on the large altarpiece of the Dominican church of Yanhuitlan in 1575, including a Saint Bernardino of Siena wearing the papal tiara; in Valadés's *Rhetorica christiana* (1989), a plate illustrating the church hierarchy shows a pope seated beneath a canopy in a niche, cross in hand (176–177).

28. Sahagún (1977), II: vi, 159.

29. Jeanneret (n.d.), 159.

30. *Cantar* XIX, 1, in Bierhorst (1985), 179; *Cantar* LXIV, 19, Ibid., 317; *Cantar* XIX, 13, Ibid., 181.

31. On the Tecamachalco Apocalypse, see Gruzinski (1994), 91–128.

32. Bierhorst (1985), 334–337.

33. Durán (1967), I: 193.

34. Bierhorst (1985), 336–337.

35. Sahagún (1977), II: 64.

36. A reliquary in the shape of a butterfly, made in Paris circa 1325–1335, can be seen in the cathedral of Regensburg.

37. Gary Tomlinson, "Ideologies of Aztec Song," *Journal of the American Musiciological Society* XLVIII: 3 (1995), 364–367.

38. Molina (1571), fol. 80 v.

39. Bierhorst (1985), 336–337.

40. Jane H. Hill, "The Flowery World of Old Uto-Aztecan," paper presented at the 86th Annual Meeting of the American Anthropological Association, Chicago, November 10–21, 1987. For ancient Mexicans, brilliance and color went together—the pope's cavern-palace was multicolored. Colors also facilitated the establishment of connections and associations.

41. Bierhorst (1985), 338–339. Cf. Durán (1967), II: 400: "los nueve dobleces del cielo." [Translator's note: Bierhorst renders *chicnauhtlamantlini* as "nine divisions." Gruzinski prefers "neuf niveaux" (nine layers).]

42. Sahagún (1583), fol. 173 v; Bernardino de Sahagún, *Coloquios* (1986), chap. xii, 94.

43. Other sources mention thirteen heavens, that is to say the sum of the two regions (one with nine levels, the other with four). See López Austin (1980), I: 60–61, as well as the same author's *Tamoanchan y Tlalocan* (Mexico City: FCE, 1996), 20. On the term *chicnauhnepaniucan*, see "lugar de los neuve pisos," Ibid., 90.

44. Pomar (1986), 23. The information dates from the early 1580s, and therefore must have been familiar to performers of the *cantares mexicanos*.

45. Diego Muñoz Camargo (1984), 202–203.

46. Fernando de Alva Ixtlilxóchitl, *Obras históricas*, ed. Edmundo O'Gorman (Mexico City: UNAM, Instito de Investigaciones Históricas, 1975), I: 405.

47. During Jesuit festivities in 1578, nine angels represented the various hierarchies and the nine heavens. "Las alas eran de plumería conforme al color de la ropa," noted Pedro de Morales, *Carta* (Mexico City: Antonio Ricardo, 1579). On *voladores*, see the *Codex Azcatitlan*, ed. Robert Barlow (Paris: Bibliothèque Nationale, Société des Américanistes, 1995), plate 27. On the *capillas posas* of Calpan, the carved cherubs have been linked to glyphs that might be the traditional sign for the wind; see Daniela Riquelme Mancilla,

"La Imagen del angel en el siglo XIV novohispano," Master's thesis (University of Paris VIII, October 1997), passim.

48. *Cantar* LXII, 1 and *Cantar* LXXXVII, 45; Bierhorst (1985), 354–355 and 408–409.

49. *Cantar* LVII, 28; Bierhorst (1985), 266–267.

50. *Cantar* LVII, 21; Bierhorst (1985), 266–267.

51. *Cantar* XXXVIII, 9: "Tamoannempoyon...Moyolamox"; Bierhorst (1985), 210–211.

52. *Cantar* XVIII, 50: "Xochiquahuitl onicac in tamoan ychan dios yecha"; Bierhorst (1985), 176–177.

53. López Austin (1996), 93.

54. *Cantar* LXXX, 13; Bierhorst (1985), 370–371.

55. *Cantar* LXIV, 4; Bierhorst (1985), 312–313.

56. *Cantar* LXIV, 17; Bierhorst (1985), 314–315. This heavenly city, still resounding with an affirmation of Mexica grandeur, hints at a new sacralization linked to the presence of the Mother of God. The text of the *cantares mexicanos* was contemporary with the mid-sixteenth-century cult of the Virgin of Guadalupe, when rumors reported that an image of the Virgin in the chapel of Tepeyac performed miracles. The *cantares* prepared the way for the new cult by inscribing it within ancient beliefs. On the columns, see also *Cantar* LXXIX, 3; Bierhorst (1985), 366–367: "Where turquoise columns stand, in Mexico, Dark-Water Place, where...you hold God's mat and seat!"

57. Garibay (1993), III: 36–38, eliminates references to the Holy Father (*santo Patile*) and God (*Tiox*), and at the end changes "God our Father" (*tota Tiox*) to "the god" (*teotl*).

58. Bierhorst (1985), 338–339. [Translator's note: For reasons explained several paragraphs later, Gruzinski prefers the term "emanation" for *ixiptla*, which Bierhorst renders as "deputy" in *Cantar* LXVIII, 89–90.]

59. David Carrasco, *Quetzalcoatl and the Irony of Empire: Myths and Prophecies in the Aztec Tradition* (Chicago and London: University of Chicago Press, 1982), 30.

60. Graulich (1982), 135, 136.

61. Ibid., 263.

62. *Cantar* LIV-B, 1; Bierhorst (1985), 249: "Sing, red Sun! O Master of shields...."

63. See, for example, Sahagún (1979), II: fol. 44 r., concerning the sacrifice of captives as *ixiptla* of the *tlaloque* gods.

64. Gruzinksi (1990), 86–87, 267.

65. For example, Ripa (1992).

66. *Cantar* LVIII, 9; Bierhorst (1985), 268–269.

67. In his *Psalmodia Christiana*, the Franciscan Sahagún also made the association between the sun and the son of God.

68. But this mestizo way of thinking was also an aristocratic one, insofar as the afterworlds that the *cantar* painted for Indian eyes were reserved for members of the nobility, for warriors of glorious lineage. Like the solar heaven of the ancients, Rome and the house of the emperor welcomed only high-ranking Nahuas, pace the monks who preached—and congregations who expected—more egalitarian heavens.

69. During this same period, the Indians who supplied information to Friar Sahagún followed a different approach, which involved presenting Tamoanchan as a historic, geographically specific place on the coast of the Gulf of Mexico; see Lopez Austin (1996), 46–71. Whereas the composers of the *cantares* practiced heavenly one-upmanship, the Franciscan's informers tried to gloss over everything in the Mexica past that might seem too idolatrous.

70. Bierhorst (1985), 70–82. It would be surprising if indigenous methods of singing and dancing remained uninfluenced by Western singing in church, by the monks' theatrical productions, and by the sight of dances and other entertainment brought by the conquistadores.

71. Niv Fichman, *Yo-Yo Ma: Inspired by Bach, Struggle for Hope* (Sony, SHV 62724), 1995/1998.
72. Bierhorst (1985), 28.
73. Compare not only the neoplatonist adage, "In its simplicity, this three-in-one spirit is animal, vegetable, and mineral," but also the Renaissance "syncretic thought, steeped with animism." Jeanneret (n.d.), 50.
74. Brotherston (1992), 317.
75. Graulich (1982), 59; and *Journal de la Société des américanistes*, II (1905): 1–42. Established and annotated by E. de Jonghe, this text, titled "Histoire du Mechique," arrived in France in the sixteenth century.
76. Serge Gruzinski, *Les Hommmes-Dieux du Mexique: Pouvoir indien et société coloniale, XVIe–XVIIIe siècle* (Paris: Editions des Archives Contemporaines, 1985), 40–41. English Edition, 44–46.
77. Heyden (1983), 99.
78. Garibay (1993), II: xxxiii.
79. Umberger, "Antiques, Revivals and References to the Past in Aztec Art," *Res* (Spring 1987), 63–105.
80. Arthur Miller, "Indian Image and Visual Communication before and after the Conquest: The Mitla Case," in *Le Nouveau Monde, mondes nouveaux: L'expérience américaine*, ed. Serge Gruzinksi and Nathan Wachtel (Paris: Editions Recherches sur les Civilisations/ EHESS, 1996), 199–234.
81. Technical and formal potentialities included the use of calligraphy and its various styles; geometric virtualities included the suggestion of the third dimension and the use of rule-based perspective. Constraints and potentialities restricted and oriented capacities for improvisation and creativity.
82. I am notably thinking of the *titulos primordiales*, discussed in Gruzinski (1988), 139–188.
83. Díaz del Castillo (1968), I: 275.
84. The outline of clouds, the shape of riverbeds, the line of mountain ridges, and atmospheric turbulences correspond to extremely complex forms that cannot be reduced to familiar, classic shapes such as straight line, square, triangle, etc. Nor can they be expressed as whole numbers. Every reduction or simplification of these fractal forms irrevocably betrays the specificity of the phenomena to which they belong. A fractal object responds to none of the usual norms of topology—it entails intermediate figures situated halfway between surface and volume, between point and line. A fractal objects possesses multiple dimensions; it is what Omar Calabrese calls *teragonico* in *La Età neobarocca* (Bari, Italy: Sagittari Laterza, 1987), 130. Although fractality gives a disordered appearance to things, the extreme irregularity it produces is not totally random and is generally the product of an array of determinations that can be pinpointed with the appropriate tools. See Benoît Mandelbrot, *Fractals: Form, Chance, and Dimension* (San Francisco: W.H. Freeman, 1977).
85. Gleick (1991), 83.

CHAPTER 12

1. The humanist Cervantes de Salazar described *cantares* that were apparently addressed to the cross but were in fact "internally" dedicated to idols. See his *Crónica de la Nueva España* (Mexico City: Porrúa, 1985), 39.

2. María Sten, *Vida y muerte del teatro náhuatl: El Olímpo sin Prometeo* (Mexico City: SepSetentas, 1947), 86. In 1539, the *junta eclesiástica* prohibited *bailes con cantos* (dancing with songs) in churches, "tanto por ser cosa seglar como por usarse en sus ritos gentiles." In 1546, Viceroy Antonio de Mendoza criticized nocturnal dances and the songs that Indians "solían y acostumbraban en sus tiempos cantar." See Garibay K. (1971), II: 97.

3. *Concilios provinciales....* (Mexico City: Antonio Lorenzana, 1769), 146.

4. Cervantes de Salazar (1985), 39.

5. Durán (1967), I: 17, 236.

6. Solange Alberro, *Société et inquisition au Mexique, 1571–1700* (Mexico City: CEMCA, 1988), 36.

7. Durán (1967), I: 17.

8. Durán (1967), I: 237. "De lo cual sienten muy poco los que hablan desde fuera."

9. Ibid. I: 237.

10. Motolinía (1971), 87, 92.

11. The 1538 execution of the chief of Texcoco for idolatry is the exception that proves the rule, and even this indigenous noble seems to have be more a victim of political plotting within the Indian aristocracy than the target of the Spanish Church. On the suppression of idols, see Motolinía (1971), 87.

12. José de Acosta, *Historia natural y moral de las Indias* [1590], ed. Edmundo O'Gorman (Mexico City: FCE, 1979), 318.

13. Ibid.

14. An example of this practice in medieval Italy can be found on a record by the Mala Punica ensemble, conducted by Pedro Memelsdorff: *Missa Cantinella, Liturgical Parody in Italy, 1380–1410: Matteo de Perugia-Zaccara da Teramo* (Erato 0630-17069-2).

15. Examples include verse by Garcilaso de la Vega.

16. Mariner Ezra Padwa, *Peter of Ghent and the Introduction of European Music to the New World* (Santa Fe, NM: Hapax Press, 1993).

17. Motolinía (1971), 91–92.

18. Durán (1967), I: 195. Durán described *cantares* dedicated to the ancient gods as "divinos," as though that classification were self-evident.

19. Portuguese Jesuits in Brazil were employing the same technique twenty-five years later without raising an eyebrow: "Se nos abraçarmos com alguns custumes deste gentio... como hé cantar cantigas de Nosso Senhor em sua lingoa pello seu toom e tanger seus estromentos de musica que elles [usam[em suas festas quando matão contrarios e quando andão bebados: e isto para os atrahir a deixarem os outros custumes esentiais e, permitindo-lhes a aprovando-lhes estes, trabalhar por lhe tirar os outros." The writer goes on to add, "porque a semelhança é causa de amor." Letter from Manuel de Nobrega to Simão Rodrigues, Bahia, 1552, printed in *Monumenta Brasiliae* (Rome: Monumenta Historica Societatis Iesu), I: 407–408.

20. Acosta (1979), 317; Mujica Pinilla (1996), 237–239. On the policies of the Peruvian Church, see Juan Carlos Estenssoro-Fuchs, "La prédication au Pérou: De l'évangelisation à l'utopie," *Annales, Histoires, Sciences Sociales* 6 (Nov-Dec. 1996): 1225–1257.

21. Louise M. Burkhart, "Flowery Heaven: The Aesthetic of Paradise in Náhuatl Devotional Literature," *Res* 21 (Spring 1992): 95.

22. Jeanette Favrot Peterson, *The Paradise Garden Murals of Malinalco: Utopia and Empire in Sixteenth-Century Mexico* (Austin, TX: University of Texas Press, 1993).

23. Hernán González de Eslava, *Teatro selecto: Coloquios y entremeses* (Mexico City: SEP, 1988), 176, 204.

24. González de Eslava (1989), 58–59.

25. Letter from Jerónimo López to the emperor, Mexico City, December 20, 1541, *Colección de Documentos* (1971) II: 150.

26. "Avisen y sepan los ministros el gran mal que entre esta gente podría ser que hubiese disimulado vistiendo en los bailes algún indio al modo que su ídolo solía estar. Y esto con mucha disimulación festejándole y cantándole cantares apropriados a las excelencias y grandezas que de él fingían." Durán (1967), I: 18.
27. According to a journal kept by Juan Bautista, cited in Miguel León-Portilla, *Los franciscanos vistos por el hombre náhuatl* (Mexico: UNAM, 1985), 59.
28. Gruzinski (1990), 152–157.
29. This temple was linked to a mountain cult: "Avirtiendo que aquel beneficio de la lluvia les viene de aquellos montes [las gentes] tuvieronse por obligados de ir a visitar aquellos lugares y hacer gracias a aquella divinidad que allí residía."
30. Sahagún (1977), II: 352–353.
31. Ibid., 353.
32. On the role of ambiguity and misconception in all transfers of a visual nature, see S. Gruzinski (1990), passim.
33. José A. Llaguno, *La Personalidad jurídica del indio y el III concilio provincial mexicano* (Mexico City: Porrúa, 1963), 201.
34. Francisco Fernández del Castillo, *Libros y libreros en el siglo XVI* (Mexico City: FCE, 1982), 84.
35. Durán (1967), I: 237.
36. Ibid., I: 237.
37. *Arte adivinatoria,* fol. 101 v. Facsimile in *Cantares Mexicanos*. See also Jesús Bustamante García, *Fray Bernardino de Sahagún: Una revisión critica de los manuscritos y su proceso de composición* (Mexico City: UNAM/Instituo de Investigaciones Bibliográficas, 1990), 375–377.
38. Sacchi (1997), 132.
39. The Indians consistently painted the administrative center with all its surroundings, whereas the Spanish would have merely produced a schematic indication of the town.
40. Sacchi (1997), 130–132 and passim.
41. *Santoral Mexicano,* 13 r.—15 v., quoted in Burkhart (1992), 102–103.
42. López Austin (1980), I: 378.
43. Sahagún (1977), vol. II: Book II, Chap. xxvi, 14 (p. 173); Burkhart (1992), 91.
44. Reyes-Valerio (1978), passim.
45. Gruzinski (1985), 109–179. The fragility of mélanges explains why George Kubler deliberately overlooked the phenomenon on the grounds that colonization had eradicated all formal vestiges of pre-Columbian art and that the little that had survived was perpetuated only in an impoverished, degraded form. Referring to the carved pillars at Tlalmanalco, he wrote: "in this process the original design loses articulation, hierarchy, variations and individuality in increasingly schematic stylisations" Kubler (1985), 67. This means conceiving the transformation of a tradition exclusively in terms of extinction and decadence.

CONCLUSION

1. Bernand and Gruzinski (1993), II: 492.
2. *HK, Orient Extrême Cinéma* 4 (October 1997), 66.
3. *HK, Orient Extrême Cinéma* 0 (October 1996), 38.
4. *HK, Orient Extrême Cinéma* 3 (July 1997), 9.
5. Jean-Marc Lalanne et al., *Wong Kar-Wai* (Paris: Dis Voir, 1997), 13.
6. See also the role of the tune *California Dreaming* in the 1994 film, *Chunking Express*.

7. Born in Shanghai in 1958, Wong Kar-Wai left the People's Republic of China for Hong Kong. Since 1988 he has made a series of feature films that are intricately linked to the final years of British colonial control.

8. Hong Kong appears surreptitiously in *Happy Together* in inverted form, sky downward, in daylight (in contrast to the glum night of Buenos Aires). In this film, Chinese port and Argentinean port occupy positions simultaneously equal and antithetical, as though Buenos Aires had become a double of Hong Kong, located on the other side of the earth.

9. Lalanne (1997), 10, 13, 45, 52.

10. Ibid., 27.

11. Ibid., 18, 19.

12. Ibid., 19; Gruzinski (1991), 33

13. Ibid., 11, 19, 22, 27, 41.

14. One section of *Documenta X* in Kassel (1997) explored "a new form of urban coexistence." It showed the mind-boggling urban complex of the Pearl River Delta as "a city of exacerbated difference...based on the greatest possible difference between its parts—complementary and competitive."

15. Lalanne (1997), 53.

16. Ibid., 45.

17. John Woo, *HK* 4 (October 1997), 69.

18. Ackbar Abbas, *Hong Kong: Culture and the Politics of Disappearance* (Minneapolis: University of Minnesota Press, 1997), 53.

19. Ibid., 54.

20. Ibid., 11.

21. Or postcolonial, if this term has any meaning in a Hong Kong now reverted to China.

22. Abbas (1997), 8.

23. Ibid., 48.

24. Ibid., 40. Two major works deal with this subject: *Rouge* (1988) and *Actress* (1991). *Rouge* tells the story of Fleur who, after having committed suicide in the Hong Kong of the 1930s, reappears fifty years later in search of her vanished lover.

25. Ibid., 41.

26. Ibid., 35.

27. In the Sala della Scimmietta, painted in the late sixteenth century. See Carla Di Francesco, ed., *Le Sibille di Casa Romei: Storia e restauro* (Ravenna: Longo Editore, 1998).

BIBLIOGRAPHY

INAH   Instituto Nacional de Antropología e Historia
FCE   Fondo de cultura económica
UNAM   Universidad Nacional Autónoma de México

Abbas, Ackbar (1997). *Hong Kong: Culture and the Politics of Disappearance*. Minneapolis: University of Minnesota Press.

Acosta, José de [1588] (1984–1987). *De procuranda indorum salute*. Madrid: Centro Superior de Investigaciones Científicas.

——— [1590] (1979). *Historia natural y moral de las Indias*. Edited by Edmundo O'Gorman. Mexico: FCE.

Aguirre Beltrán, Gonzalo (1970). *El Proceso de aculturación*. Mexico City: Universidad Iberoamericana.

——— (1973). *Medicina y magia: El proceso de aculturación en la estructura colonial*. Mexico City: Instituto Nacional Indigenista.

Alberro, Solange (1988). *Société et inquisition au Mexique, 1571–1700*. Mexico City: CEMCA.

——— (1992). *Les Espagnols dans le Mexique colonial: Histoire d'une acculturation*. Paris: Armand Colin.

Albornoz Bueno, Alicia (1994). *La Memoria del olvido: El lenguaje del tlacuilo. Glifos y murales de la Iglesia de San Miguel Arcángel, Ixmiquilpan, Hidalgo. Teopan dedicado a Tezcatlipoca*. Pachuca, Mexico: Universidad Autónoma de Hidalgo.

Alciat, André (1997). *Les Emblèmes, fac-simile de l'édition lyonnaise Macé-Bonhomme*. Preface by Pierre Laurens. Paris: Klincksieck.

Alpers, Svetlana (1990). *L'Art de dépeindre: La peinture hollandaise au XVIIe siècle*. Paris: Gallimard.

Alva Ixtlilxóchitl, Fernando de (1975). *Obras históricas*. Edited by Edmundo O'Gorman. Mexico City: UNAM, Instituto de Investigaciones Históricas.

Alvi, Geminello (1996). *Il Secolo americano*. Milan: Adelphi.

Amselle, Jean-Loup (1990). *Logiques métisses: Anthropologie de l'identité en Afrique et ailleurs*. Paris: Payot.

Anania, Lorenzo de (1576 and 1582). *Fabrica del mondo ovvero Cosmografia divisa in quattro trattati*. Venice.

Andrade, Mário de (1996). *Macunaíma: O herói sem nenhum caráter*. Edited by Telê Porto Ancona Lopez. São Paulo: Allca XX, Edusp.

Ares Queija, Berta, and Serge Gruzinski (1997). *Entre dos mundos: Fronteras culturales y agentes mediadores*. Séville: Escuela de Estudios Hispanoamericanos.

Arrellano, Alfonso (1996). *La Casa del Deán: Un ejemplo de pintura mural civil del siglo XVI en Puebla*. Mexico City: UNAM.

Arróniz, Othón (1979). *Teatro de evangelización en Nueva España*. Mexico City: UNAM.

Baird, Ellen Taylor (1979). *Sahagún's Primeros Memoriales: A Structural and Stylistic Analysis of Drawings*. Ph.D. dissertation, University of New Mexico, Albuquerque. Ann Arbor, MI: University Microfilms.

Barkhan, Leonard (1986). *The Gods Made Flesh: Metamorphosis and the Pursuit of Paganism*. New Haven, CT.

Barlow, Robert H. (1948). "El Códice de Tlatelolco." In Heinrich Berlin, *Anales de Tlatelolco: Unos annales históricos de la nación mexicana y Códice de Tlatelolco*. Mexico City: Porrúa.

Barlow, Robert H. (1989). "Los caciques coloniales de Tlatelolco 1521–1526." *Obras*. Mexico City: INAH/Universidad de las Américas.

Bate, Jonathan (1998). *Shakespeare and Ovid*. Oxford: Clarendon Paperbacks.

Baudot, Georges (1977). *Utopie et Histoire au Mexique: Les premiers chroniqueurs de la civilisation mexicaine, 1520–1569*. Toulouse: Privat.

Baxandall, Michael (1986). *Painting and Experience in Fifteenth Century Italy*. Oxford: Oxford University Press.

Bénat-Tachot, Louise (1997). "Ananas versus cacao. Un exemple de discours ethnographique dans la *Historia general de las Indias* de Gonzalo Fernández de Oviedo." In Ares Queija and Gruzinski (1997).

Bencivenni, Alessandro, and Anna Samueli (1996). *Peter Greenaway: Il cinema delle idee*. Genoa: Le Mani.

Benzoni, Maria Matilde (1994). "La cultura italiana et il Messico: Storia de un'immagine da Temistitan all'Indipendenza (1519–1860)." Dissertation, University of Milan.

Bernabé, J., et al. (1989). *Eloge de la créolité*. Paris: Gallimard.

Bernand, Carmen (1997). "Mestizos, mulatos y ladinos en Hispano-América: un enfoque antropológico y un proceso histórico." Typescript.

Bernand, Carmen, and Serge Gruzinski (1988). *De l'idolâtrie. Une archéologie des sciences religieuses*. Paris: Seuil.

—— (1991). *Histoire du Nouveau Monde*, Vol. I, *De la découverte à la conquête*. Paris: Fayard.

—— (1993). *Histoire du Nouveau Monde*, Vol. II, *Les Métissages*. Paris: Fayard.

Bernand, Carmen et al. (1994). *Descubrimiento, conquista y colonización de América a quinientos años*. Mexico City: FCE.

Bhabha, Homi K. (1994). *Location of Culture*. London: Routledge.

Bierhorst, John (1985). *Cantares Mexicanos: Songs of the Aztecs*. Stanford, CA: Stanford University Press.

Bonfil Batalla, Guillermo (1973). *Cholula, la ciudad sagrada en la era industrial*. Mexico City: UNAM.

Boschloo, A. W. A. (1974). *Annibale Carraci in Bologna: Visible Reality in Art after the Council of Trent*. The Hague, Netherlands.

Brotherston, Gordon (1987). *Aesop in Mexico: Die Fabeln des Aesop in aztekischer Sprache. A 16th Century Aztec Version of Aesop's Fables*. Berlin: Gebr. Mann Verlag.

—— (1992). *Book of the Fourth World. Reading the Native Americas through Their Literature*. Cambridge, UK: Cambridge, University Press.

Brown, Jonathan (1991). *The Golden Age of Painting in Spain*. New Haven, CT: Yale University Press.

Brown, Peter (1998). *L'Autorité et le sacré*. Paris: Noêsis.

Buarque de Holanda, Sergio (1957). *Caminhos e fronteiras*. Rio de Janeiro: José Olympio.

—— (1996). *Visão do Paraíso*. São Paulo: Editora Bresiliense.

Burity, Glauce Maria Navarro (1988). *A presença dos Franciscanos na Paraíba através do convento de Santo Antônio*. Rio de Janeiro: Bloch Editores.

Burkhart, Louise M. (1988). *The Slippery Earth: Nahua-Christian Moral Dialogue in Sixteenth Century Mexico*. Tucson, AZ: University of Arizona Press.

—— (1992). "Flowery Heaven: The Aesthetic of Paradise in Nahuatl Devotional Literature." *Res* 21 (Spring).

—— (1995). "The Voyage of Saint Amaro: A Spanish Legend in Nahuatl Literature." *Colonial Latin American Review* IV: 1.

Bustamante Garcia, Jesús (1990). *Fray Bernardino de Sahagún: Una revisión crítica de los manuscritos y su proceso de composición.* Mexico City: UNAM, Instituto de Investigaciones Bibliográficas.

—— (1997). "Francisco Hernández, Plinio del Nuevo Mundo: Tradición clásica, teoría nominal y sistema terminológico indígena en una obra renacentista." In Arés Queija and Gruzinski (1997).

Calabrese, Omar (1984). "Catastrofi et teoria dell'arte." *Lectures: Analisi di materiali e temi di espressione francese* 15 (December).

—— (1987). *La Età neobarocca.* Bari, Italy: Sagittari Laterza.

—— (1992). *Mille di questi anni.* Bari, Italy: Sagittari Laterza.

Camille, Michael (1992). *The Margins of Medieval Art.* London: Reaktion Books.

Cantares mexicanos (1994). Facsimile edition edited by Miguel León-Portilla. Mexico City: UNAM.

Carrasco, Davíd (1982). *Quetzalcoatl and the Irony of Empire: Myths and Prophecies in the Aztec Tradition.* Chicago and London: the University of Chicago Press.

Cartari, Vincenzo (1556). *Le imagini con la spositione dei Dei degli Antichi.* Venice: Francesco Marcolini.

Castelli, Patrizia (1979). *I Geroglifici e il mito dell'Egitto ne Rinascimento.* Florence: Edam.

Céard, Jean (1977). *La Nature et les prodiges. L'insolite au XVIe siècle, en France.* Geneva: Droz.

Cecchi, Alessandro (1977). "Pratica, fierezza e terribilità nelle grotesche di Marco da Faenza in Palazzo Vecchio a Firenze." *Paragone* 327.

Cervantes de Salazar, Francisco [1560] (1985). *Crónica de la Nueva España.* Mexico City: Porrúa.

Chastel, André (1972). *Le Sac de Rome.* Paris.

Chastel, André (1988). *La Grottesque: Essai sur l'ornement sans nom.* Paris: Le Promeneur.

Chimalpahin Cuauhtlehuanitzin, Domingo Francisco de San Antón Muñón (1965). *Relaciones originales de Chalco-Amaquemecan.* Trans. by Silvia Rendón. Mexico City: FCE.

Chiusa, Maria Cristina (1996). *Alessandro Araldi: la "maniera antico-moderna" a Parma.* Parma, Italy: Quaderni di Parma per l'arte, II: 3.

Cisneros, Luis de (1621). *Historia del principio origen . . . de la santa imagen de Nuestra Señora de los Remedios.* Mexico City: Juan Blanco de Alcaçar.

Codex Azcatitlan (1995). Edited by Robert Barlow. Paris: Bibliothèque nationale, Société des Américanistes.

Codex Magliabechiano (1970). *Codices Selecti*, XXIII. Graz, Austria: Akademische Druck u. verlagsanstalt.

Codex Vaticanus A (1979). Rome: Biblioteca Apostolica Vaticana.

Colección de documentos para la historia de México (1971). Published by Joaquín García Icazbalceta. Mexico City: Porrúa.

Concilios provinciales primero y segundo (1769). Published by Francisco Antonio Lorenzana. Mexico City: Antonio de Hogal.

Conti, Natale (1551). *Mythologiae sive explicationum fabularum libri decem.* Venice.

Cough, Christopher (1987). "Style and Ideology in the Durán Illustrations." Ph.D. dissertation, Columbia University 1987. Ann Arbor, MI: University Microfilms.

Dacos, Nicole (1969). *La Découverte de la Domus Aurea et la formation des grotesques à la Renaissance.* London and Leiden: The Warburg Institute.

Delâge, Denys (1991). *Le Pays renversé: Amérindiens et Européens en Amérique du Nord-Est, 1600–1664.* Quebec: Boréal.

Díaz del Castillo, Bernal [1568] (1968). *Historia verdadera de la conquista de la Nueva España.* Mexico City: Porrúa.

Didi-Huberman, Georges (1990). *Fra Angelico. Dissemblance et figuration*. Paris: Flammarion.

Di Francesco, Carla (1998). *Le Sibille di Casa Romei. Storia e restauro*. Ravenna: Longo Editore.

Documenta X (1997). *Short Guide/ Kurzfürher*. Kassel, Germany: Cantz Verlag.

Durán, Diego [1581] (1967). *Historia de las Indias de Nueva España e Islas de la Tierra Firme*. Mexico City: Porrúa.

Duverger, Christian (1978). *L'Esprit du jeu chez les Aztèques*. Paris: Mouton.

Estenssoro-Fuchs, Juan Carlos (1996). "La prédication au Pérou: De l'évangélisation à l'utopie." *Annales, Histoires, Sciences Sociales* 6 (November-December).

—— (1998). "Du paganisme à la sainteté: L'incorporation des Indiens du Pérou au catholicisme." Ph.D. dissertation, Paris: Ecole des Hautes Etudes en Sciences Sociales.

Farago, Claire (1995). *Reframing the Renaissance. Visual Culture in Europe and Latin America 1450–1650*. New Haven, CT, and London: Yale University Press.

Farris, Nancy M. (1984). *Maya Society under Colonial Rule. The Collective Enterprise of Survival*. Princeton, NJ: Princeton University Press.

Favaretto, Celso (1992). *A invenção de Hélio Oiticica*. São Paulo: Edusp/Fapesp.

Favrot Peterson, Jeanette (1993). *The Paradise Garden Murals of Malinalco. Utopia and Empire in Sixteenth-Century Mexico*. Austin, TX: University of Texas Press.

Feest, Christian (1986) "Koloniale Federkunst aus Mexiko." *Gold und Macht: Spanien in der neuen Welt*. Edited by Christian Feest and Peter Kann. Vienna: Verlag Kremayr & Scheriau.

Fernández de Oviedo, Gonzalo (1547). *Crónica de las Indias. La historia general de las Indias*. . . . Salamanca: Juan de la Junta.

Fernández de Recas, Guillermo (1961). *Cacicazgos y nobiliario indígena de la Nueva España*. Mexico City: UNAM.

Fernández del Castillo, Francisco (1982). *Libros y libreros en el siglo XVI*. Mexico City: FCE.

Figueiredo Ferretti, Sérgio (1995). *Repensando o sincretismo*. São Paulo: Edusp/Fapema.

Flores de varia poesía (1987). Edited by Margarita Peña. Mexico City: SEP.

Florescano, Enrique, et al. (1980). *La Clase obrera en la historia de México. De la colonia al imperio*. Mexico City: Siglo XXI.

Foster, George M. (1960). *Culture and Conquest: America's Spanish Heritage*. New York: Wenner-Gren Foundation, Viking Fund Publications in Anthology 27.

Foucault, Michel (1966). *Les Mots et les choses: Une archéologie des sciences humaines*. Paris: Gallimard.

Fragmentos del pasado. Murales prehispánicos (1998). Mexico City: INAH, Antiguo Colegio de San Ildefonso, UNAM, Instituto de Investigaciones Estéticas.

Fraser, Valerie (1990). *The Architecture of Conquest: Building in the Viceroyalty of Peru 1535–1635*. Cambridge, UK: Cambridge University Press.

Gallego, Julián (1987). *Visión y símbolo en la pintura española del Siglo de Oro*. Madrid: Catedra.

Gallini, Clara (1996). *Giochi pericolosi: Frammenti di un immaginario alquanto razzista*. Rome: Manifestolibri.

Gante, Pedro de [1553] (1981). *Doctrina cristiana en lengua mexicana*. Mexico City: Centro de Estudios Históricos Fray Bernardino de Sahagún.

García Canclini, Néstor (1990). *Culturas híbridas: Estrategias para entrar y salir de la modernidad*. Mexico City: Consejo Nacional para las Artes, Grijalbo.

—— (1995). *Consumidores y ciudadanos: Conflictos multiculturales de la globalización*. Mexico City: Grijalbo.

García Granados, Rafael (1995). *Diccionario biográfico de historia antigua de Méjico*, vol. III, *Indios cristianos: Bibliografía e índices*. Mexico City: UNAM.

García Icazbalceta, Joaquín (1981). *Bibliografía mexicana del siglo XVI*. Mexico City: FCE.

García Icazbalceta, Joaquín (1986–1992). *Nueva colección de documentos para la historia de México*. Mexico City: Díaz de León.

Garibay K., Angel María (1971). *Historia de la literatura náhuatl.* Mexico City: Porrúa.

—— (1993). *Poesía náhuatl, Cantares mexicanos. Manuscrito de la Biblioteca Nacional de México.* Mexico City: UNAM.

Garrido Aranda, Antonio (1980). *Organización de la Iglesia en el reino de Granada y su proyección en Indias.* Séville: Escuela de Estudios Hispanoamericanos, Universidad de Córdoba.

Gellner, Ernest (1985). *Relativism and the Social Sciences.* Cambridge, UK: Cambridge University Press.

Gennes, Pierre-Gilles de, et al. *(1992). L'ordre du Chaos.* Paris: Belin.

Gentili, Augusto (1980). *Da Tiziano a Tiziano: Mito e allegoria nella cultura veneziana del cinquecento.* Milan: Feltrinelli.

Gerbi, Antonello (1978). *La Naturaleza de las Indias nuevas: De Cristobal Colón a Gonzalo Fernández de Oviedo.* Mexico City/FCE.

Gibson, Charles (1964). *The Aztecs under Spanish Rule: A History of the Indians of the Valley of Mexico, 1519–1810.* Stanford, CA: Stanford University Press.

Gillespie, Susan D. (1989). *The Aztec Kings: The Construction of Rulership in Mexica History.* Tucson, AZ: the University of Arizona Press.

Gilroy, P. (1987). *There Ain't No Black in the Union Jack.* London: Hutchinson.

Giraud, Michel (1997). "La créolité: Une rupture en trompe-l'œil." *Cahiers d'Etudes africaines* 148: XXXVII-4.

Gisbert, Teresa (1980). *Iconografía y mitos indígenas en el arte.* La Paz, Bolivia: Editorial Gisbert and Cía.

——, and José de Mesa (1997). *Arquitectura andina, 1530–1830.* La Paz, Bolivia: Embajada de España en Bolivia.

Gleick, James (1991). *La Théorie du chaos: Vers une nouvelle science.* Paris: Champs/Flammarion [*Chaos: Making a New Science.* New York: Viking Penguin, 1987].

Glissant, Edouard (1990). *Poétique de la relation.* Paris: Gallimard.

Gómez Martínez, Javier (1997). *Fortalezas mendicantes.* Mexico City: Universidad Iberoamericana.

González de Eslava, Fernán (1988). *Teatro selecto: Coloquios y entremeses.* Mexico City: SEP.

—— (1989). *Villancicos, romances, ensaladas y otras canciones devotas.* Edited by Margit Frenk. Mexico City: El Colegio de México.

González Torres, Yolotl (1985). *El sacrificio humano entre los Mexicas.* Mexico City: FCE.

Grafton, Anthony (1995). *New Worlds, Ancient Texts: The Power of Tradition and the Shock of Discovery.* Cambridge, MA: Belknap Press of Harvard University Press.

Granger, Gilles-Gaston (1998). *L'Irrationnel.* Paris: Odile Jacob.

Graulich, Michel (1982). *Mythes et rituels du Mexique ancien préhispanique.* Brussels: Académie Royale de Belgique.

Greenaway, Peter (1991). Prospero's Books, *A Film of Shakespeare's "The Tempest."* New York: Four Walls Eight Windows.

—— (1996). *The Pillow Book.* Paris: Dis Voir.

Grenier, Jean-Yves (1996). *L'Économie d'Ancien Régime: Un monde de l'échange et de l'incertitude.* Paris: Albin Michel.

Gruzinski, Serge (1985). *Les Hommes-dieux du Mexique: Pouvoir indien et société coloniale, XVIe-XVIIIe siècle.* Paris: Editions des Archives Contemporaines.

—— (1987). "Confesión, alianze y sexualidad entre los indios de Nueva España: Introducción al estudio de los confesionarios en lenguas indigenas." *Seminario de Historia de las Mentalidades, El placer de pecar y el afán de normar.* Mexico City: Joanquín Mortiz.

—— (1988) *La Colonisation de l'imaginaire: Sociétés indigènes et occidentalisation dans le Mexique espagnol, XVIe-XVIIIe siècle.* Paris: Gallimard.

—— (1989) *Man-Gods in the Mexican Highlands—Indian Power and Colonial Society 1520–1800.* Stanford, CA: Stanford University Press.

—— (1990). *La Guerre des images de Christophe Colomb à Blade Runner, 1492–2019*. Paris: Fayard.

—— (1992a). *L'Amérique des Indiens peinte par les Indiens du Mexique*. Paris: Flammarion/Unesco. [*Painting the Conquest*. Trans. by Deke Dusinberre. Paris: Flammarion, 1992.]

—— (1992b). "Vision et christianisation. l'expérience mexicaine." In *Visions indiennes, visions baroques, Les métissages de l'inconscient*. Edited by Jean-Michel Sallmann. Paris: PUF.

—— (1994a). *L'Aigle et la sibylle, Fresques indiennes des couvents du Mexique*. Paris: L'Imprimerie nationale.

—— (1994b). "Las repercusiones de la conquista: la experiencia novohispana." In *Descubrimiento, conquista y colonización de América a quinientos años*. Edited by C. Bernand. Mexico City: FCE.

—— (1994c). "Le premier centenaire de la découverte du Nouveau Monde: Témoignages de la Nouvelle-Espagne." *Mémoires en devenir, Amérique latine XIVe–XXe siècle*. Bordeaux: Maison des pays ibériques.

—— (1996). *Histoire de Mexico*. Paris: Fayard.

—— (1997). "Entre monos y centauros: Los indios pintores y la cultura del renacimiento." In Berta Ares Queija and Serge Gruzinski, *Entre dos mundos: Fronteras culturales y agentes mediadores*. Séville: Escuela de Estudios Hispanoamericanos.

——, and Nathan Wachtel (1996). *Le Nouveau Monde, mondes nouveaux: L'expérience américaine*. Paris: Editions Recherches sur les Civilisations, Ecole des Hautes Etudes en Sciences Sociales.

Guadalupe Victoria, José (1995). *Una bibliografía de arte novohispano*. Mexico City: Instituto de Investigaciones Estéticas.

Guaman Poma de Ayala, Felipe (1980). *El Primer nueva corónica y buen gobierno*. Edited by John Murra and Rolena Adorno. Mexico City: Siglo XXI.

Guidieri, Remo (1992). *Chronique du neutre et de l'auréole: Sur le musée et les fétiches*. Paris: La Différence.

Guzmán, Décio de Alencar (1998). *Les Chefferies indigènes du Rio Negro à l'époque de la conquête de l'Amazonie, 1650–1750: Le Cas des Indiens Manao*. DEA dissertation, Paris: Ecole des Hautes Etudes en Sciences Sociales.

Hassig, Ross (1988). *Aztec Warfare: Imperial Expansion and Political Control*. Norman, OK, and London: University of Oklahoma Press.

Hebdige, D. (1983). *Subculture: The Meaning of Style*. London: Methuen.

Heikamp, Detlef (1972) *Mexico and the Medici*. Florence: Edam.

Hellendoorn, Fabienne Emilie (1980). *Influencia del manierismo-nordico en la arquitectura virreinal religiosa de México*. Delft: UNAM.

Herbert, Christopher (1991). *Culture and Anomie: Ethnographic Imagination in the Nineteenth Century*. Chicago and London: University of Chicago Press.

Hernández, Francisco (1960). *Obras completas*. Mexico City: UNAM.

Heyden, Doris (1983). *Mitología y simbolismo de la flora en el México prehispánico*. Mexico City: UNAM.

Hill, Jane H. (1987). "The Flowery World of Old Uto-Aztecan." Paper presented at the 86th Annual Meeting of the American Anthropological Association, November 10–21.

Hill, Jonathan (1988). "Introduction: Myth and History." In *Rethinking History and Myth: Indigenous South American Perspectives on the Past*. Edited by Jonathan Hill. Urbana, IL: University of Illinois Press.

Horapollo [1505] (1993). *The Hieroglyphics of Horapollo*. Translated by George Boas with a new foreword by Anthony T. Grafton. Princeton, NJ: Princeton University Press.

Horcasitas, Fernando (1974). *El teatro náhuatl: Epocas novohispana y moderna*. Mexico City: UNAM.

Iriarte, Isabel (1992). "Tapices con escenas biblicas del Peru colonial." *Revista Andina* I (July).

Jeanneret, Michel (n.d.). *Perpetuum mobile: Métamorphoses des corps et des œuvres de Vinci à Montaigne.* Paris: Macula.

Jones, Grant D. (1989). *Maya Resistance to Spanish Rule: Time and History on a Colonial Frontier.* Albuquerque, NM: University of New Mexico Press.

Kemp, Martin (1995). "Wrought by No Artist's Hand: The Natural, the Artificial, the Exotic, and the Scientific in Some Artifacts from the Renaissance." Claire Farago. *Reframing the Renaissance: Visual Culture in Europe and Latin America, 1450–1650.* New Haven and London: Yale University Press.

Kirchhoff, Paul, Lina Odena Güemes, and Luis Reyes García (1976). *Historia tolteca-chichimeca.* Mexico City: INAH.

Klor de Alva, Jorge, H. B. Nicholson, and Eloise Quiñones Keber (1988). *The Work of Bernardino de Sahagún, Pioneer Ethnographer of Sixteenth-Century Aztec Mexico.* Studies on Culture and Society, vol. II. Institute for Mesoamerican Studies. Austin, TX: University of Texas.

Konetzke, Richard (1983). *Lateinamerika: Entdeckung, Eroberung, Kolonisation.* Cologne/Vienna: Böhlau.

Kroeber, Alfred L. (1963). *Culture Patterns and Processes.* New York and London: First Harbinger Books.

Kubler, George (1984). *Arquitectura mexicana del siglo XVI.* Mexico City: FCE.

——— (1985). *Studies in Ancient American and European Art: The Collected Essays of George Kubler.* Edited by Thomas E. Reese. New Haven, CT, and London: Yale University Press.

Lalanne, Jean-Marc, et al. (1997). *Wong Kar-Wai.* Paris: Dis Voir.

Laplantine, François, and Alexis Nouss (1997). *Le métissage.* Paris: Flammarion.

Las Casas, Bartolomé de [1559] (1986). *Historia de las Indias.* Mexico City: FCE.

——— [1559] (1967). *Apologética historia sumaria.* Edited by Edmundo O'Gorman. Mexico: UNAM.

León Hebreo (1989). *Dialoghi d'amore.* Edited by Miguel de Burgos Nuñez. Seville, Spain: Padilla Libros.

León-Portilla, Miguel (1985). *Los Franciscanos vistos por el hombre náhuatl.* Mexico City: UNAM.

——— (1992). *Le Livre astrologique des marchands.* Paris: La Différence.

Leonard, Irving (1996). *Los libros del conquistador.* Mexico City: FCE.

Lestringant, Frank (1991). *L'Atelier du cosmographe ou l'image du monde à la Renaissance.* Paris: Albin Michel.

Lévi-Strauss, Claude (1977) *L'Identité.* Seminar conducted by C. Lévi-Strauss. Paris: P.U.F.

Libera, Alain de (1991). *Penser au Moyen Age.* Paris: Seuil.

Llaguno, José A. (1963). *La Personalidad jurídica del indio y el III concilio provincial mexicano.* Mexico City: Porrúa.

Lockhart, James (1992). *The Nahuas after the Conquest: A Social and Cultural History of the Indians of Central Mexico, Sixteenth through Eighteenth Century.* Stanford, CA: Stanford University Press.

López Austin, Alfredo (1973). *Hombre-Dios. Religión y política en el mundo náhuatl.* Mexico City: UNAM, Instituto de Investigaciones Históricas.

——— (1975). "Algunas ideas acerca del tiempo mítico entre los antiguos nahuas." *Historia, religión, escuelas* XIII. Mexico City: Sociedad Mexicana de Antropología.

——— (1980). *Cuerpo humano e ideología. Las concepciones de los antiguos nahuas.* Mexico City: UNAM.

——— (1996). *Tamoanchan y Tlalocan.* Mexico City: FCE.

Lorimer, Joyce (1989). *English and Irish Settlement on the River Amazon. 1550–1646.* Cambridge: Hakluyt Society.

Lupo, Alessandro (1996). "Síntesis controvertidas. Consideraciones en torno a los límites del concepto de sincretismo." *Revista de Antropología Social 5*.

Lyell, James P. R. (1976). *Early Book Illustration in Spain*. New York: Hacker Art Books.

Macera, Pablo (1993). *La Pintura mural andina. Siglos XVI–XIX*. Lima: Editorial Milla Batres.

MacGregor, Luis (1982). *Actopan*. Mexico City: INAH.

Madonna, M. L. (1979). "La biblioteca: Theatrum mundi e theatrum sapientiae." *L'Abbazia benedittina di San Giovanni Evangelista a Parma*. Edited by Bruno Adorni. Milan.

Mainzer, Klaus (1996). *Thinking in Complexity: The Complex Dynamics of Matter, Mind and Mankind*. Berlin: Springer.

Maldonado, Humberto (1995). *Hombres y letras del virreinato*. Mexico City: UNAM.

Manrique, Jorge Alberto (1993). *Manierismo en Nueva España*. Mexico City: Textos Dispersos Ediciones.

Martino, Ernesto de (1980). *Furore, simbolo, valore*, Milan: Feltrinelli.

Mason, Peter (1990). *Deconstructing America: Representations of the Other*. London: Routledge, Chapman and Hall.

Mathes, Miguel (1982). *Santa Cruz de Tlatelolco: la primera biblioteca académica de las Américas*. Mexico City: Secretaría de Relaciones Exteriores.

Maza, Francisco de la (1968). *La Mitología clásica en el arte colonial de México*. Mexico City: UNAM, Instituto de Investigaciones Estéticas.

Megged, Amos (1996). *Exporting the Catholic Reformation. Local Religion in Early-Colonial Mexico*. Leiden/New York/Cologne: E. J. Brill.

Meira, Márcio (1994). "O tempo dos patrões: extrativismo, comerciantes e história indígena no Noroeste da Amazônia." *Cuadernos Ciencias humanas 2*. Museu Paraense Emilio Goeldi.

——— (1996). "Indios e Brancos nas águas pretas: Histórias do Rio Negro." Seminar on *Povos Indígenas do rio Negro: Terra e cultura*. Universidade do Amazonas, Manaus, August 1996.

Mello e Souza, Gilda de (1979). *O tupi e o alaúde: Uma interpretação de Macunaíma*. São Paulo: Livraria Duas Cidades.

Mello e Souza, Laura de (1993). *Inferno atlântico: Demonologia e colonização, Séculos XVI–XVIII*. São Paulo: Companhia das Letras.

Mendieta, Gerónimo de [1596] (1945). *Historia eclesiástica indiana*. Mexico City: Salvador Chávez Hayhoe.

——— (1971). *Historia eclesiástica indiana*. Mexico City: Porrúa.

Michaud, Philippe-Alain (1998). *Aby Warburg et l'image en mouvement*. Paris: Macula.

Mignolo, Walter D. (1995). *The Darker Side of the Renaissance: Literacy, Territoriality and Colonization*. Ann Arbor, MI: University of Michigan.

Miller, Arthur (1996). "Indian Image and Visual Communication before and after the Conquest: The Mitla Case." In *Le Nouveau Monde, mondes nouveaux: L'expérience américaine*. Edited by Serge Gruzinski and Nathan Wachtel. Paris: Editions Recherches sur les Civilisations, Ecole des Hautes Etudes en Sciences Sociales.

Minelli, Laura Laurencich (1992). *Terra America: Il mondo nuovo nelle collezioni emiliano-romagnole*. Bologna: Grafis.

——— (1992). "Museografia americanista in Italia dal secolo XVI fina a oggi." *Bulletin des musées royaux d'Art et d'Histoire 63*. Brussels.

Molina, Alonso de (1569). *Confesionario mayor en lengua mexicana y castellana*. Mexico: Antonio de Espinosa.

——— (1571). *Vocabulario en lengua castellana y mexicana y mexicana y castellana*. Mexico City: Antonio de Espinosa.

Morales, Pedro de (1579). *Carta*. Mexico City: Antonio Ricardo.

Morel, Philippe (1997). *Les Grotesques: Les figures de l'imaginaire dans la peinture italienne de la fin de la Renaissance*. Paris: Flammarion.

Moreno, Roberto (1966). "Guía de las obras en lenguas indígenas existentes en la Biblioteca Nacional." *Boletin de la Biblioteca Nacional* XVII: 1–2.

Motolinía, Toribio de Benavente (1971). *Memoriales o libro de las cosas de la Nueva España y de los naturales de ella*. Edited by Edmundo O'Gorman. Mexico City: UNAM.

Mundy, Barbara E. (1996). *The Mapping of New Spain: Indigenous Cartography and the Maps of the Relaciones Geográficas*. Chicago and London: University of Chicago.

Muñoz Carmargo, Diego (1984). "Descripción de la ciudad y provincia de Tlaxcala." In *Relaciones geográficas del siglo XVI: Tlaxcala*. Edited by René Acuña. Mexico City: UNAM.

Nettel, Patricia (1997). *El precio justo o las desaventuras de un confesor en el siglo XVI*. Mexico City: Universidad Autónoma Metropolitana-Xochimilco.

Neveux, Hugues (1985). "Le rôle du 'religieux' dans les soulèvements paysans: L'Exemple du pèlerinage de Niklashausen (1476)." In *Mouvements populaires et conscience sociale*. Paris: Editions Maloine.

—— (1997). *Les Révoltes paysannes en Europe XIVe–XVIIe siècle*. Paris: Albin Michel.

Nicholson, H. B. and Eloise Quiñones Keber (1983). *Art of Aztec Mexico: Treasures of Tenochtitlán*. Washington, D.C.: National Gallery of Art.

Osorio Romero, Ignacio (1979). *Colegios y profesores jesuitas que enseñaron latín en Nueva España (1572–1767)*. Mexico City: UNAM, Instituto de Investigaciones Filológicas.

—— (1990). *La Enseñanza del latín a los indios*. Mexico City: UNAM.

Ovid (1826). *Metamorphoses*. Translated by Garth, Dryden, et al. London.

Padwa, Mariner Ezra (1993). *Peter of Ghent and the Introduction of European Music to the New World*. Santa Fe, NM: Hapax Press.

Paleotti, Gabriele (1960). "Discorso intorna alle immagini sacre e profane" [1581–1582]. P. Barocchi, *Trattati d'arte del Cinquecento fra Manierismo e Controriforma*. Bari, Italy.

Palm, Erwin Walter (1973). "El sincretismo emblemático de los Triunfos de la Casa del Deán en Puebla." In *Comunicaciones: Proyecto Puebla-Tlaxcala* VIII. Puebla: Fundación Alemana par la Investigación Científica.

Panofsky, Erwin (1961). *The Iconography of Correggio's Camera di San Paolo*. London: The Warburg Institute.

Pascoe, David (1997). *Peter Greenaway: Museums and Moving Image*. London: Reaktion Books.

Paso y Troncoso, Francisco del (1930). *Epistolario de Nueva España*, IV, 1540–1546. Mexico City: Antigua Librería Robredo.

—— (1940). *Epistolario de Nueva España*, X, 1564-1569. Mexico City: Antigua Librería Robredo.

Pérez de Moya, Juan [1585, 1611] (1910). *Philosophia secreta donde debajo de historias fabulosas se contiene mucha doctrina provechosa a todos los estudios, con el origen de los ídolos o dioses de la gentilidad*. Edited by E. Gómez de Baquero. Madrid.

Phelan, John L. (1970). *The Millennial Kingdom of the Franciscans in the New World*. Berkeley, CA: University of California Press.

Pinelli, Antonio (1993). *La Bella maniera: Artisti del cinquecento tra regola e licenza*. Turin: Einaudi.

Pomar, Juan (1986). "Relación de Texcoco." In *Relaciones geográficas del siglo XVI: Mexico*. Edited by René Acuña. Mexico City: UNAM.

Prigogine, Ilya (1994). *Les Lois du chaos*. Paris: Flammarion.

Quiñones Keber, Eloise (1995). "Collecting Cultures: A Mexican Manuscript in the Vatican Library." In Farago (1995).

Quiroga, Vasco de (1988). *De debellandis indis.* Edited by René Acuña. Mexico City: UNAM.

Ransmayr, Christoph (1990). *The Last World.* Translated by John E. Woods. New York: Grove/Weidenfeld.

—— (1997). *The Dog King.* Translated by John E. Woods. New York: Knopf.

Reichel-Dolmatoff, Gerardo (1971). *Amazonian Cosmos: The Sexual and Religious Symbolism of the Tukano Indians.* Chicago: University of Chicago Press.

"Relación de Cholula" [1581] (1985). In *Relaciones geográficas del siglo XVI: Tlaxcala.* Edited by René Acuña. Mexico City: UNAM.

Reyes-Valerio, Constantino (1978). *Arte indocristiano: Escultura del siglo XVI en México.* Mexico City: INAH-SEP.

—— (1989). *El Pintor de conventos: Los murales del siglo XVI en la Nueva España.* Mexico City: INAH.

Riess, Jonathan (1995). *The Renaissance Antichrist: Luca Signorelli's Orvieto Frescoes.* Princeton, NJ: Princeton University Press.

Ripa, Cesare [1593] (1992). *Iconologia.* Edited by Piero Buscaroli. Milan: Editori Associati.

Riquelme Mancilla, Daniela (1997). "La Imagen del angel en el siglo XIV novohispano." Master's thesis, University of Paris VIII.

Robertson, Donald (1959). *Mexican Manuscript Paintings of the Early Colonial Period.* New Haven, CT: Yale University Press.

—— (1968). "Paste-Over Illustrations in the Durán Codex of Madrid." *Tlalocan* 4.

Roosevelt, Anna (1997). *Amazonian Indians from Prehistory to the Present.* Tucson, AZ, and London: University of Arizona Press.

Russo, Alessandra (1996). "Arte plumaria del Messico coloniale del XVI secolo: L'incontro di due mondi artistici." Dissertation, University of Bologna.

—— (1997). *Les Formes de l'art indigène au Mexique sous la domination espagnole au XVIe siècle: Le Codex Borbonicus et le Codex Durán.* DEA Dissertation, Paris: Ecole des Hautes Etudes en Sciences Sociales.

Sacchi, Duccio (1997). *Mappe del Nuovo Mondo, Cartografie locali e definizione del territorio in Nuova Spagna (Secolo XVI-XVII).* Milan: Franco Angeli.

Sahagún, Bernardino de (1953). *Florentine Codex. General History of the Things of New Spain, Book 7. The Sun, Moon and Stars and the Beginning of the Years,* No. 14, Part VIII. Translated by Arthur J. O. Anderson and Charles E. Dibble. Sante Fe, NM: School of American Research and University of Utah.

—— (1963). *Florentine Codex. General History of the Things of New Spain, Book 11. Early Things,* No. 14, Part XII. Translated by Arthur J. O. Anderson and Charles E. Dibble. Sante Fe, NM: School of American Research and the University of Utah.

—— (1969). *Florentine Codex. General History of the Things of New Spain, Book 6. Rhetoric and Moral Philosophy,* No. 14, Part VII. Translated by Arthur J. O. Anderson and Charles E. Dibble Sante Fe, NM: School of American Research and University of Utah.

—— (1977). *Historia general de las cosas de Nueva España.* 4 vol. Edited by Angel María Garibay K. Mexico City: Porrúa.

—— (1979) [1580] . *Códice florentino.* Mexico City: AGN.

—— (1982). *Historia general de las cosas de Nueva España.* Edited by Alfredo López Austin and Josefina García Quintana. Mexico City: Banamex.

—— (1983). *Psalmodia christiana y sermonario de los sanctos del año en lengua mexicana.* Mexico City: Pedro Ocharte.

—— (1986) [1564]. *Coloquios y doctrina cristiana.* Edited by Miguel León-Portilla. Mexico City: UNAM, Fundación de Investigaciones Sociales A.C.

Salazar-Soler, Carmen (1997). "Alvaro Alonso Barba: Teorías dela antigüedad, alquimia y creencias prehispánicas en las ciencias de la tierra en el Nuevo Mundo." In Ares Queija and Gruzinski (1997).

Saldivar, Gabriel (1934). *Historia de la música en México: Epocas precortesiana y colonial.* Mexico City: Cultura.

Sartor, Mario (1992). *Arquitectura y urbanismo en Nueva España, siglo XVI.* Mexico City: Azabache.

Schwartz, Stuart, et al. (1994). *Implicit Understandings: Observing, Reporting and Reflecting on the Encounters between European and Other Peoples in the Early Modern Era.* Cambridge, UK: Cambridge University Press.

Serna, Juan de la (1953). "Manuel de ministros de indios." *Tratado de las idolatrías.* Mexico City: Fuente Cultural.

Seznec, Jean (1993). *La Survivance des dieux antiques.* Paris: Flammarion.

Shônagon, Sei (1991). *The Pillow Book.* Translated and edited by Ivan Morris. New York: Columbia University Press.

Solórzano y Pereyra, Juan de [1647] (1776). *Politica indiana.* Madrid: Imprenta Real de la Gazeta.

Sten, Maria (1974). *Vida y muerte del teatro náhuatl. El Olímpo sin Prometeo.* Mexico City: SepSetentas.

Stevenson, Robert (1968). *Music in Aztec and Inca Territory.* Berkeley, CA: University of California Press.

Taylor, René (1987). *El Arte de la memoria en el Nuevo Mundo.* Madrid: Swan.

Terra America. Il Mondo nuovo nelle collezioni emiliano-romagnole (1992). Edited by Laura Laurencich Minelli. Bologna: Grafis.

Tomlinson, Gary (1995) . "Ideologies of Aztec Song." *Journal of the American Musicological Society* XLVIII: 3.

Toussaint, Manuel (1981). *Claudio de Arciniega: Arquitecto de la Nueva España.* Mexico City: UNAM, Instituto de Investigaciones Estéticas.

——— (1982). *Pintura colonial en México.* Mexico City: UNAM.

Tovar de Teresa, Guillermo (1988). *Bibliografía novohispana de arte, Primera parte: Impresos mexicanos relativos al arte de los siglos XVI y XVIII.* Mexico City: FCE.

——— (1992). *Pintura y escultura en Nueva España (1557–1640).* Mexico City: Azabache.

Trejo, Pedro de (1996). *Cancionero.* Edited by Sergio López Mena. Mexico City: UNAM, Instituto de Investigaciones Filológicas.

Tylor, Edward B. (1951). *Primitive Culture.* New York: Harper.

Umberger, Emily (1987). "Antiques, Revivals and References to the Past in Aztec Art." *Res,* Spring 1987.

Vainfas, Ronaldo (1995) *A heresia dos Indios: catolicismo e rebeldia no Brasil colonial.* São Paulo: Companhia das Letras.

——— (1997). *Confissões da Bahia.* São Paulo: Companhia das Letras.

Valadés, Diego [1579] (1989). *Rhetorica christiana.* Mexico City: UNAM, FCE.

Vasari, Giorgio (1550). *Le Vite dè piú eccelenti architetti, pittori et scultori italiani, da Cimabue insino à giorni nostri.* Florence: Lorenzo Torrentino.

Veliz, Zahira (1986). *Artists' Techniques in Golden-Age Spain. Six Treatises in Translation.* Cambridge, UK: Cambridge University Press.

Vicencio, José Victoria (1992). *Pintura y sociedad en Nueva España. Siglo XVI.* Mexico City: UNAM, Instituto de Investigaciones Estéticas.

Wachtel, Nathan (1971). *La Vision des vaincus: Les Indiens du Pérou devant la Conquête espagnole.* Paris: Gallimard [*The Vision of the Vanquished: The Spanish Conquest of Peru through Native Eyes, 1530–1570.* Trans. by Ben and Sian Reynolds. New York: Barnes & Noble, 1977].

Wagner, Roy (1992) , *L'Invenzione de la cultura.* Milan: Mursia.

Warburg, Aby (1939). "A Lecture on Serpent Ritual." *Journal of the Warburg Institute* II: 4.

——— (1996). *La Rinascita del paganesimo antico.* Florence: La Nuova Italia Editrice.

Warman, Arturo (1972). *La Danza de Moros y Cristianos.* Mexico City: SepSetentas.

Wasson, Robert Gordon (1980). *The Wondrous Mushroom: Mycolatry in Mesoamerica*. New York: Mc Graw-Hill Book Company.

Whitehead, N. L. (1988). *Lords of the Tiger Spirit: A History of the Caribs in Colonial Venzuela and Guayana, 1498–1820*. Royal Institute for Linguistics and Anthropology, Caribbean Studies Series, 10. Dordrecht and Providence: Foris Publications.

Wittkower, Rudolf (1987). *Allegory and the Migration of Symbols*. New York: Thames and Hudson.

Yhmoff Cabrera, Jesús (1989). *Los Impresos mexicanos del siglo XVI en la Biblioteca Nacional de México*. Mexico City: UNAM.

Zanchi, Mauro (1998). *Lorenzo Lotto et l'imaginaire alchimique. Les "imprese" dans les marqueteries du choeur de la basilique de Sainte-Marie-Majeure à Bergame*. Bergamo, Italy: Ferrari Editrice.

Zeron, Carlos (1998). *La Compagnie de Jésus et l'institution de l'esclavage au Brésil: Les Justifications d'ordre historique, théologique et juridique, et leur intégration dans une mémoire historique* (XVIe–XVIIe siècles). Ph.D. Dissertation. Paris: Ecole des Hautes Etudes en Sciences Sociales.

INDEX